A Neurophilosophy of Libertarian Free Will

A Neurophilosophy of Libertarian Free Will

Peter Ulric Tse

Great Clarendon Street, Oxford, OX2 6DP,
United Kingdom

Oxford University Press is a department of the University of Oxford.
It furthers the University's objective of excellence in research, scholarship,
and education by publishing worldwide. Oxford is a registered trade mark of
Oxford University Press in the UK and in certain other countries

© Oxford University Press 2024

The moral rights of the author have been asserted

All rights reserved. No part of this publication may be reproduced, stored in
a retrieval system, or transmitted, in any form or by any means, without the
prior permission in writing of Oxford University Press, or as expressly permitted
by law, by licence or under terms agreed with the appropriate reprographics
rights organization. Enquiries concerning reproduction outside the scope of the
above should be sent to the Rights Department, Oxford University Press, at the
address above

You must not circulate this work in any other form
and you must impose this same condition on any acquirer

Published in the United States of America by Oxford University Press
198 Madison Avenue, New York, NY 10016, United States of America

British Library Cataloguing in Publication Data

Data available

Library of Congress Control Number is on file at the Library of Congress

ISBN 978–0–19–887695–3

DOI: 10.1093/oso/9780198876953.001.0001

Printed in the UK by
Bell & Bain Ltd., Glasgow

Oxford University Press makes no representation, express or implied, that the
drug dosages in this book are correct. Readers must therefore always check
the product information and clinical procedures with the most up-to-date
published product information and data sheets provided by the manufacturers
and the most recent codes of conduct and safety regulations. The authors and
the publishers do not accept responsibility or legal liability for any errors in the
text or for the misuse or misapplication of material in this work. Except where
otherwise stated, drug dosages and recommendations are for the non-pregnant
adult who is not breast-feeding

For my children Eliza Jane, Henry Christian and Lilia Grace

One ship sails East,
And another West,
By the self-same winds that blow,
'Tis the set of the sails
And not the gales,
That tells the way we go.

—**Ella Wheeler Wilcox**

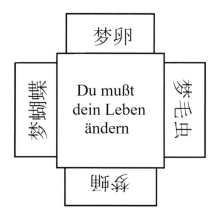

The German says "You must change your life," and the Chinese says "Dream egg, Dream caterpillar, Dream chrysalis, Dream butterfly."

Contents

Acknowledgments		xi
Introduction		**1**
I.1	Introduction to Libertarian Free Will	1
I.2	The Associated Online Lectures	19
1. The Basic Questions		**21**
1.1	What Is Freedom?	21
1.2	What Is Subjective Truth?	30
1.3	What Is Objective Truth?	31
1.4	What Is "Real"?	34
1.5	How Do We Know?	36
1.6	What Illusions Teach Us	39
1.7	What Are Information and Meaning?	41
1.8	What Is Causation?	50
1.9	What Is the Mind–Body Problem?	51
1.10	What Is Consciousness?	53
1.11	Against Pan-Psychism and Computational Reductionism	60
2. The Philosophy of Free Will		**69**
2.1	Defining the Problem of Free Will from a Scientific Point of View	69
2.2	Defining the Term "Free Will"	71
2.3	Volition Involves Various Brain Processes	71
2.4	Determinism versus Indeterminism	73
2.5	Possible Positions on Free Will	75
2.6	Two Types of Libertarian Free Will	76
2.7	Necessary Conditions for Free Will	84
2.8	The Consequence Argument against Compatibilism	85
2.9	The Exclusion Argument against Mental Causation	86
2.10	How to Overcome the Exclusion Argument	88
2.11	What Is Necessary for a Libertarian Free Will?	108
2.12	Why I Am an Indeterminist	110
2.13	What Is Criterial Causation?	120
2.14	Information as Pattern Decoding	128
2.15	The Luck Argument against Free Will	134
2.16	Criterial Causation Can Counter the Luck Argument	137
3. Scientific Arguments against Free Will		**151**
3.1	The Libet Experiment	151
3.2	Debunking Libet's Conclusions	155

x   Contents

3.3	Hypnosis versus Libet	157
3.4	Libet's Confusion about Causation in the Brain	158
3.5	Wegner's Theory of Apparent Mental Causation	163
3.6	Is the Feeling of Agency Retrodictive?	164

4. The Neuroscience of Free Will   169

4.1	Why Did Free Will Evolve?	169
4.2	The Two Valleys of Information Processing Death	172
4.3	How Neurons Function	174
4.4	Ionotropic and Metabotropic Receptors	179
4.5	Synchrony and Bursting	182
4.6	AMPA and NMDA Receptors	186
4.7	Why Is There a Synaptic Cleft?	188
4.8	How Neurons Realize Informational Criteria	191
4.9	A Synaptic Reweighting Neural Code	195
4.10	Indeterminism in the Brain, Part 1	200
4.11	Indeterminism in the Brain, Part 2	203
4.12	Indeterminism in the Brain, Part 3	206
4.13	What Is a Top-Down Brain Executive?	211
4.14	Global Cortical Architecture	214
4.15	Phineas Gage and Self-Governance	216
4.16	Executive Control Circuits of the Brain	219
4.17	Cybernetic Cingulate Cortex and Willpower	222
4.18	Top-Down Causation in the Brain	227
4.19	The Neural Basis of Volitional Attention	230
4.20	The Neural Circuitry of Nonvolitional Thought	235
4.21	The Neural Circuitry of Volitional Thought	238
4.22	How Volitional and Nonvolitional Circuits Interact	242
4.23	The Neural Basis of Willpower	246
4.24	The Cultivation of Willpower and Attention	249
4.25	The Neural Basis of Mindfulness	256
4.26	The Cultivation of Hope and Meaning	260
4.27	The Neural Basis of Volitional Imagination	266
4.28	The Relationship of Consciousness to Free Will	273
4.29	The Neural Basis of Self-Transformation	280
4.30	Chunking	286
4.31	Habit Formation and the Basal Ganglia	288
4.32	Second-Order Free Will and Virtue Ethics	292

Notes	297
References	299
Name Index	315
Subject Index	317

Acknowledgments

My deepest thanks go to my mother, Helga, who provided the deep emotional and intellectual scaffolding that every child needs during the formative years, when brains and minds are burgeoning with plasticity and openness. Even though we were not rich with money, my mother took full advantage of everything that NYC had to offer in the 1960s and 1970s. Thanks to her get-up-and-go and positive attitude about life, I practically grew up in the Museum of Natural History and Central Park, exploring and learning by doing.

I am also deeply indebted to my father, Kim Fung, who, through his gentleness and cultivation, taught by example what it means to be kind yet tough, idealistic yet practical. His long-term perspectives on history and life were often steadying in the cultural chaos of America back then and ever since. His voice has often guided my choices over the years, even since his passing in 2008.

My brother Mike and sister Barb have been with me since the beginning, and always bring me back to Earth with their humor. Thanks to them, we as a family have been rich in the deeper forms of wealth centered on health, love, and learning.

We come to life in a first family not of our choosing, and may, if we are fortunate, come to form a second family that is of our choosing. I am indebted to Melinda for being such an excellent and loving mother to our children Lilia Grace, Henry Christian, and Eliza Jane, who have become such fine adults. The four of you have filled my years with much more laughter than sorrow.

If the greatest wealth in life stems from health, learning, and connection, I reserve my deepest heartfelt thanks for Sienna Craig, for making life so rich and fun. Your depth, integrity, connectedness and generosity are truly inspiring. If only there were more people like you in this world.

Several P.S.173, junior and senior high school teachers had long-lasting influences on my thinking, especially Doc Sawyer in biology and Mei Lee, in literature. In eleventh grade I attended Hamphire College Summer Studies in Mathematics, which was transformational for me, in part by introducing me to other budding scientists like myself, especially Julie Ahringer and Lisa Randall. Once at Dartmouth as a physics/math major, my primary mentor was Joe Harris who took me to the bottom of quantum mechanics, and then helped free me from academia, at least for a while.

Misha Gronas is a kindred spirit among the faculty at Dartmouth. Thank you for all the conversations, laughs, and shared ideas over the years, and for accepting me into your large "moai" of friends.

Marcelo Gleiser, Jay Beaudoin, Mike Goudzwaard and Erin DeSilva made it possible for me to publish a Massive Open Online Course (MOOC), providing an abridged and simplified version of the ideas in this book for the public. Marcelo funded its production in 2018 using a part of his Templeton grant, and for that I am very grateful. It allowed me to reach many more people than I possibly could have reached with books.

I owe a lot to Dartmouth. I have been associated with the college, in one way or another, since I was seventeen. Over four decades later and I still appreciate how well it occupies a sweet spot in higher education that is centered on teaching, experiential learning, research, and freedom to explore. More undergraduates than I can possibly thank individually have year over year brought me back to life's deep questions. I could not have found a better home to work on diverse efforts to understand visual consciousness, work on octopus EEG, or write books like this one.

Special thanks go to past and present Dartmouth colleagues Sian Beilock, Dave Bucci, Yale Cohen, Scott Johnson-Frey, Mike Gazzaniga, Scott Grafton, Jenni Groh, Howard Hughes, Jay Hull, Dave Kraemer, Jeremy Manning, Kate Nautiyal, Jonathan Phillips, Jen Richeson, Caroline Robertson, Adina Roskies, Kiara Sanchez, Kyle Smith, Alireza Soltani, Arjen Stolk, Viola Stoermer, Jeff Taube, Mark Thornton, Matt Van der Meer, Tor Wager, Thalia Wheatley, and George Wolford among many others. None of it would be possible without our amazing support staff: Lisa Aubrey, Debbie Edwards, Andrew Knutsen, Lisa Lee, Michelle Powers, and Bess Ritter. Gratitude also for guidance concerning human evolution goes to Jerry DeSilva and Nate Dominy of Dartmouth's Anthropology Department, and Miles Blencowe of our Physics Department concerning quantum physics.

My first introduction to philosophy began with a year at the University of Konstanz, where I read *Philosophische Untersuchungen* very slowly. My gratitude to the Wolf family of Litzelstetten for hosting my stay there long ago.

I also owe a lot to my seven years at Harvard as a graduate student, where I had the pleasure of learning from many big thinkers who shaped me intellectually. I was educated in the Gestalt perceptual psychological tradition by my PhD advisors Patrick Cavanagh and Ken Nakayama. I learned so much from them and from my fellow grad students, post-docs and colleagues over those happy years, including Arash Afraz, Bart Anderson, Lorella Batelli, Marvin Chun, Jody Culham, Russell Epstein, Zijiang He, Sheng He, Alex Holcombe, James Intriligator, Arni Kristjansson, Steve Macknik, Vera Maljkovic, Susana Martinez-Conde, Paolo Martini, Rob McPeek, Sara Mednick, Kevin Ochsner, Josee Rivest, Nava Rubin, Brian Scholl, Adriane Seifert, Shin Shimojo, Joo-Hyun Song, Satoru Suzuki, Frank Tong, Maryam Vaziri-Pashkam, Franz Verstraten, Martin Wainwright, Takeo Watanabe, David Whitney and Yaoda Xu. Some professors who influenced my thinking were John Dowling, Nancy Kanwisher, Steve Kosslyn, Steve Pinker, Lothar Spillman and Charles Strohmeyer. One class in particular got me thinking about things that later led to certain aspects of my interest in free will that I will write about in the third volume of this trilogy; Around 1995 I took a seminar course with Amartya Sen and Robert Nozick that set me on a path toward trying to understand what political and economic institutions might maximize human flourishing and freedom.

My three post-doc years at the Max Planck Institute for Biological Cybernetics in Tübingen in the lab of Nikos Logothetis were formative. Special thanks to people from those years go to Heinrich and Isabelle Bülthof, Igor Bondar, Zoe Kourtzi, David Leopold, Christof Koch, David Sheinberg, Mike Silver, and Stelios Smirnakis.

Special gratitude goes to Al Mele for including me in his Big Questions in Free Will project, supported by the Templeton Foundation. That support allowed me and my dear collaborators at Dartmouth—Thalia Wheatley, Walter Sinnott-Armstrong, Adina Roskies, Alex Schlegel, and Scottie Alexander—to redo many of the Libet studies and then go beyond them. As a result, we concluded that the field was "barking up the wrong free," as we titled one of our papers. In my case, I reached the conclusion that Libet's work was largely irrelevant to issues of imagination and deliberation, which, I realized, were where the action actually is in free will. Through Al's meetings I came to know numerous philosophers, such as Eddy Nahmias and Thomas Nadelhoffer, and scientists interested in this topic who helped me to hone my own views. As a first result, I wrote *The Neural Basis of Free Will* (2013, MIT), followed by my MOOC (2018, EdX) on free will, followed by this book. Al's outreach to scientists and creation of collaborative interactions between scientists and philosophers reoriented me from my lab work toward the bigger picture implications of scientific findings for philosophy, life, and society. Thanks also to Robert Kuhn for making such fine documentaries about the deep questions.

Jaegwon Kim extended kindness to me when I went through a kind of crisis of doubt concerning his exclusion argument, back in 2006. I spent one long day talking with him at Brown, but he set me on a good track. He might be the only philosopher I have ever met who said of his views "I must be wrong because . . . ."

Philosopher Gabriel Mograbi was very kind to invite me down to Rio in 2021, and then to take me for a fantastic week of exploration in the Pantanal.

As I was writing this book, I also started an octopus lab to try to understand one of the most different complex brains and minds in the world. I thank Walt Besio, Gideon Caplovitz, David Edelman, Kelly Finn, Jonathan Fritz, Carl Harris, Marie-Luise Kieseler, Marvin Maechler, Marcus Missal, Sharif Saleki, and Jay Vincelli for helping me get that project off the ground.

I owe special gratitude to my graduate students. Concrete experiments and wide-ranging conversations with them have helped me in numerous ways to define what it is that I stand for. Special thanks go to Gideon Caplovitz, Eunhye Choe, Sergei Fogelson, Sebastian Frank, Kevin Hartstein, Nate Heller, Po-Jang Hsieh, Jiahan Hui, Peter Kohler, Sirui Liu, Marvin Maechler, Mert Ozkan, Eric Reavis, Sharif Saleki, Alex Schlegel, Liwei Sun, as well as NSF EPSCoR students Taissa Lytchenko, Mohsen Rakhshan, Adam Thuen and Kirsten Ziman.

I have collaborated with many scientists over the years. Special thanks goes to Mark Greenlee at the University of Regensburg. I am also grateful to Alfonso Caramazza, Jens Schwarzbach, and Angelika Lingnau for hosting me at CIMEC in Rovereto, Trento and Mattarello for a year, where I began jotting down notes for this book. I am also grateful to my many colleagues who helped lead the NSF EPSCoR consortium on the neural basis of attention for almost six years, in particular, Marian Berryhill, Gideon Caplovitz, Barry Connors, Theresa Desrochers, Charlie Gray, Barbara Jobst, Jamie Mazer, Alan Peterfreund and David Sheinberg. I also thank Cody Plante and Natalie Stephenson, my coordinators, who are so much more organized than I could ever hope to be.

I thank computer scientist Clint Ehrlich, who wrote me one of the most gratifying and uplifting emails I have ever received. Our subsequent interchanges clarified certain philosophical points for me, some of which I have incorporated into this book. I copy a part of his first email below, with his permission.

> Realizing that my brain was endowed with true free will was as intense a revelation for me as a stereotypical religious conversion. I had spent years believing that the compatibilist substitute was wholly satisfactory, but once I realized that elaborate intellectual rationalizations for unfree will were no longer necessary, it felt like a weight was lifted from my soul. Criterial causation gave me the mental framework I needed to take responsibility for making choices of moral consequence. Some of them have had profound impacts beyond my own life. After reading your book, I used my newfound agency to start my own investigation into a high-profile murder that I suspected the local police and FBI had mishandled. It was the right thing to do: I freed an innocent man who had served more than a decade of a life sentence. Even if the media and philosophy community never give your work the credit it deserves, please know that it has already had a tremendous impact in the world. I can tell you unequivocally that I never would have been inspired to take on that challenge and follow my moral intuition had I not read *The Neural Basis of Free Will*. Due to your writings, Sgt. Raymond Jennings is a free man enjoying life with his five children, instead of being locked in a cage for a crime he did not commit.

Finally, I thank the hundreds of people around the world who have contacted me, thanking me for my MOOC and other defenses of libertarian free will. Many have thanked me for convincing them that they do have free will. Many wrote of their suffering from the endless drum-beat of demoralizing and, I feel, faulty arguments coming from various outspoken popular writers, such as Hebrew University History lecturer Yuval Harari ("*organisms as little more than biochemical algorithms*"), Sam Harris (science "*reveals you to be a biochemical puppet*"), or Jerry Coyne ("*we're puppets performing scripted parts written by the laws of physics*").[1] They assert, sometimes dogmatically and with dismissive certainty, that we have no free will. Such popular writers generally ignore the deep and complex philosophical debates on these issues.[2] Similarly, the biologist Robert Sapolsky recently wrote a book titled "Determined," in which he argues that there can be no free will because biological determinism is the case. He said "We are biological machines who know our machine-ness. And some of us flee from that with responses that are ... delusional insofar as irrationally based, confabulatory, and comforting. Some of us face it and feel utterly depressed ...."

This book is therefore also written for the many who have despaired over the misinformation that free will is an illusion. With the ideas and arguments in this book, as well as in my upcoming books *Free Imagination* and *Reenlightenment*, I hope to persuade skeptics and offer the more hopeful message that we do have a say in the matter of what becomes of us, and that life truly can turn out otherwise, depending on what we now choose to do, and who we choose eventually to become. This book is the first in that trilogy of books and begins with the brain. The second book focuses on the imaginative sources of freedom, and the third asks what societal organizations and institutions optimally foster human freedom.

Hanover, NH, January 2024

Introduction

I.1 Introduction to Libertarian Free Will

In this book I defend an indeterministic naturalism. By "naturalism" I mean the monistic stance that there is only Nature, or that everything in this universe is natural. In other words, there is nothing supernatural, and all causes are natural causes, realized in whatever the ultimate realizer of patterns turns out to be.

My goal is to develop a naturalistic account of how a libertarian free will is realized in the human brain. Libertarian accounts of free will are deemed incoherent by those who (incorrectly) think that such accounts posit causes that lie outside of the succession of energetic patterns permitted by the laws of physics, whatever those might be. If libertarianism meant supernatural causation, or if it entailed a violation of the laws of Nature, or posited immaterial agents or souls, I would agree. But libertarianism does not have to entail supernatural causes, beings, or things. There are no supernatural miracles, and a case for libertarian free will can be made that dispenses with magical thinking and substance dualism. To give a coherent libertarian account of free will requires giving an account of causation that is consistent with natural successions of patterns of energy in spacetime.

Implicit in naturalism is an assumption of monism. Monism is the idea that there is just one fundamental underlying type of existence, in which all else is realized, whether neurons, baseball games or love. Naturalism has no room for dualism, which is the view that there are two or more fundamental types of existence, such as spirit and matter, or mind and matter. The basic problem facing dualism is that it cannot explain how two or more fundamental types of stuff could ever interact. (For example, take their interaction and divide it into the two mutually irreducible types, rather like separating intermixed salt from pepper; we can then ask again "But how do the two fundamental substances, say, mind and matter, interact?", and so on, *ad infinitum*).

I add "indeterministic" before "naturalism" to make clear that I defend a libertarian position concerning free will, in contrast to the currently dominant deterministic variants of naturalism, according to which events could not have turned out otherwise. Naturalism need not (and should not) be conflated with determinism. As I argue when I discuss Jaegwon Kim's exclusion argument, I believe that the possibility of free will is eliminated on the basis of exclusion if determinism is the case, contrary to the now-dominant compatibilist view that a form of free will is compatible with determinism.

There are many common misconceptions about free will. One is that free will is necessarily incompatible with determinism. It is not; although I am an incompatibilist, there are many compatibilist philosophers who advocate versions of free will that are compatible with determinism. Another is that free will is incompatible with indeterminism. Again, it is not; here I defend an account of free will that is compatible with indeterministic chance in the universe that does not reduce solely to randomness or present luck. Rather, I argue for a form of channeled chance, or one in which natural systems can harness chance to their own prespecified aims. My philosophical position (namely, that future chance outcomes can be pre-parameterized to satisfy present reasons) does not collapse into either utter randomness or dumb luck over which seeming agents have at best an "as if" form of control. Many scientists and philosophers mistakenly assume that to be fully caused means to be determined. In describing "criterial causation" or "parameter causation" I describe a form of probabilistic causation that Nature created through evolutionary processes. This is a type of causation that is neither deterministic nor utterly random.

If most naturalistic accounts of free will are compatible with determinism, my aim is to give an account that is compatible with indeterminism; that is, an account in which true randomness plays a role, but one where agency is not utterly lost to chance outcomes that just happen for no reason, regardless of what the agent wants. If utter randomness reigned, then causation on the basis of the brain's wants, reasons, and intentions would be lost. The solution is constrained randomness, wherein the nervous system places parameters, criteria, or constraints on future chance outcomes that will meet those preset limitations. Or, framed in terms of agency, an agent's will or intentions can place conditions on valid possible outcomes before any chance outcomes occur.

Within naturalistic views, the perspective that I develop here is diametrically opposed to that laid out in Robert Sapolsky's book "Determined," which came out just as I was going through the final proofs for this book. In terms of Philosophy, there is nothing new in his position. Sapolsky elaborates traditional philosophical causal determinism for the special case of biological determinism, leading to his main conclusion:

The intent you form, the person you are, is the result of all the interactions between biology and environment that came before. All things out of your control. Each prior influence flows without a break from the effects of the influences before. As such, there's no point in the sequence where you can insert a freedom of will that will be in that biological world but not of it.[1]

This view is based on a simplistic and incorrect conception of causation in which a cause A impacts some recipient of that cause B, such that B has no say in the matter of what shall happen to it. It is not really different from a Newtonian conception of causation in which billiard ball A hits billiard ball B, and B responds to the impact according to the deterministic laws of classical physics. Taken to a biological system, such as the brain, according to the implicit Newtonian metaphor behind Sapolsky's position, neuron A's inputs drive neuron B's outputs as deterministically as colliding billiard balls. But this Newtonian view of causation fails to apply to neuronal interactions or other classes of biological causation. When A causes B, B is not a passive recipient of A's effects. Especially in the case of biological systems, B evaluates A's inputs using criteria that can be altered, including, for some classes of neural events, altered volitionally for reasons held by an agent. For example, returning to the billiard ball metaphor, such criteria can be informational, as in "if even and striped, do this, but if odd and solid, do that." Even if these criteria could not be changed volitionally, this would lead to a radically non-Newtonian type of causation in the world. But criteria can be changed. For example, neuron A might change neuron B's criteria for future firing, without making it fire now. And, importantly, criteria for firing can be changed volitionally for reasons held by an agent. For example, a mind might think to itself: recall the name of a woman politician, in which case a person who met those criteria would subsequently percolate up from memory stores. That Margaret Thatcher came to mind rather than Victoria May, Angela Merkel, Hillary Clinton or Indira Gandhi might have been entirely random within the constraints imposed by those criteria, but it was not entirely random in that it had to be a woman politician rather than just anything at all.

Those who push the idea that we are nothing but deterministic biochemical puppets with at best epiphenomenal conscious operations are responsible for enhancing psychological suffering and hopelessness in this world. This perspective has pushed many people to the brink; some to suicide. I can understand why some philosophers might want to assert propositions with certainty, given that philosophers rely on persuasion, rather than collecting data. I have less understanding reserved for scientists who have made the radical and sweeping claim that there is no free will, given that scientists should know better than to make claims that go far beyond what is warranted by the thinnest of data.

Scientists such as Libet, Wegner, and Sapolsky have, I feel, done a disservice by asserting that there is no free will, when none of these authors researched the domains of human cognition where the action actually is in free will, namely, imagination and deliberation. Non-scientists, bloggers and popular writers then spread such claims by scientists to promote the falsehood that there is no room for free will within the scientific worldview. Sometimes this is done with a smugness that adds insult to intellectual injury. This is how despair propagates through our world, as memes of incorrect thinking.

Biological determinism is the argument that our behaviors are fully dictated by our genes and environmental inputs. This stance fails to account for behavior because the genetic and neural codes are parametric; They place parameters or constraints on outcomes, without specifying exact outcomes. That is why identical twins will always have differing pores, fingerprints, and hair locations. It is also why biological determinists, like Sapolsky, will never be able to provide the scientific community with an actual theory that predicts precisely what an animal will do next given some precise input. Such theories for them are always just one or two generations away.

The reason that such a theory is unattainable is that biological causation has inherent play that allows for an array of constrained outcomes. Biological codes are more like a recipe. A recipe might say "add one egg" without specifying its age, exact size or whether the egg is white or brown. For example, a neuron might be tuned to cat-defining criteria, but these can be met in infinitely many ways that result in an infinite set of possible inputs that would drive the neuron indistinguishably, thus defining a set of cat-like things bearing "family resemblances." Biological codes must be parametric, because there is simply not enough information carrying-capacity to specify an infinity of precise input-output-facts within a finite code. For example, there is no way one can specify the location of every atom in the body, because then the code would have to essentially be infinitely long, and our body would have to be as big as the world.

Reductionistic and linear conceptions of causation underlie intuitions that biological systems are deterministic. But these conceptions are wrong because biological systems are nonlinear, involving circular causation in which negative feedback allows a system to homeostatically (i.e. fixed setpoint) or allostatically (i.e. flexible setpoints, invoked as needed) pursue goal states in unforeseeable ways. One form of such nonlinearity arises because biological systems are capable of reparameterizing themselves. This allows animals to respond differently to identical future inputs than they did in the immediate or distant past.

In addition to criterial causation, in this book I emphasize another key aspect of causation generally absent from non-living natural systems, and also generally absent from discussions of free will, namely, cybernetic or error-correcting negative-feedback loops relative to internal reference signals, as depicted in Figure I.1 by Powers (1973a; see also 1973b, 1978). Norbert Wiener, who coined the term "cybernetics" in the 1940s, derived it from the Greek root κυβερνήτης (kubernetes), meaning "steersman" or "pilot," because the negative feedback loop of error minimization steers a process back to its set point. This is also the etymological root of the verb "to govern." It is through cybernetic processes that we govern ourselves.

Unlike a thermostat, which has no desires or preferences, and whose reference signal or setpoint is imposed externally when someone sets it to, say, 21°C (70°F), our bodies and minds generally have innate homeostatic setpoints that lead us to seek goal fulfillments. For example, if our body needs water, we start to feel thirsty and actively seek out liquids that we can drink; if we have then drunk too much, we are repulsed by the prospect of drinking any more. We cycle between satiation and thirst in order to stay close to the ideal hydration setpoint that has been sculpted into our genes by natural selection.

More generally, internal setpoints are allostatic rather than homeostatic in that there is not a single fixed setpoint. Rather, setpoints are variable, depending on need. For example, the setpoint for our blood pressure will vary depending on external factors, such as whether we are safe or under attack, and internal factors, such

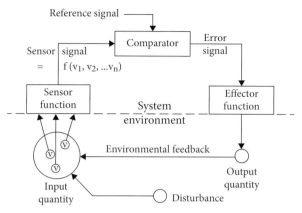

Figure I.1 Powers's (1973a) schematic of a basic control system that acts in a way that both minimizes disturbances caused by changes in the environment and causes the system to seek out inputs that will bring its sensors toward input that will allow a return to an internal reference signal. For example, if an animal is thirsty, it will seek out something to drink; and if it falls while seeking water, it will get up and continue the search, until the goal of drinking to satiation has been reached. This occurs when the comparator reports no difference between the reference signal and the sensor signal, meaning the error signal is now zero. Powers describes the above "Basic control-system unit of behavioral organization" as follows: "The *Sensor function* creates an ongoing relationship between some set of environmental physical variables (*v*'s) and a *Sensor signal* inside the system, an internal analog of some external state of affairs. The sensor signal is compared with (subtracted from, in the simplest case) a *Reference signal* of unspecified origin. The discrepancy in the form of an *Error signal* activates the *Effector function* (for example, a muscle, limb, or subsystem) which in turn produces observable effects in the environment, the *Output quantity*. This quantity is a 'response' measure. The environment provides a feedback link from the output quantity to the *Input quantity*, the set of '*v*'s' monitored by the sensor function. The input quantity is also subject, in general, to effects independent of the system's outputs; these are shown as a *Disturbance*, also linked to the input quantity by environmental properties. The disturbance corresponds to 'stimulus.' The system, above the dashed line, is organized normally so as to maintain the sensor signal at all times nearly equal to the reference signal, even a changing reference signal. In doing so it produces whatever output is required to prevent disturbances from affecting the sensor signal materially. Thus the output quantity becomes primarily a function of the disturbance, while the sensor signal and input quantity become primarily a function of the reference signal originated inside the system. For all systems organized in this way, the 'response' to a 'stimulus' can be predicted if the stabilized state of the input quantity is known; the stimulus–response law is then a function of environmental properties and scarcely at all of system properties."

as whether we are asleep or awake. Many aspects of our mind are cyclical, whether homeostatically or allostatically. For example, if we are alone too long, we may begin to feel lonely, causing us to seek out emotional connection; if we have been with people too long, we may become irritated by those around us or we may desire solitude.

William Powers preferred the term "perceptual control theory" to "cybernetics" because he felt that Wiener's term failed to emphasize the endogenous nature of reference signals such as thirst, and also failed to emphasize that feedback loops function to shift perceptual-motoric systems in the service of fulfilling aims, such as finding water. Powers's conception emphasizes consciousness and the subjective, in that error signals, such as thirst, and control of sensorimotoric systems to perceive and move through the world, exist in order to help an animal fulfill its goals, such as finding water. While it is true that Wiener tended to talk of exogenous reference signals set by an engineer, as when a thermostat is set to 21°C (70°F), and ignored the subjective, the difference between Wiener and Powers is really one of emphasis. Because it is less clunky, I will use Wiener's term "cybernetics" to mean control through error minimization relative to a reference signal, whether that be exogenously set, as in a thermostat, or endogenously set by evolution, as in the case of thirst, or endogenously set by volition or an intention, as when we choose to drive to the supermarket to buy milk.

A cybernetic architecture of control allows agents to fulfill their intentions over durations that may involve many cycles of error correction and reparameterization of the goal, or modifications of possible paths or criterial satisfactions that could lead to the intended goal, despite mistakes and setbacks. Causation in living systems is better understood in terms of this kind of nonlinear control theory, rather than in terms of linear, Newtonian equations that lack feedback. In Powers's (1973a) words, "A control-system model of the brain provides a physical explanation for the existence of goals or purposes, and shows that behavior is the control of input, not output."

Note how this turns the traditional linear understanding of minds on its head. Typically, linear thinkers argue that brain activity is driven in a bottom-up manner by sensory input. Powers says instead that the sensory input is what it is because the animal chose to move its eyes there, and it chose to look there versus elsewhere, for its own internal reasons. That is, bottom-up input is driven by prior top-down intentions and actions. For example, an animal might be thirsty (an error signal indicating deviation from the reference signal of how hydrated the body should be), so it looks for water, or moves to a place where water might be found.

Cybernetic causation and criterial causation are inextricably linked. The essence of both types of causation is that "there are many ways to skin a cat." When a cybernetic system has been disturbed, it can find its way back to the setpoint via error minimization in many possible ways. For example, if someone is shoved, they will take a first rough step to counter the shove, then finer and finer steps, until the error signal returns to zero, which occurs when they are standing upright again. There are many possible stepping sequences that will minimize the error signal back to zero. The first step might be a rough first approximation subject to substantial randomness of positioning. Indeed, for a toddler, the first steps might be entirely random until it has learned which rough steps correct which kinds of errors. On the next loop, the new error signal will lead to another, presumably smaller, step, and so on. Note that nothing complex need be computed. Nothing about the state of the world need be considered when shoved. All that is needed is a way to minimize the error signal defined by the difference between the current state of imbalance relative to the internal setpoint of balance.

Similarly, criterial causation can operate over the informational parameters of some internal task, say, "think of a mammal," in which case any mammal will do. Moreover, criterial causation can operate over goals, effectively specifying an endogenous reference signal or setpoint of a cybernetic process. For example, the task might involve finding an escape route from a predator. The whole organism would be thrust into the fight or flight response, not to compute the ideal escape route, but to find any escape route in an opportunistic manner. Any escape route would be good enough, just as any pattern of steps upon being shoved is good enough, so long as we come to stand upright again. There are generally many possible ways to meet any criterially defined goal.

When criteria can be set volitionally, the entire hierarchy of cybernetically looping causal chains can come to serve higher level reasons. For example, if we decide to find something to drink, the neurally realized cybernetic loops that underlie balance and body movement will operate in the service of that goal. Again, nothing highly specific needs to be computed in advance. A first step toward finding something to drink might involve going to the fridge in any number of possible ways, then looking inside at what is available with any number of eye movement sequences, then picking one among several possible drinking options up, then finding any cup that happens to be available, and so on. While the goal can be precise, the path to its fulfillment need not be—it can simply be good enough.

Many fail to understand free will because they implicitly believe that all causation must bottom out in linear "F = ma" types of deterministic causal relationships, in which there is no feedback and no error correction in service of reaching a goal. Moreover, linear thinkers tend to believe that all causation proceeds from the lowest level to the highest, with no possibility of top-down causation. However, a nonlinear causal relationship, even one at a higher level, imposes causal nonlinearity at all levels, assuming indeterminism, in the sense that top-down parameter causation biases which possibilities at the bottom-most level can become real. Moreover, people locked into a linear perspective concerning choice and goal-seeking tend to fall into the conceptual trap that everything must be computed within a complex internal world model if actions are to be successful. But that is not how free will typically works. Once a goal has been set volitionally, the path to the fulfillment of that goal can take many forms. It can unfold in a semi-haphazard way. We can overcome unforeseen hurdles and recover from many setbacks even in the absence of a very precise world model or precise computations about optimal paths. We deal with things as they arise, in the absence of complete information, and do what is needed to get us back on track to fulfilling our goals.

We can infer from our own experience and behavior what the internal reference signals must be that drive us to seek out the fulfillment of our diverse goals. Many of these are physiological and are associated with various desires. Desires are the subjective aspect of error signals in control theory. We seek out warmth when we feel cold and seek out cooling when we feel overheated. If we did not subjectively experience these error signals in our consciousness, as feelings of being too cold or too hot, we would not seek out, or volitionally be able to seek out, fulfillments of our desires. Fulfillment is often itself associated with subjective reward signals, such as pleasure. That which harms us or thwarts the fulfillment of our goals is typically associated with error signals to the downside, associated with pain, disgust, and at an emotional level, fear, embarrassment, and other forms of emotional pain. These positive and negative subjective signals are not made explicit in Powers' basic schematic of control theory, but they serve to reinforce behaviors that led, in the past, to goal fulfillment and satisfaction. Experiencing pleasure and pain therefore minimizes the likelihood of future mistakes. That is, subjectively experienced reward and punishment lead to learning. If we did not feel the various types of pleasure and pain, we would not learn how to maximize and minimize those subjective experiences. Through learning, the nervous system changes itself so that error correction will be more efficient in the future. Consciousness is the vehicle of volition.

Other error signals are not associated necessarily with physiological setpoints but rather are driven by more abstract reference signals associated with needs for territory, rank, safety, and so forth. Here, error signals might be associated with various emotions, or higher-order desires for love, domination, security, defense, and so forth.

Because subjectively felt error signals associated with numerous desires and emotions are central to their fulfillment, consciousness is inherently teleological and goal-seeking. Consciousness, especially concerning felt desires and emotions, plays a central role in the minimization of felt error signals relative to our various internally specified reference signals. Subjective experience is central to goal-seeking and therefore central to volitional goal-seeking or free will.

The behaviorist's view of the organism is wrong. We are not linear mechanistic sensory input–motoric output devices. Causation does not flow linearly like that in cybernetic systems centered on control of thought and behavior toward desired ends. It is not only that perception drives behavior, but rather that behavior also drives perception. In other words, there is a nonlinear behavior–perception–evaluation–behavior cycle.

Similarly, the dominant computer metaphor governing cognitive psychology and neuroscience (Yin, 2013, 2020) is inadequate. Like the mechanistic behaviorism that it sought to overthrow by adding a computer inside the black (stimulus–response) box, it tends to view causation in the brain as driven by the stimulus. Often cognitivists will speak of bottom-up or stimulus-driven processing, and top-down processing as that which modifies how the bottom-up processing will be biased or interpreted. But processing is top-down in a much deeper sense than simply biasing interpretations of bottom-up processing. Bottom-up processing is preceded by and driven by top-down processing because the animal chooses to look, attend, or move here versus there in its search for fulfillments of its various goals. Just as we are not sensory input–motoric output devices, we are also not primarily input–computation–output devices. As Powers emphasizes, the input drives the output less than the output drives the input. For example, we look around for a restaurant because we are hungry. We do not start to feel hungry only when we happen to stumble upon a restaurant. An organism seeks out input in order to approach, again and again, the fulfillment of its inner setpoints, sometimes experienced subjectively as desires and the satiation of desires, or the teleology of emotional striving and longing. The stimulus does not trigger the action mechanistically, as linear-thinking behaviorists or cognitivists would have it; rather, the action purposefully seeks out the stimulus.

Some of our endogenous setpoints or reference signals are genetically encoded products of evolution; deviations from such setpoints are experienced in our consciousness as the teleological desires and emotions, for example, thirst, hunger, loneliness, attraction, disgust, fear, territoriality, jealousy, anger. But other goals are not set by biology. We strive to get a PhD over years, for example, or strive to be true in our marriage, because the setpoint around which our actions are evaluated is an idea, including, very often, an idea of the ideal self or situation that we hope to eventually realize through our actions. With enough striving, and with enough practice, we may, in time, become the desired ideal agent we can now only hope to attain.

It is the linear thinking associated with open-loop causation, in which there is no feedback and no setpoint, and therefore no goal-seeking, that leads so many people to believe that there can be no telos in Nature; that is, that all causation is ultimately localistic "billiard ball" causation of quarks acting on neighboring quarks, or strings, or whatever is at the rootmost level, deterministically. The open-loop analysis of causation also leads to the fallacy that causal influence is instantaneous, when in closed-loop systems, it is cyclical and extended in time, over a vast scale of durations, from microseconds to decades. When the idea of closed-loop causation is combined with indeterminism, there is room for agents to sculpt—out of all possibilities open at the rootmost level—a desired future that realizes the agent's own goals for the agent's own reasons.

Powers (1973a) emphasized that control loops do not typically operate in parallel but are instead hierarchically nested, saying:

> A systematic investigation of controlled quantities can reveal an organism's structure of control systems. The structure is hierarchical, in that some quantities are controlled as the means for controlling higher-order quantities. The output of a higher-order system is not a muscle force, but a reference level (variable) for a lower-order controlled quantity.

All biological systems are hierarchies of nested closed-loop causal systems, in which causation is circular, typically in the service of goals (Figure I.2). Because control loops can be, and typically are, nested and hierarchical, there can be control loops

10   A Neurophilosophy of Libertarian Free Will

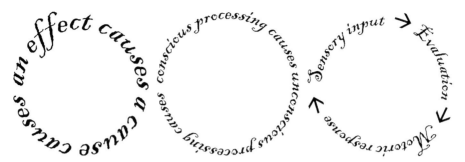

Figure I.2 Causation in the brain and body is circular, driven by a dynamic and nested hierarchy of control loops that are goal-seeking, relative to endogenous reference signals.

that lead not to external action, but to the resetting of lower-level reference signals or modulation of lower-level control loops' outputs and inputs. For example, we can feel second-order desires about our first-order desires. A lower level control loop might express an error signal that is felt as some desire, say, hunger or physical attraction to a potential mate. But a higher-order control loop might rein in the motoric response that the lower-level control loop alone might instigate, say, taking food off of someone else's plate, or grabbing someone who is physically desirable. It is not that the higher-order control loop eliminates the lower-order control loop, but it might govern its expression in light of context and higher order aims, such as abiding by societal rules. Instead of grabbing, we might accomplish our goals in a way that is optimized to minimize violations of contextual considerations to which the lower-level control loop might be blind. For example, we might politely ask for a piece of food rather than grabbing it, or we might develop a plan to court the focus of our attraction, rather than attempt to take a person against their will.

A sign of the cultivation of a person is the degree to which they govern themselves through higher-order control of lower-order control systems. As my father taught me, the essence of being civilized, rather than brutish, is appropriate restraint and discipline, while furthering longer-term and greater goods beyond those dictated by local self-interest.

In control theory, the cause causes the effect as much as the effect causes the cause. For example, we might begin to feel hungry, so we actively move our bodies and eyes to look for food, which leads us to finding food, and then reaching for it. If the error signal, namely, the deviation from the setpoint, did not trigger a conscious desire for food, namely, the subjective experience of hunger, animals would not be able to invoke volitional operations, such as volitional attention and associated volitional eye movements, to find food in a contextually appropriate way. The food stimulus alone did not lead to the reaching, as Pavlov or other behaviorists might have imagined. Similarly, the contents of consciousness do not emerge as a linear causal chain from sensory input to unconscious processing to conscious experience. Rather, operations in consciousness, such as mind-wandering, might lead to a thought of, say, Italy, which then invokes a desire to remember where we ate that delicious meal ten years ago, which in turn leads unconscious processing to search and then deliver "Assisi!" into our consciousness. That name just popped into consciousness, but only because prior conscious operations evoked its recall.

Bringing this idea specifically home to the issue of free will, it is linear (open-loop, Newtonian) thinking that leads many people to believe that matter cannot be truly teleological, agentic, or self-governing. Under the linear paradigm, expressed in the Sapolsky quote above, which works well for planets and billiard balls, the effect follows necessarily from preceding causes, which are sufficient to account for what happens next, except perhaps for some randomness. Under this linear causal paradigm, free will makes no sense, because what happens, happens purposelessly, obeying deterministic descriptions of the laws of Nature, which are not cybernetic; basic laws, like Newton's, involve no negative feedback loops, no control, and no internal setpoints or goals, especially ones associated with purposeful conscious experiences, such as hunger or thirst. But unlike planets and billiard balls, living systems have closed-loop causation, involving complex hierarchies and systems of interacting feedback signals that exist in order to continually return the organism to a dynamic equilibrium point of health, safety, and desire fulfillment.

Under the linear view of causation, what an organism does next is, in principle, dictated by all of its impinging causes, external and internal; this view requires knowing, in principle, infinite amounts of information concerning the positions, momenta, and other attributes of perhaps all the particles in the universe. Not only is this impossible in principle, it is misguided. Very little information is needed to understand why an organism seeks to correct a discrepancy between its endogenous reference signal and its current state; for example, it seeks water because it is thirsty, and it starts to feel thirsty because its body is below the setpoint of optimal bodily hydration. Nothing need be known about other factors in the universe. And if a discrepancy arises unexpectedly because of some external disturbance, say, it is shoved while searching for water, counteractive measures will immediately reduce the discrepancy, in this case, bringing it back to a position of standing. Counteracting disturbances requires little (or even no) knowledge about the causes of the disturbance or the state of the world. It just requires a way to minimize the discrepancy in order to return to the inner setpoint.

The free will problem, viewed from the perspective of closed-loop dynamic processes that play out over multi-scale durational cycles, becomes one of goal fulfillment despite setbacks and mistakes. The goal can be achieved in many possible ways, none of which is necessary; an animal can search for water in many ways, whether in the world or in its memory; a human can have a goal, say, of learning Tibetan, and accomplish this in countless possible ways. Free will is a cybernetic process of negative feedback and error correction in which biologically given and reason-based agentically specified goals might be attained with effort and striving over perhaps long durations of want and tribulation.

Let us now turn from causation to chance. Indeterminism alone is not enough to attain a libertarian free will. Ontologically real indeterminism is only a necessary condition for that attainment. A universe that was utterly random would be as unfree as a universe in which events unfolded as deterministically as the playing out of a movie on a reel of film. In addition to indeterminism, agents must be able to shape the likelihoods of the events that they intend to realize, so that those envisioned events have an enhanced likelihood of actually coming to pass, relative to other, less-desired outcomes. This is where causation via reparameterization comes into play. Depending on the problem or choice we are trying to make, we might set parameters rather tightly. For example, we might try to recall from our long-term memory some fairly specific fact such as "She was an actress on the TV show *Friends* who was not Jennifer Aniston." Other times, we might set parameters loosely, such as "Who should I visit today?" or even very loosely, such as "What should I do with my life given all the things that I can do and want to do?" Possibilities that might come to mind in a seemingly bottom-up way will not be random, because they will have to first meet the prespecified criteria to even count as possibilities. Such upward percolations from the unconscious are not entirely bottom-up, because they will have emerged in interaction with prior top-down impositions of willed parameters, many forged during conscious deliberations. Willing channels randomness in order to shape the likelihoods of possible realizable futures.

One way our nervous system does this is to place constraints on imagined outcomes. For example, try this: imagine a chimera with the head of one animal and the body of another. There are infinitely many ways to satisfy these constraints, but the results are not utterly random, because the outcome of such an act of imagining will be a chimera. In order to be able to do this, we need an information-processing system that allows such informational constraints to be placed on the products of mental operations carried out in the imagination, and physically, in the physical realizers of mental events: patterns of intra- and inter-neuronal activity.

A free will denier might respond that the parameters that were imposed on subsequent bottom-up processing themselves had to come from somewhere; did they themselves not simply emerge in the absence of free choice? The answer is that it depends. Some parameters are truly beyond our control: we did not choose to be born as a human who can only survive within a narrow range of physical conditions, being genetically xx or xy, or the century or country of our birth. But even if we did not choose what we are, what we are only defines our potential, not how that potential will be realized, including the realizations that follow from choices we make. Just because we are limited to a life within, essentially, an infinitesimal proportion of the universe, does not mean that we must regard Earth as a prison. There are many possibilities open to us on Earth and within the parameters that define our potential. Our world is like a Rorschach inkblot figure. If we see it as a prison, that is what it is for us. If we see it as a playground rich in possibilities that we can shape in light of our purposes and imaginings, then that is what the world is for us.

Some parameters emerge into consciousness seemingly against our will, especially those associated with the many emotions and desires. For example, we may simply start feeling hungry. This is one of many desires that nonvolitionally emerge into consciousness. Hunger will then trigger a search in memory or in the world for sources of food. This search can, but need not, be subject to volitionally imposed constraints, such as "it must be kosher," or "it must contain fewer than 400 calories," or "it must not contain peanuts." Or perhaps no volitional constraints will be imposed in a top-down manner, and whatever first comes along that meets the criterion "is edible" will do.

Other consciously imposed parameters, however, consistently arise volitionally. For example, mental operations that play out in consciousness, in particular, in the internal virtual reality of our consciously experienced deliberations and mind wanderings, might involve imagining who we could invite for dinner, which, once settled, might entail that we then search for halal possibilities, because one of our planned guests follows orthodox Muslim eating rules. The parameter "must be halal" is not akin to an inborn desire, like hunger. It itself arises as the conclusion of mental operations that take place in consciousness.

Willing can also alter the setpoints of cybernetic processes. For example, if the feeling of having to go to the bathroom emerges into our consciousness as a desire needing fulfillment, but we are in the middle of taking a proctored exam, making it impractical to immediately go to the bathroom, top-down processes can inhibit this desire, at least momentarily, so that our attention can stay focused on the more important matter of doing well on the test. A momentary hierarchy of cybernetic processes emerges in which a higher-level goal, say, completing the test, is able to rein in and even inhibit or change the setpoint or associated desire of a lower-level goal. And while we could impulsively just go and do what our body wants to do while taking the exam, this would violate even higher-level goals, such as adhering to social convention and maintaining our social standing. But the hierarchy of cybernetic processes is flexible because it can be flipped. The feeling may become so urgent that it must now take highest priority. Other goals, like focusing on the test or maintaining decorum can become subservient to this reprioritized desire, which in turn may now inhibit these "higher" desires. At this point we might take the entire context into account and decide that our best course of action is to get up and explain to the proctor that we have an emergency.

Consciousness is the domain where competing goals with associated desires can be volitionally and flexibly contextualized, prioritized, and sequenced appropriately. More precisely, desires and emotions impose a prioritization hierarchy of goals within consciousness even without volitional control; this can, however, be volitionally modulated as needed, though not eliminated, because desires and emotions cannot be willed into or out of existence (Tse, 2013; §10.9–§10.11). Unconscious processing, in contrast, lacks volitional operations, prioritization, or sequencing in light of context. In the absence of consciousness, urination, say, would be triggered as needed, decided by an unconscious process that detected the fullness of the bladder relative to some setpoint beyond which a reflex of bladder-emptying would be invoked nonvolitionally. Teleological qualia, such as desires and emotions, allow volitional operations to flexibly negotiate an optimal path to their maximal fulfillment in light of the "bigger picture." In the absence of qualia, volitional operations would have no operands upon which to operate and we would be left with unconscious automaticities, blind as they tend to be, to reasons and context. Consciousness, as the domain of experienced operands of potentially volitional operators, evolved so that animals could agentically and appropriately prioritize, sequence, and choose among possible paths to the fulfillment of their desired goals. Qualia evolved for free will as the world/body hallucination that affords our agency.

Thus, conscious and unconscious processing are in a tight symbiotic relationship, where one constrains the other in a cycle of top-down parameterization and bottom-up satisfactions. This is an ongoing dynamic that affords the possibility of evaluating how well we are doing at reaching our diverse goals in light of what has happened, both internally, in terms of our deliberations and desires, and externally, in light of our actions. The feedback afforded by the difference between what we expected to happen or wanted to happen, and what in fact did happen, allows us to make midstream corrections. Volition does not happen in an instant; it plays out over short or long durations during which we can correct our errors so that we can better fulfill our goals in light of our reasons for fulfilling them. To view consciousness solely as the passive recipient of the outputs of unconscious processing that continually just pop linearly into consciousness at each instant is wrong (e.g., Harris, 2012).

Consciousness is not a passive mirror that reflects events as they arise without processing any further. Consciousness is not a passive stage that receives unconsciously generated outcomes, ideas, scripts, and plans. Consciousness is rather an active workroom, where volitional operations can generate outcomes that affect both future conscious and unconscious processing. Perceptual consciousness does reflect events in the world, but even here top-down processing can affect the bottom-up processing that leads to subsequent contents of consciousness (Sun et al., 2017; Tse et al., 2013). For example, intending to see a Rorschach inkblot as, say, a butterfly versus a face, will bias what we will then see in the inkblot. The contents of perceptual consciousness now are the result of what was volitionally attended and intended a moment ago, which in turn affects what will be attended and intended next, and where we will next move our eyes and bodies.

Moreover, some subset of perceptual consciousness can be shunted into working memory for further mental operations in that other aspect of consciousness, that is, our internal virtual reality simulator, or imagination. Volitional operations, in particular, operate over conscious operands because their outcomes must be experienced, so that we can experience how this versus that possible future feels before trying to enact our preferred option in the world. Alternatively, if it is an outcome that we dislike in our virtual experience, we attempt to lower the likelihood that it will become actualized as our future. Imagination allows us to consciously experience what it feels like to live possible life x, virtually.

I argue that the core circuits underlying free choice involve frontoparietal, default mode, and basal ganglia (see Section 4.29) networks that facilitate deliberation among options that are represented and manipulated in executive working memory areas. Playing out scenarios internally—as virtual experience—allows a super-threshold option to be chosen before specific motoric actions are planned. The chosen option will likely have optimally met criteria held in working memory, constrained by the evaluations of reward, emotion, and cognitive circuits. The processes of volitional deliberation and nonvolitional mind-wandering involve consciousness because if a considered possibility does not experientially *feel* right, it can be rejected; and if it feels right, it can be accepted. If rejected, prior top-down constraints imposed on future bottom-up percolations can be altered, in a cybernetic consciousness–unconsciousness–consciousness feedback loop where the goal is to find a path to a solution that meets the criteria set. This process also harnesses synaptic- and ultimately atomic-level randomness to foster the generation of novel and unforeseeable satisfactions of those criteria. Once criteria are met, executive circuits can alter synaptic weights on other circuits that will implement a planned operation or action. For example, someone, say, one of the Wright brothers, can imagine possible flying machines, and then, after much deliberation, go and build an airplane that will transform the physical universe forever.

Another theme of this book is that we have free will in both a first-order (type 1) and in a second-order (type 2) sense. With first-order free will, we have the capacity to consider options, weigh them in light of our own reasons or desires, and then select and enact the one that we want to enact. With second-order free will, we have the capacity to choose to become a new kind of chooser in the future.

I am an incompatibilist whose aim is to give an account of second-order free will in the brain that is not deterministic, but that also does not boil down to randomness alone. There are pessimistic incompatibilists who argue that free will is incompatible with determinism, and who then argue that because determinism is the case, there can be no free will. I argue, optimistically, that indeterminism is the case, and that our brains have evolved to harness indeterminism toward intended and desired ends. This includes second-order ends like choosing or willing now to become a different kind of chooser or willer in the future.

We should also consider the various sources of the feeling of agency or authorship of decisions and actions. At least in some cases, these cannot be causal of subsequent actions or thoughts, because they are attributions about what just happened in the past. In other cases, an agent, defined as that which governs volitional operations, such as choosing to voluntarily attend to this versus that other possibility, does play a role in the outcome of such operations. For example, if asked why we are attending to children on a beach we can give a reason such as: we are looking for a child who ran off with a friend because we are supposed to be babysitting them. Surely, those who deny free will do not want to deny that there is a distinction between a volitional process, such as moving the eyes here versus there for known reasons in a manner flexibly influenced by context, and a nonvolitional process, such as unconscious and automatic pupillary size modulations with changing brightness of a light. What free will deniers want to deny is that there is an agent who governs consciousness and action who is an uncaused cause in the chain of causation. But we can grant that there are causes that generate the set of reasons that governs subsequent volitional action. Some of those causes might be beyond our volitional control, as when the reason we start seeking food volitionally is that we nonvolitionally simply notice that we now feel hungry. But there are other cases where the reasons that we act volitionally are themselves chosen volitionally, as when we suppress a current desire to stray because of a wedding vow we made years ago, or when we try not to read words during the Stroop task because of a voluntary decision to take part in an experiment involving top-down control of our actions.

It is reasonable to deny that there is a noun-like willer, rather like a little person in the head, who is turning attention or the eyes this way or that. But it is not reasonable to deny that there are verb-like agentic processes that govern attention or the eyes that are volitional and are applied in light of reasons that can be reported. Not all choices just happen mysteriously. Very often we can list reasons why we chose to act this way versus that way. If we deliberate, it is typically because we have good reasons for wanting to realize two or more options, but can only choose one, say, job location or life partner. If one option is the obvious winner, there is no reason to deliberate. If a long-deliberated choice just happened for no apparent reason, we would not need to agonize over it. The reason we can feel conflicted is that our reasons can be conflicting. For example, one part of us may crave deep connection, while another may crave independence, and yet another security. If we ultimately choose A over B, it is not solely a matter of chance. It is because we have played out the future with A and the future with B, and have experienced, virtually, the future with A to be more fulfilling of our most closely held reasons, even if we might let go of a possible future with B with a sense of loss, because at least along some dimensions they may have been a better satisfier of some of our conflicted desires. However, it may be that there is not a single choice that optimizes over all our needs and goals. In life, there are often trade-offs.

It would be a mistake to say that there is no difference between a volitional process and an automatic one, or to say that there are only automaticities. For example, it would be wrong to say that all eye movements are tantamount to reflexes of the pupil, because there are volitional saccadic and smooth pursuit eye movements as well. What distinguishes volitional from nonvolitional processes is that they are governed by consciously knowable reasons that can change in light of our deliberations, that we can suppress or enact for reasons that we can often state, and that are amenable to alteration on command. Say I find my lost child on the beach, and then learn that they are hungry. I would then start a search for places to eat and my attention and eyes would move for these new reasons. Such reasons cannot themselves be automatized because they need to adapt to context and circumstance flexibly. For example, not every day is the sabbath. But if it happens to be the sabbath, we might look for a different kind of place to eat than usual. Or if it is Ramadan, we might inhibit the search for food altogether until sundown, despite our intense hunger.

A free will-denying and moral responsibility-denying philosopher (e.g., Caruso, 2012; Levy, 2011; Strawson, 1994) might then assert that, while yes, it is true that you were looking for the child because you had promised someone to watch them, and you care about them, those reasons are as involuntary as suddenly feeling hungry. You might respond: "No, I promised them that I would watch their child because I needed a job." And they might then ask, "Where did that need for a job come from?" Eventually this philosophical "walking back" argument typically bottoms out in genetics, in the environment, or in events that may have happened before you were even born, none of which was subject to your volitional control. Any reason you give for having had the reasons you had for looking for the child could be subject to the same walking-back line of attack. If we walk any chain of reasons back far enough, they bottom out in some non-chosen reason. But even if this is true, so what? At any given moment, we are acting voluntarily in light of our reasons, and our actions can turn out in multiple different ways given the identical state of the nervous system, as long as subsequent actions mediated by chance are consistent with those reasons. For example, we might look for a lost child here versus there; but if we could rewind the universe, we might look for the child with a different sequence of volitional saccades instead.

Libertarian free will depends on the claim that events can turn out otherwise, subject to our reasons. If some of those reasons arise nonvolitionally into consciousness (like hunger often does), this does not eliminate the freedom we have to eat at many possible restaurants or to eat many possible types of food in order to sate our hunger, or to choose to fast despite our hunger.

Do we even always want the freedom to change what we want? Would we want the freedom to choose to find vomit delicious? We would not. We want to find something that sates our hunger that is delicious, even if we cannot choose what will count as delicious. Another example might be that a person might want to find someone to date. To that person, it does not matter that the desire itself was not chosen by them. What matters is the ability to satisfy that desire in a way that is volitionally subject to their own reasons. In fact, if you gave the person the freedom to alter the nature of their desire, say, to choose to find trees or cows sexually attractive instead of humans, they would surely find this absurd. Most people do not want that kind of free will. They want the freedom to volitionally choose given their desires and reasons. They typically do not want the freedom to volitionally change their desires and reasons to something that does not concur with their present desires and reasons. That said, there are cases when we would like to change our desire structure or even character structure. Later in this book I will more closely examine such examples of choosing to become a new kind of chooser.

Thus, we can consider a taxonomy of types of free will. First there is proximal free will. There are proximal acts of volition, and these can either involve picking between equivalent options, as in picking more or less equivalent apples from a tree branch, or they can involve deliberation about what we will next do, when options have pros and cons, as in choosing among different brands of bread at the supermarket. Then there is distal free will, in which we strive over long durations to realize an envisioned future. This might involve building a house, rebuilding our physique, honing our mental capabilities, or even transforming our own character. This book is foremost about the slow cybernetic processes underlying the volitional realization of such distal envisionings. It is about slow free will.

Powers (1973a) makes clear that animals driven by endogenous reference signals associated with internally felt desires and emotions, and indeed internally felt control, will be inherently difficult to control by others. He writes: "Behavior itself is seen in terms of this model to be self-determined in a specific and highly significant sense that calls into serious doubt the ultimate feasibility of operant conditioning of human beings by other human beings." If a person is driven by endogenous subjective desires and emotions that an external controller cannot directly access or manipulate, that external controller can at best try to harness those endogenous states through persuasion, inculcation and reward, as when we shape a dog's behavior by harnessing its desires for food and approval, or we employ punishment, as when we hit or yell at a dog for eating our dinner off the table. Governments and other systems of external control that push too hard against the endogenous desires that govern us, including a desire to be free of external control, typically fight a losing battle. Humans will eventually find a way around such external constraints placed on their freedoms and sovereignty. This is the innate sovereignty of the private mind, with its internal locus of control, and subjectively experienced goals, desires, and emotions.

Control ultimately lies with the individual because consciousness only exists in the individual, not in the collective. Only an individual can subjectively feel that what is happening is right or wrong, and then respond in light of that conviction. Only a human can be moral. Institutions, corporations, and governments are amoral. They can seem to have control, but this as-if control is always expressed through the consent of individual participants and enforcers, or the compliance of those individuals who are governed. Consent can be withdrawn, and compliance can be replaced by defiance, revealing that it was always individual choices that led to the façade of collective control. This is why the argument that "it was the system, not me" never flies. Following orders is a person's choice. This is also why the example of dissenters and those who do not comply is so threatening to those who lust for total domination. They undermine control of the narrative that governs subjects' minds by saying that the governing narrative is flawed or can be ignored. This perspective shift can spread rapidly and turn compliant dogs into defiant wolves overnight. The problem for dictators is that gulags can imprison bodies but not ideas. Bullets can kill bodies, but they cannot kill ideas.

Assuming the reality of indeterminism, this book aims to provide arguments for a libertarian conception of free will within the theoretical frameworks of criterial causation and cybernetic control. Mental and brain events really can turn out otherwise and yet are not utterly random. Prior neuronally realized informational settings parameterize what subsequent neuronally realized informational states will pass preset physical criteria for firing, which serve as informational filters or constraints. This does not mean that we are utterly free to choose what we want or want to want. Some wants and criteria are innate, such as what smells good or revolting. However, given a set of such innate parameters, the brain can generate and play out options, and then select an option that adequately meets criteria. If none are adequate it can spur the generation of further options. This process is closely tied to voluntary attentional manipulation in working memory, more commonly thought of as deliberation or imagination.

But before beginning our journey into how all this might work in the brain, we begin at the very beginning, by defining our basic concepts in Chapter 1. What is freedom? What is causation? What do we mean by the term "free will"? What is volition? Indeed, what do we really desire when we say that we are striving for greater freedom?

I.2 The Associated Online Lectures

I had already been working on this book for a few years when my physicist friend at Dartmouth, Marcelo Gleiser, suggested that I put together a version of my ideas for the general public. He suggested that I produce online lectures summarizing my views concerning what makes the human mind so much freer than those of other animals. He thought that the public would be interested in my thesis that human capacities to imagine and deliberate are at the very heart of human free will, and that these imaginative capacities are rooted in a neurally realized functionality that is unique to human brains. The online lectures that accompany this book appeared as an edx.org Massive Open Online Course (MOOC) in 2018, as well as coursera.org, and can also be found on YouTube:

https://www.youtube.com/playlist?list=PLCh78lhDREMyIOCl3-9BeOWk3Q9MtxWGv

For the most part, each short lecture is an abridged version of the corresponding chapter in this book with the same numbering. They revisit some themes of my 2013 book, and then move beyond that book in examining imagination and willpower as the foundations of free will. This book covers lectures 1.1–4.29, and the sister volumes, *Free Imagination* and *Reenlightenment*, cover the remaining lectures.

Some philosopher friends told me there was too much neuroscience in my 2013 book *The Neural Basis of Free Will*, and some neuroscientist friends told me there was too much philosophy. Here, I have tried to find a certain sweet spot, such that any educated person should be able to understand the philosophy and neuroscience presented in this book or the accompanying online lectures. If you find anything difficult to understand, then that reveals my shortcomings as an explainer, not yours as a reader or viewer.

1
The Basic Questions

1.1 What Is Freedom?

Before beginning on our journey, we will define and clarify our concepts. In later chapters we will carefully define basic terms, such as "free will," "causation," and "indeterminism." But before we get into philosophical and scientific details about how mental events might be causal in a top-down manner in the brain, let us reflect a bit on the diverse meanings of the word "freedom."

Why would we want to have a free will anyway? Presumably to maximize our freedom. But freedom from what? External control? And freedom to do what? To do whatever we want? If so, what do we really want to do in this brief life? Many people, especially many of us in the West, have a default notion of freedom as freedom *from* constraints. Many of us don't want people telling us what to do or violating our liberty in other ways. An example of this would be freedom from people stealing our things, and freedom from them harming our body, or even freedom from others violating our privacy. It seems obvious why we would want freedom from any of these violations of our personal liberty.

But let us say we actually lived in a perfect world where there were no violations of our personal liberty, that is, a world without theft or war and one without government or corporate surveillance or control. Would that be enough to feel free or even be free? If we think of freedom from constraint as the sole and ultimate form of freedom, then a conquistador or cowboy, living far away from society, outside any governmental or police jurisdiction, and beholden to no one, would be maximally free, surviving and perhaps even thriving by virtue of individual guts, wits, perseverance, and strength.

In other societies, this rugged individualism might be regarded as selfish, unwise, and perhaps even pathological. Such societies might regard real freedom as possible only within the constraints afforded by a society in which what you can do is defined by shared agreements concerning what is allowed and good. Just as you can only speak and be understood given the constraints imposed upon you by your native language and a community of speakers who follow shared grammatical rules, and, as Kant noted, just as a bird can only fly by virtue of the constraints imposed upon its wings by air, we can only be free inside of a system that constrains our actions, simultaneously defining what is possible by making certain actions impossible, wrong, or impermissible. Meaningful possibility without impossibility is impossible. Even in the West, there is an understanding that binding contracts and the rule of law, which constrain human action, afford the trust and security required to attain the freedom

A Neurophilosophy of Libertarian Free Will. Peter Ulric Tse, Oxford University Press. © Oxford University Press 2024.
DOI: 10.1093/oso/9780198876953.003.0002

to start a business or take financial risks. Even in the West there is another current of understanding human freedom as freedom not *from* constraints, but freedom *within* constraints.

Consider a great pianist, say, Vladimir Horowitz. He was born knowing nothing about the piano. He might have come to this world with plenty of genetically endowed potential in the domain of music. However, even Mozart, had he grown up without exposure to music, would have failed to realize his magnificent potential. Genetics provides potential, but whether and how that potential is realized depends on many factors, including, in the end, personal decisions regarding how we will mold the "clay" of potential we have inherited. When we are very young, most decisions are made for us, including how we might best realize our potential. Perhaps young Vladimir's parents constrained his freedom by forcing him to practice the piano against his will. Over time his nervous system chunked and automatized the recognition of notes from a random collection of black dots into coherent chord patterns, so that he could now recognize a C major chord at a glance, rather than having to attentionally work it out. The same happened in his motor system. At first a C major chord was attentionally demanding to execute. In time his fingering became automatized, and attentionally effortless. Then, whole sequences of such chunks became automatized into longer motor sequences and the mapping between perceptual and motor chunks also became automatized. His own volitional attentional circuitry functioned as a good teacher should, making itself no longer necessary.

Volitional attention played the role of a glue holding together simpler representations in his working memory, which, metaphorically speaking, hardened, allowing previously disjoint units to be stored, recalled, recognized, and subsequently executed as chunks and meta-chunks. In a word, Vladimir Horowitz began mastering the piano. He employed his volition, especially the "glue" of his volitional attention, to automatize that which he chose to master. His volition chose what would, with practice, become nonvolitional.

If consciousness is the domain of volitional operations, such as paying volitional attention to this versus that for one's own reasons, one goal of consciousness is to relegate to the unconscious that which we have attentionally glued together. Much of what we regard as the unconscious is in fact a creation of past states of attentionally glued-together components in consciousness. To the extent that we freely choose to attend to or practice this versus that, the automaticities of our unconscious processing come to encapsulate our past volitional acts, or free will. Free will depends on the automatization of volition, or the transformation of volition into nonvolition. An "archaeologist" of the unconscious would find there the fossils of previously conscious acts of volitional attention to selected contents once held in working memory.

The years-long process of transforming the Horowitz nervous system required constraints. He had to practice the piano for hours a day at the expense of many other things that he could have done with that time. In the end, this focus afforded him a deeper freedom of action within the severe constraints of the piano. This might be thought of as the freedom to play directly "from his chest," as opposed to being constrained by the cumbersome inefficiencies that plague most dilettantes and beginners. The beginner's stage of learning chunks was followed by learning meta-chunks of chord sequences and ultimately meta-chunks of these meta-chunks, and so on, until, after perhaps years of practice, he attained mastery.

We are not born as that which we eventually become. Month-old Adolf Hitler was a baby who could have gone in many directions in his life, as could have baby Martin Luther King, Jr. We become who we become gradually. We learn to speak and walk haltingly, with good or poor scaffolding. After years of our own decisions and cultivation or buffeting by circumstance, we approach a fully formed adult personality.

I believe that the determinist's notion that a baby, rich in potential, and capable of learning any language or culture, was "predestined" at the Big Bang to become, say, a prostitute or an air traffic controller, is both incorrect and absurd. This notion fails to recognize the role that agency has in shaping the play in objective events by denying the reality of such play. Later we will examine evidence for indeterminism, and then how we evolved the capacity to sculpt our envisioned realities out of what is physically possible, given the degree of ontological play that exists.

The units over which the mental operations of a master operate might be difficult for non-masters to comprehend. The adult Vladimir Horowitz likely operated over very high-level patterns involving nuances of emotion and expression, the lower-level chunked executions being relegated to the domain of automaticities. At that stage, overthinking can harm expression because, at the stage of mastery, volitional manipulation of components that have already been chunked would hinder fluid and effortless execution of well-practiced sequences. In turning off interfering volitional control over lower-level chunked sequences, it might seem to the master that his or her body was functioning in a manner tantamount to a marionette that moves itself, or that the body is even a channel for the expression of some agent outside of the self. Indeed, agency would now lie largely beyond the ken of the locus of volitional control, in particular with that sense of agency felt when governing the shifting and allocation of endogenous attention. However, given that volitional attention could still be allocated over the highest levels of meta-chunks—perhaps, in the case of Horowitz, to the emotional phrasing realized in modulations of loudness and timing—it would seem to the master that he exercised volitional control over an army of loyal subordinates. Perhaps this is how Napoleon felt about hundreds of thousands of soldier sub-agents who were ant-like vehicles of his master will, despite their own subservient sub-wills.

This is not to say that the master's processing is entirely automatized like some deterministic biochemical puppet. Whereas the beginner's volitional control is exercised over low-level patterns and chunks, the master's volitional control is exercised over very high-level patterns and chunks. For a great pianist, volition might weight subtle shades of voice meant to convey emotions, without a thought given to the motoric implementation of those expressions. But both the halting stumbles of a beginner and the flowing expressiveness of a true master involve volition, or more precisely, the allocation of volitional attention and other volitional mental operations needed to manipulate and combine chunks together in meaningful ways. The difference is that a master might volitionally attend to high-level meaning, whereas a beginner might attend to low-level motoric operations. Volitional attention can glue together arbitrary units into spatial meta-units and temporal sequences in working memory. With practice and the consolidation afforded by sleep, these can become habits or automaticities that no longer require volitional attention, which, like a good teacher, has made itself unnecessary.

A constant danger of volitionally gluing together and then setting hardened chunks in memory is the learning of mistakes. Anyone who has learned an instrument knows how difficult it is to unlearn a mistaken automatization or to overcome poor technique. This is why good teachers, mentors, coaches, and parents are key to the ideal formation of mastery and sound freedom of the will. Without their guidance, we can automatize mistakes. Bad teachers can actually harm our bodies and minds as we make their mistakes our own. In this category would fall mistaken modes of thinking, such as stereotyping or indoctrinated false dogmas.

Different cultures have different attitudes toward freedom and mastery. My father is from China and my mother from Germany. They met in England and then moved to Washington Heights, New York City (NYC), where I was born and grew up. They had very different attitudes about freedom, raising children, and the cultivation of mastery. Let me give a sort of comedic but telling example. When I was maybe five years old, my father came home and said something like "My son must learn the violin." My mother, being German, saw little point in imposing this on me. She asked me "So Peterlein, would you like to learn the violin?" I knew how to play my parents' differences against each other for maximal gain to myself. I said "What? No way, yuck, I hate the violin and you can't make me!" Then my father turned to my mother and asked "Why did you ask him? Do you ask him if he wants to brush his teeth?" My mother said "well, isn't it his choice? Doesn't he have free will?"

This story is slightly tragic because I "won," and as a consequence never learned the violin. I wish now that my father had won that battle because now I would be able to play the violin. But we can see from this example how different their two cultures were regarding freedom. My mother emphasized self-determination and freedom from constraint, whereas my father emphasized the imposition of his will for my own good, in order to foster eventual freedom within constraint, namely, mastery of the violin.

The role played by Vladimir Horowitz's parents was the role of scaffolding. Scaffolding is not part of a building but it is necessary for the building's construction. Once the building is completed, the scaffolding is removed, creating the impression that the building emerged fully formed. The lie of rugged individualism lies in the illusion that we achieved our independent minds on our own while, in reality, we are all born as helpless babies. We depend on the scaffolding and care of others for years, as they and we build the structures undergirding our future mental operations and operands. Similarly, family and society are key cultivators of the basic capacities that afford our later free action and thought.

We did not, for example, create our native language. Rather it was there as scaffolding, being spoken all around us as children. When we have incorporated our native language into the very workings of our nervous system and thought processes, we gain tremendous freedom to think in the abstract ways afforded by our language. We literally in*corpo*rate our scaffolding, or the lack thereof, into our bodies and brains.

If you look at children raised with little or no scaffolding, such as feral children raised by wild animals, it is obvious how much we owe to those who provided us with the scaffolding of love, guidance, language, and society. Data show a litany of poor outcomes prevalent in children raised in broken homes (Anderson, 2014; Garnefski and Diekstra, 1997; Teel et al., 2016). It is truly because of the scaffolding afforded to us by our parents, peers, and mentors that we have the minds and volitional capacities that we have as adults.

I think that the role of the parent has changed from being a purveyor of culture and values to one now of also having to function as a shield to keep out the negative aspects of a mass culture that undermines the cultivation of mastery (and therefore of deeper human freedoms) with endless distraction, "attentional junk food," and consumeristic shallowness. Mass culture so often undermines the deeper freedom earned by cultivating mastery in some domain through practice and attentional devotion.

One of the key decisions we made as parents was getting rid of the TV and most other screens while our children were small. It was initially harder for me than my kids, because I was a bit of a news junkie. Being very small, they just played outside more, or played board games when it was cold outside. We were lucky to have another family in our area who likewise semi-homeschooled their children, despite sending them to the public school as we did, so that our children grew up in a kind of "noisy village" of playing kids. On several occasions, older strangers commented on how nice it was to see kids actually playing outside, the implication being that, because of video games, this had become an increasingly rare sight. We kept a DVD player so that they could watch movies, but limited them to age-appropriate cartoons, their favorites being the lovely and deep animations of Hayao Miyazaki. The main reason we limited their screen time was that the onslaught of advertising not only distracted them from their hours of daily exploration and play (where real learning takes place), but was actually damaging their minds via the incessant explicit and implicit messaging that happiness is only found in buying things. Most advertising implies that we lack a desired quality (e.g., beauty, thinness, or youth) or thing (which, for most children's toys, would likely end up in the trash within a year anyway).

By the time the kids were teenagers, they started demanding cellphones. Their winning argument was: "Papa, just because you're a freak doesn't mean that we have to be freaks too!" So I relented, and they got their first smartphones. Predictably, they became glued to their screens and also (I would say) less happy, though some of that is confounded with the normal growing pains of adolescence.

I do not regret having functioned as a shield to keep the manipulative consumerism of our society at bay during their formative years. I believe they have internalized what they learned from playing with their friends, and now have the rich imagination and confidence that can only come from having used their bodies and minds in the real, natural world with friends who were physically present. Hopefully, the scaffolding we helped foster will allow them to further scaffold themselves—in effect, becoming their own parents, guiding themselves toward greater fulfillment of their potential.

A message that I hope they internalized is this: how we choose to spend our minutes and days is how we will have chosen to spend our life. Life is a succession of freely chosen moments, and someday there will be a last one. This is why we should strive to live as fully and rightly as possible and work every day toward the fulfillment of our visions. That is the only way to now have a fulfilling life, rather than a life of squandered could-have-beens. It is commonly said that we reap what we sow, but more importantly, we do not reap what we do not sow. Think of a farmer who, by planting seeds now, cultivates and reaps rewards later in the season.

It seems, in the phases of life, that it makes sense to have a period of exploration as freedom from constraint, before one commits to a path (e.g., career, spouse, community), and willingly submits to the constraints required to attain a deeper freedom within those constraints. A young person might try this instrument or that for some years before committing to the piano. But if we met them at age 50 still just trying out this and that, having mastered none, we might feel sorry for them. On the other hand, if a child is forced to commit too early, without having ever explored other options, we might feel sorry for them, as well.

Tiger parents make the mistake of forcing their children to strive for praise for their accomplishments. Extrinsic rewards may lead children to excel at the piano or violin, but will these children have the internal wildness and passion required to compose music that is moving to themselves or others? Or are they constrained like a bonsai tree to be obedient and perfect in a miniature, cultivated version of the real thing? Exploration allows them to discover for themselves that which is intrinsically rewarding, and only that discovery will lead them to dive deeply and spend the time required to attain creative mastery.

There seems to be a sweet spot in life, where we first explore in order to find out that which best suits us, and only after this discovery, do we go for depth. We trade in some freedom *from* constraint, hopefully, for a lot more freedom *within* constraint. Exploring and then mastering an instrument is a metaphor for the commitments we make in life in search of deeper freedoms and meanings, whether a commitment to a life partner, a cause, a career, or something else. Ideally, exploration while we are young reveals a passion that gradually yields to devotion as we mature. We open ourselves to that which naturally moves us, or that which we find enjoyable and fun.

During childhood it is the guidance provided by our parents and community that provides the scaffolding we need until we are ready for freedom. Too much external constraint and a child may end up with a "bonsai personality." Too little constraint, and the child, like a vine, may not grow upward at all.

Most of our volitional decisions probably don't matter to our life outcomes in the long run. For example, if I choose to eat a pizza for dinner tonight, or a piece of salmon, it probably won't make much difference in the long run. Next month I probably won't even be able to recall what I ate tonight. Similarly, if I want to point at something,

I might choose to do so with my left or right hand. Since it does not matter which hand I move, I simply pick one, seemingly randomly.

But some of our volitional decisions are consequential in that they affect many other decisions that follow. These include decisions about where to go to college, whether to marry (if so, whom), whether to have kids (if so, how many), what country to live in, and what career to pursue. Consequential decisions are ones that we do not take lightly. We typically deliberate. We go over the pros and cons of, for example, choosing a life partner. If we have two or more options, we might deliberate for weeks, months, or even years. We might imagine different scenarios, where one potential mate is kinder, more intelligent, and better looking, but the other is richer, comes from a better family, and speaks our native language.

The perspective developed in this book is that free will lies most fundamentally in the domain of such deliberations. That is, human imagination is where the action is in volitionally choosing among deliberated options. Free will has little if anything to do with meaningless and arbitrary picking decisions that might be selected randomly. If the deeper freedom that we humans strive and long for is the ability to act as we want, within a domain where we have that freedom, because we have mastered that domain, then rugged individualism and freedom from constraint are hardly enough. Freedom *from* constraint is only useful in that it gives us time to explore and then choose the domains where we might eventually attain freedom *within* constraints. One of the most important domains of mastery is mastery within and over the events that happen in our own minds.

Different cultures again seem to take radically different attitudes toward the notion of self-mastery or self-cultivation. Interestingly, there is a metaphor of the self that pops up again and again in world literature, probably because it captures some essence of the disunity of the human mind and the internal struggles we all go through. The metaphor describes a rider and his horse (or riders and horses). It appears in the *Epic of Gilgamesh*, Plato's *The Republic*, and even in Sigmund Freud's theory of the relationship between the ego and the id. In one version, a charioteer (representing reason, volition, or executive control) is in a chariot pulled by several horses (which represent the desires and emotions). Perhaps one horse represents greed, another lust, another fear, and so on. The ancient Greeks interpreted this metaphor to mean that a good life is one in which the charioteer governs the horses well and harnesses their inherent power toward the attainment of glory. In contrast, medieval Christians largely regarded the horses as evil, and in need of constant flagellation to keep them from leading the charioteer astray into temptation. In Buddhism, the metaphorical horses might not be regarded as evil, but they are also not to be followed or allowed to govern the charioteer's mind or actions. Rather they should be watched, and then gradually reined in, over and over, until they no longer wander off on their own, but instead obey the will of the charioteer.

If deeper freedom is attained through mastery of some domain of thought or action, and if the most central freedom is that which we attain through mastery over our own minds, then free will is most centrally about what we choose to master and what kind of person we intend to and then strive, through practice, to become. Later in this book I return to this notion of free will as not only having the (type 1) capacities that afford our freedom to act, but also, more importantly, the deeper (type 2) free will expressed in our capacity to choose to become a new kind of chooser in the future. That is ultimately what this book is about: imagining a future self or world, and then setting about realizing it. Second-order free will, then, is in part a question of the nonvolitional automaticities we volitionally choose to create in ourselves in the future.

Naysayers will deny that we have this kind of slow free will, which is the freedom to shape our minds and sculpt our characters over long durations of commitment and effort, despite setbacks and fumbles. They will typically argue from a perspective of genetic determinism or fatalism, according to which our characters are fully determined by our genetics and environment, neither of which we chose. While it is true that about half the variance in character traits of monozygotic twins can be accounted for by genetics and shared environmental factors, such as growing up in the same family, the fact that about half the variance is *not* accounted for by these factors means that this form of fatalism is unwarranted by the data (Dar-Nimrod and Heine, 2011; Turkheimer and Waldron, 2000). Monozygotic twins can end up with very different values, personalities, characters and lives because, as Turkheimer (2011) put it, "the nonshared environment, in a phrase, is free will." That is, we are agents who play a role in the shaping of our genetically given potential in a manner that is not reducible to the interplay of our genes with our external environment. The internal environment constructed in part by our volitional decisions and commitments is central to the formation of who we become. We are not slaves to our genes or upbringing. Our life and character outcomes depend as much on how we play the hand that we were dealt as on the hand itself. In particular, what automaticities and habits will form in us over long durations depends on what we choose to pay attention to and practice now. An attended, indeed, carefully tended vision, including a vision of a future self, can function as a cybernetic setpoint or compass that allows us to gradually realize that vision in spite of setbacks and mistakes. We can correct our errors, learn from them, then get back on track toward realizing our vision.

None of this is easy. Harnessing one's potential begins with recognizing where one has potential. Fire can keep us warm if harnessed well, but can destroy us if left unconstrained. Similarly, talent, if not handled well, can be destructive. For example, a given trait, which may be in part innate, such as tenacity, might be expressed negatively as pig-headedness, or positively, as perseverance. Just as a hammer can be used positively, to build a home, or negatively, to murder someone, a trait like tenacity can be applied in life wisely or unwisely. Given the capacity to persevere, one must still exercise discernment if one is to apply this trait in a positive way. Just because we are capable of persevering does not mean we should. Sometimes the right decision is to give up. Tenacity is a gift that can become a curse if we persevere on a path that is destructive or foolish. Another two-edged gift is empathy, or the ability to feel another's pain as if it were one's own. If harnessed well, empathy might allow one to become a great therapist, elder, or teacher. But if applied without discernment, inappropriate empathy might allow people into one's heart who emotionally damage it. Without appropriate boundaries, letting such people into one's heart can undermine other relationships that are premised on trust and commitment. Many marriages have failed because of such a lack of discernment and an absence of strong boundaries. Lost trust is hard to recover.

In the West we tend to romanticize the infatuation stages of love. If someone says "I am so in love" we tend to be happy for them or even feel envious. In other cultures, this is not the case. For example, I was a Peace Corps volunteer from 1984 to 1986 in Nepal. One way the Nepalese say "I love you" is "Ma (I) timilai (you) maya (love) garchu (do)." But the word "maya" has several meanings, ranging from bewilderment to magic to illusion and delusion. When one is madly in love, one may not be seeing things as they truly are. Older people in Nepal might regard infatuation as dangerous, and might respond with an offer to help those "in maya" through the situation, rather than expressing happiness for them.

Feeling in love can be a beautiful and complex rush of emotions. But love is built on a more basic foundation than fluctuating emotions. That foundation is one of trust, respect and connection. These things do not come and go. They are strongly present, or weakly so, or entirely absent. If these become damaged, the foundation can collapse, and with it the "house of love and family" built upon that foundation of trust. Many marriages fail because trust is broken. As my Chinese Aunt would say "Build trust three years, destroy trust three seconds." People tend to be liberal in detecting cheating or deception, but conservative in assigning trust. When trust and respect are gone, love and romance often eventually falter or collapse. So rather than romanticize infatuation, it would be better to laud trust and respect, as the foundations of true love.

The path to building trust and respect is not complicated and can be found in the perennial values of many traditions: be honest, respectful, kind, reliable, non-hurtful, true and non-deceptive in your actions and words. A more mature society would lionize not infatuation but love in the sense of devotion and dedication. Beyond that, more foundationally, behaviors that foster trust would be highly valued and honored.

Just as there is proximal and distal free will, there is proximal love and distal love. Whereas the former is flush with emotions and the intensity of new or deepening connections, the latter is a matter of calm devotion, dedication, and commitment to a shared vision over years.

But how does one learn discernment or wisdom, so that the luck that one had in being blessed with some trait is harnessed well, and for good ends, whether for oneself or others? Partly, wisdom can arise through mentorship and the guidance of a culture. Partly, it can be learned by having made mistakes, and learning from them. However, none of this is easy. Some say nothing is more common than unfulfilled potential. Some say nothing is more common than repeating old patterns. But many people do escape self-destructiveness and learn to harness their gifts for good. If we can harness the fire of emotions and desires, they can generate warmth for ourselves and others. But if left untended and ungoverned, they can burn down everything we love. Change begins with recognizing our harmful patterns.

In order to fully harness our powers of self-transformation we must ask "what is this self?" that we want to transform. One kind of self decides where to allocate volitional attention, as the highest mental operator (or meta-operator) that aligns so many subordinate mental operations to its goals. But there are other meanings of the self that are not specifically attentional. Another self is the narrative edifice upon which perch the stories we tell about our body, its experiences, and its present and past actions, all of which explain who we are to others and to ourselves. Another meaning of "the self" is that shield of egoic character armor that protects us from emotional harm, but which can also imprison us like a tank.

In mastering our selves we would want to subject all these aspects of our self to our will. This should begin with recognizing what we are dealing with, so that we can begin the process of demolition or remodeling wisely, with a plan that stands a chance of succeeding. For example, if we find intransigent armor that is so rigid that it imprisons us in automatized patterns of emotional response barely subject to volitional constraints, rather than express our will over such automaticities, we might volitionally engage in therapy or even psilocybin-assisted therapy under the guidance of a wise guide capable of helping us dismantle the tank that both shields our hearts from harm and imprisons us in psychological armor that undermines the possibility of deeper connections and freedoms.

Let me close this section with the example of my father. So often we think of Free Will as having to do with action and what we choose to do. But equally important is what we choose not to do, or "free won't." When my parents were falling in love in Manchester England, he promised my mother that he would never hit their future children. He had himself been beaten as a child, as had his father's father, possibly back across many generations. There were rare times when he raised his hand in anger at us as children, but each time he walked away without going through with this pattern that he had learned as a boy. He said the buck will stop here. And through the power of his will and willpower and love, it did.

1.2 What Is Subjective Truth?

What is truth? Many people say they seek the truth. But what do they mean? A problem arises because there are multiple meanings associated with "truth," some of which are objective, and others that are subjective. In this section and the next I talk about four meanings of truth. In this book we are interested in objective truth, but first, let us look at two kinds of subjective truth.

The first meaning of truth refers to what is true from someone's perspective. For example, if someone believes in Santa, for them he is real. A great old film about this kind of truth is Akira Kurosawa's *Rashomon*, in which a samurai, his wife, a thief, and a woodcutter give radically different accounts of a single crime. Each account is inconsistent with the others, but because each person has their own perspective, for each of them, it is *subjectively* true. Their accounts can't all describe what really happened because they are conflicting. Nonetheless, it can be true that each person fully believes their account of what happened. This can get a little tricky, because it can be objectively true that someone subjectively believes that Santa exists, but for now, let us put aside the complicated relationship between subjective experience of events and events as they presumably really are.

The second meaning of truth is also a subjective one. According to the "pragmatic" notion of truth advocated by psychologist William James and philosopher Charles Sanders Peirce, truth is what works for a person. What does that mean? Most people are motivated to act on their ideas, as well as to eliminate doubt. Doubt occurs when a person thinks that their model of reality might be incorrect. In a sense, for pragmatists, truth just is the cessation of doubt. For example, while most children are comfortable with uncertainty, asking a lot of questions—why is the sky blue? Where do I come from?— it often happens that as people get older, they become less comfortable with uncertainty and start to look for certainty. Often they will search for and then find some ideology that they can believe in, and then for them, there is a cessation of that awful feeling of doubt. Pragmatists would say that when their doubts finally go away, they have found their truth.

1.3 What Is Objective Truth?

Scientists and philosophers are not very interested in what someone *believes* to be true. They want to uncover what is *really* true. But how do scientists and philosophers define truth? Scientists and philosophers start at opposite ends of a search for objective truth. Science specializes in one type of truth-seeking, while philosophy specializes in another, leading to two different meanings of "objective truth." These are our third and fourth theories of truth.

Scientists start from the world as it is and try to figure out how some real world thing is or how some process works. The third theory of truth, one advocated by scientists, is "the correspondence theory of truth," according to which "truth" is defined as correspondence between a proposition or model and facts in the world. For example, if I announce that "it's raining," and I look out the window and see rain, then the statement is true because my proposition about the world and the state of the world correspond. But if I look outside and find that it is sunny out, my statement is false because it does not correspond to what is happening.

Usually, truth, in the sense of correspondence, is taken to be about the degree to which a model (about what is now the case in reality) matches reality. But there is an equally important case of correspondence, namely, the degree to which our *imagined* futures correspond to what is *actually* possible. If the match is poor—if I believe I am God and I am in fact not God, or that I can fly and I cannot in fact fly—we might say that I am delusional. But if I believe I cannot fly, but in fact can fly, I would be subject to a different form of delusion. What we as individuals strive for, and what evolution presumably fostered in our brains, is a realistic imagination, in which we can assess the possibilities in fact open to us, so that we can successfully go about realizing the optimal set, given our present reasons. But because the future is inherently not observable, we can only hone the match between our models of our possible futures, and the objective possible futures that are open to us, by doing. Only by doing, succeeding and, at times, failing to realize our envisioned goals, can we learn to assess our options and possibilities more realistically. Mistakes are therefore our ally in honing the maturity of our imaginations, so long as we learn from them, and try not to repeat them. Only through genetic and personal learning can the garden of forking paths in our heads come to resemble the garden of forking paths open to us in reality.

We must therefore divide the correspondence theory in two: there is correspondence between a model of what is and what actually is, and then there is correspondence between a model of what could be and what actually could be. The former concerns science, because observations can only be made in the present concerning what is. The future, being inherently non-observable because it has not yet happened, is not the concern of science in a direct way. Indirectly, science can say "if such and such is really possible in the future, then we should observe such and such upon measurement in the present with such and such probabilities." If correspondence between imagined possibilities and world-possibilities cannot be compared, what can be compared? We can compare what was predicted with what actually happened. And when the prediction turns out to be wrong, we can use that error signal to correct our model of likely future possibilities.

It turns out that predictive coding is central to every complex nervous system because nervous systems evolved to allow animals to act in the real world in order to bring about expected goals. Thus even local goal fulfillment (e.g., reaching for a branch) has an aspect of imagination to it, in that the system predicts what the feedback from the muscles and real world will be before the action is ever executed. The error between the prediction and what actually occurred can be used to hone a realistic assessment of one's capacities, so that future actions will be more likely to succeed. This low-level form of imagination is largely unconscious, and very different from the internal virtual-reality type of imagination that permits us to envision experiences and actions without necessarily carrying them out in the real world.

In contrast, philosophers, at least analytic philosophers, start from logic. Philosophers tend to think about how things must work, or cannot work, given their starting assumptions. The fourth meaning of truth, then, is the one that philosophers emphasize. It is the coherence theory of truth, according to which, a proposition is true if it logically coheres with the other propositions of some propositional system, or follows from the assumptions, axioms or premises of that system (about the world or God or whatever you like). For example, if I assume that all humans are mortal, and find that Socrates is a man, it logically follows that he is mortal.

Science and philosophy are both in search of truth but approach it from different angles, employing different tools and strategies. Both fields care about both fundamental meanings of objective truth, but science emphasizes the correspondence of models with facts while philosophy emphasizes the logical coherence of a set of propositions about facts.

The most devastating weapon of Science is disconfirming real world data or evidence, because it proves non-correspondence between a model and the facts. For example, if I say that no animal can talk, and a farmer finds that his pig Wilbur can talk, well, that falsifies the claim that no animal can talk. In contrast, the main weapon of philosophy is a demonstration of logical inconsistency through argument, because it proves non-coherence and therefore falsity. In one sense, philosophers don't need to look at the world or neural circuits or to collect data at all, because any view that is logically impossible or incoherent, or any proposition about the world that does not logically follow from accepted premises, cannot be true about the world.

However, philosophy can only get part way to the truth on its own. Since many competing propositions about the world are each logically possible or plausible even when they are mutually exclusive, we must, in the end, look at the world and collect data to settle metaphysical debates such as the ongoing debate over free will. For example, an eternity of logical debate, in the absence of examining facts about the world, could never have settled what the physical laws are, what the behaviors of various types of matter are, or how the brain works. For this reason, I believe that metaphysical debates about what is the case, including what the case is regarding free will, can only be settled by science.

That said, science needs philosophy too, much more so than most of my neuroscientist colleagues care to admit, because without subjecting ourselves to withering logical criticism, we might make and indeed have made, arrogant and wrong-headed claims such as "there is no free will" on the basis of the thinnest of data, or misinterpretations of data.

In this regard, in Chapter 3 we will dismantle the wrong-headed claims of two scientists, Benjamin Libet and Dan Wegner, who claimed that the conscious feeling of having willed something to happen is not the actual cause of it having happened, since unconscious processes can fully account for that happening. Even if the conscious feeling of willing something to happen was not causal of our actions in certain cases, it would be a logical error to conclude that it can never be causal; it would be an even bigger mistake to conclude that nothing about consciousness can ever be causal of our actions. But these are the types of basic logical mistakes neuroscientists have made for decades until philosophers pointed out flaws in their logic and reasoning.

In summary, we have considered four meanings of the word "truth." The first two are subjective notions of truth and the latter two are objective notions of truth. They are: 1. Truth as your perspective on an event, or your belief about an event. Let's say your cat is dead but you believe it is still alive. Then, for you it is true that your cat is alive, even though, objectively this is not true. 2. Truth is what works for you, or settles a matter of doubt for you. For example, you feel doubt about whether your cat is alive or dead, so you begin to try to find out more information. You call your trusted friend, who says that your cat is still alive. You cease having doubts. This cessation of doubt is what pragmatists mean by something being true for someone. 3. Truth as

correspondence between a claim and what is the case. Here you say "my cat is alive" and if it is really alive, then that statement is true because it corresponds with the facts.
4. Truth as logical coherence with a set of unproven assumptions. If one assumes the truth of the statement that all cats are mortal, then it logically follows that your cat is mortal.

1.4 What Is "Real"?

We are interested in discovering what is objectively true about free will, and how it might work in the human brain. We will begin by examining certain philosophical claims about free will, which will take us into logic, and then, later, we will consider scientific claims that there is or is not free will.

We asked what the meaning of "truth" is. We concluded that there are several different definitions of "truth," both subjective and objective. Our aim is to develop an objectively true understanding of reality regarding mind and mental causation, in particular, regarding that subset of mental events that are freely willed. In order to do that we have to come up with a model of brain function underlying free choices that corresponds to how the brain really works.

We can see that for science, the meaning of truth is tied up with what is real. But what is real? People have been struggling with that question for a very long time.

In our attempts to answer the question "What is real?", we are left with the odd picture first portrayed in Plato's allegory of the cave and later elaborated by Immanuel Kant. All that we have access to and all we can describe is the contents of our consciousness, and these contents presumably correspond to something about the events- or objects-in-themselves in reality-in-itself. Because many people can look at the same, say, red flower, and have largely consistent experiences, it is not likely that everyone just happens to be hallucinating a red flower at the same time. That said, is the flower really red?

Perceptual neuroscientists largely agree that there is no redness out there in reality. Redness is a construction of our perceptual systems that exists in our conscious experience, but is not a property of the rose-in-itself. What is presumably real are pigments in the surfaces of the rose-in-itself, that reflect light in a certain way, and those surface reflectance properties we experience as red. But redness and those pigments seem to exist in two different domains, one in consciousness and the other in the world-in-itself, regardless of how it is being experienced or even whether it is being experienced.

Consider the dramatic art by Akiyoshi Kitaoka in Figure 1.1. On one eye in (a), the girl's iris looks yellow, while in the other eye it looks blue, when in fact both irises are an identical gray in the image. In (b), the strawberries appear to be red, but are in fact the colors indicated by the rectangles on the right, at the locations indicated by the black lines. This makes apparent that we do not experience the input detected at the retina. We experience a highly preprocessed representation of color that discounts

The Basic Questions   35

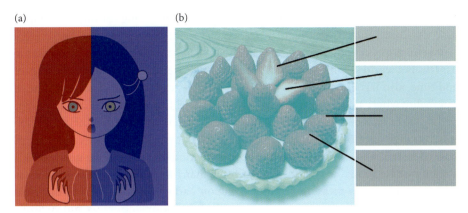

Figure 1.1 This girl's irises appear to be blue and yellow but are in fact both an identical gray in the image, while the strawberries appear to be red, but are actually shades of gray and cyan in the image, as indicated by the colored rectangles on the right.
Images by Akiyoshi Kitaoka, with permission.

many irrelevant or extrinsic factors, such as the overall illuminant, in order to recover the intrinsic reflectances of surfaces in the world. This is because we evolved to infer and then experience facts about intrinsic properties, such as pigments and materials.

Color is a property of our conscious experience that is constructed. We cannot experience the color values detected at the retina. Instead, we can only experience the color that is computed by operations that happen in the quarter to a third of a second between retinal activation by light and our conscious experience of what is presumed to be the case in reality, even though we can never step outside of our conscious experience to experience the world as it truly is. Moreover, some, though not all, of these preconscious, unconscious operations are cognitively impenetrable, in the sense that we cannot will them not to occur, and cannot will them to turn out otherwise. These preconscious operations precompile interpretations of what is real so that conscious operations, such as volitionally attending to this versus that, can take these precompiled representations as their input operands (Özkan et al., 2020).

But Kant did not just argue that there is a schism between the "noumenal" world of things-in-themselves, and our "phenomenal" experience of them. He emphasized that our phenomenal world is constructed on the basis of presupposed organizing principles of spatial and temporal relationships that rest on assumptions about how events are causally linked. In other words, the phenomenal is not detected, it is constructed. Consciousness is a construction inferred on the basis of what is detected. It can be thought of as a "veridical hallucination" of what is real, in the case of perception, or a hallucination of what might be or could be, in the case of imagination and dreams.

In addition to our senses, we have a capacity to reason. Using reason, however, we have developed models that paint a strange picture of the nature of reality. Present claims from physics describe a bizarre reality radically unlike the world as it seems to us. This is a world in which a particle, seemingly located at a single position in space and time, also has the properties of a wave, which is extended in space and time. It is a reality where non-locality reigns, namely, where two events, perhaps hundreds of thousands or even billions of light years apart, can be correlated in their behavior. It is a strange universe in which some kind of "dark matter," which we cannot see, is posited to exist and even to be the most common kind of energy in the universe. It is a reality where virtual particles are thought by many to be real in the specific sense that they can exert a measurable influence upon particles that exist. Indeed, virtual particles have recently been observed to jostle macroscopic objects (Chu, 2020; Yu et al., 2020) and some have even argued that "to exist" means to be in an excited state of the underlying vacuum of seething virtual particles (Battersby, 2008). This would in turn seem to imply that nothing exists or is real at all except this underlying vacuum, a theme we will return to in section 2.12. Finally, none of our physical models, whether in physics or in neuroscience, has so far succeeded in giving a complete explanation of consciousness and its physical realization.

So, science has a long, long way to go. There are some things we can be confident of, like that the heart has four chambers. Then there are many things that we are not so sure of, like whether invisible dark matter really exists. Then there are things we know that we don't yet know, like what the neural basis of consciousness is or what the neural code is. Then there are things that we don't even know yet that we do not know. And finally, there are things that may be in principle not knowable. For example, some ideas may be undefinable. What came before the beginning? That might not be a definable concept because it appears to involve a contradiction: before the beginning. Similarly, the question "what caused the first cause?" might not be answerable. We can add to the list of unknowables the answer to the question "what lies outside of everything?" This might not be definable because how can there be something that is not included in everything? The question "are there multiple universes or just one?" might not be answerable. Should we give up? Not at all. Science has a lot to explain even if it cannot explain everything.

Nonetheless, it seems reasonable to assume that there is a way the world really is, independent of our experiences of it. The only problem is this: all we have to go on are our experiences. The world as it really is may forever be beyond our ability to know. But using reason and the constructions of our senses, we can go much farther than we have so far in our quest to understand the nature of reality.

1.5 How Do We Know?

What we call "light" is an incredibly tiny portion of the vast spectrum of electromagnetic radiation. We have evolved sensors that are sensitive to the domain of electromagnetic energy emitted by our sun. It makes sense to become sensitive to information where the information lies. If we ever found the body of an alien, we could tell a lot about its sun and world by looking at the sensitivities of its sensory detectors. However, in a sense we are all also blind. We are blind to the vast majority of energy around us. We cannot see those parts of the electromagnetic spectrum that we call radio waves, cosmic rays, x-rays, or cell phone signals. For us, it is as if they did not exist. But we know they must exist because our TVs, radios and cellphones work.

But what if everyone else but us could see ultraviolet light or magnetic field lines? Then our blindness might bother us, because then we would feel like we were missing out, relatively speaking. The only reason it does not bother us too much that we are blind to the vast majority of energy, events and structure around us, is that everyone else is also blind to them.

Plato's *The Allegory of the Cave* describes people locked in a cave who can only see the shadows cast onto the cave wall by events in the outside world, but not the events themselves. They are limited to indirect inferences about what might be happening in the world that could cast the shadows that they see. This is of course a metaphor for our difficulty in discerning what is real based solely on the indirect "shadows" that we have from our senses. For example, the retina detects two-dimensional patterns of light that have been cast upon the "wall" of the retina. These images are not objects in the world and, in fact, any image or sequence of images could have been cast by many possible events in the world. So how do we go from an ambiguous sequence of two-dimensional patterns cast upon the retina to a conscious experience of a three-dimensional world?

Following in Plato's footsteps two millennia later, the philosopher Immanuel Kant argued that all we have access to is our subjective experience of events in the world. We have no access to events as they are in themselves, independent of our perception of them. Our conscious experience is the only thing that we know for sure. And yet our conscious experience is a construction that can be mistaken. We know this because visual illusions, hallucinations, visions, fantasies and dreams may have nothing to do with what is really happening out there in the world. If all that we have access to is our constructed and potentially faulty conscious experience, how can we possibly ever know what is real, outside of our perception of it?

Perhaps we cannot know the world in itself. But our consciousness is the result of unconscious inferences about the nature of events in the world, made on the basis of assumptions about the image to world mapping. We experience a fully interpreted pre-compiled analysis of what is going on. A mantra for this point of view might be "perceiving is perceiving as." But sometimes the system infers the wrong thing, and we see what is not there or fail to see what really is there. We call these illusions or hallucinations. These are the exceptions that prove the rule that consciousness is a construction about a world of events and meanings from the perspective of a moving self. This is very much like a hallucination, but one that is meant to be about what is really going on in the world and in our bodies. Even if we come to terms with the idea that this construction exists solely as a creation of neural activity in the utter darkness of our skulls, it is very hard not to regard consciousness as being about a world that is out there. The correspondence is presumably so good that we firmly believe we are experiencing the world as it in fact is. This is almost surely incorrect.

In addition to the perceptual inferences that go into the construction of the "veridical hallucination" of our consciousness, we can carry out cognitive inferences about the world based on what we experience. We can infer what must be happening in the world based on the evidence we have from perception and we can extend perception using scientific devices that extend our senses into domains that we normally cannot perceive, such as into the invisible domain of the very small using a microscope or into the invisible domain of the very distant using a telescope. Thus, consciousness is constructed on the basis of unconscious, preconscious "perceptual inferences," and is then itself used as the basis for making later cognitive inferences about the world. For example, going outside and seeing the sidewalk as wet is a perceptual inference, but inferring that it must have rained or that a gardener hosed it down would be a cognitive inference based on what we have seen. Perceptual inferences go into the construction of the world as experienced, while cognitive inferences are made on the basis of what is experienced along with other assumptions about what may be going on. Conscious experience results from perceptual inferences and affords cognitive inferences.

But consciousness is not only a veridical hallucination about what is visible or apparent. Much of what we call seeing, for example, involves representing what is invisible. Seeing is also seeing the invisible. Some of what we "see" is concretely invisible. In that category fall the occluded parts of things, the backs of things, and continuation in space and time despite momentary occlusion, as when a bird flying behind trees is represented as the same bird, rather than as a series of different birds going in and out of existence. These are things that would be visible if we could see through occluders. But then there is another category of things that are in principle invisible, like causation and the contents of other minds, that we "see" as well. They are precompiled interpretations built into the unfolding "narrative" of what is going on in the world and that is delivered to us as our conscious experience. For example, if we turn off a light switch just before a blackout strikes, we will inevitably have the feeling that the one caused the other, when it was a mere coincidence. This is because temporal juxtaposition is a key cue used by unconscious processing to infer causation.

Then, in addition to representing what is going on in the world in terms of our perceptual, emotional, and bodily experiences, including imagined experiences, we have a second level of representation of the invisible. This is a meta-consciousness of mental models and narratives about what is going on in the world, whether they pertain to the scene at hand or to worlds unseen. For example, if I internally model a scene as a restaurant, it would be inappropriate to join a table of strangers; yet, if I model the same scene as a casino, it would be fine to sit at a table of strangers. So, the mental model that informs me is not only part of my conscious experience, but also fundamentally influences the meaning of the world and the actions I might consider taking in it.

It is this second imagined world that makes our consciousness so different from that of a chimpanzee. In this second world there are narratives that weave the visible together with the nonvisible, whether these involve gods, or other models and meanings in our heads. It is truly remarkable to listen to two people who are lost in conversation jointly constructing shared mental models on the fly, then discarding them as soon as the topic changes. This capacity to model is dependent in part on memory, that servant of imagination, which enables us to make visible again in our internal virtual reality traces of past visible things. Sharing mental models is also, no doubt, one of the secrets of our intense sociality and capacity to create together while following a shared narrative, whether this involves building pyramids or scientific theories. Chimpanzees and bonobos can do nothing of the sort because their consciousness is not bifurcated into a base level and a level of narratives.

Problems arise for us, however, when our memories, models, or narratives are wrong, false, or delusional, or when we catastrophize the future and live in dread of what might happen. French Renaissance philosopher Michel de Montaigne once said: "My life has been full of terrible misfortunes, most of which never happened." Part of the price we pay for having this kind of bifurcated architecture of consciousness is that we can go mad with imagined "realities." We can enter the fight-or-flight response, perhaps chronically, because of some perceived threat due to a believed narrative about, say, the devil or hell. In the past, humans have convinced themselves that it is essential to sacrifice people or animals on some altar to appease an imagined god because it may not have rained for many months. It is as if we, as a species, are schizotypal. Being able to model and construct narratives about the invisible causal forces that created the visible world may have allowed us to grasp patterns that really exist, but it came at the cost of essentially false-alarming, that is, seeing patterns as real that only exist in our heads. The price we pay for having a higher hit rate, in terms of discerning stories that are true, is having a higher false alarm rate, in terms of believing stories that are not true.

1.6 What Illusions Teach Us

Neuroscience has largely worked out the basic information-processing steps that lead to the construction of our conscious experience of seeing. Light reflects off surfaces in the world. This reflected light passes through the cornea, pupil, and lens before being detected by photoreceptors in the retina. Let us call the moment that light is detected by retinal photodetectors "time zero."

Our conscious experience of events in the world does not happen at time zero, but rather, roughly, a third of a second later. Within that brief duration, a tremendous amount of very complex unconscious and preconscious processing turns the two-dimensional pattern of pixel-like activations at the retina into a highly constructed three-dimensional conscious experience of objects and events occurring in the external world. Some of the work in my lab has focused on the operations that happen in this third of a second before we become conscious of what is apparently happening in the world.

I have been especially interested in visual illusions because they are mistakes made by the constructive processes that go into the construction of our conscious visual experience. They are mistakes that can tell us useful information about the processing steps that usually construct non-illusory percepts. In the case of illusions, we might see something that we know is not really there or that is happening that we know cannot really be happening.

Take the example of what is called "apparent motion." In one frame of a two-image sequence, I show two dots on diagonally opposite corners of an invisible square, and in the other frame I show two other dots on the other two opposite corners. When I toggle back and forth from .˙ to ˙. every half second or so, even though there is no actual motion in the image sequence, I see the dots as jumping positions as if in motion. But this motion sequence is ambiguous. Some people see the dots jump vertically back and forth, while others see horizontal motion back and forth. Whatever you see, you can force your visual system to construct the opposite motion. Let's say you are seeing vertical motion. To force your brain to consruct horizontal motion, you can cover the bottom two jumping dots with your hand, leaving the remaining two dots to jump horizontally. Now, when you take your hand away, you should continue to see the motion jump back and forth horizontally. Likewise, if you wanted to force your visual system to see vertical motion, you would cover the right two dots with your hand.

In apparent motion, none of the dots is actually moving. We consciously experience a motion that does not exist. It is a construction created by those unconscious, preconscious processes that create our conscious experience. Because the dots appear at different times, it cannot be that the motion is computed starting with the appearance of the first dot, because there may never even have been a second dot at a later time. It must be the case that the motion is computed only *after* the second dot has appeared. However, that means that the first dot's position must be maintained for a while in some buffer, so that a motion can be inferred to have occurred to the second dot's location from the first dot's location. So, the mere existence of apparent motion is evidence that there must be a preconscious buffer that allows comparisons over space and time in order to infer what must have just happened in the outside world. This buffer must have a finite duration, which in turn implies that our conscious experience of apparent motion is not about what is happening now. It is about what has happened in the past one third of a second.

It gets even more interesting because we have shown that volition can reach down into the preconscious buffer and alter the results of matching operations that then result in seeing the intended motion. Call time zero the time when the dots switch from .˙ to ˙.. If you will to see horizontal motion at −300 ms, say, you will be more likely to see horizontal versus vertical motion. Even more amazingly, if a command to see horizontal motion (or vertical motion) happens as long as 300 milliseconds *after* .˙ has been replaced by ˙., volition can bias what we will consciously experience

(Sun et al., 2017). Not only is our consciousness delayed relative to events in the world by a third of a second, but also while the preconscious processing is taking place that will result in our conscious experience, our volition can reach down into the preconscious buffer and bias how preconscious processing will turn out. Those who argue that consciousness is nothing but the epiphenomenal output of prior unconscious processing are wrong. Conscious volitional operations, such as intending to see this versus that motion, can alter unconscious operations, which then alter their future consciously experienced outputs, resulting in the experience of the intended motion.

Apparent motion is a case where we see something that we know is not really out there in the world. There are other cases where we fail to see something that we know is in fact out there in the world. A beautiful example of this occurs in a phenomenon known as "motion-induced blindness." If you find the animated demo on wikipedia (https://en.wikipedia.org/wiki/Motion-induced_blindness), you will see that there are three yellow dots and a blinking fixation point. In addition, there is a rotating array of blue crosses. What you will notice, if you carefully look at the blinking green dot in the middle, is that one or two or all three of the yellow dots will vanish from your consciousness. But if you make a sudden eye movement, poof, all three yellow dots appear again.

We have cases where we consciously experience something that we know is not really happening in reality, as when we see horizontal or vertical apparent motion in a sequence of static dots; and we also have cases where we fail to see something that we know is happening in reality. What are we to take from all this? While it is safe to assume that there is a reality-in-itself, it might turn out to function in a radically different way than it seems to function to us given what we can glean from our flawed sensory constructions. Yet, all that we have to go on in deciphering what is happening in reality comes from our senses and the quasi-hallucinatory constructions of our conscious experience. Given these limitations, we can only try to do the best we can in our efforts to figure out the nature of reality as it really is, beyond how it may seem to us.

1.7 What Are Information and Meaning?

Sometimes it is useful to look at the roots of a word to figure out what it might mean. For example, the words "will" and "volition" both descend from the root "to want" in Indo-European languages; in German "I want" is "ich will" whereas in Italian it is "voglio." You can also hear the same root in our word "voluntary"—meaning done of one's own free will, that is, because one wants to.

We can also do this for the word "information," which is related to the verb "to inform." This descends directly from the roots "in" and "former" in Latin, implying the formation of something new in the mind of the person who is informed; it refers to teaching or instructing someone about something that they did not know before.

In ordinary language, information is commonly thought of as a noun describing a thing that we locate out there, whether a book in a library or a webpage on a server. But a pattern of energy, whether a book, a webpage, or a compact disc, is only informative for an interpreter or decoder capable of decoding it. Change the system of interpretation from English to Mandarin, and the pattern "women" goes from referring to "female adults" in English to meaning "we" in Chinese, which is pronounced "waw men." Similarly, if you read the word "Bad" assuming it to be an English word, it means something very different from what a German would read "Bad" to mean, because in German that word would be decoded to mean "bath." So, the informational content is not specified by the pattern of input itself, but by how it is decoded. The meaning "bad" or "bath" is not inherent to the pattern of ink "Bad" but depends on how it is interpreted. Things like books and webpages and CDs should therefore not be thought of as conveying information in any inherent manner. Rather, they should all be thought of as "potential information," whose potential to become information depends on whether and how they are decoded by decoders or interpreters that can take them as input to be decoded or interpreted.

Mental events cannot supervene on those brain states that realize *inputs* to a decoder because those same brain states might feed into two or more different decoders, which might each realize different information or meaning upon an act of decoding. There also need be no act of encoding or sending of information to a receiver at all, since a decoder can decode the pattern that will release it, say, make a neuron fire, even when the input is random noise. Mental events must therefore supervene on acts of decoding. The question then is how decoding happens.

Decoding is an act of pattern recognition in the sense that criteria for what counts as an instance of that pattern have been met above some threshold. A decoder therefore defines an equivalence class, such as a family of individuals who share family resemblances, as all things that meet criteria beyond a certain threshold. The neural code is effectively "late Wittgensteinian" in defining family resemblances criterially.

What particular aspects of neural activity associated with acts of decoding do mental events supervene upon? At one level, we can associate acts of decoding with the detection of some pattern among inputs to a decoder. In the case of neurons, these typically arrive as action potentials (i.e., the "firings" that speed down axons from the cell body to the axonal terminals) to which a postsynaptic neuron is prepared to respond. The ability of a neuron to detect some particular pattern among its inputs depends on several factors, including the kinds of axonal inputs it receives, the architecture of its dendritic arborizations, and the momentary synaptic weights expressed between axonal inputs and dendritic spines or compartments. If it is correct to say that acts of decoding are realized in dendritic operations, then we would conclude that mental events supervene on dendritic operations because this is at least one central way that pattern detection happens. That the neuron then fires, in order to provide future inputs to other neurons, which in turn detect patterns among their inputs, is secondary. Action potentials provide inputs to neurons, but the act of decoding patterns, such as temporal coincidence, among multiple such inputs, happens principally within the dendrites. It is therefore likely that the neural basis of mental events, including conscious mental events, is, at least in part, dendritic in its realization. If this reasoning is correct, then the neural basis of mental events would not be primarily realized in action potentials traversing axons as such. Rather, mental events would be realized in the postsynaptic detection of patterns of coincidence among arriving presynaptic action potentials. The tuning properties of a neuron or ensemble of neurons would depend on what precise pattern of dendritic coincidences would make the neuron(s) fire above the baseline rate.

The key pattern that decoders in the brain are sensitive to is co-incidence of two or more inputs. It is this temporal co-inciding that allows a decoder to distinguish signal from noise. It is as if decoders operate under this assumption: coin*cid*ence is not a co*in*cidence. As we explore in greater depth in Section 4.5, synchrony and bursting are two avenues whereby neurons enhance the likelihood of post-synaptic coincidence of presynaptic inputs. It is therefore likely that synchrony and bursting are central to neural coding.

That said, it is unlikely that the sole path to detecting patterns is at the level of single neurons. An act of decoding might be realized in the response of populations of neurons or circuits of neurons to collective inputs, in which case mental events would supervene upon that higher level of neural activity and not just dendritic activity in single neurons.

There is a bias in neuroscience that the neural code will be some code among action potentials. But the neural code cannot ignore dendritic weightings and the structure of dendritic arborizations that may realize dendritic decision trees, including Boolean operations, such as "depolarize this segment of the dendrite, if the two branches feeding into it are themselves simultaneously depolarized." At an informational level, such an operation might realize an if–then statement, for example, "if two eyes are detected on a round background, then a face has been detected." The neural code is very likely to be a dendritic code, with action potentials playing the role of signals sent along "wires" that some pattern has been detected. If correct, then measuring only action potentials sent between neurons, while ignoring the synaptic and dendritic component of the neural code, will not achieve the hallowed goal of cracking the neural code.

Matthew Larkum and colleagues' (Aru et al., 2020; Larkum et al., 2022) "dendritic integration theory" offers an exciting recent conceptual breakthrough in understanding both the neural code and the neural basis of consciousness. They argue that the coincident activation of both top-down feedback input to the apical dendrites—coupled with bottom-up or feed-forward input to the basal dendrites and soma—of layer V cortical pyramidal cells, is what gates both the cortico–cortical and cortico–thalamo–cortical loops that subserve consciousness. Anesthesia, by disrupting this apical–basal coupling, eliminates consciousness (Suzuki and Larkum, 2020). Thus, it seems that the neural code and the neural basis of consciousness are realized in part within the immaterial pattern of coincident inputs to dendrites. Layer V pyramidal cells effectively decode that top-down/bottom-up coincidence.

Patterns in fact have no existence at all except for decoders that respond to patterns in inputs. There is no materiality to the temporal pattern of coincidence. Nor is there materiality to, for example, the spatial pattern of the Big Dipper. Yes, the suns themselves exist, millions of light years apart, and yes, there is an arrangement of light that exists in the sky solely by virtue of Earth's accidental placement in space. But without a decoder that says "This is the set of spatial relationships that drive my response" it would not exist in any sense. Pattern becomes causal via pattern detectors that then change the system in which they are embedded by virtue of having responded to that pattern. And the patterns do not even have to be spatial or temporal or among material things. There can be social patterns (e.g., who is dominant over whom), emotional patterns (e.g., who longs for whom), and patterns of patterns, and patterns of patterns of patterns, and so on, all realized in acts of decoding.

Is all causation merely material causation? No doubt acts of pattern detection are realized in material events, such as the dendritic operations and subsequent firings of neurons. But patterns themselves are immaterial. They exist only as spatial, temporal, and other *relationships* among material things or among patterns that are themselves ultimately realized in material things. But since patterns are immaterial, it would be misleading to say that all causation is material causation. To the extent that relationships are not themselves material, we can say that pattern causation brings a nonmaterial causation into the universe.

Claude Shannon, the founder of information theory, did not think of information as a thing but rather as a process of informing. He simplified the idea to include a "sender" that sends an encoded signal or message along some communication channel to some "receiver" who decodes it, like a speaker and listener in a phone conversation.

If uncertainty is reduced from two possibilities (0 or 1) to one certainty (say, 1)—say the answer is "yes" when we were not sure if the answer would be "yes" or "no"—that reduction in uncertainty, from two possible outcomes to one actual outcome, comprises one binary digit or bit of information. Information is therefore a process that involves a reduction in uncertainty for a receiver of inputs, who gets informed by that increase in knowing, or decrease in uncertainty.

But Shannon's conception does not capture everything about information. For example, it misses out on meaning almost entirely. If the question I asked was "will you marry me?" and the answer came back "yes" I would be overjoyed, and if it came back "no" I might be devastated. But if the question had been "do you like spaghetti?" I might not care that much, regardless of the answer. But meaning is central to what we live for. We don't want to hear "yes" when we ask someone to marry us because we want a reduction in uncertainty—we want to hear "yes" because we want to spend the rest of our life with them.

Another thing that Shannon's possibility-reduction conception of information seems to miss is its emphasis on acts of encoding and decoding. But we don't only decode or interpret encoded messages. Not everything is like a sentence that we decode. Some acts of interpretation happen in the absence of any act of encoding or sending at all. For example, a person can interpret a pile of rocks, that just happen to lie in the shape of some religious symbol, as a message from God. The pile of rocks might have been left there randomly by a glacier thousands of years ago, just by chance, so lacks any objective message, intent or meaning. But seeing that symbol in the pile of rocks might be very meaningful to the person who saw it as a message from God. An encoder or act of intentional encoding is not necessary for information to come into existence through an act of decoding or interpretation. In our example, the person finds the random pile of rocks meaningful, so for him it carries or conveys meaningful information, in this case, for him, a message to him from God. Nor is a communication channel necessary, because a receiver might decode internally generated hallucinations as messages from God as well, or as ghosts, or whatever.

The crucial point here is that information arises principally from acts of *decoding* inputs, *interpreting* signs, or *detecting* patterns in energy that is received: no *encoding* or *sending* is required. Note that information is fundamentally an epistemological construct. It is a change in the state of the knowledge of someone who comes to know something new and who is informed by that information; that is, it is all in the receiver's head. Neither a sender, intended or sent message, or channel of communication is needed, though these can be present.

Shannon's notion of information is essentially about uncertainty resolution during acts of communication. The receiver knows the sender is trying to communicate, but the communication channel is noisy. So, information theory is really a theory of information transfer, or communication. Shannon starts his famous 1948 paper with: "The fundamental problem of communication is that of reproducing at one point, either exactly or approximately, a message selected at another point." He reduces communication to detection of some change or difference, which occurs when a message has arrived via a communication channel. The reduction in uncertainty associated with this difference is a function of the likelihood of it happening. The more improbable, the more informative.

A solitary animal, say, a giant anteater, however, is not generally trying to communicate. It is trying to survive. At each moment, as it moves about its environment, there are endless detected differences, most of which do not matter to its survival. There can be a huge change or reduction in uncertainty that is of no consequence, depending on what the animal is trying to do. If it is looking for food, it might not matter very much that the sky has just gone from cloudy to sunny, making everything in its world suddenly look different. What matters is finding food. In comparison to a change in the whole sky, the appearance of one little ant might be more meaningful in terms of fulfilling its need for food. A huge difference can have no meaningful implications, whereas a tiny, detected difference can have enormous implications, depending on the context. A barely audible snap of a branch might indicate the presence of a jaguar, which, as potentially a matter of life and death, is of great consequence.

Much of our own information processing is not focused on communication. We are trying to gain information about the current state of affairs, and, as in the anteater example, a huge difference might be uninformative, whereas a tiny (or even no) difference can be hugely informative. For example, a detective might find a microscopic piece of lint at a crime scene and on that basis solve the case and identify the perpetrator.

Even more telling, even the absence of information can be informative. In the 1892 story *The Adventure of Silver Blaze* (Doyle, 1993), Sherlock Holmes is able to infer who removed a famous thoroughbred from its stall, and what led to the death of its trainer, by noting that the dog did not bark:

GREGORY (Scotland Yard detective): "Is there any other point to which you would wish to draw my attention?"
SHERLOCK HOLMES: "To the curious incident of the dog in the night-time."
GREGORY: "The dog did *nothing* in the night-time."
SHERLOCK HOLMES: "*That* was the curious incident."

Thus, the absence of information can be informative, relative to a mental model of how dogs behave: they bark at strangers. Therefore, the perpetrator must have been someone whom the dog knew and trusted. Relative to expectations that arise because of a mental model, the absence of information can be informative. Artificial intelligence (AI) systems, in contrast, which lack mental models and imagined scenarios or narratives, are confined to finding information via its presence in inputs. AI cannot as yet do so in its absence.

Sherlock Holmes later tells Watson that Gregory is one of the more competent detectives he has worked with: "Inspector Gregory, to whom the case has been committed, is an extremely competent officer. Were he but gifted with imagination he might rise to great heights in his profession." Later still, Holmes gloats a bit, attributing his own ability to solve the case to his powers of imagination: "'See the value of imagination,' said Holmes. 'It is the one quality which Gregory lacks. We imagined what might have happened, acted upon the supposition, and find ourselves justified.'" Imagination gives us the ability to see the invisible.

I believe that biologist Gregory Bateson proposed the single best definition of "information" for an animal, when he said "information is a difference that makes a difference." It is a detected difference that is meaningful to an animal, given its needs, goals, and desires. This definition of information is perhaps less mathematically precise than Shannon's, but it captures the centrality of meaning in the life and mind of an animal. Shannon's mathematization of information only concerns the reduction in uncertainty that happens upon a detected difference, weighted by its probability of having happened. But it is not the reduction of possibilities to one certainty that makes information biologically meaningful. It is the relevance of what is detected for the fulfillment of goals and drives that generates meaning. What is entirely missing from Shannon's notion of information is any concept of meaningfulness. But animals are consumed with meaning. For animals, including humans, information is but the handmaiden of meaning. Even more so than most animals, humans live for meaning above all else. This is because our invisible world of mental models, imagination, and narratives, which rides atop the perceived world, is so much more developed than is the case in other animals (more on this in Section 4.1).

If we picture the mental models of an animal as a graph, meaning can perhaps be mathematized as the degree to which nodes and edges change configuration or are added or erased with new information, weighted by their value to the animal. Again, if I ask you, "Do you like spaghetti?," the answer, yes or no—just one bit—might entail updating or adding one small subnode in my mental model of you. But if you are a woman I love, and I ask you "Will you marry me?," your answer, yes or no—again just one bit—might exhilarate or devastate me. In either case, regardless of your answer, large numbers of nodes must be updated, reconnected, or erased. Information is weighted for an animal by its value and consequentiality, much more so than its probability of occurrence.

There are different kinds of meanings associated with the many different kinds of things that we value. Some arise by virtue of their ability to fulfill drives. If you are hungry, food has great value, but less so if you are sated. If you are drowning, air takes on a value it never had before. Other things we value are more abstract, like the value associated with gaining higher status. This seemingly simple mathematization of meaning, namely as graph-level structure updating, is much harder to implement than Shannon's mathematization of information for the simple reason that we do not have decent graphs that represent mental models and narratives, let alone the dynamics of our ever-changing evaluations. But such a model is needed, if only because conceiving of animals as no more than processors of information, free of meaning and value, is not only an impoverishing view of animals, it is also incorrect. Yes, animals process information, but they do so in the service of fulfilling needs and building mental models and other systems of meaning and evaluation.

However, the notion of meaning as arising from graph-level re-conformation may be inadequate as well. If I am thirsty or hungry, water or food have meaning, not because of possibility collapse among nodes on a graph representing mental models or narratives. They have meaning for me because I desire them. If I did not subjectively experience desires for them, water and food would not have meaning for me. Meaning therefore depends on consciousness. Meaning is that which is *felt* to be meaningful, relative to subjective desires and emotions, in the service of cybernetically fulfilling goals. More abstract mental models that provide life with meaning may ultimately be grounded in desires and emotions; for example, the common belief that there is an afterlife may provide life with meaning because it fulfills desires for life and avoiding death with subjectively experienced value. Delusions can provide meaning.

Entirely missing from Shannon's conception of information is any notion of purpose, feedback, or internal setpoints that instantiate much goal-directedness in animals. But meaning is centrally concerned with purpose and teleological striving toward goals, because information for cybernetic systems, such as animals, is used to fulfill the aim of returning to the internal setpoint. That is, information affords the possibility of noting a discrepancy between where the system is and where it ought to be. And this cybernetic error signal gives rise to corrections in behavior that are purposive; their purpose is to reduce the discrepancy in the future. Corrective behavioral outputs lead to subsequent sensory inputs that either minimize the discrepancy, or fail to do so, in which case new behavioral outputs are required. Trying to understand animal behavior in terms of information alone or based on the information processing metaphor of a computer, without regard to cybernetic feedback loops that are inherently purposive, means that animal behavior will not be well modeled or understood. In humans, these discrepancies are consciously experienced as desires such as thirst, and emotions such as loneliness, that allow us to be teleologically driven in an open-ended, contextually flexible manner.

One reason consciousness evolved is so that cybernetic teleology could be embedded, as values, both positive and negative, in the world hallucination. If consciousness is the result of unconscious processing that precompiles a world, such that "seeing is seeing as," the precompiled world model is one rich with meanings and evaluations, experienced as such.

Lacking conscious desires, emotions, and goals, AI systems lack meaning and understanding of meaning. At root, they are just shuffling around zeros and ones, meaninglessly. If our goal is to create a general AI system, we may first have to solve how to instantiate consciousness in computers. For example, I can mentally model or understand what you mean when you talk of your physical or emotional pain, because I have experienced these things. An AI system that lacks consciousness cannot mentally model another's consciousness in terms of its own. If meaning is rooted in consciously felt evaluations and mental models that are themselves rooted in how we experience the world, AI will lack felt meaning or true understanding of meaning. It could at best attain a simulacrum of meaning and understanding of meaning. And yet, if we could create robots that had consciousness, we might then be faced with the immorality of slavery all over again.

The currently dominant metaphor of the mind is that it functions as an information processor, much like a computer, in which computations boil down to logical operations over inputs. But meaning cannot easily be reduced to logical operations. If mind is centrally about meaning, and logical operations fail to handle meaning, then the mind cannot be reduced to logical operations, for example, those underlying computation on a computer. For instance, the Brazilian philosopher Gabriel Moghrabi pointed out to me that there are no logical connectors (Boolean operators or any other classic logical operators) that are able to express the simplest adversation. He pointed out that we do not have a logical operator that expresses "but," "yet," "however," or any other adversive contrast, whether arising from frustration of expectations, feelings of discrepancy, or disagreement or disconformity in logical systems. For example, the sentence "He is gorgeous but dumb" would be translated as "p&q" in any traditional logic system or computer language as "He is gorgeous and dumb." But this states a conjunction of facts that fails to capture the adversation. The mental feeling of discrepancy is lost in a traditional logical translation.

Are subjective notions like irony or humor inexpressible in logic in principle? Or could a new kind of logic be created that could address this lack? Both irony and humor seem to involve a difference between a mental model of what is or should be the case, and what is in fact the case. Computers as currently configured lack mental models, so cannot contrast differences among them or between them and reality. In the case of "He is gorgeous but dumb," the expectation might actually be that gorgeous people are not typically exceptionally smart, simply because it is improbable that people would be extreme positive outliers on two or more uncorrelated dimensions. So really, if the brain operated in a Bayesian manner over probability distributions (Brette, 2019; Rahney, 2019), the violation of expectation would have been "He is gorgeous but intelligent." Interestingly, people would rarely say that. Why not? The word "but" here does not seem to communicate a violation of expectation concerning what is probable. Rather, it seems to communicate a contrast not with what was expected, but a contrast with what might have been hoped for; in other words, an expression of disappointment or even schadenfreude. Because logical operations do not consider mental models or consciousness, they cannot express discrepancies among mental models or subjective experiences, such as disappointment, schadenfreude, irony, and humor, that are associated with such discrepancies. Attempts to reduce mental processing to logical operations or computations that by their very nature cannot capture core aspects of the mental are therefore likely to fail. The brain is not a Turing machine. AI, as impressive as it is, has a long way to go. That said, we are ourselves living proof that consciousness is physically realized. So, conscious AI may yet come to pass.

Nonetheless, the notion that there could be a purely digital realization of the mind is a pipe dream. Our minds are rooted in the analog animality of the needs of our body. Hunger, for example, could never be sated by virtual food in some digital metaverse for the simple reason that our cells require physical sugars, fats, and proteins, and cannot process bits. We are processors of meaning, and meaning has its meaning because of the needs and desires of our analog bodies. Various futurists who imagine us downloading our consciousness onto computers, or the digitalization of our analog bodies through the implantation of chips into our brains that allow us to merge our consciousness with all the information of internet, are advocating pipe dreams. We do not understand how memories are stored or retrieved at the level of synaptic weight changes, and we do not yet understand, in a deep way, the neural code. So, reading out information, such as memories, from neural activity, and merging it with some digital supermind, is, at least so far, pure science fiction.

There can be a discrepancy between our mental model of our agency and our felt agency. Many people feel depressed at the thought that they might lack free will because they are determined to choose as they choose. But why should this be? Why not feel relieved that, whatever happens, it simply had to be? The depression arises because a universe in which our agentic choices are "set in stone" by events before we were even born is a universe in which our agentic choices appear not to be made by us, but by events that lie outside of our control. This can make us feel helpless, like a biochemical puppet.

Meaning and meaningfulness are tied up with our ability to choose in a way that our choices make a difference. We want to, ourselves, comprise a difference that makes a difference. That is, we want our choices to make a difference to the outcomes that we make happen in our lives. We are the meaning-makers because we make the difference, with our choices, that makes a difference to our life outcomes, and had we made other choices, we and others would have experienced different life outcomes. Thus, free will and meaning are inseparable in that both arise when our enacted choices make a difference that makes a difference to ourselves and others.

For the purposes of this book, we will think of information not as a thing, but as a process of informing, where some difference is detected by a detector, for example, a neuron. And that information will be meaningful if it is a difference that makes a difference, given the current needs and goals that an embodied mind has. If it is meaningful information, then decoders will cause other events to happen in a cascade of such acts of meaningful informing. A mind and its meanings supervene upon such acts of evaluative decoding.

1.8 What Is Causation?

Two events can behave in a seemingly causally connected way without necessarily being causally connected. They might simply be correlated. For example, it might seem that a rooster crowing at dawn causes the sun to rise. Certainly, the rooster's crowing consistently precedes the sunrise in a very systematic way. But how can we be sure that the rooster does not actually cause the sun to rise? We can intervene in some way that makes it impossible for the rooster to crow, and nonetheless the sun will rise. So, consistent pre-occurrence is not sufficient to distinguish true causation from a mere appearance of causation.

There might be what is called "a lurking variable" that can account for the apparent link between events that appear to be causally linked. For example, consider the amount of clothing that people wear and the amount of ice cream that they eat. The more clothing they wear, the less ice cream they eat, and the more ice cream they eat, the less clothing they wear. Does eating ice cream cause people to wear less, or does wearing more clothing cause people to eat less ice cream? No; we can see that there is a lurking variable, in this case temperature, that drives both outcomes. As it gets hotter outside, people tend to want to wear less clothing and they also tend to want to eat more ice cream. Therefore, neither temporal correlation nor any other kind of correlation in outcomes is sufficient to establish true causation between events.

How can we establish the existence of a genuine causal relationship between two things that both vary in time? The most popular models of causation nowadays are so-called interventionist or manipulationist models of causation, defended in recent years by philosophers such as Judea Pearl (2000) and James Woodward (2003). Their models of causation are rooted in the intuition that if some variable associated with event A causes something to change in another event B, then one should be able to manipulate A in some way and see corresponding changes in B that happen after changing A. If A is modeled as causing B, then there should be an intervention on A that results in B changing its value.

These kinds of models of causation basically describe what scientists have done for centuries to determine causal relationships among variables. Scientists try to control for all independent variables. Woodward calls this "screening off" the other variables besides A that likely partially cause B, by holding their values constant. Then we vary the single variable A in order to see the consequences or changes expressed by some outcome or dependent variable B. If B changes with an intervention on A, it is concluded that A causes B, at least in part. For example, if you manipulate the thermostat and the furnace goes on and it gets warmer, that is a causal relationship because turning the thermostat on makes the furnace turn on. But causation is not always so simple, especially in the brain and mind, where criterial causation, a different kind of causation, reigns.

1.9 What Is the Mind–Body Problem?

There isn't just one mind–body problem. There are several. Here we consider different mind–body problems. They all relate to the difficulty we have in understanding how mental events can be realized in physical events.

The first mind–body problem concerns the issue of how mental events are realized in physical events, in particular, in neuronal activity. The philosopher Leibniz said that identical things must have identical properties. This seems reasonable enough. How can two things be the same thing, but have incompatible or contradictory properties? Let's say mental events are identical with physical events. If this were so, we would expect mental and physical events to have the same properties. But mental and physical events obviously don't have the same properties. Physical events have mass and momentum, whereas mental events, like perceptions of redness or pain, lack mass and momentum. Physical events are publicly observable. I can open up your skull and brain and observe the activity of neurons in your head. But mental events are not publicly observable. I can't open your mind and observe your experiences or comprehend your experiences of redness or pain. So, we probably have to let go of the idea that the mental and physical are identical in any simple sort of direct identification, where we argue that they are one and the same thing.

Since a direct identity relationship runs into the problem of mutually incompatible properties between the mental and the physical, we have to uncover a different relationship between the mental and the physical. One proposal is that the mental is realized in, or "supervenes" upon, the physical. Mental events supervene on physical events when there can be different sets of physical events that realize the same mental event, but there cannot be different mental events that are realized in a single physical event or single brain state. So, a given mental state can be realized in many different brain states, but two different mental events must be realized in different brain states.

To make the supervenience relationship clear, think of how the architecture of a house is realized in the material of the house. Two houses can have the exact same architecture but be made of different particular instances of wood or metal or plaster forms. But two houses cannot have different architectures and be made of identical instances of those physical things in the same spatial relationships. So, the supervenience relationship suggests that there is an asymmetry between the physical and the mental. The mental is realized in a particular instance of the physical but could have been realized in other physical instantiations. In contrast, the physical is not realized in the mental. A given mental event, say, having the experience of a toothache, can be realized in many different neuronal states, but if there are two different mental states, they must be realized in two different physical states of the nervous system.

Even if we accept that the mental supervenes on the physical, or is entirely realized in the physical, we still have to ask: in what aspect of the physical is it realized? Is it realized in the material aspect of the physical? The shape of the physical? The dynamic patterns over time of physical events? In spatiotemporal relationships among physical things, even when such relationships among physical things may not themselves be physical?

We return to this first mind–body problem later. But for now, let me just say that in this book I argue that information is realized in acts of decoding patterns in input, particularly in patterns of coincidence. Since patterns in input are immaterial, even if realized in matter, and since acts of decoding do not themselves have mass or momentum, we can get around the problem that the mental and physical seem to have properties that cannot be linked in a direct identity relationship.

A second mind–body problem concerns what the neural code is or what the neural codes are. What information are neurons communicating to each other as they fire or decode patterns or rates of firing in their inputs? How do neurons encode and decode information in patterns or rates of neuronal firing?

The field of neuroscience is still waiting for its Watson and Crick to decipher the neural code. In fact, neuroscience has not even had its Darwin yet—someone who offers an overarching understanding of neural processing that can explain a vast span of observations, as Darwin's idea of evolution by natural selection did for biology. My guess is that once the neural code is cracked—and I am an optimist, I believe it will be cracked—this could be as momentous for our civilization as the cracking of the genetic code.

A third mind-body problem is the problem of mental causation. If information is assumed to be realized in physical events, why not just talk of causation among physical events, say, of atoms bumping into atoms, or quarks interacting with quarks? If all causation reduces to causation at the bottom-most level of reality, say, of quark-on-quark or string-on-string interactions, where there is no need for mental descriptors like "It looks red," "it hurts," or "it feels immoral to me," then mental causation is epiphenomenal. Any apparent causal powers of the mind are illusory. For example, I can make the shadows of my two hands look like they are knocking into each other and causing each other to move, but we all know that shadows cannot really be causal in that way.

If all causation is physical causation and if information cannot be causal in the universe, then there can be no free mental causation, or free will. And yet the mind seems to be causal in a very undeniable way. If I ask someone to please describe the contents of what they are now experiencing, it is hard to see how the contents of their consciousness play no role whatsoever in what they subsequently say, or in the motions of atoms in their jaw, that follow from what they say. For example, if they say "my tooth hurts" it is hard to understand how their conscious experience of pain can play no role in the trajectories of the calcium atoms in their jaw when they describe what they are experiencing. But if this is correct, then consciousness and mental events are indeed causal of at least some physical events in the universe. How can this be? One of our goals is to understand how mental events can be causal, in a top-down manner, of physical events, such as the trajectories of calcium atoms, or, indeed quarks.

We return to all three of these mind–body problems again and again throughout this book. Great minds have grappled with these problems since at least the time of the ancient Greeks. But neuroscience has advanced to a point that it can now shed valuable light on possible solutions unimaginable to the ancient Greeks, or even to philosophers of a century ago. One of the goals of this book is to grapple with what modern neuroscience can offer in terms of possible solutions to these ancient, fascinating, and frustrating problems collectively known as "the mind–body" problem. For me, the greatest mystery in the universe (beyond there being a universe at all) is the fact that matter can give rise to consciousness and mind. Our goal is to try to understand how this can happen in the brain.

1.10 What Is Consciousness?

Rene Descartes, the founder of modern philosophy, famously said "I think, therefore I am." Perhaps a better maxim would be "I experience, therefore I am." The only thing we cannot doubt is that we have this conscious experience right now. We cannot be sure that other people or animals are conscious, although it seems reasonable to assume that they are. We cannot even be sure that we are not a brain isolated in a vat being fed inputs that mimic an exterior world, such that we are hallucinating our experience, as in the movie *The Matrix*. But even if we are hallucinating the world, we can be sure that we are experiencing whatever it is that we are hallucinating right now. The present content of our conscious experience is the only thing we can truly know for sure.

Although our conscious experience is the sole content to which we have access, namely, that we can volitionally attend and describe, some scientists and philosophers deny that consciousness is real, or causally efficacious. It is ironic that scientific theories based on conscious observations then try to explain consciousness away as an illusion or as noncausal. I think this is a big mistake.

It is undeniable both that we have subjective experience and that it is causal in the universe, at least when we talk about it and act based on its contents. In science, our task is to figure out exactly how consciousness is realized in the brain, and how it can be causal.

A lot of the work in my own lab has examined what we can and cannot do without conscious operands. For example, conscious object positions drive smooth pursuit eye movements, apparent motion perception, attentional pop-out, and volitional attentional tracking (Hui et al, 2020; Maechler et al., 2021a,b; Özkan et al., 2020), but saccades to an object can happen on the basis of unconscious information about the position of an object (Lisi and Cavanagh, 2015). But memory-guided saccades are again driven by the position that was consciously perceived (Massendari et al., 2018). This implies that visual memories are stored in the spatial coordinate system of consciousness, not the retinotopic coordinates of a detected stimulus.

But what is consciousness, exactly? Consciousness to a first approximation is the set of all things that we are now subjectively experiencing. Since we are humans and can talk, this includes the set of experiences that we can talk about. So, for humans, a rough stand-in for determining whether something is conscious or not is whether we can describe what it is like for us to have such-and-such an experience.

But reportability is not a very general way to specify the domain of consciousness because there are animals (and some people) who are conscious but cannot speak. So, we need to have a better definition of consciousness than just reportability. A better definition of consciousness links the idea of consciousness to the ideas of volition and attention. On this view, consciousness is the domain of operands upon which volitional operators can operate. The most important volitional operator or executive process is volitional attention. On this view, consciousness includes everything that you are now volitionally attending and everything that you could volitionally attend in the next moment.

But what are the operations of volitional attention? Paradigmatic cases of volitional attentional control include voluntary manipulation of representations in working memory and the voluntary tracking of one or a few objects among numerous otherwise identical perceived objects. If there is a flock of indistinguishable birds, for example, there is nothing about any individual bird that makes it more salient. But with volitional attention, any bird can be marked and tracked. This salience is not driven by anything in the stimulus. Rather, it is voluntarily imposed on bottom-up information, and can lead to eventual motoric acts, such as pointing at the tracked bird.

Many wonderful experiments have been done in the past few decades showing the close link between what we attend and what we are conscious of. There is a famous video of basketball players passing a ball while a gorilla walks on stage (Simons and Chabris, 1999). The task is to count the number of ball passes that are made by the team wearing white, while ignoring the team wearing black. Into the middle of this, a black gorilla walks across the stage. The amazing thing is that more than half of the subjects who view this film for the first time, report not having seen the gorilla, even if they had been looking right at it.

Normally, if something changes in the world, there is a motion signal at the location of the change. The motion signal indicates that something has changed and where it has changed as well. But if we get rid of this motion signal, we will generally not be made aware that a change has taken place. In order to notice a change in the absence of a motion signal that indicates the presence of a change, we have to pay attention to a location or thing for a relatively long time and then compare it with our memories of its recent previous states. Only then, if there is a mismatch between the way it is now and our memory of it, do we notice that there has been a change.

In other experiments (Simons and Levin, 1997), a man is giving directions to an experimenter, not knowing that he is actually the subject of an experiment. While he is talking, two other men carry a big door right between the subject and the experimenter. As the door comes through, the experimenter switches positions with one of the men who was carrying the door. Even though a new experimenter is now standing in front of the subject, he continues giving directions because he does not notice that there is a new person standing in front of him. Simons and Levin have done similar experiments all around the world, and people more often than not fail to notice that there is a new person standing in front of them, as long as they were not paying attention, and as long as a person has not switched category of sex, race, or age. If the switch is within a category, say an young Asian woman is replaced by a new Asian woman, people more often than not regard her as the same woman.

This implies that most of us most of the time are processing inputs at the level of categories. When in inattentive "zombie" mode, we are operating on the basis of automatized schemas or scripts. We walk through the world and say "bench," "old man," "tree," and so on, without noticing the particularities of that individual bench, person, or tree. Without attention, we can still operate in the world, based upon automatized scripts, but we miss a lot.

Children are typically not like this. They might say "Mom! Look at this tree, it has white bark! Mom, look at this caterpillar! It has red eyes!" and the mother says "Stop talking so much Jimmy! Can't you see I'm busy?" And over time Jimmy loses his childlike enthusiasm and attentiveness and becomes ever more inattentive and no longer notices the intricacies of the bark or the caterpillars. He becomes less conscious of his world because he becomes less attentive. Like so many adults, he comes to process the world in terms of familiar categories. But categories exist in our head, not in reality. Each tree or bench or person is in fact particular and unique, and had we paid attention, we would have noticed this. When in "zombie" mode, we perceive a simplified story that we have concocted about events and things in the world, rather than the world as it is.

Without attention we might not notice that there is a gorilla right in front of us. This does not mean that we experienced nothing at the location of the gorilla. We may have experienced undifferentiated black features moving about at that location, rather than a gorilla. If that is the case, without attention, we would experience something like "qualia soup" or "feature soup." But with attention, we would experience a gorilla because attention can function like a "feature glue" that combines features (and previously glued-together chunks of features) into objects and events. Another possibility is that an unconscious representation of a gorilla is activated even in the absence of attention, as might be evidenced by semantic priming, with attention being required for activation of this representation in consciousness (Cavanagh et al., 2023).

Why do we become automatized as we grow up? Automatization allows us to save energy. We can act on auto-pilot, freeing up mental resources for other tasks. For example, when we drive, at first we have to pay attention to every little thing. It is exhausting, but as we become a better driver, we can drive on automatic pilot, so to speak. We can divert some attention to our inner thoughts.

But notice that our zombie scripts cannot handle the unexpected and the novel. Let us say that a clown suddenly starts skipping across the highway. We have no unconscious script to handle this situation automatically—our daydreams are interrupted and we are forced to pay attention to the clown. This is a good thing, because entering conscious–volitional mode, we can consider many options. We might slow down, swerve around the clown, honk, or even consider the option of opening the window and yelling at the clown. Volitional conscious-mode is slow in comparison to automatized scripts for thinking or behaving, but unlike them, it is flexible and open ended. It allows us to weigh our various options and play out events before executing one of them. It allows us to try things out internally, in the virtual reality of our imagination, before committing to a path of action. As the philosopher Karl Popper put it rather poetically, "consciousness evolved so that our hypotheses could die in our stead."

Why must the results of imagining operations be consciously experienced, even if some of those operations are not conscious? It is so that we can feel what it is like to "live" through various options, and thereby learn from experience which option we should later realize and which options we should avoid.

It is not enough to say that consciousness is that set of highly preprocessed mental representations that either are now being volitionally attended or could be so attended in the next moment. From where do such "precompiled" representations come? Volitional attention cannot get under the hood, so to speak, and be allocated to earlier representations, such as those present at the retina. Rather, unconscious and preconscious processes operate on the input, and after they are done with their rapid operations, volitional attention can then further process a subset to be processed in working memory even more deeply. For example, we can track something as it moves around the world with our attention, even if we are not directly looking at it.

The set of "precompiled" potential operands offered up to attention, like a smorgasbord of things possibly worthy of attention, is the evaluated perceptual world model. It emphasizes what has been preconsciously inferred to be the intrinsic properties of things and events. For example, the world model might reveal that there is an intrinsically white cat that happens to be moving under a blue light, of that intrinsic size and distance, moving in that world direction. Moreover, preconscious processing assigns values to them, such that objects are seen as attractive, potentially threatening, or delicious. As much pre-evaluation takes place as possible before cognitive evaluation kicks in.

Because the world model of what is intrinsically the case is a (hopefully veridical) hallucination, any particular component of experience, say the whiteness of the cat, is itself a hallucination. Concerning the subjective nature of such hallucinations, why does white look white and not blue? Why does the sky look blue and not taste sweet? The answer is that a hallucination can have any property whatsoever since it is entirely concocted. If it had enhanced survival value that we hallucinate sweetness instead of blueness when looking at the sky, evolution would have sculpted that experience into the world model that we call our perceptual consciousness. There is no objective whiteness or blueness or sweetness in the world out there. Qualia are simply hallucinations in our head, and hallucinations can have any property we like whatsoever. For example, the experience of redness can be taken to represent, like a symbol, the presence of certain pigments or light in the world. But the qualities experienced, or qualia, should reflect what is intrinsically true about objects and events in the world, and our body acting in that world. The experience of saltiness encapsulates information about the intrinsic chemical nature of a substance whereas the experience of blue evolved to encapsulate information about the intrinsic reflectance of a substance. If we could look at a blue wall and experience it as salty, that would mean that we are recovering information about the chemistry of the wall by looking at it. But information about such chemistry is not present in light generally. Conversely, if we tasted ocean water and experienced it as blue, that would mean that we are able to recover information about reflectance by tasting it. But again, that information is generally not recoverable from information about chemistry.

To ask why red feels subjectively red and not sweet is a bit like asking why the symbol "$" represents dollars and not the symbol "¶." The assignment is arbitrary, but these meanings had to be represented by something. However, the symbol metaphor breaks down in the sense that redness can be bundled with other qualia in a superposition, such as a desire, as might happen when we look at a healthy ripe cherry whose red pigments trigger a desire to eat it.

The hard problem was solved by evolution as those hallucinations were selected for that had the properties that best represented useful facts about the world and our bodies in it, generally corresponding to what is intrinsically true (e.g., this is a white pigmented cat under blue light, rather than a blue pigmented cat) and what is valued (e.g., this is attractive, delicious, painful, etc.). Evolution sculpted the set of qualia hallucinations we have because they got the job done, that is, they afforded us a world of representations corresponding to what is intrinsically the case (the true pigment, size, distance, value), which executive operators, such as volitional attention, could then operate on in light of contextual reasons, in order to decide what to do next. If the hallucinated world model was true, in the sense of representing and evaluating well that which was relevant and really the case in the colorless, valueless world-in-itself, then animals would survive and pass on their genes. Those who mis-hallucinated or failed to hallucinate what was of relevance to survival did not survive. We are the inheritors not only of those whose bodies worked well enough so that they could bring offspring into the world, but also of those animals who hallucinated correctly enough to accomplish the same.

Only a very specific subset of neural decodings in brains should realize consciousness, because consciousness, in animals, exists to create a world model of what is intrinsically true about the world and the body, which is then used in a perception-action cycle that affords choices among options for behaving in the world. Preconscious and unconscious operations, and the consciousness that they construct, have evolved to represent what is intrinsically the case in the world, despite spurious deformations, ambiguity and noise at the level of sensory detectors. This conscious representation of what is intrinsically the case has evolved in order to allow an animal to do things in the world correctly. Animals must operate within a "true" model of what is taken to be intrinsically the case in the world, including of itself in the world, or else they will operate within an incorrect world model. The "veridical hallucination" of animal consciousness usually corresponds to the world so well, that it is for the animal as if it operates within the world itself, rather than within a model of the world.

The vast majority of information processed by the nervous system is not and should not be conscious. Information processed prior to stages where information about intrinsic color, shape, size and so forth has been made explicit, could actually damage the chances that an animal might survive in the world, because the animal would not operate over information that is its nervous system's best estimate of what is currently intrinsically true about the state of the world. Operating on the basis of false information, whether sensing what is not the case, or not sensing what is the case and relevant to survival, could lead to fatal mistakes.

Moreover, only information that affords selection among options should be made available to executive planning areas and operators, such as volitional attention, because evaluating and selecting options open to possible action is just what executive planning areas are for. Anything that has only one option or has been fully automatized should not be presented to planning areas as part of the conscious world model. Doing so would be like having a pop-up menu occur on your desktop that said "The operating system has only one option and will now execute it." The only reason that such pop-up menus are needed is when a volitional decision must be made among two or more options on the basis of personal or contextual reasons. If there is only one option, the fastest and most efficient response is to simply execute it. Thus, most information processing that has been automatized by the nervous system should remain unconscious. Only that which affords volitional selection among possible options of behavior or volitional attending, and only that which is true about the world and the body in the world, should comprise the consciousness world/body model.

Qualia are necessary for volitional mental causation because they are the only informational format available to volitional attentional operations. Actions that follow volitional attentional operations, such as volitional tracking, cannot happen without consciousness. Qualia on this account are a "precompiled" informational format made available to attentional selection and operations by earlier, unconscious information processing. The relationships between qualia, free will, working memory, and volitional attention are therefore very intimate. The domain of qualia is the domain of representations that either are now being volitionally attended or that could be so attended in the next moment in light of current criteria held in working memory. In other words, qualia are the possible operands of volitional operations.

But what exactly are qualia, beyond being the operands of volitional attentional operations? In my previous book, *The Neural Basis of Free Will*, I argued that a quale is a simple feature or chunked combination of features that can pop out in a search array in which distractors lack the feature in question. On this account, we must be born with a basis set of basic feature sensitivities, say, in the taste domain: sweet, sour, salty, bitter, and savory. But because of automatization, whether due to repeated passive exposure or the active exposure of volitionally attending to chosen combinations, we can "wire up" sensitivities to complex combinations of these features (Frank et al., 2014, 2016, 2018, 2022; Reavis et al., 2015, 2016, 2018). If we think of the basis set as vectors, we can create new vectorial dimensions, expanding the dimensionality of our representational space. For example, the taste of pineapple might involve a certain novel vector in the basis set space, which can then be orthogonalized (sparsified) so that a complex curry can then be projected onto this chunked neo-dimension, and we can then say, "I can taste pineapple in this curry." This process allows us to master sensitivities to the things present in the world in which we find ourselves. If born in Thailand, we can automatize sensitivities to pineapple, coconut, and mango, and if born in Greenland, perhaps to the taste of narwhal versus seal blubber.

At a neural level, this process of sparsification and sensitization to basis vector combinations is likely realized in the development of precise new tuning properties among pyramidal neurons to, say, the taste of pineapple, such that the neuron or population of neurons only becomes active in a certain way if pineapple is present in something we are tasting.

Because the feature combinations we learn are not only a matter of frequency of passive exposure, but also a matter of what we choose to attend to and practice, we can create willed chunks or automaticities. That is, with practice, things that were no more than qualia soup to us initially, will now pop out immediately as obvious. We can will to change the nature of our consciousness, meaning the world as we experience it, by willing to automatize chunks that we want to bring into existence. Free will can alter the very structure of our own future conscious experience. For example, we can choose to learn Nepali, and, with practice, for us the sound of Nepali will transform from disorganized sounds into meaningful chunked words and sentences. If the contents of consciousness are that which pops out, because we have specialized detectors for such features and feature combinations (Cavanagh et al., 2023), we can will our consciousness in the future to be a different type of consciousness by willing to chunk, say, new classes of sounds into Nepali words. Once we master Nepali, its words will be automatically decoded. We will not only have willed a new brain into existence, namely, one that can now process Nepali, but also we will have willed a new kind of consciousness into existence, namely, one where Nepali words are now automatically decoded, which then seem to pop out effortlessly.

In sum, consciousness is the set of all operands (qualia) that we are volitionally attending (comprising the figure), or could attend in the next moment (comprising the unattended background). But the background might involve highly complex chunks, if we have automatized these, whether through exposure or past volitional choices (Cavanagh et al., 2023; Reavis et al., 2016, 2018). We can therefore see that there are four concepts that are deeply connected: volition, attention, the kind of learning associated with chunking or automatization, and consciousness.

1.11 Against Pan-Psychism and Computational Reductionism

Dualism or any other form of substance pluralism is difficult to defend because it seems impossible that mutually irreducible fundamental substances could ever interact. But there are a variety of monisms. It is possible to posit that energy, action, mind, information, consciousness, spirit, or even the vacuum is the fundamental substrate within which all higher patterns are realized.

Broadly speaking, there are two classes of monisms: materialist and non-materialist. In this book I argue from a materialist stance and in this section I argue against non-materialist positions.

The most common type of non-materialist monism is pan-psychism. There exist various versions of pan-psychism, but all tend to argue that the fundamental substrate of reality is in some vague sense conscious. The pan-psychist view tends to run into problems in that it is not at all clear how the "consciousnesses" of quarks could be unified into the unified consciousness of an animal. And having conscious experiences, at least for an animal, generally means having a functioning brain. Moreover, in animals, consciousness is "intentional" in that it tends to be about something going on in the world, the body, or in the imagination. If a photon, say, were conscious, in what sense would it be intentional, namely, about or pointing to something else? If NYC were in some sense conscious, of what would it be conscious? To avoid such problems, those of a more hard-headed persuasion tend to be physicalists rather than mentalists, idealists or pan-psychists.

An even more far-fetched monism argues that we are all realized in an informational matrix or virtual reality in which we are analogous to avatars in a video game. Just as it is difficult to disprove the solipsist's claim that we are figments in their world-hallucination, it is difficult to disprove this radical claim. But the view seems implausible because the virtual reality in which we live would have to be realized in some substrate, as video games are realized in computers. Would that substrate be real? Saying that the substrate is itself virtual could lead to an infinite regress in which nothing is fundamental or real. Moreover, why would virtual avatars have to be conscious, as we know that we ourselves are? And, if reality were virtual, it is not at all clear why there should be any physical limits at all, such as the laws of physics. In a virtual reality, virtually anything could happen, as in a video game. Since possible events are in fact severely constrained by physical factors, such as conservation of energy, spin, and momentum, physicalists tend to view consciousness as realized in material processes, rather than seeing material processes as the consequence of conscious processes.

A more plausible mentalistic monism is that everything, fundamentally, is information, rather than physical energy in spacetime. But what would we mean by "information?" Scientists and many philosophers (e.g., Dretske, 1981; but cf., e.g., Millikan, 1989) tend to adhere to the traditional view of Shannon (1948) that information is effectively epistemological in the sense that it arises as a function of possibilities collapsing in the state of the knowledge of some reader, decoder, or receiver of information sent over some channel by a sender who (or encoder that) shares a common informational encoding scheme.

Neuroscientists generally take for granted that neural circuits process information in Shannon's epistemological sense. In trying to understand how the brain works, it is natural to make analogies with computers, because we understand how information is processed by computers. And, at a superficial level, computers and brains do seem to have a lot in common. Both have short-term (RAM) and long-term (ROM) memory stores, for example. Moreover, in the context of computers, we know exactly what we mean by the word "information." Information in the context of computers is well-described by Shannon's information theory; the magnitude of information gained by a decoder is a function of the number of possible inputs that could have been received, weighted by the likelihood of respective outcomes. The less likely an outcome, the more informative or surprising it is. If neurons process information in this epistemological sense, then a post-synaptic neuron gains information from pre-synaptic neurons by receiving "messages" whose informational content depends on how many possible messages could have been sent at any given moment, weighted by their probability of occurrence.

It is also possible to create an "ontological" conception of information that has nothing to do with knowledge or changes in uncertainty of a receiver, but instead depends on the likelihood that a system can occupy its present physical state, given all the physical states that it could occupy. Whereas an epistemological reading of "information(x) = $-\log(p(x))$" would require $p(x)$ to be the subjective probability of a message in the mind of a receiver, an ontological reading would require $p(x)$ to be the objective probability of occupying a state of the system x in the absence of any receiver.

Tononi and colleagues (Oizumi et al., 2014; Tononi, 2004; Tononi et al., 2016) proposed a mathematically elaborate ontological conception of information. According to their information integration theory (IIT), information arises from the nature of all cause–effect relationships that could happen within a system. This could, in principle, be determined by perturbing the system in all possible ways to learn how a given state of the system alters the probabilities of future and past states of the system. Such a causal "transition probability matrix" links each momentary state of the system to the likelihoods of all other possible physical states of the system in the past and future. According to IIT, consciousness in the hard sense of qualia is equated with the objective causal properties of the system described by this matrix.

Information is fully integrated when perturbing any part of the system can affect every other part. If any part cannot influence or be influenced by other parts, it is not part of the integrated system. Information so defined is intrinsic to the physical system, that is, it does not depend on inputs to the system. In contrast, information for Shannon only occurs when a decoder receives inputs that reduce uncertainty in knowledge of that decoder.

According to IIT, any integrated system that can occupy many states has a "phi" value corresponding to the amount of its intrinsic ontological integrated information. A phi value is a function of the number of other states that the system could occupy, even if it happens to occupy just one state at present, or indeed, even if it were to occupy the same state forever. The higher the phi value, the more integrated information is present, and the more conscious a system is or the more consciousness that it has. It does not matter that it is never made clear how phi would actually be measured. Even if the goal of developing a "phi-o-meter" would never be practically attainable, the theory can be criticized at the level of a theory of information and consciousness.

Note that IIT assigns a phi value to every physical system, even if the phi value is very low, as for, say, a rock. Since phi is taken by IIT to also be a measure of the amount of consciousness present in a system, IIT would seem to imply pan-psychism. Indeed, Tononi and colleagues argue that everything in the universe is conscious, differing only in the degree to which it is so. If so, how do we go from the minimal "consciousness" of quarks to the consciousness of animals?

In the case of the brain, the description of the particular state of the system that would correspond to the particular conscious state that is currently occupied (i.e., its "shape in Q space") depends as much on the neurons that are firing as those that are not. According to Fekete and Edelman (2011), this is a major conceptual flaw of IIT because it cannot explain how neurons' mere potential to fire, even when silent, contributes to conscious experience. Bartlett (2022) argues that the claim is not even testable.

IIT is rather the opposite of the micro-consciousnesses view (Koch, 2004; Zeki, 2008) that the neural correlates of consciousness (NCC) are realized in specific *active* neurons that are the minimal sufficient set required for the having of a specific experience. For example, a believer in the micro-consciousnesses account might argue that the firing, in a particular way, of deep layer pyramidal cells in motion-processing area MT is the NCC corresponding to the experience of a particular perceived motion. Holding this set constant, but changing the potential for firing of silent neurons elsewhere in the brain (by, say, hyperpolarizing them further), would (according to IIT) change the conscious state of the observer. Whereas those who believe that consciousness depends on the state of neural activity would regard this as wrong, Tononi (2008) predicts that cooling—and thereby changing the potential for firing—of inactive neurons should change qualia. In our example, Tononi might predict that cooling an inactive nonvisual area, such as, say motor cortex when we are not moving our bodies, should alter our conscious experience of visual motion. This certainly seems counterintuitive but is at least a testable and therefore falsifiable claim. It would lead to unintuitive predictions; for example, a person whose arms were momentarily paralyzed because motor strip outputs that are associated with arm-control motor neurons have been blocked should see or hear the world differently than if such arm paralysis were not the case.

Another problem with an ontological conception of information is that it does not depend on the decoding of informative inputs. That is, defining information relative to possible physical states that could be occupied, or relative to the causal influences that a physical state could exert, does not link the concept of information to physical state changes that depend on how input is decoded. Returning to our example from Section 1.7, the pattern of ink "Bad" would be decoded by German readers to mean "bath," whereas English readers would read it to mean "not good." The meaning does not arise from the input itself, but rather from how the input is decoded. We could even say that there is no information whatsoever in "Bad," and that it contains only the *potential* for information, relative to a given decoder that decodes it as input. We can imagine countless languages, each of which assigns this pattern of ink a different message. But the potential for realizing information relative to any decoder is not the same as actually realizing information via physical state changes of a particular decoder. For example, a ribosome that "reads" mRNA will build proteins. But relative to a different decoder, the same mRNA strand might be used to build cities or write sonnets.

We can even imagine two identical people with brains in identical states, save for a single differing neuron that decodes inputs from the rest of the brain using a German decoding scheme in one brain and an English one in the other. That single neuron difference might lead the first person to interpret "Bad" to mean "bath" and the second person to interpret it to mean "not good." In this thought experiment, it does not matter how integrated the other billions of neurons in rest of the brain are; the conscious experience, upon reading "Bad" will come down to the decoding scheme of a single neuron.

A central problem for any theory of information is that given any physical configuration, a physically realized decoder can be designed that does whatever you would like in response to that configuration. Fashion the right decoder, and even cracks on a burned tortoise shell can be thought to carry information about the future, the temperature on the sun, or anything else. Information arises from acts of decoding, not the decoded thing or input itself.

However, this decoder-dependent conception of information might seem to some to run counter to common sense because it seems that, for something to be informative about some event in the world, it must derive from that event in the right way. The "right way" is thought by externalist philosophers of mind to be in part a causal chain between the event and our experience of (or knowledge of) the event that makes our experience or knowledge of the event true (i.e., making it correspond to facts). On this account, even though generations of ancient Chinese thought that cracks in tortoise shells carry information about the future, they do not; this kind of causal chain is generally regarded as impossible within the modern scientific worldview. Even though we may now think that they were deluded, the ancient Chinese who cracked tortoise shells in fire to divine the future believed that the cracks were very much informative about the future. If information is only realized within a physical state change of a decoder, the decoder itself has no way to determine whether that which it decodes corresponds to some event in the world. Indeed, we may undergo a scientific revolution someday and come to see that the ancient Chinese were right about tortoise shell cracks after all, and that we so-called modern thinkers were wrong. But then again, in the even more distant future, we might find that in fact we were right after all, and so forth. Does the informativeness of the cracks change with our transient scientific theories? No—the cracks were informative for the ancient Chinese but are not for us because they were decoding them according to a different decoding scheme than we use today. If someone believes in astrology, horoscopes are informative for them, relative to their decoding scheme, even if objectively, astrology is complete bunk. Thus, information has no necessary link to truth, or correspondence to events in the world. Information arises from acts of decoding; whether or not that information is true is irrelevant to the existence of that information. Information has no necessary link to what is ontologically the case.

Information arises only in the context of some decoding read-out mechanism (cf. Buzsáki, 2010). Information does not even require that a message be sent by a sender; even a random pile of rocks left by a melted glacier can be decoded as informative by a decoder prepared to interpret such input as a pattern that matches its criteria. For example, a pile of rocks randomly shaped like a crucifix could be interpreted by a religious person as a personal message confirming the existence of a caring God.

I reject the notion that a name (or word or symbol) can only refer to a thing if it has a causal link to that thing in the world. Instead, information and reference arise in the context of the physical re-conformation of a decoder or read-out mechanism when its physical/informational criteria are met, regardless of whether the thing exists (or could exist) in the world. According to traditional "descriptivist" theories of reference, like those of Frege, Russell, Wittgenstein, and Searle (1990), a proper name refers to a thing by virtue of its being—or being associated with—a set of descriptions which that thing uniquely satisfies. My view of reference is related to a descriptivist account in that reference arises from the satisfaction of criteria, which, although they can be satisfied in many and even partial ways, can be thought of as descriptions. Note, however, that the physical/informational criteria that neurons place on their inputs need not be, and typically cannot be, understood in terms of words, semantics, descriptions, or names.

Another key problem with IIT is that informational states are intrinsic, or internal to the system, and have nothing to do with the state of the world outside the system. That is, states of the system are not "intentional" or about extrinsic facts outside the system. A physical system has a higher phi value the more ontological states that it could occupy or influence, and to the extent that phi measures the degree of consciousness of a physical system, a physical system such as NYC will have a phi value. Obviously, NYC can occupy many states and is causally complex and well-integrated, but what would NYC be conscious of exactly? Do Queens, Manhattan, and Brooklyn have different conscious contents under IIT? What would unify them into a greater NYC consciousness? I would argue that NYC is not conscious because it does not realize acts of decoding inputs.

Consciousness in humans and animals is generally consciousness of something. This "intentionality" arises in the brain because the conditions for the firing of some neurons that primarily fire only when those conditions are met have, in fact, been met. That is, intentionality in the brain arises because of the specificity of the tuning properties of particular neurons to their inputs, which in animals are typically perceptual inputs concerning states of the world, as occurs in exteroception, or the body, as occurs in interoception.

The notion of phi lacks this aspect of intentionality, and so lacks a key aspect of the only kind of consciousness that we know exists, namely, our own. NYC could in principle exist as a closed system in a manner whose states or state changes are not dependent upon the organization of inputs into the system. But the states of our normal waking consciousness are usually dependent upon the organization of our inputs. For example, we are conscious of a cat when we see one, in part because of the pattern of light that falls upon our retina when a cat in fact stands before us. Even in cases like dreaming or hallucination, where we may become conscious of a cat solely by virtue of endogenously generated inputs, our decoders for a cat (i.e., neurons that fire differently when the criteria for a cat being present are met) are presumably activated, or otherwise we would not dream of or hallucinate a cat.

Perceptual systems evolved in order to provide animals with information about goings-on in the world and in the body so that perceiving animals could act in the world appropriately. Biological consciousness is generally intentional because, in order to survive, animals need information about food, terrain, and objects such as potential predators, prey, and mates. The intentionality of consciousness arises because of neural acts of decoding. Since there is no necessary role in IIT for acts of decoding, there is nothing inherently intentional about the ontological type of information that phi purports to be a measure.

The centrality of a perception–action cycle that arises in animals that need to move about and respond to a world in order to fulfill biological needs is missing from IIT. Consciousness, in the context of biological agents, is a world model constructed on the basis of preconscious, unconscious processing that allows an animal to fulfill its biological goals within that world. The animal operates within a model of the world, including a model of itself in the world. This "veridical hallucination" usually corresponds to the world so well that for the animal it is as if it operates within the world directly, rather than within a hopefully veridical hallucination of the world.

Chalmers (1995) and others have pointed out that theories, like IIT, that attempt to reduce consciousness to computation or function, do not answer the hard problem. In this context we could ask why occupying this state versus any other in a multistate system, say a particular state of NYC, should be associated with a subjectively felt experience at all. So IIT simultaneously backs adherents into an almost religious assertion of universal consciousness, while failing to account for the hard aspect of consciousness, namely, its subjective phenomenology.

Against pan-psychism, I see the vast majority of nonbiological nature as nonconscious because it does not involve decoding inputs on the basis of informational criteria. Against IIT and other versions of pan-psychism, I argue that consciousness can emerge only in those systems that instantiate physically realized decoders whose state changes depend on the meeting of informational criteria by inputs, and in systems whose informational causal chains are based on successions of such acts of decoding. For example, the weather on Jupiter would lack consciousness for the simple reason that the weather's state changes are not necessarily about anything. Against pan-psychism, the vast majority of nonbiological nature would be nonconscious because it does not involve decoding inputs on the basis of informational criteria, and those parts of it that are conscious but not biological we have yet to discover.

Neuroscience needs to abandon ontological conceptions of information and return to an epistemological conception of information; namely, one that depends on changes of a decoder's state upon the arrival of inputs that then affects downstream decoders that receive its outputs as their inputs.

On a decoding account, only those physical causal chains that are also informational causal chains can give rise to mind, and only the subset of those that comprise the world model that affords ongoing planning among options gives rise to consciousness. In animals, the kind of physical causal chains that are informational causal chains involve the meeting of criteria for neural firing.

Interestingly, those criteria depend on the phase relationships among energetic inputs, in particular the simultaneity of neural spikes arriving at post-synaptic neurons. This type of "phase causation" is very different from types of physical causation based solely on energy transfer or chemical transformation found typically in nonbiological systems. Indeed, the path to biological systems began when physical systems responded to the phase relationships among energetic inputs (say, the shape of a molecule that would trigger the opening of a receptor pore, or the timing of spike inputs), and not merely to the amount or frequency of energetic inputs.

Once state changes that could alter the system came to depend on energetic patterns of input, patterns became causal in the universe, as patterns in inputs triggered patterns of outputs. Such a state change can be regarded as an act of decoding of a pattern among inputs. Information and the special class of information that is conscious is realized in physical decoders whose state changes are driven by a sensitivity to the phase relationships among energetic inputs. As such, information in biological systems is inherently intentional in that a state change of a decoder depends upon some proportion of informational criteria being simultaneously met at a given time.

While I reject Tononi's attempt to ontologize information, and instead view information as inherently a product of acts of decoding, I acknowledge deficiencies in the current Shannonesque epistemological conception of information. Namely, the dominant metaphor underlying psychology and neuroscience, that the brain processes information no differently than a computer does, requires a good dose of skepticism. One reason to be skeptical of the computer metaphor is that there is no distinction between software and hardware in the brain. Information processing in the brain leads to physical changes in circuitry, which influence how subsequent information is processed. Even if software could alter hardware on a computer, it would not be separable from the hardware. You could always run the same software on a computer built on different hardware. In the case of the brain, however, how neurons process information is directly dependent upon the physics of hardware components such as channel proteins and membranes. The functionalist notion that mental processing could be carried out by any other physical system that carries out the same computations is limited by the fact that how computations are carried out in the brain is given by the hardware of the brain. In order to transfer a person's mind to a computer, for example, the physical workings of that person's brain would likely have to be replicated by the computer.

Moreover, the brain occupies teleological states. It enters "attractor" states, like hunger, that lead the organism to seek an attractive object or sensation, and it enters "repeller" states, like fight or flight, that lead the organism to seek relief from a repellant object or sensation. Computers, in contrast, have no goals, desires, or fears. Whereas causality in brains is cybernetic, driven in part by subjectively experienced error signals, such as thirst, in computers causality tends to be non-cybernetic. Teleological states influence how information is processed by animals. For example, it might turn out that food-like stimuli are more perceptually salient when an animal is hungry. However, teleological states like hunger are not easily reducible to Shannon's definition of information. The information I gain when I see a hamburger as opposed to anything else depends critically on seeing the hamburger as opposed to any other possibility. An attractor state, like hunger, however, need not be about any particular set of inputs. For example, an animal can be hungry or fearful and not have a particular food or threat in mind.

Because the brain has desires, not all information is equal. Shannon's theory generally does not place value on information because information is a function of the number of possible states a system can occupy, weighted only by the probability of their outcome. A high-probability event might carry more significance for an animal than a low-probability event, if the former has greater value relative to the desires and goals of the animal. The notion of value could be incorporated into Shannon's theory by adding weights to various outcomes that reflect their value to an animal, given its current states of desire. But this is no longer the type of information processed by a computer, which places no value on outcomes. And Shannon's account of information processing entirely lacks cybernetic setpoints and negative feedback loops that are so central to the processing of meaningful information in nervous systems, or even within cells.

The harnessing of true randomness appears to be central to neural processing, whereas a computer in a given state, with identical inputs, will yield identical outputs. Because randomness is by definition not computable in terms of an algorithm—if it were, it would not be random—the succession of brain states biased by randomness is not computable. For this reason alone, the brain is not reducible to a Turing machine.

Finally, the brain is rewiring itself on a millisecond timescale, in that synaptic weights (the degree to which neurotransmitter released at a synapse can drive postsynaptic depolarization or hyperpolarization) are changing as a result of channel opening and other factors. In contrast, no computer as currently instantiated is rewiring itself at all, let alone on a millisecond timescale.

Thus, while I reject pan-psychism, and IIT's ontological conception of information that is used by some as a theoretical framework for pan-psychism, I fully recognize the need to rethink our ideas of information so that they better capture the kind of information processing realized in biological systems.

2
The Philosophy of Free Will

2.1 Defining the Problem of Free Will from a Scientific Point of View

In this chapter I use the words "willed" and "volitional" interchangeably. A volitional action is one we could have chosen to do otherwise for our own consciously knowable reasons. A nonvolitional action is one we could not have chosen to do otherwise, regardless of what we might have consciously wanted to happen. There is no question that there are some processes in the brain that are not subject to volitional control, and some processes that are. For example, breathing usually proceeds automatically, without our conscious awareness. But breathing can be brought under volitional conscious control. Note that to say that it can be brought under conscious control means that it can be altered subject to one's will, for whatever reasons one might have to do so. For example, if I say to you, please breathe slowly, you can easily do so. If I say, now breathe to the rhythm of the song "Jingle Bells," you can do that too. But there are other processes that we cannot bring under conscious or volitional control, even if we wanted to, no matter how hard we try. You have no direct conscious control over your blood pressure, and you cannot will to make your heart beat to the rhythm of your favorite song. You cannot choose, or will, to alter unconscious processes rapidly, even if you can modify them very slowly via the process of automatization. If you could do so, how would you even know that you had succeeded, given that you have no conscious access to unconscious processing?

The vast majority of decisions and processes carried out in your brain and body are not subject to conscious volitional control. That is to say, they happen automatically and unconsciously. A small subset is volitionally consciously controllable, but what sets these volitional processes apart from the automatic ones? The eyes offer another good example. You cannot willingly stop making pupillary adjustments to light levels. Shine a bright light into your eyes, and your pupils will get smaller, no matter what you want or will to happen. Remove the light, and they will get bigger again. However, the eyes also offer a good example of a case where you do have volitional control. Consider the large eye movements that you make when you look around the world. These are known as "voluntary saccades." Indeed, where you next move your eyes is a decision that you make three or four times a second, and this is a decision that you can volitionally regulate.

The decision where to look next is no doubt the most common decision you make in your life. People make this class of voluntary decision thousands of times a day.

A Neurophilosophy of Libertarian Free Will. Peter Ulric Tse, Oxford University Press. © Oxford University Press 2024.
DOI: 10.1093/oso/9780198876953.003.0003

For example, you can choose to look at anything that you want, and you can even choose not to move your eyes at all. What we decide to look at next is not given by anything in the stimulus. It depends on factors in us, such as what we might desire, or what we maintain in working memory as our present goal. For example, the psychologist Alfred Yarbus showed people Ilya Repin's 1884 painting *An unexpected visitor*. What people looked at depended on what task he gave them. If he told them to estimate the material circumstances of the family they exhibited a sequence of saccades that allowed them to evaluate how rich or poor they were, by, for example, looking at their clothes. But if subjects were told to assess the ages of the characters, their eye movements were quite different. They looked more at people's faces, as you might expect.

It seems obvious that what we look at depends on our goals, and that we could have moved our eyes differently than we did, because we could have had different goals than we did. But who is this "you" inside your brain who decides to look at clothes rather than faces one moment, and vice versa the next? Neuroscientists and philosophers wouldn't want to argue that there is a little person (known as a "homunculus") in your brain who decides where to move your eyes. This would lead to an infinite regress because who then would decide where this little homunculus will decide to move your eyes? Another homunculus inside his or her head? And so on.

To avoid the problem of an infinite regress, neuroscientists talk about executive circuits, typically thought to be located in the frontal lobes, that can decide to search for red things or trees or children or whatever, based upon operations in neural circuits that we call "working memory." Voluntary eye movements can serve the flexible and arbitrarily redefinable aims of the moment, processed in working memory.

One of my goals as a neuroscientist is to try and discover how such volitional acts and decisions are realized at the level of neural circuits. One of the major goals of neuroscience is to understand how volitional decisions, such as where we choose to look next, or where we choose to attend next, are carried out in the brain.

Philosophers who deny the existence of free will commonly declare that there may *appear* to be a difference between nonvolitional and volitional eye movements or other decisions, but even the seemingly voluntary decisions that we make are not really voluntary, because where we voluntarily choose to next move our eyes is itself a decision that was made unconsciously and automatically, not subject to our consciously knowable reasons.

Later in the book we explore reasons to doubt such rejections of free will, but for now let me just say that over hundreds of millions of years, Nature came up with neural processing that underlies willed or volitional decision making. Whether or not philosophers decide to attribute "free will" to such volitional neural processes is largely irrelevant to the scientific goal of discovering how volition or will works in the brain. By way of analogy, arguing about whether Greenland is a large island or a continent is simply irrelevant to figuring out what Greenland is in the world or how it functions as a physical system. Similarly, arguing whether or not volitional processes are free has no bearing on how they are realized in neural circuits.

Neuroscientists think that studying what actually evolved is more urgent than discussing what can logically exist, especially since what evolved did not evolve to obey any logic. Whatever worked stuck around, and what did not, got eliminated. I do not think we can get very far in understanding volition in general, or free will in particular, without looking at how the nervous system actually realizes volitional decisions and actions.

2.2 Defining the Term "Free Will"

It is important to get our terms straight. "Free will" is a philosophical term referring to the ability of choosers to choose to do something from among alternatives. A lot needs to be unpacked here.

What is freedom? What does it mean to choose? What is a chooser? Does the chooser need to be conscious? How are alternatives generated? Must they be real alternatives in the sense of alternate future possible states of the universe? Can they instead be alternatives that we only imagine? What is the relationship of imagined possibilities to the possibilities that are really open to us?

In this book, free will refers to the capacity to choose freely. Free choosing in turn is the capacity of a chooser or agent to influence the probabilities of occurrence of future events, perhaps by internally considering or modeling those possible future events, and then choosing to implement or execute internal or external actions that will enhance the likelihood that the desired alternative will be realized. Free will is not a thing. It is a process that has many component subprocesses.

So here is our working definition of "free will": *If a mind can alter the probabilities of future events, in light of its own reasons, and if it can knowingly choose among alternatives, each of which might really happen, then we can say this mind exhibits free agency or has a free will.*

Of course, people want to enhance the odds of those events happening that they want to have happen and decrease the odds of undesirable outcomes. People change their odds by enacting concrete plans that open up real possibilities. For example, if someone wants to increase the odds of meeting a potential partner, and decrease the odds of spending their life alone, they can join a dating site. They might pay a little money, set their criteria, and then evaluate potential mates. In addition to these freely willed acts, with a little luck, they will meet the love of their life.

2.3 Volition Involves Various Brain Processes

The idea of will, whether free or not, is not monolithic. Willing is not a momentary event but a durationally extended process. Consider an everyday process, such as driving a car, which involves numerous procedures and nested subprocedures. For example, in order to drive, we need a driver or executive who has a plan about where to drive. This driver must be able to control the workings of the car by manipulating the steering wheel, accelerator, brakes, and transmission. All these things have to be in working order. In addition, we need fuel. Without fuel, it does not matter how good our driver is. Conversely, a car can have fuel, but without a driver who has a destination in mind, we will also not be going anywhere. The driver's inner setpoint is the destination he has in mind. If there are setbacks, such as a detour, or if he takes a wrong turn, the discrepancy between his present state and his setpoint is corrected; he changes course. There is no single way to reach his destination, so he remains flexible. If his car should break down, he can get it fixed, or, if need be, he can reach his destination some other way. Of course, this driving example is a metaphor for how volitional processes might work in the brain.

In neuroscience we are pragmatic. We want to understand how volitional processes work in the brain. The palm-sized extent of frontopolar cortex behind your forehead (Brodmann area 10) might underlie the ability to generate multiple possible plans or play them out internally. Reward circuitry in the ventral medial and orbital prefrontal cortex allows you to evaluate possibilities for their positive or negative reward value. Attentional areas, such as the frontal eye fields and posterior parietal cortex, may enable you to select from among optimal options. The anterior cingulate cortex, about an inch behind the middle of your forehead, allows you to evoke motivation or evoke appropriate emotional and physiological responses for a given plan while inhibiting suboptimal or inappropriate plans. Motor planning areas afford you the ability to plan motor acts appropriately.

Because the cascade of steps from an abstract plan to a concrete action occurs in such rapid succession in a normal brain, it may seem that willing is a single process, when actually it is a concatenation of many subprocesses. And because of cybernetic feedback, these processes are not realized in an instant, but over durations that allow the possibility of midcourse error correction.

Some might want to primarily associate the act of willing with the ability to freely choose a plan; others might want to associate it with the feeling of effort associated with trying to implement a plan. Confusion arises when people talk about the operations of different neural circuits using the single word "will." Here, willing means doing something or thinking something volitionally, for reasons you might have.

We won't only focus on volitional actions. In fact, some of the most important volitional acts don't involve doing anything in the world at all. A person might have locked-in syndrome and could still choose to volitionally attend to the radio or to the television when both are playing. We want to understand what is behind such volitional acts of the mind and brain, from which volitional motoric acts of the body follow.

Consider, for example, the disks in Figure 2.1. If you look at the central fixation spot, and attend to any of the gray disks, the one you choose to attend will appear to change in brightness. We want to understand what it is that allows you to freely choose to attend to one disk or another, which then subsequently affects what you consciously experience, which then in turn affects what you do in the world. You might say: "I attended to the lower disk, and it turned darker in my experience."

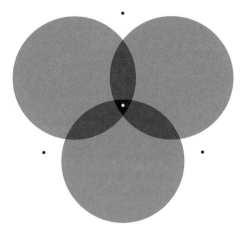

Figure 2.1 Fixate the middle dot and attend to any disk you like. Notice how the attended disk gets darker, more opaque, and seems to appear behind the other two. This is proof that we can volitionally alter our visual consciousness in a top-down manner that is not driven by the stimulus.

To sum up, free will means the ability to volitionally and knowingly choose to do this option versus some other option that is really open to you. This need not involve an act in the world. It can simply mean choosing to attend here versus there, for reasons that are consciously knowable by you. Before we try to unpack how this might work in the brain, we must first explore philosophical arguments for and against free will.

2.4 Determinism versus Indeterminism

Determinism entails a universe that is like a movie that unfolds with only one possible future. What happens in the movie is already set before you ever hit "play." Alternative possibilities and notions of "could have turned out otherwise" just don't apply to a movie, because a movie can only turn out one way.

Another way to think of determinism is that life proceeds as if moving through a tunnel, where the tunnel never branches, because there is only one possible future for the universe. And if the universe is deterministic, then you also have just one possible future that was "laid out" for you before you were even born. In fact, every choice you would ever make was set at the beginning of the universe, just like the unfolding of a movie.

In contrast, indeterminism would be more like a tunnel that branches. At a branching point, one possible path is open to you at the very same time that other possible paths are also open to you. Which path happens is not determined. It might be that one path is more probable than another, but it is not guaranteed that any given possible path is the one that will actually happen. On this view, your life really could have turned out very differently than it has turned out, and could yet turn out in myriad ways, depending on your actions and decisions now.

But there are two types of forking paths: one in our heads made of the various possible courses of action and thought that we imagine, and the other in reality. If determinism is the case, there is only a single non-forking path in reality, and our belief that the forking imagined paths in our head correspond to reality is delusional. Only if indeterminism is the case is there a chance of correspondence between Borges's internal and external gardens of forking paths, or a chance that we are not delusional. But even if indeterminism is the case, and the two gardens lack any correspondence, we are still delusional. Only if our imagined possible courses of thought and action correspond in part with the courses actually open to us, are we not delusional. Imagination by its very nature explores multiple possible courses of action or thought, and imagination need not be rational. In the imagination, nobody models reality as being deterministic, namely, as having only one possible course of action open at a time. But some people, on rational grounds, do model the world to be deterministic. According to determinists, the feeling that we have multiple courses open to us, rooted in our ability to imagine various possible courses of action, is delusional.

Now, whether the universe is fundamentally deterministic or indeterministic is an open question. Some of our best theories in physics model the universe as deterministic. Albert Einstein's theories of special and general relativity, for example, are deterministic theories. In contrast, quantum theory suggests that events can really turn out in more than one possible way (at least as it is interpreted by some people, including two of its founders Niels Bohr and Werner Heisenberg). Quantum theory can assign different possible outcomes very precise probabilities of happening but cannot predict in advance which outcome will actually happen. Physics has yet to resolve the divide between deterministic theories and indeterministic theories of how events unfold. But only one side can be correct. The universe is either ontologically deterministic or it is not. So, one of the central goals of physics remains bridging a theory of gravitation with a theory of events in the quantum domain.

The one certainty is that the universe is, at its root and everywhere, only a quantum domain affair. This is simply because the big is realized in aggregations of the small, not vice versa. The seeming determinism of stellar and planetary paths that allows us to predict the date of an eclipse millions of years ago or in the distant future is a stochastic determinism that arises from averaging over vast numbers of atomic and other quantum domain events. But a stochastic macroscopic "as if" determinism is not the same as a microscopic determinism. The only question then is whether the quantum domain itself is deterministic or indeterministic, a question we return to in Section 2.12.

From the point of view of any subset of the universe, say, our brain, influences will come in from outside in a manner that is not predictable given past events that happened solely within that subset. For example, light or some other form of energy might enter the brain and trigger brain events. From the point of view of events in the brain, such externally triggered events might appear to happen randomly. So, even if the universe as a whole were deterministic, brain events would appear to be in part random.

One possibility is that it is not ultimately knowable whether the universe is fundamentally deterministic or indeterministic. Perhaps, in order to answer this, we would have to be able to observe all particles in the universe. Even if this were possible in practice, we would run into a difficult problem in that we ourselves are part of the universe. We would end up having to observe all events in the universe, including those events that realize our own acts of observation. Just as it is impossible to lift yourself up, or for an eye to turn around and look at itself, it might be impossible for an observer to observe his or her own acts of observation or their material realizers. This Gödelian problem would make it in principle unknowable whether or not the universe is deterministic. To complicate things, there may be events in the universe that are in principle unobservable, such as those subjective events we call consciousness. If something is in principle unknowable, there is no need to lose any sleep over it. We can just go with the preferred option. If we are forced into an either/or choice of an irrational leap of faith, whether toward determinism (which deems imagined openness to be delusional) or toward indeterminism (which deems our imagined futures as potentially non-delusional), why take an irrational leap toward delusionality when we can just as easily take an irrational leap toward non-delusionality?

2.5 Possible Positions on Free Will

The issue of whether or not we have free will is tied up with the debate regarding whether or not the universe is deterministic. Compatibilism is the view that free will is compatible with determinism. Incompatibilism is the view that it is not.

People often talk past each other when debating the reality of free will because they are arguing on the basis of different definitions of free will. For example, if, as per philosopher David Hume, someone defines free will to mean that choices and actions are made free of any external constraints that might be imposed upon them, where choices and actions are consistent with what they want to do, one has defined free will in a way that is, by definition, compatible with determinism. This definition of free will makes no reference to the need for different possible outcomes, any of which might really happen. If one defines free will in this way, then by definition, free will is compatible with determinism, and one can be a compatibilist. Of course, if you define free will in a way that is compatible with determinism, it is hardly surprising that you will think that free will is compatible with determinism.

Alternatively, if someone defines free will as the ability to make reasoned choices among several options, any of which might really happen, this is by definition incompatible with determinism, because under determinism there can be only one outcome. If you are an incompatibilist, meaning that you hold that free will is not compatible with determinism, and if you also believe that the universe is deterministic, then you will be a "hard incompatibilist" and reject the possibility that we have free will. For example, if you believe that a character in a movie cannot have free will because they cannot really do otherwise in the movie, given that all outcomes in the movie are fixed before you even hit "play," and if you also believe that the universe unfolds like such a deterministic movie, then you would reject the idea of free will.

But if you are an incompatibilist who believes that the universe is not deterministic, you can develop what is known as a "libertarian" conception of free will. Although most people are not philosophers who have pondered questions of incompatibilism, most people take for granted a libertarian perspective regarding their own ability to choose. This is because they subjectively experience multiple courses of possible action open to themselves (I can turn left, right, or go straight) that they can evaluate in light of their own reasons (I am hungry and am looking for a bite to eat), and they daily experience the consequences of having realized their chosen courses of action (I turned right, and sure enough found the restaurant that I selected from among my options). While the folk perspective is libertarian, it would be delusional if our subjective experiences of the forking paths open to us did not correspond to forking paths in reality. If determinism is the case, then there is only one possible course of action open to us, and we are delusional for thinking otherwise, despite the subjective experience of branching imaginary paths open to us.

The view of free will advocated in this book is a libertarian conception of free will. As long as people can (in their imaginations) realistically model the possibilities that are really open to them, and have a way of realizing their choice, the folk view is not delusional.

2.6 Two Types of Libertarian Free Will

Libertarian incompatibilists talk about two different kinds of freedom of will, both of which, by definition, are incompatible with determinism. The first type of "libertarian" free will requires that one could have done otherwise. This is by definition not possible under determinism. Choosers can only have chosen otherwise if some physical events themselves could have turned out otherwise. This makes indeterminism a necessary condition for the truth of libertarian free will. The second type of libertarian free will concerns the capacity to choose to eventually become a new kind of chooser in the future. We will talk about this type 2 free will a bit later.

The reality of indeterminism is not sufficient to grant us a libertarian free will, because indeterminism might turn out to be true, and yet a chooser could lack the freedom to shape the likelihoods of future events coming to pass. Unless a chooser plays some role in defining which chance events can happen, or in altering the probabilities of events turning out this way or that, chance just happens to the chooser randomly.

This is the point where Hume and many other thinkers got stuck, seeing no alternative between determinism, where outcomes are set before birth and are beyond one's control, and blind chance, where one has no control whatsoever over random events. Later, when we talk about criterial causation, I argue that there is a middle way between determinism and utter randomness.

Hume (1739) wrote "'tis impossible to admit of any medium betwixt chance and an absolute necessity." Many other philosophers have seen no middle path to free will between the equally "unfree" extremes of determinism and randomness, concluding either that free will does not exist or arguing that a "weak" version of free will (i.e., "freedom from coercion") is compatible with determinism. A weak free will, where events could not have turned out otherwise than they were "destined" to turn out since the beginning of a deterministic universe, is by definition compatible with determinism in that our determined decisions are uncoerced while certainly playing a causal role in our subsequent actions. But a "strong" free will, where events could have turned out otherwise, is incompatible with determinism, because only given an ontological indeterminism can events really have turned out otherwise than they did. Indeterminism is a necessary condition of a strong free will, such as a type 1 libertarian free will, or a stronger free will, such as a type 2 libertarian free will or meta-free will. Thus, compatibilism holds regarding weak free will while incompatibilism holds regarding strong free will and meta-free will. A lot of confusion occurs because compatibilists and incompatibilists talk past each other, assuming conflicting notions of free will.

A Humean freedom from coercion offers a "weak" conception of free will that is by definition compatible with determinism, since no mention is made of a need for outcomes to have the possibility of having turned out otherwise. A libertarian conception of free will, according to which events really might have turned out otherwise, however, is not compatible with either determined or random choices. In the determined case there are no alternative outcomes, so events could never turn out otherwise, while in the random case, what happens does not happen because it was willed.

A libertarian free will requires meeting four high demands. Beings with libertarian free will:

1. Must have information processing circuits that have multiple courses of physical or mental activity open to them;
2. Must really be able to choose among them;
3. Must be or must have been able to have chosen otherwise once they have chosen, and;
4. Must not have their choice be dictated by randomness alone, but by the informational parameters realized in those circuits.

Note that although an agent is not needed at the stage that settles which option will happen, one is needed at the stage that settles that this set of criteria will be set rather than others. This is a tough bill to fill because it seems to require that acts of free will involve acts of self-causation. I argue that these conditions for a libertarian free will are indeed realized in the nervous system. We have no choice but to have a libertarian free will, because evolution fashioned our nervous systems to have it. Those animals that had a nervous system that realized a libertarian free will survived to the point of procreation better than those that did not.

Criterial causation offers a middle path between the two extremes of determinism and randomness that Hume was not in a position to see, namely, that physically realized informational criteria parameterize what class of neural activity can be causal of subsequent neural events. The information that meets preset physical/informational criteria may be random to a degree, but it must meet those preset informational criteria if it is to lead to neural firing. Since any possible outcome meets those criteria, it is not utterly random. Preceding brain activity specifies the range of possible random outcomes such that only those that meet preset informational criteria for firing are possible. Volitionally preset informational parameterization of future firing is causal in the universe, and not epiphenomenal, by virtue of allowing only that subset of possible futures open at the particle level to become real, which also realize informational causal chains. These are those that are consistent with the informational parameters or criteria that were preset by prior neural firing in present neural synaptic weights that realize informational constraints on allowable triggers of future neural firing.

But let us say that some brains can weigh options, and then select among them, thereby affecting the probability that one option will occur over another. A tiger trying to hunt down a tapir in the Sumatran jungle might have such freedom. It can see the tapir and weigh possible paths towards killing it, then choose an optimal option, given all the variables that it has internally weighed. It might want to maximize speed, minimize distance traveled, maximize quietness, and so on. Such a tiger would have "freedom of action."

A tiger would have the kind of "first-order or type 1 libertarian free will" afforded by the kind of nervous system summarized in the above points, in that a tiger can choose among considered actions freely, and those choices/actions could have turned out otherwise. This is not enough to have a truly free will in the sense that humans want. For that, a chooser would need a second-order or meta-free will or a type 2 libertarian free will. According to this notion of free will, the chooser must have freedom of thought and action that allows the shaping of the nature of future decisions and acts of choosing. In effect, the chooser must be able to shape the basis or grounds of future volitional decisions. The chooser must be able to choose the kind of being he or she will become in the future. Only if present choices can ultimately lead to a chooser turning into a new kind of chooser—that is, only if there is second-order or type 2 libertarian free will or a meta free will—do brains have the capacity to both have chosen otherwise, and to have meta-chosen otherwise. Only such a meta-free will allows a brain to not only choose among options available to it now, but to cultivate and create new types of options for itself in the future that are not presently open to it. Only then can there be responsibility for having chosen to become a certain kind of person who chooses from among actions consistent with being that kind of person.

Thus, in addition to meeting the four conditions that must be met by a first-order libertarian free will, a second-order or type 2 libertarian free will must meet a fifth condition: present choices must trigger actions that, after perhaps long durations of training or practice, ultimately lead to the re-conformation of the nervous system such that a brain or chooser can decide to train itself to become a new kind of brain or chooser in the future. The human brain can choose to become a new kind of brain in the future, with new choices open to it then, which may not be open to it now. This is possible because of a slower kind of neural plasticity, rooted in long-term potentiation of synaptic weights, dendritic spine formation, myelination, and other slow changes among neurons and glial cells that lead to the re-conformation of neural circuits. For example, one can choose to learn Chinese, and then, within a year of practice and study become a brain that can adequately process and produce Chinese inputs and outputs (Schlegel et al., 2012).

Philosopher Harry Frankfurt (1971) draws a link between second-order free will and second-order desires:

> freedom of action is … freedom to do what one wants to do … freedom of the will means … that he is free to want what he wants to want … it means that he is free to will what he wants to will, or to have the will that he wants. Just as the question about the freedom of an agent's action has to do with whether it is the action he wants to perform, so the question about the freedom of the will has to do with whether it is the will that he wants to have. It is in securing the conformity of his will to his second-order volitions, then, that a person exercises freedom of the will.

Frankfurt's conception of free will is generally viewed as supportive of a compatibilist position. He wrote:

> My conception of the freedom of the will appears to be neutral with regard to the problem of determinism. It seems conceivable that it should be causally determined that a person is free to want what he wants to want. If this is conceivable, then it might be causally determined that a person enjoys a free will (1971, p. 19).

But if I am right, and free will is not compatible with determinism, then it becomes necessary to develop an account of human second-order wants and free will that is compatible with indeterminism. Frankfurt continues: "On the other hand, it seems conceivable that it should come about by chance that a person is free to have the will he wants." Thus, his view is also compatible with the existence of ontologically real chance occurring in the universe, and, in particular, in the brain.

A tiger has type 1 libertarian free will but lacks type 2 libertarian free will. We humans have the capacity for type 1 and type 2 free will because only we, among all animals, have second-order or type 2 desires, as far as we know. While a tiger has a first-order desire to eat, it does not appear to have desires about that desire. No tiger thinks to itself, "next year I would like to be a different kind of tiger, one that eats fewer tapirs and instead eats more pangolins." This is why animals are amoral, despite having type 1 freedom of choice and action. While animals can choose, they cannot choose to become a new kind of chooser. We humans, in contrast, bear a degree of responsibility for having chosen to become the kind of chooser we now are. This may be due to our capacity to time travel in our imagination beyond the here and now to a world different than the present world. We can not only choose what to do, think, or feel now. We can also choose what we want to become, and then set about making that imagined vision of ourselves a reality.

Choosing to become a new kind of chooser in the distal future seems like a tall order, but really the seeds of this idea were already discussed in Aristotle's *Nicomachean Ethics*. According to his virtue ethics, a person's decisions and the moral consequences of those decisions flow from the fact that a person has made past choices that have cultivated them into being the kind of person they are now, in particular, by having reached a point where certain kinds of (ideally virtuous) decisions have been automatized because of habit formation. The idea is that humans, at least, can choose to transform their characters or minds or behaviors, just as they can transform their bodies by going to the gym or doing yoga. This might involve years of practice. But a libertarian advocate of free will like myself would argue that this is doable. For example, while transforming character might be difficult, it is not so difficult to learn a foreign language. You can install an app on your phone and begin teaching yourself. After one year of practice you might be pretty good. After three years of hard study and practice, you would likely be quite fluent. You will have effectively willed to become a new kind of nervous system, namely, one that can process sentences in the foreign language that you chose.

I believe that the human brain has evolved to realize both kinds of libertarian free will. We can consider options, and choose among them, thereby affecting the likelihood of one possibility happening over others. This we have in common with other complex animals like tigers. But unlike other animals, I believe we have second-order libertarian free will as well. Namely, we can choose, with practice, to become a new kind of chooser in the future. Your future self might have options that are not open to you now, like choosing to speak in a foreign language that you cannot yet understand.

The first type of libertarian free will requires that one could have done otherwise. This is by definition not possible under determinism barring exotic philosophical moves like granting agents the capacity to change the past or the laws of physics, which most people would argue no one could actually accomplish. Choosers can only have chosen otherwise if some physical events themselves could have turned out otherwise. This makes indeterminism a necessary condition for the truth of incompatibilism. But the reality of indeterminism is not sufficient, because indeterminism might turn out to be true, yet an agent could lack the freedom to shape future events; unless the agent plays some role in defining which chance events can happen, chance just happens to the agent randomly. The freedom afforded by a nervous system that meets the four conditions of a libertarian free will, such as might be realized in the brain of a tiger or other non-human vertebrate, would be what Robert Kane (2007) might call "freedom of action." But this would not be what Kane would mean by a truly free libertarian free will. For that, an agent would need type 2 incompatibilist free will or meta-free will: the capacity to choose to become a new kind of chooser in the future. According to this notion of meta-free will, the agent must have freedom of action that allows the agentic shaping of the nature of future volitional decisions. In effect, the agent must be able to shape the basis or grounds of future volitional decisions. The agent must be able to volitionally choose the kind of volitional being they will become in the future.

To reiterate, there are at least two kinds of free will demanded by incompatibilists. One is what Kane regards as freedom of action, and the other is what might be regarded as the freedom to choose one's capacity to choose, not right now, but in the perhaps distant future after much cultivation or training. This type 2 incompatibilist free will requires the capacity to develop one's nervous system, or the character realized in it, in an intended way. This is the freedom to choose what kind of chooser one will become weeks, months, or years down the line.

According to Kane, ultimate responsibility for an action and its immediate consequences requires responsibility for anything that is a sufficient cause or motive of that action. Thus, if an action follows necessarily from having a certain character (which we can use as a shorthand notion for the conglomeration of desires, values, tendencies, capacities, and principles that one has), then to be ultimately responsible, even if in part, one must be in part responsible for the character that one has. This again hearkens back to Aristotle's insight in his *Nicomachean Ethics* that in order to be in part responsible for the wicked acts that follow from having a wicked character, one must be in part responsible for having the wicked character that one has.

Kane recognizes that there would be a logical regress if we chose our present character based on the character we had in the past, which we in turn chose based on the character we had in the more distant past, and so on, until we came into existence. To escape this regress, Kane argues that there must be a break in the chain of sufficient causes. This happens when a character-forming decision is made that is not sufficiently caused by one's present character or state. This, Kane argues, requires that this "self-forming" decision is not determined, because if it were, it would be sufficiently caused by the preceding state of affairs. Only under indeterminism is an outcome not sufficiently caused, because identical causes can lead to various different effects or outcomes just by chance. But if a self-forming act or decision were utterly random, then our resulting new character would not have been one that we willed. It would instead be one that just happened by chance. We might make a random self-forming decision and find that suddenly we are a murderer for no reason at all.

To get around this, Kane, in *Four Views on Free Will* (2007) and Mark Balaguer, in *Free Will as an Open Scientific Question* (2010), focus on a very special class of decisions that occur when people are torn between two options, both of which they have willed. These "torn decisions" might happen only rarely in a person's life, but unless at least one such self-forming act happened in their life, they could not be even partly ultimately responsible for anything they decide or do on the basis of their present character, because of the above regress. To break the chain of sufficient causes, at least these kinds of decisions have to be undetermined, even if every other act or decision in a person's life is determined.

Kane writes:

> undetermined self-forming actions ... occur at those difficult times in life when we are torn between competing visions of what we should do or become ... yet the outcome can be willed (and hence rational and voluntary) either way [that we decide] owing to the fact that in such self-formation, [our] prior wills are divided by conflicting motives ... When we ... decide in such circumstances, and the indeterminate efforts we are making become determinate choices, we make one set of competing reasons or motives prevail over the others then and there by deciding (2007, p. 26).

Even though which way we will decide is not determined, since either choice is one some part of us wants and has reasons for, Kane argues that it is willed because it reflects our purposes and intentions and is not utterly random. Indeterminism in essence selects among a class of options, each of which some part of us has agentically specified as one "we" (note the need for a divided self here) want and intend to do. No matter how we decide by chance, we succeed in doing what at least one part of us knowingly and willingly was trying to do. Note that the reasons and motives for the two options have to be different for this to work, because otherwise we are like Buridan's ass choosing between options that are equivalent to us (see Balaguer, 2009, p. 74–75; it is unlikely that Buridan's ass kinds of decisions will transform our character, so reduce to type 1 libertarian free will choices). Kane considers, as a prototypical example of a torn decision a businesswoman who wants to help someone out of empathy, but who also wants to get to an important meeting, because of ambition, yet she cannot do both, because the clock is ticking. She must choose, either/or.

In order to break the chain of sufficient causation in the formation of character, neither Kane nor Balaguer need to try to rest the possibility of the existence of a type 2 libertarian free will on such rare events as torn decisions, or the notion of a divided self with conflicting sub-agendas or sub-desires, even if this is a valid way of grounding them. All that is required to ground both type 1 and type 2 libertarian free will is that options reflect our reasons and motives, and that the option selected is undetermined.

Criterial causation can help break the chain of sufficient causation that so worries Kane and Balaguer. To ground a type 1 libertarian free will it is enough to specify some criterion such as "I need an escape route." Many possibilities can be generated, and one, just by chance, can be selected, whether in our brains or the brain of a tiger. The selected escape route is not utterly random, because it had to be an escape route. But it is not determined, because a different escape route might have been selected by chance. This is what Kane regards as freedom of action. Kane thinks we need more than this to have true free will, because unless we can intentionally reshape our characters, we are subject to the above regress.

To ground a type 2 libertarian free will, we can imagine, given the constraints imposed by our present character, the kind of future character that we want to achieve. This then sets criteria for the (in part) random fulfillment of those character-defining criteria. For example, in light of our present character, which, let us say, is dissatisfied with our present level of integrity in late December, we might set a criterion that we need to resolve to increase our level of integrity somehow. Now, in part just by chance, we might resolve to be more honest, and set that as our New Year's resolution. But we could have just as easily decided, again by chance, to be more kind, or to keep our word better, or to be less impetuous, or less jealous, or less greedy, or more reliable, or to henceforth be a better friend, or be more organized. Let us say, just by chance, the possible resolution to be more punctual arose from unconscious information processing to the level of consciousness for consideration of adequacy. This criterion, held in working memory, would act as a downward or top-down cybernetic setpoint against which upward or bottom-up possible satisfactions of that criterion would be evaluated. Consciousness plays a role in this evaluation because it is important to deliberate in order to virtually experience how this possibility feels in the imagination. If above threshold, it could be selected. If below the threshold for criterial satisfaction, the conscious–unconscious–conscious processing cycle would begin anew. Then, a new possible resolution might come to the fore of consciousness, percolating up from unconscious processing set in motion by the conscious demands to find possible solutions, this time, say, to keep our word better in the future. Let us say that this passes the threshold, after some conscious consideration, for meeting our integrity-enhancing criteria. So why did our New Year's resolution turn out to be "to be more honest" rather than "to be less selfish and greedy?" Well, just by chance the one passed our criteria for integrity enhancement first and became a self-forming resolution. This is not an utterly random resolution, because it had to be an integrity-enhancing resolution. But it is not determined, because it could easily have turned out otherwise, even though we could not change our character at the moment of threshold crossing. However, once a resolution is in place, in part just by chance, it will shape our actions come January, and over several months we may be able to accomplish the improved character we envisioned. Note that because we chose this resolution for self-improvement in part just by chance, we did not determine which resolution we would settle on; what we did settle were the criteria that possible self-forming resolutions would have to meet, and an adequate one passed threshold first, which we then chose.

Type 2 libertarian free will is a slow and bootstrapping, cybernetic, goal-directed process because changing one's character takes effort and time. It breaks the chain of sufficient causation among self-forming acts and decisions because chance plays some role in their outcome; if events can turn out otherwise, they are not sufficiently caused by prior states or events.

Criterial causation can ground both type 1 and type 2 libertarian free will, and is not rare, like Kane's or Balaguer's torn decisions. We are constantly engaging in this kind of criterial decision making at multiple levels, and also constantly correcting deviations from our paths to our envisioned goals in a cybernetic process involving feedback. This is why both contingency and goal-directed agency are everywhere you look in human action and decision making.

As we form ourselves over many years, we are continually reparameterizing criteria that must be met locally so that, despite setbacks, we can adaptively approach our global life goals, including our goals for the kind of person we hope to become. Just as we can slowly reparametrize our physical capabilities by training our bodies to, say, become capable of running a marathon two years hence, we can reparametrize our brain to, say, become one that can speak Tibetan two years hence, or one that will prefer veganism in the future, even if currently we like eating meat. Such criterial resetting is happening at multiple levels in us, and, because of causal feedback that we can harness, we can go from an *idea* of having bigger biceps to *having* bigger biceps by doing curls regularly; we can go from an *idea* of learning Tibetan to *speaking* Tibetan by studying regularly; we can go from an *idea* of becoming kinder to *actually being* kinder by intentionally putting ourselves in others' shoes. The existence of feedback loops can take an idea and concretize it in our future constitution and character. We can also prepare ourselves for future setbacks. We are reparameterizing ourselves at multiple levels in our efforts to transform ourselves into the self that we envision. We can prepare ourselves for future challenges, and check our readiness, like building and testing a sluice before the flood comes down.

2.7 Necessary Conditions for Free Will

To get our terms straight, what does it mean for something to be necessary for something else to happen? And what does it mean for something to be sufficient for something else to happen? Let us start with necessity. A condition is necessary if, without the necessary fact being true, a consequence of that fact could not follow or happen or be true. There are lots of examples of necessary conditions. For example, in order for you to exist, it is necessary that the universe exists. But the existence of our universe is not sufficient for your existence, because the universe existed for a long time without you in it. Similarly, a condition can be *necessary* for the existence of free will but not *sufficient* for the existence of free will. For example, it is necessary but not sufficient for you having free will that this universe exists. Without this universe you cannot exist, and obviously you cannot have free will if you don't exist.

Now, what does it mean for something to be a sufficient cause of something else? It means that the mere occurrence of the cause is enough to bring about the consequent outcome. For example, there are lots of ways for you to travel from your house to the next city. In order for you to get there, all it takes (it is sufficient) is for you to drive there. It is also sufficient to take the train. But neither the car nor the train is necessary for you to get there, because you could have gotten there in lots of other ways (walking, bicycle, etc.).

Now that we understand what necessary and sufficient mean we can address key philosophical arguments against the possibility of free will. The next sections focus on two such arguments: the consequence argument and the exclusion argument.

2.8 The Consequence Argument against Compatibilism

Peter van Inwagen's consequence argument is one of the leading philosophical arguments that free will is not compatible with determinism. Its logic runs like this:

1. Determinism entails that any state of the past entails every state of the future, because events unfold according to the deterministic laws of nature.
2. The past is not under our control.
3. The laws of nature are also not under our control.
4. It follows that our actions are entailed by the past and the laws of nature.
5. This means that our actions are not under our control.

In a nutshell, the consequence argument concludes not only that our actions and choices are entailed by the state of the universe at the beginning of time, but also the consequence argument concludes that our actions are not under our control. In fact, everything we believe that we voluntarily choose to do was "set in stone" long before our birth.

As mentioned earlier, determinism effectively pictures the universe as a movie reel that exists with all of its moment-frames fixed before the film begins. When we see a character in that movie jumping up and down, insisting that he has free will, that action was set in the reel before the movie was played.

Some philosophers have tried to wriggle out of the consequence argument by arguing that we can, in fact, change the past or can change the laws of physics. I find the idea preposterous that I or anyone could actually change the past or the laws of physics. I find the consequence argument to be an effective argument against the idea that free will is compatible with determinism.

I once said to a group of philosophers that I find it surprising that so many philosophers argue for compatibilism, when the evidence is overwhelming that the basic necessary conditions of a libertarian account of free will appear to be met by the universe as we find it. That is, indeterminism and amplification of quantum domain randomness to a level of macroscopic neural function are supported by the evidence from physics and neuroscience, respectively. John Fischer said that having a version of compatibilism ready was like an insurance card that he and other philosophers could whip out just in case physicists ever come along with a theory to replace quantum mechanics that proves determinism to be the case once and for all. That may be prudent, but I believe this stance is exceptionally cautious, given that the evidence is overwhelming that the conditions necessary for a libertarian free will appear to be met both by the universe (indeterminism appears to be the case, ontologically) and the brain (amplification of microscopic to macroscopic randomness as well as criterial causation appear to be realized by neural activity). Taking out this kind of insurance card is like taking out insurance that space station debris or a meteor might hit you in the head. If we have won the existential lottery, so to speak, why not be happy about it? Some sage once said, "sometimes you are lucky and you just have to learn to accept it!"

Personally, I am not worried about the consequence argument that free will cannot exist under determinism, because I feel there exists overwhelming evidence that our universe is indeterministic. Moreover, as we shall unpack in Chapter 4 (neuroscience), the conditions necessary for having a libertarian free will are met in our brains.

We address the conditions necessary for a libertarian free will in a later chapter. I believe we have evolved to have a libertarian free will because animals with this capacity survived better than those who lacked the capacity to weigh their options internally and then choose among those options on the basis of their own reasons. So, in a sense, evolution gives us no choice about the matter. We did not choose to arrive in this universe with free will. We have, so to speak, no choice but to have free will. The question for us, as volitional beings who shape the probabilities of our own futures with our current choices, is: how do we want to apply this human capacity to volitionally shape the future to better our own future or the future of the world?

2.9 The Exclusion Argument against Mental Causation

Jaegwon Kim's exclusion argument against the possibility of mental causation is a deeper, logically prior problem than the free will and moral responsibility problems. The most fundamental question regarding free will and moral responsibility is whether mental events can be causal at all. If not, then the conscious deliberations that we so treasure as the basis of both free will and moral responsibility are epiphenomenal. For example, a shadow can be made to look like it causes another shadow to move, but shadows cannot really be causal in this way. If mental events are similarly only apparently causal of their intended consequent actions, but not really causal of them, then there can be no mental causation, and therefore also no free mental causation.

Ruling out mental causation would rule out free will. Similarly, if a fundamental component of any definition of moral responsibility is that an act of willing causes consequences to happen for which we are in part blameworthy or praiseworthy, but willings cannot be causal because mental events cannot be causal, then moral responsibility is not possible either. The epiphenominality of mental causation implies both no free will and no moral blameworthiness.

In my view, the exclusion argument is a more devastating argument against compatibilism than the consequence argument. The exclusion argument is explicitly about causation, not implicitly so like the consequence argument.

Let us walk through the exclusion argument. The exclusion argument rests on the premise of the causal closure of the physical. "Causal closure" means that causality at the level of particles is sufficient to account for all outcomes and interactions at the level of particles. Kim advocates the "exclusion of over-determination" when modeling physical causation. In his words, "If event e has a sufficient cause c at time t, no event at t distinct from c can be a cause of e" (2005, p. 17).

If particle-level causality is sufficient to account for particle behavior, and neurons are made of particles, mental events (assuming that they are realized in—or "supervene" upon neuronal and particle events) can play no causal role in neuronal or particle behavior. In other words, mental events cannot cause fundamental particles to behave differently than they otherwise would have behaved if they had only interacted according to the deterministic laws obeyed by particles. And the same goes for neural events.

Put succinctly, Kim's exclusion argument can be stated as a logical syllogism:

Major premise: All physical events are caused by preceding sufficient physical causes. In other words, all microphysical states are completely and sufficiently caused by antecedent microphysical states.

Minor premise: Mental events are realized in physical events. In other words, mental events are realized in and determined by underlying microphysical states.

Conclusion: The physical events that realize mental events have preceding sufficient microphysical causes. In other words, mental events are not causal even if they appear to be, because particle-on-particle causation is a sufficient account of how events unfold. There is no causal work left for mental events as such to do. All causation boils down to particle-on-particle causation, which is a level where mental and moral descriptions simply do not apply.

One way to try to skirt this would be to let go of mental causation, and simply try to ground free will and moral responsibility solely on the neural basis of mental events. Someone making this philosophical move would redefine free will away from mental free will and the conscious deliberations that nearly everyone really hopes to find to be causal. The philosopher Al Mele, for example, hedges his bets when he frames causation disjunctively by saying that a mental event such as an intention *or* its physical basis causes a decision and the consequences of acting on that decision. If the exclusion argument holds, however, a mental event cannot be causal, leaving open only the possibility that its physical basis is causal as a physical-on-physical event. That might be a way to save free will from the exclusion argument but would come at the cost of having to accept that mental willings cause nothing. I think this move is too little too late because the exclusion argument makes neural causation itself epiphenomenal as well, assuming determinism, since it also reduces to particle-on-particle causation. If we lose both mental causation and neural causation to the exclusion argument under determinism, we lose free will and moral responsibility utterly.

I believe the exclusion argument holds if determinism is the case, ruling out mental causation, and thereby mental free will and mental moral responsibility. If determinism is true, then the major premise is true because then events are sufficient causes of their subsequent outcomes, as Newton or Einstein believed. A physicalist like me must accept the minor premise that mental events are entirely realized in their neural, and ultimately particle-level, basis. Thus, if determinism is true, Jaegwon Kim's brutal conclusion follows, namely that mental causation is not really causal at all, which in turn rules out the kind of mental free will and moral responsibility most people want. Therefore, free will and moral responsibility are not compatible with determinism.

The exclusion argument is so deadly for compatibilism in its simplicity because it follows from widely held assumptions of reductionistic physicalism about mental realization and physical causation. For me the big problem for a compatibilist position regarding free will is not the consequence argument, but rather Kim's exclusion argument. I believe it holds true if determinism is the case. No non-epiphenomenal mental causation entails no non-epiphenomenal free will.

2.10 How to Overcome the Exclusion Argument

If the logic of the exclusion argument is valid, then only if one or both of its logical premises is incorrect is there potentially room to develop a theory of mental causation, including one for which mental acts of willing are actually causal of their intended consequences. So, any theory of mental causation that attempts to overcome Kim's exclusion argument must explicitly state which premise is incorrect.

Here is the short argument. In my 2013 book *The Neural Basis of Free Will* I concluded that the exclusion argument does not hold under *in*determinism but does hold under determinism. The sufficiency of physical causation is crucial if the exclusion argument is to succeed at excluding mental causation. Under determinism, because only one outcome in the next moment can follow any cause, that cause is a sufficient cause of that outcome. In contrast, under indeterminism, the major premise (namely, that physical causation acting at the rootmost physical level is sufficient to account for what will happen next) does not hold because any particular present microphysical state is not necessitated by its antecedent microphysical state or states back through the past. In other words the traditional definition of causal closure, namely, that "every physical event has an immediately antecedent sufficient physical cause" is not satisfied, because when a cause can be indeterministically followed by any number of possible effects, then that cause is not a sufficient cause of any of the possible effects. Sufficient causation is lost under indeterminism because they might not happen if they have not yet happened, and they might not have happened even after they have happened. In conclusion, if determinism is the case, then the exclusion argument holds, and mental causation, free will and moral responsibility are ruled out, as is compatibilism. However, if indeterminism is the case, the exclusion argument does not hold and mental causation and free will and moral responsibility are not logically ruled out, at least by the exclusion argument.

This still leaves open the hard work of explaining how mental causation might work in a brain that harnesses indeterministic events to make information downwardly causal, which I will take up in the upcoming section on downward causation.

In the remainder of this section,[1] I argue against the exclusion argument in much greater detail, but for readers who are satisfied with the short argument above, it would be fine to skip the rest of this section. It is necessary to counter this rather extreme philosophical claim in detail because if it is correct, a central assumption of neuroscience and psychology, namely that mental information can be causal of subsequent brain events, falls apart. A philosopher might object that Kim's argument is only an argument against anti-reductionism or nonidentity theories, and that if one adopted a type identity theory, then mental information would indeed be causal, but only by virtue of being physical. But that would still make mental events, like pain, not causal in the universe by virtue of their informational or experiential characteristics, such as hurting, but only causal via their physical instantiations having physical causal efficacy. If mental events cannot be causal by virtue of being informational and, for the conscious subset, experiential—and they would not be if the exclusion argument is correct—then it would follow that there can be no free will (i.e., free mental events) that makes a difference to physical outcomes. It would also follow that there can be no morality or immorality. Mental decisions cannot be held accountable for their having made a difference to physical outcomes, when, as would be the case if the exclusion argument holds, mental decisions can make no difference in a universe where quark-on-quark interactions (or whatever types of energy are at the very lowest level) are sufficient to fully account for all causal chains. So, confronting the exclusion argument is a first step to any argument for mental causation or free will, since informational or mental causation is necessary (though not sufficient) for forms of free will and moral agency that make a difference to physical outcomes.

Let us now examine Kim's (1996) exclusion argument more closely. If true, his exclusion argument would logically rule out that mental information can be causal. (Note that this argument could also be used to argue that all macroscopic causation (Baker, 1993), including genetic causation, is epiphenomenal, though no one argues that, probably because we understand the genetic code quite well now, whereas we do not yet fully understand the neural code.) The argument rests on the premise of the causal closure of the physical.

"Causal closure" means that causality at the level of particles is sufficient to account for all outcomes and interactions at the level of particles (Kim, 1996). Kim applies Occam's razor and advocates the "exclusion of over-determination" when modeling physical causation. In his words, "If event e has a sufficient cause c at t, no event at t distinct from c can be a cause of e" (Kim, 2005, p. 17). Note that without the sufficiency of c, Kim cannot apply the "exclusion of over-determination" principle, so cannot rule out mental causation. The sufficiency of c is crucial if the exclusion argument is to succeed at excluding mental causation. If particle-level causality is sufficient to account for particle behavior, and neurons are made of particles, then mental events (assuming that they supervene on neuronal events) can play no causal role in neuronal behavior. In other words, mental events qua mental events cannot cause fundamental particles to behave differently than they otherwise would have behaved if they had only interacted according to the laws obeyed by particles.

Put succinctly (Kim, 1996, p. 206–210): If (i) the "realization thesis" is the case, then each mental state is synchronically determined by underlying microphysical states, and if (ii) "the causal or dynamical closure of the physical thesis" is the case, then all microphysical states are completely diachronically necessitated by antecedent microphysical states, then it follows that (iii) there is no causal work left for mental states as such to do.

If the logic here is valid, then only if either (i) or (ii) is incorrect, is there potentially room to develop a theory of mental causation. So, any theory of mental causation that attempts to meet "Kim's challenge" must explicitly state which premise, (i) and/or (ii), is incorrect.

If quantum domain indeterminism is correct then (ii) is incorrect, because any particular present microphysical state is not necessitated by its antecedent microphysical state or states. In other words, the traditional definition of causal closure that "every physical event has an immediately antecedent sufficient physical cause" is not satisfied, because when a cause c can be indeterministically followed by any number of possible effects e_i, then c is not a sufficient cause of any of the possible e_i, because they might not happen if they have not yet happened, and they might not have happened even after they have happened.

Papineau (2009) tries to handle the problem of causal non-sufficiency of c introduced by indeterminism by appending a qualifier to the more traditional definition of causal closure as follows: "Every physical effect has an immediate sufficient physical cause, in so far as it has a sufficient physical cause at all." Davidson's (1970) similar attempt to make a definition of causal closure consistent with indeterminism is to say that "every physical event that has an explanation has a physical explanation." But neither of these attempts to dodge the non-sufficiency of c imposed by indeterminism gives existing physical explanations enough credit. Quantum domain effects are not unexplained. It is not the case that just anything can happen inexplicably. Rather, the set of possible outcomes and their likelihoods of occurrence are very precisely defined by quantum theory, arguably the most accurately predictive theory in the history of science.

Classical deterministic laws are laws that hold among sufficiently causal actualia, where both c at t_1 and e at t_2 are actual events. Quantum mechanical laws are deterministic at the level of possibilia, but indeterministic at the level of actualia, because which possible outcome will occur upon measurement is only probabilistically specifiable. Nonetheless, under quantum mechanics c is sufficiently causal of its entire set of possible outcomes e_i with their associated probabilities of occurring. It is just that c is not a sufficient cause of any particular one of its many possible effects that happens to happen when measured. Classical deterministic and modern quantum mechanical laws both operate deterministically, and causation is sufficient, but over different types of physical entities, actualia and possibilia, respectively.

Actualia and possibilia, while both physical, have mutually exclusive properties. Actualia are real and exist now or in some past moment; they have a probability = 1 of happening or having happened. Possibilia are not yet real and may never become real, exist in the future relative to some c, and have a probability of happening (i.e., of becoming actualia) between zero and one. A given event cannot be both actual and possible at the same time, relative to the same c.

Closure, therefore, applies to different types of physical events under ontological determinism and indeterminism. "Closure" entails that the set of physical events is closed; any particular effect will be a member of the same set to which a sufficient cause itself belongs. A deterministic universe is closed at the level of actualia; any particular cause or effect will be a member of the set of all actual events in the universe across all time. An indeterministic universe, in contrast, is not closed at the level of actualia. This is because a non-sufficient actual cause and one of its possible outcomes that may never happen are not both members of the set of actualia. Rather, quantum theory is closed (and deterministic!) at the level of possibilia: any particular outcome or event will be a member of the set of all possible outcomes or events in the universe across all time, and any possible cause is sufficient to account for the set of all of its possible effects.

Under indeterminism physical explanations are of a different type than under determinism, though both actualia and possibilia are physical, and theories of either actualia or possibilia are physical explanations. The Schrödinger equation, for instance, provides a model of how possibilia evolve over time deterministically. Possibilia are modeled to have the properties of waves and can interfere with each other like waves. But the interference pattern is a probability density function that describes the probability of detecting a particle at each position in space and time. Actualia, then, are modeled to be particle-like, whereas possibilia are modeled to be wave-like, with the transition from a possibility to an actuality being a matter of chance.

An indeterministic causal closure thesis could be restated as follows: "(ii*) the set of all possible microphysical states is completely diachronically necessitated by antecedent possible microphysical states." The realization thesis for the indeterministic case might be: "(i*) all mental states are synchronically determined by underlying sets of possible microphysical states." But claim (i*) is contrary to the definition of supervenience. Mental events do not supervene on sets of possible physical states; rather, they supervene on specific, actually occurring physical states. Since it is absurd to maintain that mental events synchronically supervene on sets of possibilia, we can rule out (i*). It remains to be shown whether (i), that is, supervenience on actualia, can be combined with (ii*), that is, causal sufficiency and closure among possibilia, to yield (iii). I demonstrate below that this combination fails to deliver causal closure.

An actual microphysical state and the set of all possible microphysical states are different kinds with mutually exclusive properties (e.g., real/~real; present/~present). The essentially syllogistic structure of the exclusion argument requires staying within a logical kind. It is logically valid to draw from the major premise (ii) "All physical events are caused by preceding sufficient physical causes" and the minor premise (i) "mental events are realized in physical events" the conclusion that (iii) "the physical events that realize mental events have preceding sufficient physical causes." But now we are splitting "physical" into two types with mutually exclusive properties: possibilia and actualia. The conclusion (iii) of the syllogism holds only if both the major and minor premises hold and are both about actualia as in (ii) and (i), or both are about possibilia as in (ii*) and (i*). If one premise is about possibilia and the other about actualia, the conclusion does not follow, because the premises are about exclusive entities. For example, (ii) and (i*) would read "All actual physical events are caused by preceding sufficient actual physical causes" and "mental events are realized in sets of possible physical events," which violates syllogistic logic as much as "all men are mortal" and "Socrates is a robot." Conversely, (ii*) and (i) would read "The set of possible physical events are caused by preceding sufficient possible physical causes" and "mental events are realized in actual physical events," which similarly violates syllogistic logical form. Thus, assuming indeterminism, mental causation is not logically ruled out by Kim's argument.[2]

I wrote a version of this argument first in my 2013 book, and then on the philosophy blog *Flickers of Freedom*, where I battled with free will denier Neil Levy. He wrote that the above argument

> is badly confused. It rests on a misunderstanding regarding the causal closure principle. Tse understands the principle to claim that physical causes are sufficient for the occurrence of physical effects. If indeterminism is true, then physical causes sometimes or often are not sufficient for the occurrence of later events. Tse therefore concludes that the closure principle is false for indeterministic systems, so it is no obstacle to mental causation. But the causal closure principle is, roughly, the principle that physical events can be accounted for by physical causes, or (equivalently) that physics is causally complete. It is silent on whether physics is deterministic or not. The brain may be indeterministic; causal closure remains an obstacle to mental causation.[3]

In response to Levy, I did not invent the definition of causal closure as "every physical effect having an immediately antecedent sufficient physical cause"; many philosophers have written variants of just such a definition, including Papineau and Kim, cited above. If we eliminate the requirement that c be sufficient to cause its physical effects, we lose Kim's elegant "exclusion of over-determination" argument against any possible causal role of the mental qua mental and can no longer rule that out. In the absence of sufficient physical causation, we could at most argue that an action or outcome would be overdetermined if it had both a physical cause (whether deterministic or indeterministic) and a mental cause. Under that move all the causal work is still done by, presumably, particle-on-particle interactions, not by mental events qua mental events (e.g., when pain, by virtue of consciously hurting, causes a trip to the dentist).

As a physicalist I agree that "physical events can be accounted for by physical causes." But there is an ambiguity in Levy's phrase "accounted for" here. Deterministic physical laws account nonprobabilistically (or rather, with a probability of 1) for a deterministic succession among actualia, whereas indeterministic physical laws account probabilistically for an indeterministic succession among actualia; or as is the case with the evolution of the wave function in quantum mechanics, physical laws account deterministically for a changing probability distribution of possible outcomes of measurements. If we are to take the idea of closure of the physical seriously, then a physical cause c and its physical effect(s) must belong to the same closed set. We agree that this closed set includes only physical events regardless of whether determinism or indeterminism is the case. But under determinism that closed set of physical events includes physical actualia across time whereas under indeterminism it includes physical possibilia across time. In principle, classical physics is a causally complete and deterministic account of the sequence of actualia over time, and quantum physics is a causally complete and deterministic account of the sequence of possibilia over time. But standard versions of quantum physics do not give a complete account that can explain why one possible outcome becomes actual upon measurement or observation rather than other possible outcomes that did not occur. It just happens, with no reason given beyond chance.

If c does not provide sufficient grounds for why one possible outcome occurs over another, exclusion of overdetermination cannot be used to rule out the possibility that the physical realization of present mental events might bias which particle possibilia will become actualia in the imminent future. Note that this does not require positing any bizarre notions like consciousness collapsing the wave packet. It just requires that present physically realized informational criteria placed on inputs can be met in the future in multiple possible ways.

In sum, Kim's exclusion argument amounts to saying that the physical substrate does all the causal work that the supervenient mental state is supposed to do, so mental or informational events can play no causal role in material events. One might say that this does not hold if the mental and physical are identical, but even then it is the physical side of the equation where causal efficacy resides. On Kim's reductionistic view, all causation "seeps away," as Ned Block puts it, to the rootmost physical level, that is, particles or strings or whatever physicists next model the most basic level to be. Add to that an assumption of determinism, and the laws of physics applicable at the rootmost level are sufficient to account for event outcomes at that level as well as every level that might supervene on that level. So, informational causation, including voluntary mental causation or any type of libertarian free will that relies on information being causal in this universe, is ruled out. I argue that indeterminism undermines this sufficiency, which provides an opening whereby physically realized mental events could be downwardly causal.

Exploiting this opening, biological physical systems evolved to emphasize a new kind of physical causation, one based upon triggering physical actions when detected spatiotemporal patterns in energy meet the criteria for releasing some action, such as an action potential. This is a very different kind of causation than traditional Newtonian conceptions of the causal attributes of energy, such as mass, momentum, frequency, or position, which seem to underlie deterministic and exclusionary intuitions. But unlike amounts of energy, patterns lack mass and momentum and can be created and destroyed. They only become causal if there are physically realized pattern detectors that respond to some pattern in their energetic inputs. For example, the 5HT2a serotonin receptor is indifferent to the mass or momentum of a molecule; it responds to some portion of a molecule that has the correct shape among a potentially infinite class of molecules that have various masses. What is important about inputs, given the Newtonian metaphor of causation as local impact (namely, mass, momentum, inertia, velocity, and the like), is of little importance under criterial causation because this type of causation emphasizes global spatial and temporal patterns in inputs. Basing causal chains upon successions of detected patterns in energy, rather than the transfer of energy among particles, opens the door not only to informational downward causation but also to causal chains (such as mental causal chains or causal chains that might underlie a game of baseball or a romantic relationship) that are not describable by or solely explainable by the laws of physics applicable at the rootmost level.

Yes, a succession of patterns must be realized in a physical causal chain that is consistent with the laws of physics, but many other possible causal chains that are also consistent with physical laws are ruled out by informational criteria imposed on indeterministic particle outcomes. Physically realized informational criteria set in synaptic weights effectively sculpt informational causal chains out of the "substrate" of possible physical causal chains.

Information is not causal as a force. Rather, it functions more like a filter in that it is causal by allowing only those possible physical causal chains that are also *informational* causal chains (i.e., that meet particular preset informational criteria) to become real (i.e., to switch ontological status from possibilia to actualia).

The tired argument that there is no middle ground between utter randomness and determinism is wrong. If indeterminism is ontologically the case, then parameters placed on possible outcomes can select from among possible particle paths an instance of the small subset that also satisfies specified informational parameters. Causation via informational reparameterization would not be possible if the neural code were based on spikes ballistically triggering spikes like Newtonian billiard balls colliding deterministically. But if presynaptic neural spikes reparameterize the informational criteria that will make post-synaptic neurons spike, given possible future presynaptic neural spike inputs, then many neural causal chains are possible that would be consistent with those reset informational parameters or criteria for firing.

By itself neural causation via informational reparameterization does not get us the control or the ability to settle outcomes that is needed for free will and moral responsibility. Much more is needed and has indeed evolved to be present in our brains, which I return to later. But an informational criterial neural code is a necessary condition for having such control. For example, if I say to you "Name a female politician with red hair" your response will likely not be utterly random, because you will state a name that meets these three criteria of being a woman, a politician, and having red hair. But your response is also not determined, because your answer might have turned out otherwise. For example, if you responded "Angela Merkel," had I been able to rerun the universe again from the moment of my question, this time you might have said "Margaret Thatcher." This is because (as I go into in depth in my 2013 book) the brain has in fact evolved to amplify quantum domain randomness up to a level of neural spike timing randomness. And since neurons are effectively spike coincidence detectors, this randomness affords the possibility of other solutions to any given finite set of informational criteria. This kind of criterial neural code in turn affords the possibility that events might turn out otherwise, yet not be utterly random, because they will have to meet the informational criteria that were preset. Information, then, is not causal as a force, but rather as a filter that allows possibilia (at the particle level) that are consistent with informational parameters to become actualia. Those that are not consistent with informational parameters get weeded away in that they do not transition from possibilia to actualia.

The brain will need more causal powers, which have also evolved, to get to a full-blown libertarian free will, as I argue later. But a criterial or parametric neural code is necessary (even when not sufficient) for free will and moral responsibility, because informational reparameterization via synaptic weight resetting is the core engine whereby information can be causal of subsequent events in the brain. Thus, all possible or actual informational causal chains are also possible or actual physical causal chains, whereas the vast majority of possible physical causal chains are not informational causal chains. Only those who have yet to appreciate that causation in the brain can proceed via informational criterial or parameter resetting via rapid synaptic weight changes can continue to bring out the tired Humean argument that there can be no libertarian free will realized in the brain because there is nothing between determinism (where events could not have turned out otherwise) and utter randomness (where an agent plays no role in the chance events that happen next).

Accounts of free will that require supernatural or contra-causal interventions have given libertarianism a bad name and violate basic assumptions of physicalism and science. For any naturalistic variant of libertarian free will to exist, several necessary conditions must be met. First, indeterminism must be ontologically real, rather than just a matter of epistemic uncertainty. I argued earlier that, under indeterminism, Kim's exclusion argument fails to rule out mental causation, leaving us with an opening to develop a believable account of mental or informational causation that is not epiphenomenal. To get there, the following facts must in turn be true of neural processing: (1) quantum domain randomness must be amplified up to the level of randomness in macroscopic neural information processing, which (2) would have to be able to harness this randomness to fulfill information processing aims, and (3) there would have to be a role for the subclass of information processing that we call "mental," particularly the subclass of the mental that we regard as consciously volitional, in the specification of the ends to which such harnessing will apply, if conscious willing is to be agentic or causal of the realization of such aims. In my 2013 book I laid out a detailed case that these conditions are met, permitting the physical realization of a "type 1 libertarian free will."

In order to have a "type 2 libertarian free will," however, an additional fifth condition would have to be met, namely, the nervous system would have to (5) be able to make decisions about how it would like to change itself, and then have the means to change itself, over time, into the intended type of chooser.

Libertarian free will requires non-illusory downward mental causation. "Downward" here means that events at a supervening level can influence outcomes at the rootmost level. In this context it would mean that information can bias which possible particle paths are realized. There is no wiggling out of this. If we want mental causation, and a free will and moral responsibility rooted in mental events that cause real consequences, we must defend the position that an informational entity, such as an intention or plan developed or held in working memory, can bias which possible particle paths that are open at the rootmost level can and do become real.

But an entity at a supervening level at time t cannot, logically, change its own physical basis at time t because there can be no *causa sui*. This is where criterial causation via informational reparameterization comes in, because this allows what supervenes now to place informational constraints on what can supervene in the future.

How might such constraining work in the brain? The key pattern to which neurons respond is temporal coincidence. A neuron will only fire if it receives a certain number of coincident inputs from other neurons. Criterial causation occurs where physical criteria imposed by synaptic weights on coincident inputs in turn realize informational criteria for firing. This permits information to be downwardly causal regarding which indeterministic events at the rootmost level will be realized; only those possible rootmost physical causal chains that meet physically realized informational criteria can drive a post-synaptic neuron to fire, and thus become causal at the level of information processing. Typically, the only thing that the set of all possible rootmost physical causal chains that meet those criteria have in common is that they meet the informational criteria set. To try to cut information out of the causal picture here is a mistake; the only way to understand why it is that only this subset of possible physical causal chains—namely those that are also informational causal chains—can occur, is to understand that informational criteria delimit that class of possible outcomes.

As Eddy Nahmias put it on my October 2013 thread on Thomas Nadelhofer's blog *Flickers of Freedom*:

> the fact that informational state S_1 could be realized by a range of physical states P_1–P_N and that informational state S_2 counterfactually depends on S_1 but *not* any one of the specific physical states, including the one that actually realizes S_1 on this occasion (e.g., P_3) suggests that S_1 is what makes a difference to S_2 in a way that P_3 does not. If we want to causally manipulate S_2, manipulating P_3 may not do it (e.g., if we alter it to P_1 or P_4, or one of the other S_1 realizers); rather, we need to

manipulate S_1 (yes, by altering its realizers in the right way, but the right way will involve considerations of the S-level, not the P-level). S_2 *rather than* S_7 occurs *because* S_1 *rather than* S_1' occurred, and not because P_1 rather than P_4 occurred.

Counterfactual relationships between informational states do not depend on any particular physical realization. In my 2013 book I argued that information causing information is the "parsimonious model" (p. 265). But why would we regard parsimony as the appropriate standard for evaluating whether a phenomenon exists? Well, like Kim, we could invoke Occam's razor under an assumption that explanations should be as simple as possible, without recourse to duplicate causation. But a critic might say that I am multiplying causal entities unnecessarily because criterial causation is an additional phenomenon that supervenes on rootmost microphysical causation.

A more nuanced formulation of parsimony than Occam's razor is philosopher Jonathan Schaffer's (2015) "the Laser," which only forbids multiplying "fundamental" entities beyond the minimum necessary to account for the facts: "By the lights of The Laser, derivative entities are an 'ontological free lunch', in the sense that they are genuinely new and distinct entities but they cost nothing by the measure of economy." Schaffer argues that this type of epistemological parsimony is necessary to scientific progress, because a "deeper, more unified, and more elegant theory ought to replace a shallower, less unified, and less elegant theory."

Criterial causation is deeper and more elegant than strictly lowest-level microphysical causation because it explains causal equivalencies that exist between nonidentical physical states. If information state S_2 depends counterfactually on S_1, and S_1 is realizable by physical states P_1-P_N, Kim's account of reductionistic materialism can explain why P_1-P_N individually cause S_2, but Kim cannot explain why P_1-P_N *each* result in S_2 even though they are physically nonidentical. Criterial causation provides the missing explanation: P_1-P_N each produce S_2 because they each realize S_1, in the sense that they each adequately meet S_1-defining criteria, and S_1 causes S_2.

Computer scientist Clint Ehrlich, who kindly suggested that I add the above paragraph, suggested that I call this "the overspecification argument," since it is effectively a rejoinder to Kim's "overdetermination argument". "Overspecification" means that Kim's model of the world requires more information than is actually required to understand the causal relations in question. Criterial causation allows one to predict S_2 without knowing which of P_1-P_N occurred, so long as S_1 was realized by any one of them. If informational states had no causal power, we would instead need to know the particular physical state realizing S_1; knowledge of S_1 alone would not allow us to predict S_2. But because knowledge of S_1 *does* allow us to predict S_2, informational states do have causal power. Overspecificationists like Kim ignore the higher-level causal relationships that emerge as an equivalence class that meets some criteria. The criteria define a potentially infinite class of nonidentical physical causes, each of which is adequate by virtue of meeting those criteria. Overspecificationists fail to see higher-level causal relationships among adequacy-specified equivalencies, each comprised of nonidentical constituents.

Because, under the Laser's notion of parsimony, criterial causation posits fewer causal entities than Kim's theory of causation (because there are fewer equivalence classes of microphysical states than there are microphysical states), criterial causation is a more fundamental theory of causation than Kim's notion of causation (i.e., an individual microphysical state causing the next individual microphysical state).

The mistake that overspecificationists like Kim make is in looking at causation as an issue of sufficiency and necessity when it is really a question of *adequacy*. If the criteria are met, then that is an adequate trigger for the effect, whether that be the opening of an ion channel (e.g., psilocybin or DMT or LSD or serotonin are adequate for the re-conformation of a 5HT2a receptor), or at the level of a neuron (e.g., if the criteria are "cat-defining conditions are present" then input about any cat-like patterns will drive the neuron), or at the level of life (e.g., if the criteria are what we want in a mate, then many mates will do and which one we marry becomes a matter not of necessity but of contingency, timing, and being above threshold first), or at the level of society (e.g., if the criteria are to destroy the enemy in war, then there are many ways to do that adequately).

Causal adequacy differs from causal sufficiency. If A causes B, A is a sufficient cause of B if, should A occur, B always occurs. B follows passively, if A is a sufficient cause of B, and B effectively has "no say in the matter" of what occurs. But if B actively imposes informational or other criteria on A in order for B's effects to be released, A is an adequate causal releaser of B if those criteria are met. However, if A is an adequate cause of B, B does not always follow. For example, if B is a person who is hungry and who therefore wants to eat something, a sandwich A might be an adequate way to satisfy that hunger. But this does not mean that the sandwich has to be eaten. Perhaps the person is fasting because of Ramadan, and refrains from eating the sandwich, even though it is an adequate satisfier of what counts as edible. The difference is that adequacy is about satisfaction of B's criteria above some threshold, whereas sufficiency is about A's causal power. If B imposes no criteria on A to be satisfied, as occurs with billiard balls, A can be a sufficient cause of B (say going into a corner pocket), without being adequate. Conversely, A can also be adequate, but not sufficient, as in the uneaten sandwich example.

Another example that clarifies the distinction between sufficiency and adequacy concerns acquiring something that one wants. If one wants to come into possession of some object at a store, it is sufficient to buy it with a credit card. It is also sufficient to buy it with cash. It is also sufficient to steal it. A passive object has no say in the matter of how it is acquired. But if one wants to marry someone who themselves has free will, that person has final say in the matter of whether that comes to pass or not. They might find the suitor inadequate, no matter whether the suitor considers themselves to be sufficient to convince the suited or not. Or else they could find the suitor adequate in many different ways. That is, they could, in sum, assess them to be above threshold as a life partner in many different ways, along the numerous dimensions that matter. And the adequacy might not only concern attributes of the suitor per se. They might concern the *relationship* with the suitor. For example, two minds might resonate or not, which is an attribute of the relationship between two things, and not an attribute of either thing independently. Because most modal logic emphasizes the necessary and sufficiency operations, and ignores the adequacy operation, existing forms of modal logic are entirely inadequate at capturing the meaning of propositions that themselves capture what is important about life and consciousness as they are experienced.

Causation among neurons, and therefore also in the brain and mind, is about adequacy, not necessity or sufficiency. It is for this reason that any form of causal overspecificationism, such as Kim's, fails to capture the nature of causation in the real world, especially among biological causes and effects, whether at the level of channels, dendrites, neurons, neural circuits, human or societal interactions. Each of the "special sciences" is special in the way criteria are defined and can be satisfied. Each, therefore, also sculpts out of the substrate of possible paths that are open at the rootmost level different levels of criterial causation by filtering out possibilities open at the microphysical level from becoming real (i.e., from happening).

Criterial causation entails also that physical causation loses information about particular realizers, because many realizers P_1-P_N can realize S_1 which causes S_2; but that S_2 has happened leaves us unable to recover which realizer among P_1-P_N preceded the occurrence of the particular physical realization of S_2. This is not only true epistemologically (we cannot discern which P_i caused S_2), but also ontologically (given S_2, we cannot run the universe backward and uniquely recover P_i), since any one of P_1-P_N might have been the realizer of S_1. For example, if a neuron functions as a cat detector and fires equivalently when criteria for "catness" are met among its inputs, then, that it has fired does not reveal exactly how those criteria were met by any particular cat-like inputs; potentially infinitely many cat-like inputs could have been the cause. This loss of information enforces a direction on the ontological arrow of time beyond an epistemological account of the second law of thermodynamics, according to which there is ensemble-level irreversibility of time when there is dissipation of energy, as occurs in the case of friction, heat loss, or diffusion, but, nonetheless, maintained ontological microphysical reversibility. Criterial causational information-loss, in contrast, imposes an arrow of time ontologically, below the level of ensemble states. That is, it imposes an arrow of time on the succession of microphysical states.

By way of analogy, imagine rolling a marble down a funnel whose spout is just wide enough to allow the marble to pass through. Many paths will all lead to the same outcome, namely, a marble coming out of the spout. When a marble comes out, there is no way to recover the path around the inside of the funnel that it took to get there. Information about the past is irretrievably lost when all paths emerge indistinguishably out of the same "door" or informational threshold.

The emergence of causation via adequacy is not only a matter of the criteria preset in dendritic weights before any inputs arrive, in the sense that there are multiple ways to meet any criteria set; adequacy also emerges from play in the timing of inputs that will drive a neuron to fire. Most pyramidal cells will count inputs that arrive within a characteristic time window, typically on the order of 25 ms, as coincident or simultaneous.

Excitatory post-synaptic potentials are spread out and therefore also sum up within this temporal window. Various timings of numerous spike inputs across dendritic arborizations will sum up in an equivalent way, and drive the post-synaptic neuron to fire identically (i.e., equivalently as far as subsequent decoders of firing rates and patterns are concerned), after which information about specific pre-synaptic inputs is simply lost. Just as there are many operations that can equivalently skin a cat, there are many sequences of operations that can accomplish skinning a cat.

Criterial satisfaction is an example of crossing such a threshold, and is a class of the degeneracy or functional redundancy prevalent at every level of biological systems, according to which non-isomorphic inputs can result in isomorphic outputs (Edelman and Gally, 2001). Resultant multiple realizability is especially prevalent in the body, where multiple neural instantiations can realize the same thought, and countless combinations of muscular contraction can accomplish the same goal-driven motor act (Briggman et al., 2006). It is also prevalent in evolution and genetics, where many pathways can result in a functionally equivalent phenotype (Greenspan, 2009). For example, there are many more triplet codons than there are encoded amino acids; therefore, a large number of mRNA sequences could have been read by a ribosome to generate a given protein. Looking only at a resultant protein, we cannot know with certainty how it was genetically encoded.

Countering this criterialist view, a believer in an epistemological (but not ontological) account might say that really no information about the past is lost because there is billiard ball-like determinism at the rootmost level, and no indeterminacy at all at this "ultimately real" level. But if causation is also parametric at the rootmost level, such that various causal tokens are each adequate in meeting those parameters, then criterial indeterminacy is central to the nature of reality. The quantization of action, given by Planck's constant, is the ultimate parameter undergirding what possibilities can become real out of the sea of virtual particles. That a photon can obey all the conservation laws and yet be detected here or there on the photographic plate of the double-slit experiment suggests that causation may be parametric all the way down. We take up the theme of virtual particles and criterial causation again in Section 2.12.

Certainly, causation is parametric at the level of biological causal sequences. For example, there is simply not enough information specified within a genome to specify the precise positions and actions of every atom, molecule, organelle, or cell in an organism. What the genome recipe book contains are *constraints* on what is to happen when in a sequence, just as a recipe demands that one add an egg next, without specifying any details about the egg's weight, color, age, or the species of bird that laid the egg. This is why the same spider makes slightly different webs each time. It is also why the pores and hair follicles of identical twins are in nonidentical positions. Moreover, natural selection operates in terms of constraint satisfaction as well. This is why convergent evolution leads to similar functional and behavioral outcomes, even if realized in radically different anatomical or genetic forms, whether the flapping wings of birds, pterosaurs, and bats, or the similarity of dogs and thylacines, or ichthyosaurs and dolphins, or the remarkable similarity of the octopus and human eye. In each case, constraints were fulfilled adequately and yet differently.

It would be a hopeless task to try to create a deterministic physics wherever criterial causation holds. Contrary to the biological determinism of Sapolsky (2023), there *can* never be a deterministic account of biology or evolution at a genetic or cellular level. Nor will there ever be a deterministic account of life as it is subjectively experienced or contingently lived because life, both physically and mentally, is the most elaborated example of criterial causation that has evolved among physical systems. Adequate satisfaction of criteria that can be met in countless ways entails causal chains that could have gone this way or that. Having many ways to functionally "skin the cat," or generate the same output, at virtually every level where inputs are evaluated criterially, affords great flexibility to animal behavior and goal-driven problem solving. It is not surprising that evolution has selected for the adaptability and looseness afforded by criterial causation over systems that can only generate a given output in a single reflexive manner.

Indeed, indeterminism may follow because causation is criterial or parametric or underspecified all the way down. In other words, just as inputs may meet parameters for the release of a response in multiple possible ways, the response may also meet parameters defining adequacy in multiple possible ways. Given an interaction, there are multiple ways to release the required energy, each of which is adequate. For example, when I hit an E string on a guitar, it will have a certain fundamental frequency, but it can have various amplitudes, phases, and harmonics, while still meeting the criterion of having that fundamental frequency.

Criterial causation is usually thought of as creating equivalence classes of inputs in the immediate past that are equivalent in the sense that they each adequately meet whatever criteria were set for the release now of some action. But indeterminism can be thought of as creating equivalence classes of different outputs in the immediate future because they each adequately count as the release of that action. For example, many possible cat-like configurations can drive a cat-detecting neuron to fire, but once detected, the neuron can fire in many different ways that adequately meet the parameters that define a type of firing that will be read out by subsequent neurons as "catness has been detected." For example, the firing rate increase triggered by this criterial detection might have to be greater than some threshold in order to count as informative by downstream neurons, but the particular interspike intervals might vary randomly around some above-threshold mean, and the threshold can be exceeded in multiple ways.

Thus, the indeterminacy concerning which past inputs meet criteria now may be the mirror image of the indeterminacy concerning which future outputs will be the particular realization of that act of criterial satisfaction. Indeterminacy concerning inputs and outputs happens for the same reason: parameter satisfaction demands only adequacy, not necessity, sufficiency, or the overspecification of microphysical states, which in any case cannot (in principle) be overspecified in the quantum mechanical sense of precise local variables (see Section 2.12).

Note, indiscernibility of two objects relative to a criterion does not satisfy Leibniz's "identity of indiscernibles principle" ($\forall P(Px \leftrightarrow Py) \rightarrow x = y$): namely, if, for every property P, object x has P if and only if object y has P, then x is identical to y. Under criterialism, a property is not intrinsic to the object, but *relational*, that is, relative to the satisfaction of some criteria. For example, we might have a criterion C "can pass through this hole." That both a straw and a pencil can pass through the hole, and are indiscernible relative to that criterion, does not make a straw identical with a pencil, even if they are equivalent as far as meeting that criterion. What causes both to pass through is the relational fact that their diameter is less than that of the hole.

Yet an overspecifier like Kim would deny the reality of "relational causation" between the size of the object and the hole. An overspecifier would only accept an infinite array of "fits" or "does not fit" outcomes for every possible combination of hole and object analyzed at the level of the rootmost level of strings or quarks. Anything more than that would be "overdetermination."

But this is not in fact how causation works in nature at all, where adequacy rules. If we think A causes B, adequacy of B's parametric satisfaction by A reigns, not sufficiency of A to cause B, regardless of the parameters imposed by B on A.

Causal overspecifiers' central mistake lies in their commitment to a form of radical material reductionism that misses the causal efficacy of the immaterial *relational* aspects of matter. A relationship is immaterial in that does not have the properties of matter, such as mass or inertia, even when the relationship is realized in matter that does have mass and inertia. Overspecifiers desire to have all causation seep down to local impacts among the rootmost things, whether quarks or strings. But relationships among things are not themselves things, whether this be relationships among particles or stars. It is the immaterial relationship between the size of the pencil and the hole that causes it to pass through. It is relationships between constituent parts that distingush a smiley face :) from a frowny face): that can trigger the firing of a decoder of smiles in the former but not the latter case. Causation cannot seep away to the level of strings under pattern or phase or criterial causation because the pattern of a smile is not explicit, and therefore not assessable, at the rootmost level.

The causal efficacy of relationships does not only hold at the macroscopic level of things passing through holes or neural decoding of patterns. Microscopic, quantum domain causation is also rooted in relationships that do not themselves have material properties such as mass. A phase relationship between two vibrating systems cannot be reduced to non-relational aspects of energy, such as amplitude or frequency, because phase only exists in the relationship between fields/particles. And yet phase relationships can be causal, as when a photon can be absorbed by a metal "plasmon" only if there is phase matching (e.g., Kretschmann and Raether, 1968; Otto, 1968). Similarly, precise phase relationships between an incident electromagnetic field and atom are also required for both photon absorption and emission by the atom at the resonance frequency of its electron cloud transition (Pollnau, 2018). In particular, "emission of a photon at the resonance frequency of an atomic transition must occur with a phase that is 90° in lead of an incident field, whereas absorption must occur with a phase that lags 90° behind the resulting field. Only in this way energy is conserved" (Pollnau, 2019).

Overspecifiers like Kim are blind to the actual higher-level relational causal chains that govern our world, which are visible only in the equivalencies that arise from nonidentical physical realizations. For example, any ball that gets batted out of the park in a baseball game counts equivalently as a home run. And all that matters in the causal sequence of a baseball game is that there was a home run. How it happened to be instantiated does not matter. The mistake that causal overspecifiers make is in looking at causal sequences as an issue of sufficiency and necessity (of A's properties as they impact B) when it is really a question of criterial adequacy (of B's assessment of A as a releasing condition of B's action).

A consequence of this is that we cannot look at the state of the world now and know with precision what past states led to its present state, since at each decision point (which is to say at each moment), infinitely many past states could have triggered the present state. This information loss means time or change can only go from past to future, and not backward. Another way to put this is, as far as criterial causation goes, most microphysical facts don't matter. Only relational facts matter at the level of criterial assessment, whether physical, as in the hole example, or informational, as in the cat detector example. Causation then proceeds on the basis of nonlocal relational Gestalts or patterns, not as localistic, reductionistic overspecifiers like Kim want, namely, on the basis of local precise values of microphysical states. Their intuition of causation is rooted in the faulty metaphor of change due to local billiard ball-like impact among particles with instantaneously precise values of all variables at each instant. But that is not how our nonlocal reality works. Instead, causation unfolds whenever a multiply realizable global pattern serves as the key that opens the release of another multiply realizable global pattern.

But what is a pattern? It is tantamount to an abstraction that finds equivalence among many arrangements of microphysical constituents on the basis of their (at least partially) shared criterially defined attributes. If patterns are labeled as, say, "a cat," "a democracy," or "a smile," they comprise a category. Abstraction and categorization require dispensing with irrelevant and extraneous details. Pattern specification entails discarding the nonessential and/or extraction of (or even enhancement of) the essential. The essence of a pattern or of a thing is in effect a caricature of its set of defining attributes.

Because the neural code is criterial, rooted in detecting "abstract" patterns in concrete patterns of simultaneity and deviations from baseline firing rates and patterns, the neural code is essentialist. But the patterns that neurons respond to are not equivalence classes among real world things or their constituent particles. For example, neurons that respond to the pattern of neural inputs that realize the spatial pattern "the Big Dipper" are responding to a set of relationships among parts of information detected at the *image*; they are in no way delimiting equivalence classes of microphysical states among seven suns separated by scores of light years from both each other and from the Earth. Such equivalence classes among root-level particles would be useless to us or any animal who instead needs to know how to do practical things, like crack nuts or escape predators. Neurons delimit equivalence classes among informational states, not physical microphysical states, because the former is the level where useful predictions can be made, such as "If I throw a rock behind that deer, it might run towards me." The patterns decoded are pragmatic, in the sense that they work, not because they necessarily encode anything true about microphysical events in the world.

Even the descriptors of physics, used in our best-performing models of reality, are pragmatic abstractions. Even if it were practically and computationally possible to have a microphysically complete model of the quark- or string-level events that comprise the solar system, most of this information would be irrelevant, if our goal is to put Neil Armstrong on the moon. To accomplish that goal, the abstract representation of points obeying trajectories predicted by Newtonian mechanics is enough. Truth in physics is not about correspondence between laws or equations and the goings-on of root-level events, even when some philosophers incorrectly think that Kim's overspecificationist perspective represents the scientific worldview. The trajectories predicted by Newtonian mechanics are true because they work; they accurately describe the behavior of vast conglomerations of particles such as "Moon," "Earth," and "spaceship." And when they don't work, as in the precession of Mercury, someone comes along with an even more abstract theory that can account for this. Modeling reality using abstractions such as moving points to stand for objects, as physics in fact does, gives us the ability to predict and control objects, despite our limited knowledge and limited time to compute.

Only an overspecificationist would say that the Moon is not real, or that the laws that allow us to land Armstrong on the Moon are not true, because they fail to say anything complete about the rootmost level. Kim's radical seeping away of all causation and explanation to the rootmost level would in fact undermine science and common sense. Ordinary descriptors such as "the Moon" and the laws are true because they are useful, and they are efficient and useful because they dispense with irrelevant detail, including detail about the microphysical level.

The same is true for neurons: they dispense with irrelevant detail. Informational causal chains are multiply realizable at the level of particles. Analyzing causation among informational entities and criteria, whether for brains or computers, is more efficient than analyzing irrelevant P_i events at the rootmost level, when S_i-level analyses suffice, and indeed are necessary, if we are to efficiently make predictions about S_i-level informational outputs.

Information only comes into existence by virtue of a decoder receiving input that matches its conditions (typically placed on the phase relationships or patterns in incoming energy) for the release of some effect, say, an action potential sent to other such decoders. But a decoder also serves as a "filter" on the set of all potentially causal inputs, since it will only change the system of decoders in which it is embedded, namely, by firing, if its physically realized informational criteria are met.

We should also try to avoid the alluring trap of thinking of the neural code as solely a spike code. A synaptic account of the neural code that supplements a spike-centric account can help us get around some thorny problems that a spike-level account alone cannot. For example, a synaptic account can skirt accusations of self-causation that have been used to argue against the possibility of mental causation, free will or moral responsibility (e.g., Strawson, 1994). The traditional argument is that a mental event realized in neural event x cannot change x because this would entail impossible self-causation. Criterial causation gets around this "no *causa sui* argument" by granting that present self-causation is impossible. But it allows neurons to alter the physical realization of possible future mental events in a way that escapes the problem of self-causation of the mental upon the physical.

Mental causation is crucially about setting synaptic weights. These serve as the physical grounds for the informational parameters that must be met by unpredictable future mental events realized in unpredictable future spike inputs to a neuron that will fire above its baseline firing rate or not, depending on whether or not those physically realized informational parameters were met.

Information cannot be anything like an energy that imposes forces because it is not material even when it is realized in the material substrate. Information's causal power consists in "filtering" informational causal chains out of the set of all possible physical causal chains by constraining which sets of possible physical causal chains can occur. Although every informational causal chain is also a physical causal chain, most physical causal chains are not informational causal chains. Information is downwardly causal not as a material force, but as constraints that only allow the realization of sets of possible physical causal chains at the rootmost level that *also* comprise informational causal chains. Physical laws are not violated by this. Every possible physical causal chain conserves energy and momentum, and so forth. But only those possibilities allowed by physical laws that also meet informational criteria pass the physically realized informational filter, and become informationally causal, either by reparameterizing the criteria by which other neurons will assess future input, namely, by changing their synaptic weights, or by triggering other neural firing.

Information in the brain is multiply realizable because which particular set of spike inputs—and thus what particular information—will make the neuron fire is unforeseeable, so long as the physical/informational criteria for firing are met. If neural causal chains are also informational causal chains, and informationally equivalent informational causal chains are realizable in multiple different neural or particle causal chains, then the parsimonious model is one of information causing information. Yes, there must always be some physical realization of information, but under physical/informational criterial causation, which one it happens to be is irrelevant so long as informational criteria are met. Chains of successive informational criterial satisfactions and criterial resettings afford the physical realization of downward mental causation.

On the same *Flickers of Freedom* blog debate about my work, Derk Pereboom said:

> if on some proposal, a dualist or a nonreductivist one, M and P are distinct causes of E, the threat posed by exclusionary reasoning will be neutralized by any response

on which the number of causes is reduced to just one. There are two ways to achieve this: a first is by eliminating all but one of the causes, and the second is by identifying the causes.

If mental events are a type of information, and information is identical to acts of decoding immaterial (i.e., not made of mass) relationships or patterns among physical inputs, then mental events are identical to some class of acts of decoding. But note that this identity does not make mental events have physical properties like mass or momentum because the identity is not with physical events at some instant, but rather with a process that is realized in physical events over durations. Moreover, acts of decoding patterns cannot be reduced to a level where the patterns are not explicit, say, the rootmost level of strings or quarks, because the decoder only responds to a pattern of global relationships at a level where those patterns are explicit. And at that level, potentially countless configurations of rootmost events are equivalent in that they each realize the same pattern as far as the decoder is concerned. Thus, the identification is not with events at the microscopic level or even the neuronal level, but at the level of decoding the nonphysical patterns to which the decoder is sensitive. Mental events, including the subset of these that afford volitional mental operations, namely consciousness, are identified then with a special class of the immaterial phase relationships among material events: acts of criterial decoding and decoder criterial resetting. Mind is both realized in material events and yet is in itself immaterial because relationships are immaterial.

Under determinism, supervening informational criteria cannot filter out possible but noninformational causal chains at the rootmost level, because there is only one possible causal chain. But if indeterminism is the case, supervening informational criteria can make a difference regarding which possibilities at the rootmost level happen (shift from possibilia to actualia). That is, under indeterminism but not determinism, there is nonredundant causal work for informational criteria to do.

But how does this give the brain the capacity to freely will? It is not enough for neurons to filter out non-informational possible physical causal chains. It must be the case that some neural activity that we associate with volition can control the parameters that neurons will apply in the future to enact such acts of filtering. Control comes from executive circuits that can plan, imagine, deliberate, and make decisions in light of highest-level demands and needs, and that can "rewire" circuits and reparameterize neurons, by changing synaptic weights, to embody new informational criteria for firing that will fulfill current executive ends. The downward causation afforded by the informational filtering of possible rootmost causal chains becomes agentic downward causation when executive circuits can rewire lower-level circuits to fulfill whatever criteria they demand.

Downward causation means that events at a supervening level can influence outcomes at the rootmost level. In this context it would mean that information could influence which possible particle paths are actualized. While it would be impossible self-causation if a supervening event changed its own present physical basis, it is not impossible that supervening events, such as mental information, could bias future particle paths. How might this work in the brain?

The key pattern in the brain to which neurons respond is temporal coincidence of arriving action potentials from other neurons. A neuron will only fire if it receives a certain number of coincident inputs from other neurons. Criterial causation occurs where physical criteria imposed by synaptic weights on coincident inputs in turn realize informational criteria for firing. This permits information to be downwardly causal regarding which indeterministic events at the rootmost level will be realized; only those rootmost physical causal chains that meet physically realized informational criteria can drive a post-synaptic neuron to fire, and thus become causal at the level of information processing.

Typically, the only thing held in common among members of the set of all possible rootmost physical causal chains that meet particular informational criteria is that they meet the informational criteria set. To try to cut information out of the causal picture here is a common but serious mistake; the only way to understand why it is that only this subset of possible physical causal chains (those that are also informational causal chains) can occur is to understand that it is informational criteria that dictate that class of possible outcomes. For example, if some government edict demands that "All chickens and toasters are to be brought to the nearest police station by noon tomorrow," the only way to understand what happens as a result of this edict is to analyze physical causation as informationally driven. Nothing at the level of strings or quarks or atoms or causation among them could explain why it is that just chickens and toasters undergo trajectories toward police stations.

The information that will be realized when a neuron's criteria for firing have been met is already implicit in the set of synaptic weights that impose physical criteria for firing that in turn realize informational criteria for firing. That is, the information is already implicit in these weights before any inputs arrive, just as what phoneme your mouth will pronounce is implicit in its shape before vibrating air is passed through it, even when there is still play in terms of possible pitch, voice loudness, or even whisper. Assuming indeterminism, many combinations of possible particle paths can satisfy given physical criteria, and many more cannot. The subset that can satisfy the physical criteria needed to make a neuron fire is also the subset that can satisfy the informational criteria for firing (such as "is a face") that those synaptic weights realize. So, sets of possible paths that are open to indeterministic elementary particles which do not also realize an informational causal chain are in essence "de-selected" by synaptic settings by virtue of the failure of those sets of paths to meet physical/informational criteria for the release of a neural spike. A neural code based on informational reparameterization of subsequent neural firing affords the possibility of top-down causation because an informational command such as "think of a woman politician with red hair," whether externally heard or internally generated by executive processes, can reparameterize subsequent physical neural activity such that the result is, randomly but adequately within those parameters, say, Angela Merkel or, equivalently, Margaret Thatcher.

2.11 What Is Necessary for a Libertarian Free Will?

In this section we ask what is necessary for the existence of a libertarian free will. In other words, we want to know what must be true of any universe in which a libertarian free will could exist. Remember, libertarian free will is the type of free will where we can entertain alternative options that really have some non-zero probability of happening, and that we can then bias to become more likely to happen, in light of what we want to cause to happen.

The Reality of Indeterminism

By definition, a libertarian free will requires first and foremost the reality of indeterminism. This does not mean that events are utterly random. What indeterminism means is that events happen with certain objective probabilities that are less than one. In other words, things can really turn out in more than one possible way, and whatever happens, they could have turned out otherwise.

Bottom-up or Microscopic-to-Macroscopic Causation

This is a second necessary, but not alone sufficient, condition for the possibility of free will. Regarding bottom-up causation, it is necessary for a libertarian free will that macroscopic events, such as neurons firing, can be influenced by amplified chance events in the microscopic domain. If indeterminism primarily originates in the quantum domain, and quantum domain indeterminacy could not somehow get amplified up to a level where it made a macroscopic difference to, say, the timing of neural firings, then the macroscopic universe would be deterministic even if the microscopic domain was indeterministic. It therefore is necessary for a libertarian free will that there be microscopic-to-macroscopic amplification of chance from the quantum domain to the domain of neural firings. There is evidence for this that I will get into later in the book, in the neuroscience discussion in Chapter 4.

Top-down or Macroscopic-to-Microscopic Causation

A third condition for the realization of a libertarian free will is the existence of top-down (macroscopic-to-microscopic) causation. Given that our minds are realized in our kinds of brains, it is necessary that a macroscopic brain state, realizing, for example, an intention to learn this foreign language rather than those others, can bias microscopic events, such as which possible paths open to atoms or quarks, or whatever lies at the root-most level, will become realized. Again, there is evidence for top-down causation that I return to later in the book. For now, we are just listing what is necessary for free will to be possible.

Consideration and Biasing of Probabilities of Event Outcomes

A fourth necessary condition for the realization of a libertarian free will is that the present state of that physical realization of a mind, in our case, the present state of our brain, must be able to entertain and then bias the real probabilities of event outcomes, in light of reasons for making this choice versus other possible ones. I say "real probabilities" here to emphasize that what we need is an ontologically real indeterminism where there are multiple possibilities of event outcome, each of which has a nonzero probability of actually happening. We are not talking about subjective "epistemological" probabilities, which are really just our best guesses regarding what might happen. However, it is necessary that a mind can internally represent objectively open possibilities realistically, along with their estimated likelihoods, in order to effectively alter the objective likelihood that a desired outcome will transpire over other, less desired outcomes. If internal estimates of outcomes are unrealistic, or if outcomes themselves are represented unrealistically, then it is not likely that a person can bias a desired outcome to more likely come to pass before such efforts were made. For example, I can decide that I want to fly like a bird, and I can believe I have wings when I do not. With such an unrealistic assessment of the possibilities that are actually open to me, it is unlikely that I will be able to increase my probability of flying like a bird.

Free will is most centrally about bringing about a desired future over other less desired futures through one's own efforts to bring it about. Under determinism there is only one possible future, so our impression that we can bring about this future versus other possible futures is a delusion if determinism is the case. Even if indeterminism is the case, we would be delusional and lack free will if our internally modeled possible futures did not correspond to actually (i.e., ontologically real) possible futures. To have free will, our internally modeled possibilities and actual possibilities must at least approximately correspond. Free will is in part a matter of having a realistic imagination.

In future chapters we will summarize evidence for the reality of these four necessary conditions for having a libertarian free will. We will summarize evidence for the reality of:

1. indeterminism;
2. amplification of quantum domain events to the level of neural spike timing;
3. evidence of top-down mental causation; and
4. evidence of how we entertain possibilities and then set about enacting one option over others.

In this book I argue that our brains have evolved to realize both type 1 and type 2 libertarian free will. Type 1 free will, again, is the ability to entertain options, deliberate among them, and then select one in light of our reasons. And type 2 free will is the capacity that we have to now choose to become a different kind of chooser in the future, say, one that can play an instrument that we now cannot play, or one that can speak a foreign language that we now cannot speak, or even, one that has a different character than the character that we now have.

The key mechanism, I argue, whereby atomic level indeterminism has its effects on macroscopic neural behavior is that it introduces randomness in spike timing. There is no need for bizarre notions such as consciousness collapsing wave packets or any other strange quantum effects beyond this. For example, as described in detail in my 2013 book, quantum-level noise expressed at the level of individual atoms, such as the single magnesium atoms that block NMDA receptors, is amplified to the level of randomness and near chaos (criticality domain) in neural and neural circuit spiking behavior. A single photon can even trigger neural firing in the retina in a stunning example of amplification from the quantum to macroscopic domains. The brain evolved to harness such "noise" for information processing ends. Since the system is organized around coincidence detection, where spike coincidences (simultaneous arrival of spikes) are key triggers of informational realization (i.e., making neurons fire that are tuned to particular informational criteria), randomizing which incoming spike coincidences might meet a neuron's criteria for firing means informational parameters can be met in multiple ways just by chance.

We have won the existential lottery because our brains appear to satisfy the necessary conditions required to have a libertarian free will. Certainly, evolution did not have to come up with a physical causal system that harnesses chance to fulfill its intended or envisioned ends. And we in no way played a role in the evolution of the human brain that we inherited. But again, sometimes we are lucky, and we just have to learn to accept it.

2.12 Why I Am an Indeterminist

$$\Delta E \times \Delta t \geq \hbar/2$$
—Werner Heisenberg, 1927

Physicalism is the monistic framework within which causality is understood by most scientists and philosophers of mind, and it is the framework that I adopt here. Physicalism maintains that there is only one fundamental substance or substrate, namely, physical matter or energy changing within space-time, in a manner that is best described by the laws of physics.

Physicalist stances fall into different camps. One division occurs between deterministic and indeterministic versions of physicalism. Determinism essentially asserts that there is only one possible future course of events, whereas indeterminism asserts that there are many possible future courses of events that might occur at any moment, perhaps with different likelihoods, even when only one actually occurs. Another division lies between reductive and nonreductive versions of physicalism. My own physicalist views are nonreductive and indeterministic and even start to border on a seeming anti-physicalism or "immaterialist physicalism" in the sense that I am open to the possibility that what is ultimately real may be patterns of excitation propagating through an underlying vacuum of virtual particles, a view I develop further later in this chapter.

For centuries following Newton, causality was understood in terms of a "colliding billiard ball" model of particles, based on the idea of "energy transfer" among particles that obey the laws of classical mechanics, including the fundamental laws of conservation of energy and momentum. Fundamental particles were assumed not to transform into different fundamental particles. Particle trajectories were thought to be entirely dictated by their physical properties, for example, mass and momentum. This "energy transfer" conception of causality was deterministic.

Pierre Laplace argued that if a demon could know with absolute precision the locations, masses, momenta, and all other physical properties of all elementary particles everywhere, the whole future and past of the universe could in principle be known to it. This is not only impossible in practice, but it is also impossible in principle, because such a demon is himself a part of the universe and would have to know about the physical basis of his act of knowing, and then the physical basis of that act of knowing, and so on, which leads to an infinite regress, in an interesting variant of a Gödelian paradox. So, Laplace's demon argument cannot work. This raises the worrisome problem that it might not be knowable in principle whether or not the universe is deterministic. If that turns out to be the case, then adherence to determinism versus indeterminism might end up being a leap of faith either way, based upon one's biases, rather than attainable knowledge. But many things are in principle unknowable, and that is fine. Many things may not even be definable, let alone solvable, including questions such as "What is the cause of the first cause?," "Is there anything outside of everything?," or "What preceded the beginning of time?" We may simply have to grow more comfortable with uncertainty, the unknown, and, indeed, the unknowable.

With the advent of modern chemistry, greater attention was paid to how energy undergoes transformations and exhibits new properties as fundamental particles combine and recombine in chemical reactions. Even though this "energy transformation" conception of physical causation was no longer a simple Newtonian "billiard ball" conception of particle collisions, it remained in essence deterministic. Physical causality was thought by most scientists to be fully or very nearly fully described by the laws of classical physics and chemistry until approximately the turn of the twentieth century. These laws described how energy was transferred among particles and fields, and how energy was transformed through chemical reactions.

That said, some chemists began to realize that a reductionistic, localistic physicalism might not be possible in light of data from chemistry in the sense that the properties of parts depended on relationships to the whole. For example, ethyl alcohol

(CH_3CH_2OH) has five hydrogen atoms or protons that share three types of spatial relationships to other parts of the molecule. Nuclear magnetic resonance spectra show that there are three different peak frequencies at which its hydrogen atoms absorb radio waves (technically, undergo spin reorientation with respect to the external magnetic field), depending on the proton's relationship in space to other portions of the molecule (Earley, 2008). The protons themselves only differ in their global relationships, and yet exhibit different local physical properties, such as peak absorption frequencies, solely by virtue of relationships that are not local.

Once causation is delocalized, and the door is opened to global patterns influencing local interactions, one is faced with new and unfamiliar problems: what counts as a nonlocal influence? How global is global? That is, must the whole be considered in order to precisely account for any local interaction? Must the entire universe be taken into account if we are to fully understand any local event, such as inertia (Rothman, 2022)?

The first hint that the fundamental laws governing particle behavior might be probabilistic rather than deterministic arose with the realization that closed systems tend to approach equilibrium. For example, if water at one end of a bathtub is hot, and at the other end cold, the probability is higher that the two will tend to mix than the probability that they will remain segregated. The second law of thermodynamics implies not only that nature might be probabilistic, but also that time might have a directionality that contradicted the temporal reversibility implicit in classical mechanics. However, thermodynamics could still be regarded as an instance of epistemological rather than ontological indeterminism in that underlying particle behavior might still be entirely determined by the physical properties of particles and forces acting on particles such that at each instant a particle has only one possible path open to it.

Remember, epistemology refers to how we know things, whereas ontology refers to what really exists. An epistemological indeterminist would maintain that it is only because we cannot obtain complete knowledge of these properties that we must be satisfied with higher-level probabilistic laws, such as the laws of thermodynamics.

Not until the development of quantum theory were the physical properties of particles regarded as ontologically indeterministic by many (if not most) physicists. In the famous double-slit experiment photons or particles of matter (electrons) are shot through two slits, one at a time. They land on a photographic plate and collectively make a diffraction pattern. Thinking classically, one would think that a point-like particle would have to pass through either one slit or the other. But if that were the case, then we would not get a diffraction pattern on the photographic plate. The key insight from the double-slit experiment is that the possibilities open to a particle must in some sense have wave-like properties in order for them to be able to interfere with themselves. This can be thought of as a "probability wave" that evolves through space, where the magnitude of the wave at a given location and time indicates the probability of, for example, the detection of a particle upon measurement at that location and time. That is, at every position in space, there is a nonzero probability of particle measurement.

This is a very strange and nonintuitive view of what is real. Under this view, there are ontologically real possible paths open to particles, and these possibilities in some sense interfere with each other. Despite the strong empirical evidence for this kind of quantum domain strangeness, determinists did not simply concede that Nature, as Einstein put it, "plays dice"; he and other physicists argued that the fundamental level of causation must still be deterministic, despite the probabilistic character of quantum theory. According to advocates of such "hidden variables determinism," the probability density functions whose dynamics are given by the equations of quantum physics describe uncertainty in our knowledge of particle locations and movements, not any kind of actual nonspecificity of particle locations, momenta, energies, or durations.

The dominant "Copenhagen interpretation" of quantum mechanics framed by the physicist Niels Bohr, however, regarded uncertainty concerning measurement outcomes to be a fundamental fact about reality, rather than simply a problem concerning the limits of our knowledge about particle properties.

John Stewart Bell argued against Einstein's deterministic view, which said that no physicalist theory based on local hidden variables could account for quantum level effects. He showed mathematically, and many subsequent experiments have confirmed (BIG Bell Collaboration, 2018; Rauch et al., 2018), that any local hidden variables version of quantum mechanics can be ruled out, and that allowable versions of quantum mechanics must either allow for nonlocal coordination or correlation of the states of distant physical events (i.e., outside each other's light cones), or certain properties, such as momentum or position, must lack a definite state, even when they are not measured and are not known. Bell and others argued that this is true even for a single particle, regardless of any nonlocal connectedness between its state and the states of distant particles, in a phenomenon known as "quantum contextuality" (McCormick, 2022). Since determinists are loath to give up the idea that unmeasured properties nonetheless occupy a definite state at each moment, even if that state cannot be known to us, versions of nonlocal hidden variables determinism have been proposed. Perhaps the best known of these was proposed by David Bohm. According to this interpretation of quantum mechanics, particles continually "coordinate" with all other particles in the universe instantaneously. That they do this is a claim that may be very difficult to test because, obviously, we cannot test whether a particle coordinates with all other particles in the universe, since we cannot be at all other locations in the universe. Believers in hidden variables are on the defensive until their theories can make a falsifiable claim that establishes that an underlying determinism is the case.

Extensive empirical evidence supports the reality of nonlocality. This implies that events here and now might be correlated with events light years away, lying outside of our light cone. Reality is clearly much stranger than it appears to us. Although maintaining a belief in determinism may require accepting the reality of nonlocality, that nonlocality is the case is not sufficient to prove that either determinism or indeterminism is the case.

That said, nonlocality is a logical consequence of Heisenberg's uncertainty principle according to which there is a fundamental limit to the precision with which certain "complementary" pairs of physical variables of a particle can be measured. For example, one can know with great precision the energy of a particle-level event, but then will lack certainty about the duration of that event, and vice versa. Or one can know with great precision the position of a particle-level event, but then will lack certainty about the momentum of that event, and vice versa. But again, it is an open question whether this concerns uncertainty in our knowledge or indeterminacy of underlying physical states, regardless of our knowledge. Heisenberg used the word "Unbestimmtheit," which means indeterminacy, not uncertainty, so he appears to have taken an ontological, rather than epistemological, position like Bohr.

The reason that there is this indeterminacy is the "quantization of action." Action, which has the units of energy-time, and which can roughly be thought of as energy changing in space and time, is quantized. It comes in smallest clumps that cannot be made smaller. That is to say, this seeming fundamental substance cannot be cut into smaller pieces than a certain amount given by "Planck's constant." The reasons for this are likely very deep, having to do with how energy can close upon itself, given the underlying dimensionality of space, rather like a snake biting its tail or a looped string (thus "string theory"), or even better, like a bubble. A bubble cannot be infinitesimally small but must always have an extent. One way to think about the quantization of action is that there are smallest "bubbles" of action or change.

It is because of the quantization of action that atoms have electron orbital shells (Lieb and Seiringer, 2009), allowing atoms to exist, which in turn allow suns and galaxies to exist as we know them. So, the universe as it is, with its many types of atoms and chemical interactions, is deeply rooted in the quantum domain's strangeness, in particular, ultimately, in the quantization of action. The apparent determinism of the macroscopic world of, say, planets traversing highly predictable fixed orbits, is a stochastic determinism among vast ensembles of quantum domain events that are at root each indeterministic. The universe is always and everywhere at the rootmost level a quantum domain phenomenon. Apparent determinism emerges only at a scale where theories must estimate dynamic large ensemble behavior, such as the path of the center of the Earth around the center of the Sun, in terms of average points. Determinism is a property of such estimations or models. Just because deterministic models, for example, classical physics or Einstein's theories of relativity, work well at a macroscopic scale of planets and galaxies does not require that the ultimate reality they hope to describe is at root deterministic. Ironically, the stochastic determinism observed at the macroscopic level that some mistake for determinism at the microscopic level could only have arisen in a universe in which action was quantized at the microscopic level.

The surprising stochastic determinism of large ensembles allows insurance companies to make money hand over fist. For example, around 900 people go to the emergency room every day because of dog bites in the US. Each day different people and different dogs are generally involved. Whether a scared or aggressive dog bites this person versus that one might come down to chance events in its brain, that led it to turn left versus right just before biting someone. Where then does the stochastic determinism emerge from? The appearance of determinism emerges from large ensembles subject to fixed parameters: the number of dogs is roughly constant, as is the number of people, as are the general parameters of human–dog interaction.

Another example of a kind of pseudo-determinism that arises from parameter causation occurs in the case of convergent evolution. When Nature subjects generations of different animals to the shared parameters imposed by a common niche they often convergently evolve toward common solutions of both form and function. For example, seals, whales, manatees, and plesiosaurs evolved flippers, dolphins ended up looking a lot like ichthyosaurs, and ant-eating animals converged on armor and long sticky tongues, while birds and pterosaurs both evolved hollow bones. Is it determinism that led to this convergence? Not at all. In fact, it is the randomness among genetic combinations, as well as the occurrence of mutations, that cause variability at the level of phenotypes, which serves as the raw material over which natural selection operates.

But are all macroscopic ensembles effectively deterministic in their behavior? No, not if a quantum domain event subject to quantum domain indeterminism can be amplified to a level that affects outcomes at a macroscopic scale. We discuss later in this book how there are many ways that biological systems have evolved to carry out just such microscopic-to-macroscopic amplification. But it is easy enough to think of an example of such amplification. I can decide to do something macroscopic, for example, shout "God save the Queen!" every time a Geiger counter detects a particle associated with the radioactive decay of uranium, which is a quantum domain event. No matter how absurd, if there was ever even one single such amplification anywhere in the universe at any time in the history of the universe, then the entire macroscopic universe was made indeterministic by that single amplification. But as we shall see, in brains, and especially in those parts of brains we call "retinas," such amplifications occur pretty much constantly, and underlie our conscious experience of seeing a world, or in the case of birds, magnetic fields as well.

Quantum physics implies that virtual particles are real,[4] in the specific sense that they can interact with and alter the behavior of particles that exist (i.e., that are not themselves virtual). The main difference between a virtual and a nonvirtual particle is that the former appears to come into and go out of existence, as virtual particle pairs, within a very short duration dictated by Heisenberg's uncertainty principle $\Delta E \times \Delta t \geq \hbar/2$, where $\hbar$ corresponds to a tiny but finite clump of action, which can itself be intuitively thought of as energy extended in spacetime.

The vacuum can be thought to have a kind of material existence, comprised of a seething sea of virtual particle–antiparticle pairs coming into existence, annihilating each other, and then going out of existence. During the brief duration that they exist they can interact with other existing particles and affect them. This in turn gives the vacuum a nonzero energy state: the zero-point energy. As energy is material, this implies that *the vacuum is a material medium*. For example, the vacuum has material properties such as vacuum polarization (Zeidler, 2011). Moreover, the quantum chromodynamic vacuum is paramagnetic and the quantum electrodynamic vacuum is diamagnetic (Bertulani, 2007). Interactions with the virtual particle sea comprising the vacuum have real effects. For example, an atom can interact with the zero-point energy of the electromagnetic field, triggering the spontaneous emission of a photon in the absence of any external perturbation (Parker, 2003). And this emitted photon is modeled to transition out of the vacuum itself (Dirac, 1927). The materiality of the vacuum is also thought to generate the Casimir effect (Casimir, 1948) and the Lamb shift (Lamb et al., 1947). Moreover, quantum physics models the electromagnetic force to arise through the interchange of virtual photons between electrons. Similarly, a B_0 (a bottom and down quark–antiquark pair) meson's lifetime can be predicted only if virtual particle interactions are used as the basis of the calculation. The sea of virtual particles or spontaneous vacuum fluctuations can even measurably move macroscopic objects weighing tens of kilograms at room temperature, in a process reminiscent of Brownian motion (Chu, 2020; Yu et al., 2020). This implies that everything in our universe is constantly being jostled around spontaneously by a "Lucretian swerve" caused by the virtual particles filling the nonempty ether-like vacuum (see Section 4.10). However, the particular low positive value of energy of the vacuum in our universe remains unaccounted for by physics (Wood, 2022ab).

John Wheeler (1955; see also Hawking, 1978) proposed a related view of the vacuum, which he termed "vacuum foam." He suggested that Heisenberg's uncertainty relation might imply that over extremely brief durations and tiny spatial scales, on the order of the Planck length ($\approx 10^{-35}$ m), space-time might not be smooth, but have fluctuating local geometries in which space and time are not definite (Minsky, 2019).

Real particles may themselves be excited states propagating as quantum fluctuations through the vacuum field of virtual particles dynamically coming into, then leaving existence. This could be taken to mean that the vacuum or zero-point field is the underlying reality upon which everything else supervenes as patterns of excitation within the virtual particle sea. In a sense, the ether-like quantum vacuum is the only "thing" that might exist. Just as a wave on the water can seem to have a material existence but is really no more than a pattern of excitation propagating through the substrate upon which it supervenes, an object such as your brain may be a pattern of excitation propagating through the substrate upon which it supervenes: the ether-like quantum vacuum. You, your brain, and your consciousness might ultimately be patterns realized in and propagating through a churning "nothingness" of virtual particles. You would be realized in this nothingness. A teacup would be but a standing wave in this sea of virtual particles. The gulf between matter and mind would be bridged by the fact that all supervening patterns are realized in the same sea of virtual particles comprising the vacuum. If nothing realizes everything, then everything is ultimately nothing. To those who might want to romantically or brahmanically regard the vacuum as divine, however, I say this: We can sculpt this nothingness with our intentions, actions, and volitions, in the sense that what is to become real, as a wave upon the sea, is affected, in part, by what we choose to do and how we choose to be.

The reality of indeterminism is ultimately dictated by the reality of the quantization of action as an ontological, rather than epistemological, fact. Another way to think about this is that the finite quantization of action imposes a criterion on what types of virtual particle/anti-particle pairs can come into existence before going out of existence. This limit allows for many possible momentary realizations, without specifying a unique solution. Reality is indeterministic because causation may be criterial all the way down.

Reality is criterial all the way down because many possible virtual particle excitations, none of which violates $\Delta E \times \Delta t \geq \hbar/2$, can realize any "real" particle propagating through space-time at any specified moment or duration. If so, then classical and Einsteinian physics are wrong to model time as reversible. Instead, time would be irreversible at the level of particles, not just at the level of ensembles, because information is lost about which particular lowest level virtual particles realized a real pattern, whether a particle or an object, as an excited state of the vacuum. Multiple realizability at the rootmost level imposes an arrow of time at the rootmost level.

In sum, I am an indeterminist because quantum domain events have more than one possible outcome, any of which might really happen. For example, in the double-slit experiment, the photon or electron might land here on the photographic plate with some nonzero probability, and it might land there with a different nonzero probability. And whether it lands here or there, conservation of energy and momentum and all the other laws of physics will not have been violated. This fact arises from the nature of the underlying reality on which all else supervenes: the inherently nonlocal nature of the quantum vacuum or zero-point field; the peak of a wave entails the existence of a trough elsewhere.

In science we set up experiments to test hypotheses. If our goal was to try to settle whether outcomes follow deterministically or indeterministically from identical starting conditions, we would set up an experiment that was identical on every trial, as far as we could manage it. If that experiment turned out differently on each trial, we would reasonably conclude that more than one outcome can follow from identical initial conditions. In fact, the two-slit experiment is just such an experiment.

Determinists do not accept that our best experiments settle the matter. In this way they are dogmatic fundamentalists not so very different from religious dogmatic fundamentalists who make the "God of the gaps" argument, namely, that God is still needed to explain all those chains of causation that science cannot yet explain. But instead of arguing for the existence of a God of the gaps, they are arguing for a "determinism in the gaps" that cannot yet explain how identical starting conditions can lead to different outcomes. Deterministic dogmatists insist that the universe is actually deterministic, despite the experimental evidence, and that there must be some hidden deterministic variables that are as yet unknown, and that we are not adequately controlling. These gaps, if only filled, they maintain, would deterministically account for the variable outcomes of experiments such as the two-slit experiment. Given that they take refuge in an invisible domain of hidden causes, there is as little to say to deterministic dogmatists as there is to say to religious dogmatists. Given that the pattern of variable outcomes found in quantum domain experiments is predicted by quantum theory with incredibly high precision, the burden of proof that the universe is in fact deterministic lies with determinists.

Indeterminists, in contrast, accept the data as it presents itself, non-dogmatically, according to the precepts of scientific inquiry. Those who insist on hidden factors that might not even be measurable are not following the precepts of science, and, like religious fundamentalists, will not be satisfied with any experiment that has more than one possible outcome given identical initial starting conditions. They will always deny, as a matter of dogmatic principle, that more than one outcome is possible, each with a highly predictable probability.

Until hidden nonlocal variables theories are capable of making a falsifiable claim that could offer us a crucial experiment that could settle the matter of determinism versus indeterminism, it appears that victory lies with the indeterminists. As with religious fanatics who insist that they know the truth and what is best for us, the best strategy might be to simply ignore the insistence of those who believe in determinism despite the best existing empirical evidence.

Determinism, moreover, has trouble accounting for certain facts that indeterminism can explain easily. If determinism is the case, then events can unfold either backward or forward in time. Not only is the arrow of time lost, the privileged "now" is lost. Under determinism, the universe becomes a block universe in which all events across time, rather like a film on a reel, simply exist all at once. The real puzzle, for determinists, is why there should be change at all. If the universe is in fact a block universe, why is there a changing now? Indeterminists can easily say the now is the moment that an open future joins the ranks of the closed past, namely, when possibilia transition into actualia. Under indeterminism, the now arises as possibilities collapse successively into one subset of actualities on an ongoing basis.

One strategy determinists could use to try to escape the existence of a now would be to say that the seemingly changing now is an illusion: In fact, there is no now, but all nows are instead simultaneous in the block universe just as every frame of a movie exists at the same time in a film reel. An indeterminist might respond by asking "Why do you find yourself in this now versus any other?," "Why does the succession take us into the future and not the past?," and "Why does this now succeed the just previous one, as opposed to jumping around randomly from this now to very different nows?" A determinist might try to evade the issue by arguing that each now is connected only to its neighbors, by the laws of physics (causation as spatio-temporal adjacency). But an indeterminist could press the matter and ask a determinist why there is change at all? If all that exists is the cosmic block universal "film reel," and there is no clear analog of a projector creating a now, then there is no reason to allow any frame of the reel a privileged status, let alone a succession of frames a privileged direction of succession.

Indeterminists have not only the existence of change and a now on their side, but also they have the existence of changing consciousness, which is, as Descartes pointed out, the only basis of knowing that we have at all. Since the contents of consciousness undeniably change, it follows that whatever its material realizer is, is also changing in the present. The subjective experience of motion, which arises from a comparison of a past position and an updated one, requires a changing substrate to realize such a comparison. For each of these puzzles—why there is a now, why it changes, why it is directional, why consciousness changes, and why it exists in a subjective present—indeterminists have an answer in the ongoing collapse of possibilities into the subset that becomes actual, whereas determinists are stuck with the problem of how best to finagle an appearance of change into their conception of energy in space-time as a static block universe.

A block universe, like a film reel, could be run forward or backward. Whereas determinists are left trying to explain the direction of time in terms of stochastic factors, such as the second law of thermodynamics, indeterminists can point out that only possible events can possibly happen. Since possibilities lie in the future, not in the past, only events that are in the future can possibly come to pass, accounting for the direction of time without relying on stochastic explanations. If a determinist came along and said that events in the past could also possibly happen, then those events would not lie in the past, by definition, but in the future. Indeterminists get around this by saying that the past is comprised of possibilities that actualized, but which are no longer possible.

Determinists do have a way of answering the puzzle of time's directionality, in terms of the second law of thermodynamics, but are left accounting for it in terms of the behavior of ensembles. Although an ensemble might relax into more probable ensemble states, an ensemble only exists because someone chooses to regard a collection of particles as an ensemble. It is not clear why any given individual particle should have a direction of time. Under determinism, presumably a single particle does not have a direction of time in an ontological sense. Because an ensemble is just a collection of individual particles, the collection can change equally well forward and backward in time. If an ensemble has a direction of time, it is only epistemologically so, in terms of what configurations of particles count as equivalent. So, determinists only have an epistemological argument to account for the directionality of time, whereas indeterminists have ontological arguments. Under indeterminism, an individual particle, as well as any collection of individual particles, has an ontologically real direction of time, namely, that defined by the possible states that it might express in the ongoing collapse of possibilities into actualities. Moreover, as discussed in the context of the funnel in Section 2.10, physical systems that harness criterial causation entail a loss of information about the past, so cannot, in principle be run backward.

It is interesting that humans regard only the future as open, but the past as closed. No doubt countless pasts could have resulted in exactly this present moment, just as many paths could have led me to be sitting here, just where I now am sitting. And yet nobody regards free will to be about the past, namely, to be about choosing which one of all possible pasts (each consistent with having caused the present moment) we want to be the one past that really happened. Under determinism there is only one possible future and one possible past: because the situation is symmetrical, it is instructive that determinists regard freely willing to only be about the future. It reveals that they secretly harbor the indeterminist's belief that the future, unlike the past, is open. Indeterminists, on the other hand, embrace the asymmetry between the past and the future: the past is closed because it is no longer possible, whereas the future is open because there are multiple possibilities that might yet happen. If the past were open, it would lie in the future. If altering the probabilities of events happening in the past were possible, the past would not exist; it would instead lie in the future.

Going forward, I accept the overwhelming weight of empirical evidence from modern physics and assume ontological indeterminism to be the case. A central problem for us will be whether events in the brain can harness quantum domain indeterminacy such that it makes a difference in neural and mental processing. We delve into this when we explore neural processing in Chapter 4, where we answer in the affirmative.

2.13 What Is Criterial Causation?

In 2013 I published *The Neural Basis of Free Will: Criterial Causation*, which examined the nature of causation in the brain. Its central argument was that the neural code is criterial, permitting a range of adequate satisfactions that meet any informational criteria placed by neurons upon their inputs. Neurons not only evaluate their inputs criterially but also can reset the criteria for future evaluations of other neurons, or even of themselves.

Such "play" in the system permits randomness in the brain to influence outcomes, such that, although one criterial satisfaction may have been the one that in fact did happen, many others could just as easily have happened, had randomness tipped the timing of inputs ever so slightly differently. But this is not utter randomness, because the criteria in place had to be met. To return to our earlier example, if I ask you to name a woman European politician, you might say "Margaret Thatcher." But you might also have said "Angela Merkel" or "Theresa May" instead. And if we were able to rewind the indeterministic universe to the moment of my question, you might have given a different answer, just by chance. But in no imaginable universe would you have seriously answered "tree" or "rock," because these in no way meet the criteria that were to be met.

Criterial causation combined with appropriate amplification of randomness from the microscopic domain affords a form of constrained indeterminism that lies halfway between the unfreedom of utter randomness, in which an agent cannot shape future outcomes, and the unfreedom of determinism, in which events can never have turned out otherwise than they did, effectively having been "set in stone" at the Big Bang. Only in this middle domain of criterial causation can an agent shape the probabilities of favored futures becoming real over less desired futures. The kind of neural code that we have affords us the possibility of a libertarian free will.

But the kind of neural code discussed in *The Neural Basis of Free Will* is one that we share in common with tigers, chimpanzees, and other animals. And yet we humans are freer than other animals in fundamental ways. The life of a tiger today is basically the same as the life of an ancestral tiger a million years ago. The same goes for all other animals, including our closest living relatives, the great apes.

In contrast, human lives can be radically transformed in the span of just a few years. Sometimes such change happens to us and sometimes it happens within us. For example, the world that I grew up in had no computers, laptops, cell phones or the internet. The 1960s Manhattan of my childhood was analog, and the world I live in now is thoroughly digital. At some point the dark sides of overdigitalization and social media got to me. I got rid of my cellphone and tried my best to attend to the analog flow of events in my life. I exercised my free will when I said "no" to this way of living, and "yes" to a different possible way, effectively moving back to 2007, before everyone had smartphones. The computerization of the world happened *to* me but choosing how to deal with this external change happened *within* me.

A useful metaphor for causation via reparameterization is parenting. Many parents start out thinking they will shape their child into the type of person that they envision. They think they will be able turn their child into a talented mathematician or master musician. Then they come to realize that the child comes to the world with propensities and biases. They find that one child is drawn to playing with dolls while another is drawn to playing with weapons and trucks. As a father I eventually realized that it was a mistake to think that I could mold my children into my vision of how they should be. I came to see that my role was instead to foster their growth along the lines that their own propensities revealed, especially in their play, where I could see what they found intrinsically interesting and rewarding. I realized that it was an uphill battle admonishing them not to do things that they wanted to do, since they would find a way to do what they wanted to do, regardless. Instead, my efforts were better spent guiding what they wanted to do toward healthy expressions of their nature. I also realized that where I could make the biggest difference was in reparameterizing the world in which they developed. So we bought an old farm in New Hampshire, got rid of the TV and most screens, and traveled a lot. This reparameterization afforded certain forms of growth over others. Without screens, they spent more time outside than other kids, especially with the kids of other like-minded families. And when it was rainy, they would play board games or read books, instead of playing video games. Parameter causation is more yin than yang, more indirect than direct. It is less about acting on agents directly than creating spaces where agents themselves freely make choices naturally afforded by those spaces.

What can account for this human capacity to reparameterize our own and others' lives? Partly it is that we are freed from instinct in a way that other animals are not. Unlike all other animals, I suspect, we can choose not to obey desires and instincts, as when someone who enjoys the taste of grilled steak decides to become vegetarian for moral reasons. But we are not merely less bound by instinct and other such involuntary demands placed upon our behavior. We are creative in a way that is simply unprecedented among the endless biological forms that have come and gone over the past four billion years of life on Earth. What is it that frees us, at least to some degree, from instinct? What is it about our brains that affords us our radical creativity? To understand this, we have to examine the nature of causation in the brain. In particular, we have to understand that neurons rewire each other's criteria for firing.

Before discussing neural causation, let us begin by discussing causation schematically. The most popular models of causation are "interventionist" or "manipulationist" models of causation. Interventionist or manipulationist models of causation (e.g., Pearl, 2000; Woodward, 2003) are rooted in the intuition that if some event A causes some event B, then one should be able to manipulate A in some way and see corresponding changes in B that happen after changing A. If A is modeled as causing B, then there should be an intervention on A (in at least some state of the model) that results in B changing its value. If B changes with an intervention on A, it is concluded that A causes B, at least in part. For example, if someone wants to show that a clock A plays a causal role in the time B that you leave your house, we could manipulate the clock, say, set it ten minutes behind, and see that this affects the objective time that you leave your house. This does not mean that the clock is the sole cause of the time that you leave your house, but it is one causal factor among perhaps many different causal factors. Conversely, if we want to show that an event A, say, the crowing a rooster, plays no causal role in the timing of a subsequent event B, say, the time of the sunrise, we can carry out an intervention on the rooster, silencing it by wringing its neck, and notice that this has no effect on the time of the sunrise. This way, we could show that apparent causation is just that, namely, merely apparent.

These kinds of models of causation basically describe what scientists already do to determine causal relationships among variables. Scientists have for centuries tried to control for all independent variables (Woodward calls this "screening off" the other variables besides A that likely partially cause B, by holding their values constant) save one, A, which they vary, in order to see the consequences or changes expressed by some outcome or dependent variable B. If B changes with an intervention on A, it is concluded that A, among perhaps other causal variables, in part causes B.

A counterfactual formulation of interventionism would be "If event A had not occurred, with all screened off variables that may cause B held constant, then B would not have occurred." Criterial causation emphasizes that we need to enhance the interventionist account by saying "if A had not occurred, with all screened off variables that may cause B held constant, *and with the parameters or criteria by which B evaluates its inputs also held constant*, then B would not have occurred."

Traditional interventionist models of causation carry out some intervention on A to determine what effects, if any, there might be on B (and other variables). But if instead of manipulating A, or A's output to B, we instead manipulate the criteria, parameters, or conditions that B places on its input (including on input from A), which must be satisfied before B changes or acts, then changes in B do not follow passively from changes in A as they would if A and B were, say, billiard balls. Inputs from A can be identical, but in one case B changes in response to A, and in another case it does not, depending on B's criteria for responding. For example, under a classical or Newtonian conception of causation, billiard ball B responds rather slavishly and passively if it is hit by billiard ball A. Billiard ball B follows deterministically from the mass, momentum, direction of motion, and point of collision by billiard ball A. It does not matter whether billiard ball A is striped or solid, or if it has an even number or odd number on it. All that matters are the physical, non-informational variables of mass, momentum, position, and so forth. Under criterial causation, in contrast, billiard ball B sets conditions on A. It might say "if billiard ball A is striped, go this way, and if it is solid, go this other way." That would lead to a very strange and non-Newtonian billiard ball game. Now imagine that we can change the parameters or criteria whereby billiard ball B assesses billiard ball A, just by willing it to be so or by reprogramming B. Let us say we can change its conditions to instead be "if billiard ball A is even, go this way, but if it is odd, then go this other way." This requires that B realize a decoder of informational or pattern-relational aspects of A.

In criterial assessments of A, what matters are high-level informational characteristics about billiard ball A, such as its number being even or odd, or its being striped or solid in color. These are informational variables that the classical conception of causation simply ignored. But this kind of reparameterization of B is what neurons do when they change each other's synaptic weights, such that a neuron now responds optimally to different inputs than just prior to the act of reparameterization or criterial resetting. For example, a neuron might respond optimally to a dog being in the visual scene one minute, but then optimally to a cat the next minute.

Criterial causation emphasizes that what can vary is either outputs from A to other nodes (the traditional, and I would say incomplete, view of causation), or how inputs are decoded by receiving nodes B, B′, B″, etc. How they are decoded depends on the criteria for decoding, and these criteria can be changed. On this view, standard interventionists (hearkening all the way back to "Newtonian" models of causation that emphasize energy transfer and conservation; e.g., P. Dowe's views (1992)) are a special case where B places no particular conditions on input from A that have to be met before B changes state. But the brain, if anything, emphasizes causation via reparameterization of the way that B criterially assesses inputs from A. This reparameterization of B is what neurons do when they change each other's synaptic weights, such that a neuron now responds optimally to different inputs than prior to the act of physical and informational reparameterization or criterial resetting.

Let me emphasize that I do not think that Woodward or Pearl are wrong. But they also make no mention, as far as I can tell, that causation might partly depend on reparameterizations of B. Thus, their views of causation are incomplete and need to be amended by emphasizing the role of informational reparameterization of the response characteristics of B.

Here is a higher-level example. We can think of a soccer game in Newtonian terms as the transfer of physical forces among atoms or quarks. But it would be hard to understand what happens in a soccer game without understanding the rules whereby players play the game. For example, under the normal set of rules it is forbidden to touch the ball with one's hands. If one did not know the rules, and instead was only able to measure the movements of atoms, it might seem strange that atoms happen to move in a way that never led to a hand touching the ball. A Newtonian, atom-on-atom reduction of causation could never account for causation at an informational level, such as having a rule against touching the ball with one's hands, because information does not exist at the atomic level at all. It exists at the level of macroscopic decoders, such as neurons.

Moreover, a Newtonian conception of causation could not account for causation involving reparameterizations of the rules whereby events can happen. For example, if we reparameterize the rules of playing the game, such that it is now allowed to touch the ball with one's hands, then very different kinds of actions will unfold in the world. In effect, reparameterizing what counts as driving input from event A to an assessing process B, leads to the carving out of very different chains of actual events from all the events that were possible among particle causal chains. For example, it would lead to games where players now can touch the ball with their hands.

In this book I explore the idea of causation via reparameterization of constraints or criteria for subsequent permissible actions, as opposed to the more traditional notion of causation as the imparting of force or energy. Changing the code or parameters or criteria that B uses to decode, interpret, or respond to its inputs is a manipulation that might make no apparent changes to A or any other variable in the system for long and uncertain spans of time, until just the right pattern of inputs comes along. For example, there is a case where Israeli intelligence programmed a cellphone to explode only when a particular cellphone number, known "only" to their target, was dialed. Manipulating "A" here appears to have no effect on any dependent variable "B" and might not, in principle, for as long as you like. It might take years to get this phone into the hands of their targeted Hamas leader. But when the bombmaker dialed his "secret" number, the bomb exploded.

Here is another example. Let us say the builders of the pyramids booby trapped the tomb of some pharaoh such that, should robbers ever enter the tomb, they would be killed by the booby trap. Maybe arrows would be shot at the robbers, or a big rock would fall on them, as happened to Indiana Jones in the film *Raiders of the Lost Ark*. Thousands of years might pass before something enters the tomb that satisfies the parameters of what counts as a person entering the tomb. This might kill archaeologists three thousand years after the trap was set, even though the builders of the pyramid meant to kill robbers. For all those thousands of years it would have seemed as if nothing was happening. In this case the parameterization of B would be setting the conditions for the release of the booby trap, say, arrows being shot at the intruders or a giant stone falling on their heads. Criterial causation, unlike classical causation, entails no correlation or necessary link between the timing of causes, in particular, criterial settings and resettings, and the timing of their effects.

This initial parameterization of B need not have immediate noticeable or measurable effects within the system. In this sense it would seem to violate the assumption of the traditional manipulationist or interventionist view that causation is transferred at some fast speed (say the speed of light) or that the timing of causes and effects must be correlated, as John Stuart Mill (1843) argued. But initial parameterization or reparameterization of B is a causal intervention nonetheless, even though this subclass of causation has been relatively ignored by philosophers so far. It is at the heart of what I mean by criterial causation and at the heart of biology. Other reasonable names for criterial causation might be "reparameterization causation" or "pattern causation" or "phase causation." There is indeed a tight correlation between the timing of the manipulation of B and the timing of B's criterial reparameterization. However, since it cannot be known when inputs will arrive that will satisfy B's criteria, releasing some consequence that influences the rest of the system, there is no necessary temporal correlation between the initial manipulation and the conditions that unleash an action within the system. Thus, in the case of criterial causation, unlike billiard ball causation, the temporal correlation between causes and effects can be entirely lost.

It was the "discovery" of this class of non-Millian, non-Newtonian causation by evolution that I believe led to the explosion of physical systems that we now call biological systems. Causation by reparameterization may have begun with conditions placed on physical parameters. For example, a binding neurotransmitter molecule would have to have a certain shape before an ion channel would open in a cell's membrane. Later, it might have come to also involve conditions placed on informational parameters, say, fire if and only if the criteria for a face are met in the input. These informational parameters are surely realized in physical parameters, say, for example, fire if and only if the criteria on the simultaneity of spike inputs are met.

Once causation by reparameterization came not only to involve conditions placed on physical parameters (e.g., molecular shape of a neurotransmitter before an ion channel would open in a cell membrane), but also conditions placed on informational parameters (fire above or below baseline firing rate if and only if the criteria for a face are met in the input) that were realized in physical parameters (fire if and only if the criteria on the simultaneity of spike inputs are met), we witnessed a further revolution in natural causation. This was the revolutionary emergence of mind and informational downward causation in the universe, as far as we know, uniquely on Earth, and perhaps for the first time in the history of the universe.

Criterial causation is the central innovation that got life going, as a special type of physically realized system. It is especially central to how mental causation works in the brain. It is also central to the emergence of mind itself, and the special class of mental events that are subjectively experienced or conscious. For example, if neurons associated with the subjective experience of redness respond if and only if certain kinds of wavelengths or pigments (namely those that reflect long wavelength visible light) are inferred to be in the world, based upon the visible evidence, then the meeting of those criteria for neural firing are the realization of experiencing redness. Qualia are realized in acts of decoding.

Criterial causation also allows science to better model pattern- and purpose-centered causation and to expand beyond the prejudice that all causation boils down to matter and motion among deterministically interacting particles. This localistic and reductionistic worldview was distilled into its purest logical form in Kim's exclusion argument, which, we have seen, unravels under indeterminism. This mechanistic bias was intentionally introduced into science by Francis Bacon (1605), one of its founders, who wrote: "[Science] doth make inquiry, and take consideration of the same natures: but how? Only as to the material and efficient causes of them, and not as to the forms." Bacon was here referring to two of Aristotle's four types of causal explanation: material and efficient. For example, if we ask why a house is as it is, one answer is that it is as it is because it is made of wood (the material cause), and another is that it was constructed by a builder to be the way that it is (the efficient cause). Bacon intentionally excluded the other two types, formal and final causation, which concern design and purpose, respectively, according to which the house is as it is because an architect came up with its particular design (the formal cause) and because it is supposed to be lived in (the final cause). Given that these various causal accounts are not mutually exclusive, why did Bacon exclude design and purpose from the domain of legitimate scientific explanation? Bacon was reacting against the dogmatic supernatural design- and purpose-centered explanations of Christianity, that viewed everything as designed by God for a purpose. To purge such dogma, he set up an empirical framework within which the universe could be understood as both natural and mechanistic, building on earlier empiricist efforts by Ibn Al-Haytham, Aristotle, Thales, and others. He advocated the scientific method of empirical testing to find truth, rather than relying on the dogmatic assertions of long-dead men found in religious texts.

This liberating anti-theology worked well for planets and falling apples, and eventually landed us on the Moon. It was liberating because it freed humans from the control of religious dogmatists whose control was rooted in claims of divine purposiveness; that is, things are as they are because God wants it to be so, so don't get out of line or you'll suffer. Overthrowing the medieval Christian "Taliban" by purging the world model of purposiveness came, however, at a price. While we gained a more accurate understanding of reality where a mechanistic, purposeless account was appropriate, as in planetary orbits, we imposed the metaphor of an input–output machine where it was simplistic and wrong to do so: life. Explaining biological processes within such a deterministic, mechanistic, and purpose-purged framework proved problematic for biology, psychology, anthropology, history, sociology, the humanities, and neuroscience because animals obviously have purposes: they want food and mates; they evolved teleonomic instincts to fly south in order to avoid winter; they flee predators in order not to be killed; they build nests and make tools with a design in mind; humans long to understand their life's purpose and strive for meaning; we want to love and be loved. In ongoing efforts to deny life formal and final causation, defenders of science with a hardcore mechanistic worldview had to reduce pattern- and purpose-centered causation to efficient and material causation. This reductionistic bias has led to various reactionary expressions of righteous mechanistic reductionism in recent years, including epiphenomenalism concerning consciousness (Churchland, 1986; Dennett, 1991), free will "willusionism" (Caruso, 2012; Levy, 2011; Wegner, 2002), and the view that the body and mind are biochemical puppets of genes (Dawkins, 1976; Harris, 2012; Sapolsky, 2023) and other nonconscious machinery.

The public has found some of this reductionistic fundamentalism hard to swallow, and for good reason: it is simply obvious that we want to go to the dentist mainly because our tooth hurts, or that we strive over years to save up enough to buy a house because we want to have our own house. Purpose and design are central to how we live and to what we live for, and to deny these as illusory, or to try to reduce our aspirations to colliding quarks or selfish genes is simplistic and silly. There is no awareness, hope, longing, or fear in a quark or a gene, and yet these are what drive us toward our goals.

Criterial causation brings formal and final causation back into science in a naturalistic manner that is consistent with a rigorous understanding of efficient and material causation, without recourse to souls, gods, or magic. This allows us to move beyond denying the reality of consciousness and its volitional operations as causal in the universe, without thereby succumbing to wishful thinking that the universe in itself has a purpose or was fashioned by a conscious designer.

But criterial causation alone is not enough to fully grasp why biological systems are purposive. Yes, reparameterization of B is central to criterial causation, but why does B undergo reparameterization of its criteria for action release? B gets reparameterized because biological systems are cybernetic; they are continually detecting feedback signals in order to discern whether there is a discrepancy between an internal setpoint and the present state of the organism. This setpoint is internal, not set externally, as with a thermostat. Many such processes are homeostatic, and set by evolution, because these settings led to survival and procreation, whereas other settings did not. Essentially, the desires were sculpted by evolution as much as bodies were. Other internal setpoints are learned; we come to desire more money because we learned it has value, not because we are genetically programmed to want money. And yet other setpoints are generated cognitively; we set aside some money each month to fulfill, for example, our goal of retiring by 60. Whatever the setpoint, our current state or trajectory is continually compared to where it should be. If there is a discrepancy, we set and reset ourselves onto a corrective path that will minimize that discrepancy in future cycles of the cybernetic looping process. For example, at a physical level, if the body is dehydrated, thirst will emerge into consciousness, and an animal will then have as one of its current purposes finding water, while taking into account other demands and everything else going on in the world and in its body. Or, at a mental level, if we find that we are spending more than required to save enough to buy our dream house, we might opt for a "staycation" this year instead of going on an expensive vacation.

Corrective cybernetic processes that do not require contextualization for their execution can be carried out unconsciously; for example, if more oxygen is required by our muscles as we walk upstairs, we will find that we have started to breathe faster and that our heart has started to pound. No need for volition there, so make the process automatic. Most processes in the body are purposive in this unconscious, automatized way, whether at the level of individual cells' internal cybernetic loops of causation or at the level of the whole organism. But cybernetic processes tend to enter consciousness as desires or goals when they require contextualization for their optimal fulfillment by information that goes beyond the one type of input that their setpoint seeks. For example, if rehydration could be fulfilled automatically, without recourse to knowing about sources of water in the world, it would be so fulfilled. But since water resides in an ever-changing world, it is necessary to seek it out in the world, and the only way to do that is via our experience of the world: our consciousness. The contextualization afforded by placing a goal, say, quenching our thirst, in our world model as experienced, allows us to modulate our efforts to find water while also fulfilling other goals. For example, we won't walk to the nearest watering hole if we think lions might be there. Our desire to quench our thirst is modulated by the context of other goals and desires, such as our fear of being eaten alive. Consciousness is not just informational, it is purposive; it is a contextualizing world and body state "hallucination" that evolved to help us fulfill goals like quenching our thirst without getting eaten.

If criterial causation explains *how* B is reparameterized, cybernetic looping over extended durations explains *why* B is reparameterized. Together, we have the basis of closed-loop causation found in living systems, rooted in corrective negative feedback in the service of goals, making life so very different from nonliving physical systems in which causation is open-loop. Because nonbiological causation is open-loop, it is sufficient to think only in terms of the causal efficacy of A, ignoring B's say in the matter. It is also easy to see how so many thinkers fell into the trap of localistic, reductionistic, non-relational, linear conceptions of causation. But once causation in biological systems is understood to be criterial and cybernetic, it becomes not localistic but globalistic, not reductionistic but holistic, not linear but nonlinear, not reflexive but adaptive and purposive, not instantaneous but durational, and not nonrelational but inherently relational in nature. In short, causation in living systems cannot be understood using the mechanistic metaphor of a mindless input–output machine. Open-loop causation does appear to reign in nonliving systems, and can be reduced to the Newtonian A causes B scenario, where B sets no informational criteria on A. But it would be a mistake to apply this conception to closed-loop systems, such as living organisms and ecosystems.

2.14 Information as Pattern Decoding

One of my hopes in this book is to be able to change intuitions about what counts as physical, and to perhaps change intuitions about information and informational causation. People typically have an intuition of the physical as a substantial material or weighty substance. Often people intuit the magnitude of the fundamental substance, presumed to be energy, in terms of amounts, like varying masses of, say, clay. We learn in school that energy is a substance that can neither be created nor destroyed, a fact that we might intuit using a metaphor like the reshaping of clay. If we change a lump of clay from the shape of a man to the shape of a house, it obviously remains the same amount of clay.

More abstract models of the fundamental substance that we learned about in school centered on the concepts of the amplitude and frequency of energy. We learned to picture light as having an amplitude and a frequency, that we modeled as a wave whose height corresponded to the light wave's amplitude, and whose spatial wavelength corresponded to its temporal frequency or "color."

Common intuitions based on these kinds of models can really lead us astray in our efforts to understand what information is, and how it can be causal in the universe. In my view, physicalists, and I count myself as a physicalist, need to re-evaluate what we mean by "the physical" to accommodate information and (downward) informational causation, because, I argue, information is fundamentally realized in and is about *patterns* of energy, not amounts of energy.

Whereas it makes sense to reduce global forces to the sum of local forces, and total amounts to the sum of local parts' amounts, this kind of reductionism does not make sense at all for patterns. Reductionism of global patterns to local parts of patterns and ultimately to local particle interactions fails as a program because patterns are inherently relational over space, time, and other dimensions (e.g., color relationships, social relationships, and so on). That is, patterns are not localistic and are not reducible to a mere collection of parts. The configuration of the parts matters. Two patterns such as ":)" and the similar "):" can be built out of the same parts, but because their spatial or temporal relationships differ, they can count as different patterns with potentially different meanings; a smiley and frowny face might even have opposite meanings. Patterns are inherently globalistic or holistic because they are relational. So, reductionism and localism fail for patterns. Reducing patterns to a level of interacting particles, where a decoder can no longer decode the pattern or relationship in question, is pointless.

The program of reductionistic physicalism, which conceivably could have worked for energetic amplitude and frequency, is doomed to fail for energetic relationships in space and time or the decoding of such patterns. Understanding causation at the level of information will require a holistic understanding of energy, because patterns are holistic or relational, and acts of decoding patterns have to occur at a level where those relationships are explicit, not implicit. Patterns cannot be reduced to a level below the level where relationships to which a decoder responds are detectable and explicit, or the pattern of relationships to which a decoder is sensitive will be lost.

But if an act of decoding can trigger a change in a physical system—say, a neuron that is tuned to a face detects a face in the visual input and then fires, thereby influencing other neurons—then reductionistic physicalism won't work at all, because then even noninformational causal chains, say, among local particles, become influenced by global energetic relationships. That is, once patterns and information become causal in the universe, because of the evolution of decoders (like neurons) that do things if patterns are present (like fire or trigger behaviors of animals in the world), then reductionistic, localistic physicalism fails. Reductionism fails for the entire universe even if it fails just here on Earth in a single animal.

For example, when we look at the night sky, we might recognize the constellation Orion. The same set of stars could have been linked together in some different pattern, but this is the pattern we detect because somebody *taught* this pattern to us, perhaps when we were small, so we learned the pattern of this constellation, and now can find the pattern in the night sky. But there is nothing like Orion really out there in the universe. Sure, there are several suns really out there, but these are in fact hundreds of light years apart from each other and from us. For example, the brightest of Orion's stars, Rigel, is 800 light years from us, while the next brightest, Betelgeuse, is 600 light years from us. The only reason Orion has an existence as a pattern is that we have learned to have a decoder that responds when an Orion-like pattern is in the input. Had we been taught a different pattern, then, when looking at the night sky, we would have seen that other pattern and not the pattern of Orion. And that these stars cast this pattern, even though far apart, is because of the "accidental" position that the Earth just happens to occupy. So, Orion only exists because we learned this pattern and can detect it in the visual input when we look at the night sky because of the arbitrary position of the Earth. The pattern has no objective existence as a thing with mass in the universe out there. It exists solely because we decode it as a pattern in our sensory inputs. And the pattern does not even have to exist among stars. We could recognize the pattern Orion even if it were made by arranging limes or teddy bears or whatever we like.

Another concrete example is afforded by the Moon. Most people in the West see a face in the Moon. But most people in China are taught that there is a rabbit in the Moon. The first time I was told this, I thought it quite odd, because I thought it was obvious that the Moon looked like it had a face on it. But after it was shown to me how to see a rabbit in the Moon, I found it more natural to see a rabbit there. Of course, there is neither a face nor a rabbit in the Moon. This is just how we have been taught to decode the pattern there. But it does show how identical input from A, in this case the Moon, can lead to radically different outcomes, say, how one sees the Moon, once "Moon decoder" B has been reparameterized.

To make informational causation even more alien to the causation studied by physics and described by our best physical laws, spatio-temporal patterns of energy can be created and destroyed, so conservation laws (of energy, momentum, spin, and so forth) that apply to amounts of energy, are not relevant when it comes to understanding informational causation. For example, going back to our clay example, when I form a lump of clay into a little man and then into a little house, the amount of clay is conserved, but the shape of the clay is not conserved, because I destroyed the form of the man in order to mold the form of a house. So, form is not conserved. Phase relationships are not conserved. Pattern in general is not conserved. Information, being acts of decoding of patterns, is similarly not conserved. Thus, information does not obey the conservation laws of physics, even if it is realized in a material basis that does obey laws of physics, such as (the amount of) energy conservation.

If information is rooted in acts of pattern decoding, then informational causation is about successions of pattern-decoding acts, where the occurrence of one act of pattern decoding plays a role in the occurrence of a subsequent act of pattern decoding. Ideas that were central for understanding standard physical causation among particles, such as amount, force, frequency, and conservation of energy, spin, or momentum are just no longer very relevant or useful, and in fact may hinder our thinking about informational causation. To understand informational causation means to understand decoding, particularly the decoding of energetic patterns among inputs to the decoder. It requires understanding how decoders trigger other decoders, and also how decoders reparameterize each other for possible future acts of now altered decoding.

The technical word for energetic relationships is "phase" (e.g., a sine and cosine wave of the same amplitude and frequency have a phase difference of ninety degrees). Spatial phase arises from spatial relationships (i.e., patterns) and is related to the everyday idea of shape. Temporal phase is related to the idea of timing of one event relative to another. Physicalists' intuitions have been centered on the amount or frequency of energy, resulting in the misleading intuition that causation must involve the transfer of a conserved quantity of energy. But if we instead focus on energetic phase relationships, which can vary independently of both amplitude and frequency, we can reconceive causation as occurring among inherently nonlocalistic patterns that trigger patterns, and among acts of decoding patterns that trigger acts of decoding patterns, none of which are conserved, and none of which apply forces or have amounts. A given brain pattern might trigger two or more possible subsequent brain patterns, each of which conserves energy under all the traditional physical conservation laws. As long as traditional conservation laws are not violated, thoughts realized in patterns of neural activity are free to trigger multiple possible thoughts in the immediate future. This is why, for any particular criteria that have been set, such as "think of a European woman politician," the criteria can, in principle, be met in multiple ways.

When we think of causation among energetic patterns afforded by acts of decoding patterns that then change the system, we enter a new causal world where there are no (informational) forces, and nothing (informational) is necessarily conserved. If information is just acts of decoding inputs, such acts set up equivalence classes of microphysical inputs among physical events, as well as equivalence classes among outputs. For example, there are countless possible inputs that meet cat-defining criteria, and there are countless ways a neuron could fire above its baseline so that downstream decoders will come to know that "catness" has been detected. If those equivalence classes have to do with criteria that must be met in order to count as an instance of a certain class, then neither the class nor its members is defined by physical attributes of particles, such as mass, momentum, wavelength, or position. An informational class is defined by the meeting of informational criteria, which are in turn realized in the satisfaction of physical criteria for neural firing placed on spatial configurations and temporal patterns (again, "phase relationships") among inputs, and ultimately particles. For example, the class of things that count as a cat has nothing to do with momentum, spin, mass, or particle position.

Importantly, neither an informational class nor an informational configuration or pattern has an objective or object-like existence in addition to the particles in which the pattern is realized. A pattern or configuration only comes into existence and becomes causal in the universe by virtue of a decoder that decodes its inputs such that if this pattern is present, the decoder does something to the physical system in which it is embedded, perhaps causing the system to change its physical and informational state.

In order to understand what allows one act of decoding to trigger subsequent different acts of decoding, we must first understand what counts as an act of decoding for a neuron. Successful decoding of inputs occurs when an instance from the class of all combinations of inputs that could make the neuron fire in fact occurs as input to the neuron, making it fire. But what defines this class of potential information?

A neuron will generally fire only when a certain number of signals (i.e., action potentials or neural spikes) arrive within an extremely short duration, say within about 25 ms. The inputs must share very particular temporal and spatial (phase) relationships. For example, they have to arrive very close to simultaneously, meaning within this brief window of time, and they have to arrive on very particular parts of the neuron, before the neuron will decode the input as an instance of the class that can drive it. An act of neural decoding therefore typically involves an assessment of energetic phase.

Having decoders respond to particular spatial and temporal relationships or patterns in input allowed patterns or phase in energy to become causal in the universe. Whereas pre-biological classes of physical causation generally were unresponsive to phase differences in input, being more responsive to other attributes of energy, such as its amplitude and frequency, life introduced "phase causation" or "pattern causation" into the universe. Informational causation occurs when there is a succession of pattern decoding events, as when the firing of this neuron, tuned to pattern A, in part drives the firing of another neuron, tuned to pattern B.

But informational causation is more powerful even than that because the criteria that a neuron applies to evaluate its inputs can change or be changed by other neurons' inputs. This subclass of informational causation is made possible in the human brain via the resetting of the informational parameters that will drive a neuron, realized in resetting synaptic weights and other parameters so that a neuron now effectively receives and responds to different driving inputs than it did before the act of resetting. Thus, informational causation is realized in criterial causation, which is itself an instance of the more general class of energetic phase causation or pattern causation.

A typical deterministic physicalist who thinks of causation localistically will respond to this kind of indeterministic and holistic physicalism by denying that the causal efficacy of a neural state has anything to do with the information realized in that physical state. In line with the exclusion argument, they will argue that the causal efficacy of physical states reduces ultimately to the bottom-most level of strings-on-strings or atoms-on-atoms—a level where information or mental events undeniably have no role. So, in what sense is information causal? Information arises in the form of equivalence classes of physical brain states defined by having met informational criteria such as "there is a cat in the scene."

The criteria that define an informational state will tend to create equivalence classes that look a lot like Ludwig Wittgenstein's criterially defined sets containing members who are linked only by fairly loose family resemblances. Indeed, I credit Wittgenstein with cracking this conceptual aspect of the neural code, even though he never wrote about neurons. Although informational equivalence classes of physical realizers may tend to delimit a family of physical realizers that bear physical resemblance to one another, this need not be so. An informational equivalence class can be defined in ways that lump together as equivalent physical realizers that are radically different. These very different inputs may drive a neuron equivalently, and then, as far as the next neurons in an information-processing cascade are concerned, be quite literally the same. For example, "all things that are living or red and bigger than a breadbox" delimits a set of satisfactions that bear no resemblance to one another, whether as referents in the world, or in the neural encoding of those referents. A tapir and a sunset are both either alive and bigger than a breadbox or red and bigger than a breadbox. Obviously, the tapir or sunset, as a thing in the universe, are radically different, and the neural encoding of a tapir and a sunset are also radically different. If they were not, we would confuse them, which we never do. The only way to understand a nexus in a causal chain such as "Holler 'God save the Queen' as soon as you see something living or red, and bigger than a breadbox" is to analyze inputs at the level of meeting the criteria that define a proposition or an informational structure, such as an informational satisfaction of informational criteria. In other words, the only way to understand how seeing a tapir or a sunset could lead to the same hollered sentence is to understand the informational conditions that made those inputs equivalent members of the set of driving inputs. And if all we know is that someone hollered, we would not know the particular cause.

Indeed, an informational equivalence class may have a nonmeaningful source. If, in one imaginable universe U_1, P_1 and P_4 are assigned randomly to the same set S_1, and in another imaginable universe U_2, they are assigned to different sets S_1 and S_2, then in U_2 manipulating P_1 to P_4 might trigger a decoder of S_2-ness to detect an instance of S_2, whereas in U_1 it will not, since in U_1, P_1 and P_4 are regarded as equivalent realizations of S_1. But these two universes might be physically identical in all ways except for the single random process that assigned P_1 and P_4 to the same or different equivalence classes. The only way to distinguish why manipulating P_1 to P_4 identically in the two universes leads to a realization of S_1 to S_1 (no change) versus a realization of S_1 to S_2, requires knowing whether or not P_1 and P_4 are members of the same equivalence class. And the only way to know that is to know the informational sorting process that resulted in their allocation to the informational equivalence classes in which they find themselves. The laws of physics cannot explain such a sorting process, since the sorting process has nothing to do with mass, momentum, spin, or any other physical property. The basis of sorting is informational. Causation at this level can only be understood as information triggering information or as pattern triggering pattern at the realizer level.

We return to this line of argument again in Sections 4.8 and 4.18, where I argue that information is causal in the universe not as a force but as a top-down filter that allows only those sets of particle-level physical causal paths or possibilities that are also informational causal paths to become real.

2.15 The Luck Argument against Free Will

So far, we have considered two primary philosophical arguments against the possibility of free will: the consequence argument and the exclusion argument. Here we consider a third philosophical argument against the possibility of free will: the "luck argument." It rests on the idea that there are two kinds of luck. First, there is the good or bad luck we had in being born with the constitution we have, with our particular genetics, into a world that we did not create, which fosters or harms us and our development. We can't be held responsible for the world we were born into or the genetics that we inherited, since we did not choose these things. They just happened to us, so to speak. All that we can do is to try to play the hand that we were dealt in life as well as we can. This kind of luck is called "constitutive luck."

Besides constitutive luck, there is a second kind of luck called "present luck." Let us say we decide, just by chance to go jogging around the park clockwise versus counterclockwise. Let us say a mugger is looking for someone to rob. Just by chance, the mugger also decides to run around the park either clockwise or counterclockwise. If, just by chance, we both go around the park in the same direction, we will most likely not meet each other. But if we, again, just by chance, go around the park in opposite directions, the probability that we will cross paths is very high. In one case we encounter the mugger and are attacked, while in the other case, we don't encounter the mugger and are not attacked. In either case we did not choose to be attacked or not be attacked, so we can't be blamed if we are attacked or not attacked. Getting attacked just happened by chance. We either had the good present luck of not running into the mugger, or we had the bad present luck of running into the mugger and getting mugged.

The standard luck argument against free will runs like this:

> If decisions or actions occur indeterministically, such that two or more alternative decisions might be made at a given moment, each with a nonzero probability of happening, and everything is exactly the same in the world's history until that very moment, then there is nothing about the world or the decider prior to that moment that accounts for one decision being made over the other. Which option gets chosen is just a matter of (perhaps weighted) chance, not a matter of agentic influence on specific outcomes. If one decision should turn out better or worse than another, well, that is just a matter of luck and not a matter of agentic choice. But if

decisions and consequences are just a matter of luck, then the decider cannot be responsible for the decision made or for its consequences.

It is not a matter of the chooser having some influence on the likelihood of specific outcomes. If one decision should turn out to be better or worse than another, then that is just a matter of good or bad luck and not a matter of the agent's choice. But if decisions and consequences are just a matter of luck, then the decider cannot be held responsible for the decisions they make or for their consequences. Note that if the argument from luck works at all, it works not only against libertarians, but also against everyone, including compatibilists; see Caruso (2012, 2015), Levy (2011), and Pereboom (2001, 2014).

According to the luck argument against free will, free will is ruled out by luck, regardless of the truth of determinism or indeterminism. This entails a denial that anyone bears any moral responsibility whatsoever. If this view is correct, then, even though Hitler chose to systematically murder millions of people in a premeditated manner, he did so just by bad luck, whether because of his inherited wicked character—which was his constitutive luck, and hardly his fault—or because of his present luck when deciding between options just by chance, so again, hardly his fault.

Let us try to understand the luck argument in the context of concrete examples before we try to dismantle it. The philosopher Peter van Inwagen imagines a potential thief pondering whether to steal from the church's poor box. He is in an emotionally and morally torn state before his decision is made. He feels torn because he is undergoing an internal struggle between two conflicting motives within himself. He is torn between his motive to have more money, and his conflicting motive to honor a promise he made to his mother on her deathbed to live a moral life. If he foregoes stealing the money, he foregoes something he desires, namely, the money. But if he reneges on his promise to his mother, he also loses something that he desires, which is his desire to live up to his mother's expectations and his desire to not break a promise that he made to her.

Philosophers who believe in the validity of the luck argument tend to argue that defenders of libertarian free will (like myself) fail to offer any explanation of why it is that the thief decides to steal rather than not steal the money. If he steals, well, stealing just happens. And had the decision, by chance, gone the other way, such philosophers would argue that libertarians cannot explain why the thief refrained from stealing. In that case, not-stealing just happens. The genes that the potential thief inherited are a matter of constitutive luck, so he cannot be held responsible for that or for the choices, acts, and consequences that follow because of the character that was "foisted" on him by his genetics and the environment into which he was born. But whether he chooses, by chance, to steal or not steal the money comes down to present luck, so he can also not be held responsible for stealing, or not stealing, whichever the case may be, and cannot be held responsible for any downstream consequences of his actions either.

Two philosophers, Robert Kane and Mark Balaguer, have defended libertarian free will on the basis of such torn decisions. Kane gives the example of a businesswoman who is in a rush to get to an important business meeting. On the way she sees someone who needs help. She is torn, because one part of her wants to help the person in need, whereas another part of her wants to make it to her important meeting on time. If an agent is defined as that which exerts willpower toward the fulfillment of some end, then she is a split-agent when she is torn, or even two agents occupying a single body, because one part of her exerts willpower toward the end of making it to the meeting on time, while the other part of her exerts willpower toward the end of helping someone in need. Kane says that whatever she decides—whether or not to help the person who is in need—will be an act that she wills to be the outcome, because there was a part of her who wanted and indeed fought for that to be the outcome, whether she helps the person or not.

In his book *Hard Luck* (2011), Neil Levy argues that torn decisions do not afford libertarian free will. Free will is ruled out or precluded by luck, regardless of the truth of determinism or indeterminism, making him a hard incompatibilist like Pereboom or Caruso. Levy's attack on libertarian free will is rooted in the traditional failure, he says, of libertarians to offer a contrastive account of choices (2011, p. 43, 90). Consider van Inwagen's (1983) potential thief pondering whether to steal from the church's poor box. He is in a classic torn state before the decision is made. He is torn between the motive to have money, and the motive to honor a deathbed promise he made to his mother to live morally. Levy points out that libertarians fail to offer any explanation concerning why the thief decides to steal rather than not steal. It just happens. And had the decision, by chance, gone the other way, libertarians could not explain why the man refrained from stealing the money, rather than stealing it. This allows Levy to say that:

- the character we start off with is a matter of (constitutive) luck, so we are not responsible for it or the choices, acts, and consequences that follow because of our character that was "foisted" on us by genetics, the environment, and their interaction, and
- any so-called self-forming act or choice comes down to (present) luck, so we are also not responsible for it or its consequences either.

Levy calls this his "luck pincer." This was of course the regress that drove Kane and Balaguer and other proponents of libertarian free will to rely on torn decisions in the first place. Because of luck, Levy says that torn decisions fail to afford moral responsibility, because all choices come down, he believes, to constitutive luck, present luck, or both.

Levy would say that torn decisions just come down to present luck. Indeed, the Kane–Balaguer strategy of grounding libertarian free will in undetermined torn decisions is vulnerable to the criticism that it fails to overcome the argument from luck according to which, if a critical moral choice goes one way versus another due to randomness (say amplification of quantum fluctuations to neural spike timing variability), then we cannot hold people responsible for the consequences that follow from that choice. And if every choice comes down to either constitutive luck or present luck, there can be no moral responsibility, no free will, and no blame. Terrible things just happen. This entails a denial that anyone bears any moral responsibility whatsoever.

I find Levy's denial of moral responsibility to be a nihilistic view of human beings, their choices, and life in general. The notion that Hitler deserves no blame for mass murder is as nihilistic as the denial that his mental events were causal of mass murder, which would follow if Kim's exclusion argument were correct. Free will and moral responsibility vanish either if every outcome boils down to luck or if mental causation is illusory. In the next section I defend libertarian free will against the nihilistic argument that everything we decide and do just comes down to blameless luck.

2.16 Criterial Causation Can Counter the Luck Argument

The strategy of grounding libertarian free will in undetermined torn decisions is vulnerable to the criticism that it fails to overcome the argument from luck according to which, if a critical moral choice goes one way versus another due to randomness, then we cannot hold people responsible for the consequences that follow from their random choices. Note that in Kane's and Balaguer's groundings of libertarian free will in undetermined torn decisions, there is no higher governing basis for making a choice in a torn decision. Consider the case of van Inwagen's thief, in which deciding to steal and then stealing the cash just happen. Had the thief decided not to steal, then not-stealing would have just happened. Levy's point is that if things just happen—and this is essentially also the Buddhist perspective—there can be no blame.

Note that for Kane and Balaguer the important indeterminacy happens at the moment of choice and not before it. This means that people cannot bias the chance outcome toward the morally superior choice with their wills because even if they could, their decision to bias one way versus the other would itself be subject to the argument from luck.

Balaguer thinks that it is an open empirical question whether torn decisions are made in the brain in a way that is undetermined. Neural criterial causation gives his or Kane's related theory just the sort of empirical account needed to say that we are libertarian-free and offers a way out of the argument from luck. Remember, criterial causation offers a middle ground between determinism, where things cannot turn out otherwise, and utter randomness, where what happens occurs for no reason having to do with our agentic wishes. For example, if the criteria that need to be met are "he is an American, male politician" you might have thought of Donald Trump, in part, just by chance. But if I could rewind the universe to the moment when I specified those criteria, this time, you might have said "Joe Biden." Both answers fully meet the criteria that were set. The outcome was not determined, because your answer could have turned out otherwise. But it was not utterly random, because it had to be an American, male politician.

Now consider a self-forming decision like making a New Year's resolution. We decide that we need to better ourselves in some way. We might consider various possible resolutions, say, to be more honest or more kind or less greedy. And once we have chosen a good New Year's resolution, we can set about accomplishing our goal of reforming ourselves. The result of such a decision is not solely a matter of chance or luck, because any acceptable New Year's resolution would have to meet our criteria for a decision that would improve ourselves in some way.

Unlike cases of torn decisions like van Inwagen's thief or Kane's businesswoman, in which the decision to steal the money or not, or to help the person in need or not, just came down to present luck, in the case of criterial decision making, there is a higher, but nondeterminative governing basis for making a choice. Yes, that the resolution ended up being, say, "to be more honest this year" rather than "to be less greedy this year" was a matter of luck in the sense that the first proposal passed the threshold for adequate satisfaction of integrity-enhancing criteria first. But it is not an utterly random outcome, like choosing to steal the money or not, as in the thief's torn decision, or choosing to help someone in need or go to the meeting, as in Kane's businesswoman example of a torn decision. Under criterial causation the choice is not utterly random because it had to be an integrity-enhancing resolution. It is also not determined, breaking any chain of sufficient causes that might undermine moral responsibility, because a different integrity-enhancing resolution might have won out. The regress is broken by adding indeterminism. But the luck argument is broken by forcing any choice or action to meet criteria preset by the agent.

According to a criterial account, the integrity-enhancing criteria specified by the agent imply that whatever resolution ends up being chosen was willed and was not simply a matter of luck because the decision or choice had to meet the agent's criteria. Yes, there is randomness in terms of which New Year's resolution will win, but there is not randomness at the level of the basis for choosing one option over another, as in Kane's and Balaguer's undetermined torn decisions.

Kane's defense of libertarian free will depends crucially on a person having conflicting motives. His account is vulnerable to the luck argument because there is no basis, ethical or otherwise, for choosing one way or another. One set of motives is just randomly favored over the other. But free will need not be grounded in morally torn subselves vying for control of the body, the winner decided by chance for no reason whatsoever.

Criterial pre-parameterization of the grounds for a later choice need not involve moral choices like helping someone or not, or stealing or not. Most decisions we make involve imagining options that fulfill some criteria that need to be met to fulfill some aim we have or desire we have. For example, I might inherit some money and consider all the things I could do with that money. Many decisions are not either/or types of decisions, like stealing or not. They can involve mixed commitments. I might decide to allocate some percentage of the money to a savings account, investments, travel, and charity. In weighing my options, the options often do not exclude each other, and I can realize many of them, just to varying degrees. Imagination and the realities we choose to realize are not a zero-sum game; we can try to find a sweet spot that optimizes across many parameters. Let us say I decide to allocate ten percent to travel. This then opens up new options based upon criteria given by what I enjoy. I might like sunny places in the winter, and then weigh the pros and cons of a trip to Costa Rica versus Tanzania. I might even decide to do both options, in sequence, or work toward buying a winter place in a warm country, but also keep my farm in New Hampshire.

This kind of contingency is almost everywhere you look when you look at life closely. Why are you married to your spouse instead of someone else? Perhaps you turned left one day, just by chance, instead of right, and if you had turned right, you never would have even met them. On the other hand, the outcome was not utterly random because it was severely constrained. In my case, the outcome had to be a woman who met various criteria, such as being kind, attractive, funny, intelligent, and so on. There was no way I was going to marry a cloud or a tree, which might have happened, if my decision had been truly random.

How does this kind of contingent yet criterial selection of outcomes relate to the issue of free will and responsibility? Concerning type 1 libertarian free will, we are in part responsible for our actions because we set these criteria versus others that we did not set. And we set these versus others because of the kind of agent we are when we set them. We are not completely responsible, because we are not responsible for the particular way those criteria were met (say, we chose this escape route versus another), because this was a matter of chance or luck. So, we are responsible for choosing an escape route, though not fully responsible for the particularities of choosing this escape route versus others that we might have picked had it not proven adequate first. Similarly, concerning type 2 libertarian free will, we are in part responsible for our characters because we set these criteria for self-forming resolutions versus others that we did not set. And we set these versus others because of the kind of agent we are. But we are not completely responsible for our characters, because the initial characters or capacities we inherited were a matter of constitutive luck, and the particular way in which criteria we set were met (say, we chose to be more honest for our New Year's resolution, rather than less greedy) was a matter of present luck. So, we are responsible for choosing to make a New Year's resolution to improve our character, though not fully responsible for the particularities of choosing this character-forming resolution versus others that we might have picked, had it not proven adequate first.

But even if we are only in part responsible for our actions and characters, criterial causation offers both a grounding for libertarian free will and a degree of moral responsibility. In addition, criterial causation emphasizes that self-forming acts are not primarily the result of instantaneous torn decisions, like those cases discussed by Kane, Balaguer, or van Inwagen. Self-forming acts are instead the result of a long-term cybernetic or error-correcting, temporally extended process that involve our willpower and striving. We strive to fulfill a future envisioned self, which we might attain, perhaps only after years of trying, failing, and trying again.

Both the luck argument and Kane's defense against it fail because decisions are not made in an instant, as both arguments incorrectly assume. That decisions happen in a moment, when in the just prior moment they were not made, is an example of "the fallacy of causal instantaneity." Decisions are made over durations; we prepare our nervous systems, through effort and practice, to make decisions that will meet criteria that we preset in ourselves. Decisions result from closed-loop processes in the nervous system that play out over durations, with ample time for internal evaluation, deliberation, and error correction, as we try to cybernetically fulfill our set of sometimes conflicting goals. Luck is not resolved in an instant, so Levy's pincer argument does not apply. Instead, luck, like free will, is slow, and plays out as a process over durations, sometimes years in the making.

Even if we ignore the closed-loop, processive nature of decision making in biological systems such as ourselves, the view that open-loop physical events can be reduced to a succession of independent instants that lack duration is implausible. This view of reality slices it into frames of a cosmic movie. Consider one such frame, say, of a ball suspended in the air. Given only the information available in this one instant, we cannot recover properties of the ball that require two or more frames to recover, such as the direction, speed, or momentum of the ball. Considering a somewhat earlier or later instant allows us to recover such properties, but between any two such instants, assuming that time is not quantized, there exist infinitely many other instants, just as between any two real numbers there exist infinitely many other real numbers. But this is not simply an epistemological issue; it is also an ontological one. If nondurational instants were independent, as in a movie, properties that are inherently durational would not exist. Such a ball, suspended in an instant, could be going in any direction with any speed. Causation on the basis of such properties would not exist. So, even under the localistic, reductionistic, deterministic Newtonian open-loop billiard ball metaphor of classical physics that drives such intuitions, events (such as decisions), as well as their neuronal realizations, are extended in time, as processes over durations, that are not reducible to a succession of instants. To make matters worse for Newtonian thinkers, quantum theory entails that any attempt to specify properties at an instant would make the energy of the system indeterminable. Moreover, because decision making is closed-loop, any attempt to reduce decisions to an instant of decision making becomes all the more futile.

Of course, we cannot know in advance what decisions we will have to make in the future. Unexpected situations arise, like facing a homeless person in dire need, when we urgently need to make it to an important business meeting. Instead of preparing for each possible scenario, we prepare ourselves for classes of decisions. We work on our values as the cybernetic setpoints around which we assess our moral errors. We steer our behavior with reference to principles and feelings of moral error or rightness, that serve as our moral compass. These arise as we compare our actual and possible behaviors with the control theory reference signal (see Figure I.1) of our internal moral north. Even if we stumble, morally, we can subsequently minimize the error we feel, by correcting our behavior until the error signal goes to zero, just as a person who is shoved will take one step, then another and another, until they are standing upright again. We attempt to hone our virtues and rein in our propensities for vice. To attain virtue is to attain a virtuous cybernetic setpoint or reference signal that serves to guide us, not algorithmically, but cybernetically toward error minimization. There is no correct single behavior. There are in fact many ways to minimize moral error, just as there are many ways to recover from a shove by taking small steps. With practice we come to automatize our morality, our virtues, and our vices. When we decide to help the homeless person or not, the decision does not happen in a vacuum. It happens in light of the values and character we have cultivated, which is to say, the criteria for goodness that we have realized in ourselves over long durations.

Beyond the scaffolding afforded by our parents and society to the development of our brains and minds, we gradually mature to a stage where our own efforts and intentions serve to scaffold the formation of our own envisioned future self into existence. This allows us to gradually become the person we strive to become, for example, a person who simply could not commit x, even when presented with an easy opportunity to do so. Scaffolding by others yields to self-scaffolding as we mature. Self-scaffolding involves transforming ourselves from an imagined future self into a self that has incorporated, as character, that which was once only envisioned. This is the transformation of criteria as ideas into criteria as habits and internal setpoints that will govern future cybernetic decision making.

Even so, we sometimes do find ourselves torn. But it is not usually the case that chance settles the matter. Let us say that Kane's businesswoman feels obligated to meet her clients on time. She is likely to continue to feel bad about her choice, whether out of compassion for the homeless person in need, or out of regret or guilt. In fact, guilt, as we discuss in Section 4.17, is the subjective cybernetic error signal associated with having committed social errors. After her meeting, she might try to go back to find this person and offer her help. Even if our motives are conflicting, and cannot all be satisfied at a given moment, we tend to try to fulfill them all over longer durations. We go to work, then eat, then help someone in the street, then go home, kiss the kids good night, have some wine, make love, talk about our conflicted day, then go to sleep, resolving to do a better job being the person we hope to be the next day.

Just as our motives and decisions do not play out over an instant, but instead play out over durations, the characters we form are instantiated over long durations. We, ourselves, are like the ancient sandheap or sorites paradox, according to which a single grain of sand is not a heap; nor is it a heap of sand if we add just one more grain of sand, and so on. On that account, even if we end up with a million grains of sand, it cannot be a heap of sand, because no instantaneous infinitesimal increment of a single grain could have turned that which was not a heap into a heap of sand. But at some point, integrating over enough tiny changes we obviously do end up with a heap of sand. Similarly, a baby might have an innate potential to learn to speak but cannot yet speak. At what point are grains of babbling converted into a heap of language?

Likewise, we have an inborn potential to transform. With enough time and effort toward becoming a different kind of person, we can and do become a different kind of person, even if the daily changes seem infinitesimal and of no consequence, and the inevitable setbacks and lapses seem large. Over years of practice, they integrate, and we have a new character, hopefully one with greater integrity. That is, integrating over long durations of tiny changes, we can succeed at willing to become a new kind of chooser. This capacity to choose to become a new kind of chooser, which I have called meta-free will, or second-order or type 2 free will, sets us apart, I believe, from all other animals. It is a kind of freedom that is truly central to that which makes us human. A human can become well-integrated with effort and commitment to long-term goals, including goals for development of the self. This is what integrity in fact means. It means the automatization of virtuous habits of thought and action through practice. We would never talk of a cat having integrity, because a cat is primarily driven by instincts. We also have instincts but can rise above our baser drives because we are also motivated by ideals that may require restraining, harnessing, or otherwise mastering our instincts in pursuit of our, higher, noninstinctual ends.

You might say that it is constitutive good luck that we were born as humans, with a potential for type 2 free will. Or you might say this is bad luck or a curse, since it subjects us to moral blameworthiness concerning the life we fashion or fail to fashion among all the possible lives that we could have fashioned; all the more so when we judge ourselves and feel regret, remorse, or existential guilt. But we have no choice but to be burdened or blessed by this existential freedom. We cannot will this type 2 freedom away and decide to become amoral, like a tiger. Because we can imagine distal future possibilities, including distal future selves, which we can strive to make real or not, despite our basest instincts, we have no choice but to have distal free will. We thereby become moral beings and not amoral animals ruled solely by instinct.

Distal free will is rooted ultimately in the freedom of human imagination. We can be denied this freedom and choose to accept being enslaved or not. Or we can attempt to deny this freedom in ourselves and choose to live a lie. Better than unfulfilled potential, however, is fulfilling our human potential. We can embrace our freedom and set about transforming ourselves, and thereby the world, in light of our imagined futures.

A related argument against the possibility of free will might run like this. Even if we grant that high-level criteria set constraints on possible solutions, and even if it is true that any given criterial satisfaction could have turned out otherwise, we can ask where those criteria for choosing volitionally themselves came from. If they came from the outcome of prior criterial settings, we enter a *reductio ad absurdum*, in which the earliest criteria were not volitionally set, and therefore the derived appearance of free will is rooted in the earliest criteria for deciding. And these were not themselves volitionally chosen. But just because initial conditions were not volitionally set, does not mean that volition cannot come into being. Just because a seed cannot carry out photosynthesis does not entail that the plant that the seed eventually becomes cannot later carry out photosynthesis. What is genetically given is not an outcome, but the potential for a vast diversity of possible outcomes. One of these is the potential to learn to volitionally control internal and motoric operations that are not driven by the stimulus, but instead by personal reasons. A baby might initially have no volitional control over its arms or eye movements, or the allocation of its attention, but after thrashing around, trying this and then that, it gradually discovers that it can control certain mental and motoric operations and not others. By trial and error and with practice, the toddler figures out that it can choose to look at or attend to animals or houses or whatever it so chooses. Because of chunking operations, learning and automatization take place over what is so processed, as we discuss in detail in Section 4.29; the child learns that it can will to learn what it wants, for its own reasons. That is, it can take volitional control of its own nervous system's changes. At the end of this process we have an adult who has mastered domains of behavior and thought, who can will to act or not act on the basis of very complex personal reasons, such as "at dinner I will refrain from looking at my cell phone." To equate volitional eye movements made for flexible reasons or even principles with nonvolitional eye movements such as pupillary dynamics is confused. One is responsive to reasons and the other is not.

However, a skeptic might ask "how does one decide to become a new kind of chooser? Where does the vision come from and what makes you want to act on it?" If it emerges via a process that is beyond the chooser's control, they might argue that free will is illusory because we had to come up with the type of self-forming vision that we did come up with. To answer this kind of skepticism, let us return to our working definition of free will from Section 2.2:

If a mind can alter the probabilities of future events, in light of its own reasons, and if it can knowingly choose among alternatives, each of which might really happen, then we can say this mind exhibits free agency or has a free will.

This definition does not stipulate that a mind's "own reasons" have to themselves be freely chosen. Often, though not always, they are not. For example, given what tastes good to me (which is not chosen by me), I can nonetheless choose meals that I like and avoid ones that I don't like. Does this inability to change my tastes imply that I cannot choose among possibilities given my tastes? No, of course I can choose among possibilities, even if I am not utterly free to choose all grounds for my choosing. And even if I am programmed to find vomit revolting, I can override that instinct and force myself to eat it, if, for example, the alternative is that a sadistic prison guard will shoot my child if I don't. Besides, do I really want to change my tastes? I don't want to be able to choose to make things that I find disgusting now smell or taste delicious. I want to choose among dishes I find delicious. Many predilections, such as finding vomit disgusting, evolved for the very good reason that having them set just so, helped us procreate, live, and not die. They are not subject to volitional control because being able to choose to make vomit smell delicious would likely lead an animal eating it, getting sick, and then dying. Another example: I am most likely genetically and societally programmed to like women, and cannot will to want to have a cloud or a tree as a mate. Does this mean I cannot choose among women? Of course not. It just means my freedom is constrained. That free will is constrained does not entail that it is so constrained as to leave only a single option open at each decision node, as would be the case under determinism. In fact, in the absence of constrained indeterminism, we would not have criterial causation at all, but utter randomness, which is as unfree as determinism. Free will does not mean that there are no constraints on our choosing or grounds for choosing in light of our own reasons. Just because I cannot fly does not mean I cannot choose where I will go on foot. Just because I cannot choose all my reasons does not mean I cannot choose among options that each meet my reasons.

Reasons are also not monolithic, but themselves often come into conflict. I might desire meat in a first-order way because it smells and tastes good, but also desire not to eat meat, in a second-order manner, because I do not want to cause pain to conscious beings. Although first-order desires and reasons are often set in part genetically, second-order reasons typically derive not from instincts, but from more abstract considerations, such as the immorality of unnecessarily causing pain to conscious beings. If our second-order desires can initially suppress the enactment of first-order desires (say, we decide to become vegan despite finding the smell of grilled steak delicious), often, with time, our first-order desires change. For example, we may, in time, find the eating of meat disgusting, as do many vegetarians after some time. Habit formation does not only act upon motoric actions, perceptual chunking, or cognitive sequences of mental operations. It also acts upon the desires, even the first-order desires.

The first step, then, is to ask ourselves which habits we wish to form within our future selves. The next step is to train ourselves, through a practice, to automatize that habit. And that habit can even reach down into the desire structures that we mistakenly believe to be immutable, and we may find that that which we now desire becomes repulsive, or that which we now find repulsive becomes something we desire. Coming to find meat-eating repulsive is an example of the former sort, whereas coming to want to meditate or go to the gym when we initially found doing these practices onerous are examples of the latter sort. The reason for this is that habit formation is not only a matter of automatization, but also a matter becoming addicted, in a good way or a bad way. Just as habit formation can be regarded as our ally in reforming our self, if the habits that we automatize in our nervous system are good habits, addiction can be our ally, if we become addicted to practices that benefit us. We may find that meditating or going to the gym makes us feel better, look better, or live better, as forms of internal positive feedback.[5] We may find external positive feedback in the comments of others about how we have changed (become calmer, kinder, or healthier). If we attend to these internal and external positive feedback signals, we may find that we have changed; we may now want to meditate or go to the gym, whereas in the beginning we had to make ourselves do so. In becoming addicted, in a good sense, we will have restructured ourselves from a merely imagined possible self into a new kind of self that now loves doing what we once resisted.

If we understand how habit formation and addiction operate within ourselves, we can harness these abilities for our own good, and serve as our own scaffolding into a new self. Knowing how our habit and addiction systems operate, we can optimally implement our imagined self by, for example, scheduling our training regularly to occur at a consistent time of day; we can create a support system that does not allow us to put training off or give up; and we can measure our results and create for ourselves other forms of positive feedback. Once the positive habits and desires that we wanted to cultivate have been automatized within us, we can dispense with the scaffolding, and it will be as if that initial support had never been needed at all. Central, then, to the project of self-transformation, is a correct understanding of habit formation and addiction, and the best methods for automatizing good habits and desires. With this understanding, and a clear vision of what we want to realize in ourselves, the rest remains disciplined commitment to a practice, until it no longer takes volitional effort, but rather becomes part of who we are and how we live. What was once an intention becomes integrated into our structure of thinking, doing, and desiring.

Returning now to the matter of luck, a self-forming New Year's resolution is not solely a matter of luck because it would have to meet the integrity-enhancing criteria set in place by the agent. Even though this resolution might have been chosen versus many possible others, it had to be one that met those criteria, so was not utterly random, and so was not solely a matter of blind luck. On my account, the integrity-enhancing criteria specified by the agent imply that whatever resolution ends up being chosen was willed and not simply a matter of luck because the decision or choice had to meet the agent's self-forming criteria. Because agents play this criterial role in their self-forming decisions, and continually adjust such criteria in a cybernetic or feedback-based process over years of self-formation (am I in fact getting closer to the envisioned future me?), agents are in part responsible for developing negative or positive characters over years of development. Yes, there is randomness in terms of which resolution will win, but there is not randomness at the level of the basis for choosing one option over another, as in Kane's and Balaguer's undetermined torn decisions. But even if we are only in part responsible for our actions and characters, criterial causation offers both a grounding for libertarian free will of both types 1 and 2, and a degree, therefore, of moral responsibility.

A key moment of indeterminacy for "undetermined torn decisions" happens at the moment of choice. But criterial causation gives an account of a higher-order governing process that constrains the outcome of such moments, and in that way addresses present luck. Someone might say that criterial causation only gets us out of present luck but fails to get us out of constitutive luck because the nature of higher-order choosing processes are themselves constrained by an individual's constitutive luck. In response: we cannot choose our genetics or where we are born. But what genetics gives us is not a fixed outcome; genetics gives us a potential to develop in many different ways. That potential can be realized fully or somewhat or even be thwarted by others or ourselves. Part of the environment that leads to the fulfillment of our potential is our own mind, namely, our own decisions to harness our potential in order to realize it. One of those capacities that unfolds as we develop is the capacity to volitionally weigh options and select among them. There are a number of capacities that unfold like a program, that are not themselves present at birth, just as a seed cannot photosynthesize, but has in it a program that will allow the later form to realize that potential.

It is true that there are capacities that a person cannot develop because that potential was never there. For example, you cannot choose to fly because you lack wings. But there are things you can do given the potential that you have. Everything starts with a vision. After that there is implementation and willpower to see it through. For example, you might envision a thinner, stronger self in three months, and can set about harnessing your potential to get there. For example, you might go to the gym with a partner who will not let you slack off, or you might go on a keto diet (Volek et al., 2002). A mistake people make about constitutive luck is that they think it is a done deal at birth, as if you were born with a fixed ability to do x. But that is not true. We can get better at x if it lies within our potential to do so.

But does someone who is born with low potential have less free will than someone who was born with high potential in some domain? To take an extreme case, someone in a coma has less of a range for choosing among options or envisioning a new version of themselves that they can then try to realize. We are highly constrained by many factors. But that does not mean that we are utterly unfree or have only one possible future open to us. Having *limited* options does not mean we have *no* options. There are many of us who were dealt a bad hand and have nonetheless learned to play it well. For example, George Washington, Bill Clinton, and Barack Obama were all fatherless or became so as children, yet each became president. Nobody would assert that luck plays no role in life. Luck plays a huge role. However, those who use the luck argument to argue that all choices just come down to luck are wrong. There is the chance associated with the hand you are dealt (luck) and then there is how you play the hand you are dealt (discernment, wisdom, savvy, willpower, commitment to the realization of a vision).

The luck argument is based on the faulty idea that outcomes, such as deciding this versus that, are made at an instant. In fact, they play out over sometimes long durations with ample feedback and mid-course corrections. This process allows us to make our own luck. For example, we might have a vision of becoming an actor, without a clear idea how to accomplish that goal. We might start by moving to LA to get closer to where the action is. When an opportunity arises we can seize it because we have prepared ourselves for it. Having a long-term goal allows us to keep trying, despite setbacks. Let us say things don't work out in LA. We can then move to NYC, start over, and try our luck there.

In addition to the fast luck of, say, finding money on the ground, there is slow luck. Because decisions and actions do not happen in an instant, but instead play out cybernetically over durations, we can correct our errors or deviations from our path toward a goal along the way to that goal. Some of these goals can lie in the distant future. For example, we might want to become a professor, so we do things now that enhance the likelihood that such a future will come to pass years hence. We might volunteer in a lab, for example, in the hopes of increasing our chances of getting into a good graduate school. The notion of present luck is built on the assumption that decisions and actions play out over an instant. But this is not true because there is room for the idea that we make our own luck in the sense that we can walk step by step toward a distant envisioned goal. And if we stray or are dealt a setback, we can get back on track toward that goal. We create our own luck by creating situations in which the kind of opportunities that we want to arise might arise. And we have a mindset prepared to seize such opportunities as they arise. Luck is no accident. As Bruce Lee said, "To hell with circumstances, I create opportunities." Luck arises in a cultivated optimistic approach to life. It is why some people seem to be lucky again and again, and also why others seem to have repeated bad luck.

We make our own bad luck as well, by undermining opportunities that might have arisen, perhaps because of a pessimistic, bitter, or cynical attitude that becomes its own self-fulfilling prophecy. Reality is like a Rorschach inkblot: if we see a scowling or smiling face, then that is what it is for us. So much is in how we choose to regard what happens.

In addition to fast and slow luck, there is given luck, namely, the opportunities that others give us. If we have a positive attitude, others are more likely to want us to join their team or otherwise give us a chance. If others open doors for us, is it wrong for us to walk through? If others do not choose to open doors for us, it might be due to their biases or ill will against us, or it might be due to our attitude toward them, or both. It is harder to change others' attitudes than our own attitude.

Imagination and how we regard are where the action is in free will. Entertaining what might occur allows animals to consider possible courses of present action (type 1 libertarian free will), and, at least for the case of humans, entertaining allows us to consider what kinds of choosers we want to strive to become (type 2 libertarian free will). Our capacity to entertain allows us to imagine learning this language or that, and then, once a choice has been made, to actually become, with effort and practice, a new kind of nervous system that can eventually speak the chosen language. It allowed Wilbur Wright to lay in bed and imagine flying machines, then go build what he imagined, and thereby change the physical universe forever. It allows us to imagine a better self that we can then set about realizing through practice. And that future self will be able to make new kinds of choices that are not yet open to us now.

A perfect example of the power of imagination in driving the slow luck that emerges over long durations is the case of Jane Goodall. She was too poor to go to college. In her teens she worked as a secretary and then as a waitress in England in order to save up money to go to Africa to work with animals. Many tried to convince her to give up her unrealistic, foolish dream. They advised her to marry some bloke and have children, as was the norm in the late 1940s. Her mother,[6] however, helped her buy a one way ticket to Mombasa. Once in Kenya she met the great paleoanthropologist Louis Leakey, who offered her a job at the museum of natural history in Nairobi. He hired her first as a secretary, then as a field assistant while he looked for fossils, and then, finally, he asked her if she wouldn't mind observing chimpanzees in the wild. Leakey was surrounded by chest-pounding students who wanted to be the next Louis Leakey, but he was on the lookout for someone who could patiently blend in with a troupe of wild chimps, and who was not blinded by excessive academic training. Goodall said "yes"; this opportunity was the very reason she had travelled to Africa. This was the moment for which her acts of willpower and imagination had prepared her. She seized the opportunity, and the rest is history (Figure 2.2).

Negative opportunism involves taking advantage of others, but positive opportunism involves taking advantage of chances that have been intentionally cultivated into being. The poverty of the luck argument is that it misconceives of events as disjoint, happening at infinitesimal moments. But events play out over long durations, and an act of imagination, such as Goodall's plan to work in Africa, even while just a poor waitress in London, can result in the realization of that very dream, given perseverance and a willingness to seize opportunities when they come along.

Just as the kind of luck that sponsors slow free will is itself slow, bad luck can be also slow. For example, an empire like Rome's or America's can rot slowly because it has not renewed its moral core, instead descending into rackets wherein winners win by imposing losses on society as a whole. Or a person might not take care of their health for years. Then suddenly some terrible thing happens. Barbarians attack or viruses invade the body, perhaps leading to collapse. Is this event instantaneous bad luck, when a healthier body would easily have fended off the attack? No, the failure of a corrupted, bankrupt, or otherwise weakened system was a near inevitability given the years of

Figure 2.2 Here I am with Jane Goodall, one of my greatest heroes.

neglected health. That it happened to be this wind versus that wind that caused the tree to fall may be a matter of chance, but to say it was bad luck at that instant fails to recognize all the slow decay within the trunk of the tree that led to the possibility of rapid failure in the event of a strong wind.

If imagination is our greatest tool in transforming ourselves and our world, it is also our greatest weapon. The airplanes that the Wright brothers imagined and subsequently built are now used for both intended good and evil aims: they transport travelers, and they drop bombs on sleeping children. The Holocaust was imagined long before Hitler's team enacted his wicked imaginings. Luck, imagination, and indeed free will can serve evil as well as good intentions. There is therefore a moral core that precedes and shapes any choice or act. The ultimate freedom afforded by second-order libertarian free will is therefore the freedom to shape our character slowly toward an ideal. While we can try to invent our own ideal, in general, the ideal human is emphasized implicitly or explicitly in the scaffolding that society offers to children.

3
Scientific Arguments against Free Will

3.1 The Libet Experiment

In this and coming sections I review neuroscientific evidence against the claim that we have free will, and then discuss why I think this is in fact not valid evidence against free will in the human brain. There are two main bodies of evidence often taken as "proof" that we lack free will. One stems from the experiments of Benjamin Libet, and the other from the experiments of Dan Wegner. Here, I will discuss the Libet experiment and then in the next chapter I will discuss why Libet's findings really have little bearing on the issue of free will. After that I will do the same with the Wegner experiments.

In discussions of volition and will, it is useful to distinguish *distal* acts of willing, for example, willing to take part in an experiment and all that that entails, from *proximal* acts of willing, for example, willing to move one's finger during a particular trial of an experiment. Distal willing involves coming up with a plan that plays out over minutes, hours, days or even years, whereas proximal willing generally involves choosing to do this or that in the immediate future, perhaps some hundreds of milliseconds or seconds from now. Experiments in the tradition of Libet test the assumption that acts of proximal conscious willing play a causal role on each trial where a movement is made. What Libet and his followers have studied is whether the conscious experience of proximally willing to make a hand movement at a particular time plays a causal role in the sequence of events that culminate in that motor act. If in part yes, then the hand movement can be deemed a willed act. But if not, then the hand movement, at best, has only an illusory appearance of being a willed act.

Despite Libet's strong claims about the causal inefficacy of consciousness, none of his experiments tested the possible causal efficacy of distal willing, which could be causal of subsequent motor acts, even if proximal acts of willing are not. Thus, Libet's data cannot be used to support or rule out any possible role for free will in the domain of distal willing, that is, intending to perform a future action or complex series of actions. One main thesis of this book is that deliberation and imagination are where the action is in free will, not in picking between inconsequential options arbitrarily, whether they are all equivalent, like apples on a tree or pointing with the left hand versus the right, or nonequivalent, as in choosing this brand of milk over all the others at the supermarket. Libet's experiments focused on inconsequential "picking" choices, as in apples, not even "choosing" choices, as in brands of milk. His experiments had

A Neurophilosophy of Libertarian Free Will. Peter Ulric Tse, Oxford University Press. © Oxford University Press 2024.
DOI: 10.1093/oso/9780198876953.003.0004

nothing to do with the consequential choices we deliberate about when we plan for the distal future, as in deciding whom to marry.

Now that it is clear that we are only talking about proximal acts of willing, we can get into the details of Libet's main electroencephalography (EEG) experiment. EEG measures brainwaves at the scalp and the strength of electrical signals is highly attenuated after passing through the skull and skin. If you do enough averaging of trials, the noise gets averaged away, and you can get a pretty good average waveform. This average waveform is called an "event-related potential" (ERP) and requires averaging relative to some common timepoint, which is the event in question, such as the time that a hand movement begins.

Libet and colleagues (1983) reported that an ERP called the readiness potential (RP) precedes a volitional hand movement. Subjects were told to move their hand whenever they freely chose to do so. They also watched a rapidly rotating clock and were told to report the position of the clock when they first had an awareness of wanting to move. Figure 3.1 shows a simple drawing that sums up the basic results. Let us call the time of the hand movement time M. It is the point in time relative to which Libet did his event-related averaging. W is the average time at which people reported feeling a conscious urge or intent to move. Figure 3.1 shows how the beginning of the RP precedes time W by several hundred milliseconds. Because it precedes the reported time of the conscious experience of wanting or intending to move, it is presumed to reflect unconscious processing that precedes becoming conscious of wanting or intending to move, and indeed be causal of that conscious urge.

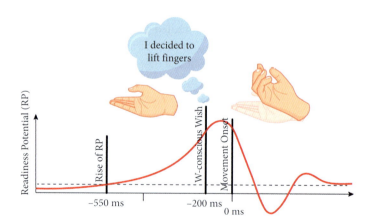

Figure 3.1 A schematic of the readiness potential. Time 0 is set at the time of hand movement detection (M). Awareness of an intention to move (time W) occurs at around minus 200 ms. The first detectable rise in the readiness potential above baseline occurs more than half a second before time 0.

Reproduced with permission from Elsevier, from Jamali, M., Golshani, M., & Jamali, Y. (2019). A proposed mechanism for mind–brain interaction using extended Bohmian quantum mechanics in Avicenna's monotheistic perspective. *Heliyon*, 5(7), e02130.

The RP is a slowly rising change in potential or "voltage" that is strongest in an area known as the supplementary motor area (SMA), thought to be involved in the planning of motoric movements (Figure 3.2). It should not be surprising that measurable brain activity precedes a volitional action, because brain activity presumably causes that action, so has to precede it. What was surprising to many people was that the beginning of the RP also precedes the conscious awareness of willing a movement to occur. Over the last few decades, the RP has proven to be one of the most controversial topics in neuroscience and philosophy due to its perceived relevance in elucidating the role of conscious will for action. Put succinctly, Libet's key innovation was to investigate the temporal relationship between the onset of the RP and time W: the reported time at which subjects' "subjective experience of 'wanting' or intending to act" began. His data revealed that on average the RP begins several hundred milliseconds before the time of conscious awareness of feeling an act of willing at time W. This called into question the ability of the conscious choice to influence the timing of the movement. Basically, if something preconscious and unconscious precedes our conscious willing

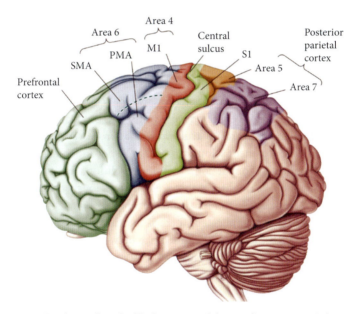

Figure 3.2 Areas implicated as the likely source of the readiness potential are Brodmann areas 4 and, especially, the medial portion of area 6. Area 4 lies in the precentral gyrus. It is also known as "M1" or "primary motor cortex." Using cortical stimulation in epilepsy patients, Wilder Penfield discovered that area 4 contains a somatotopic "map" comprised of motor output neurons governing muscular contraction on the contralateral side of the body. Area 6 is subdivided into the more medial supplementary motor area (SMA) and more lateral premotor area (PMA), each of which also contains a somatotopic "map" of the body.
Source: operativeneurosurgery.com

by several hundred milliseconds, maybe that unconscious process is the actual cause of our volitional movement. Maybe the conscious willing itself only seems to cause our motor act. Since we do not seem to have control over our unconscious processes, and cannot even report what they are, if everything is decided unconsciously, there is no room for our consciousness to be in control of our actions or, presumably, to have chosen otherwise than those unconscious processes had already decided for us.

To make this worry clear, here is an analogy. When I am about to sneeze I feel a tingle in my nose that precedes my sneezing by a fraction of a second. But just because something precedes my sneezing does not mean that it causes me to sneeze, just as a rooster crowing before dawn does not mean that the rooster's crowing causes the sun to rise. When it comes to my sneezing, there are other things going on, before I become aware of that tingling sensation in my nose, that are the actual causes of my sneezing. There are unconscious processes that detect dust or something in my airways that needs to be ejected, and these unconscious processes both trigger my later tingling conscious awareness of being about to sneeze, and they trigger the actual sneeze that happens a bit later still. In this sense, the feeling of tingling in my nose is epiphenomenal. It is not the actual cause of my sneezing. It is just a conscious feeling that precedes and accompanies sneezing, which is really started unconsciously before I become aware of that conscious feeling of nose-tingling. On this analogy, the feeling of being about to sneeze would be analogous to the feeling of willing to move my hand in the Libet paradigm. And the unconscious processes that make me sneeze would be analogous to those unconscious processes associated with the start of the RP. The analogy breaks down in that sneezes are not really volitional, whereas the hand movements that Libet investigated were volitional. But really, if Libet is right, it is questionable whether there are any truly volitional processes at all. Maybe mental causation all boils down to unconscious causes that lie beyond our conscious control. Maybe, if Libet is right, all of our actions, seemingly volitional or otherwise, might be variations on sneezing. We might feel that we can consciously control them, but in fact that feeling would be epiphenomenal and illusory.

To make matters more complicated, there is another ERP, called the lateralized readiness potential (LRP), which is the difference between voltage signals measured above the left and right motor output areas. When I move my right hand, the contralateral or left side typically shows more activity than the ipsilateral or right side, and vice versa. The LRP also precedes the time of first conscious awareness of wanting to move. That is, it begins approximately 600–800 ms before time M, namely the time of moving one's hand, and also precedes time W, which precedes time M by 200–400 ms. So, we actually have two different ERPs that begin to be detectable before we consciously become aware of intending or wanting to move.

However, it remains unclear how either the RP or the LRP is causally related to either conscious willing or movement, or even whether they are really related to them at all. Section 3.2 presents evidence that the Libet experiment cannot be used to support the claim that we have no free will and also cannot be used to support the claim that consciousness is not causal of any of our actions.

3.2 Debunking Libet's Conclusions

Acts of willing cannot be free in the radical sense of being uncaused because they are realized in brain events, which are not supernatural. However, we can ask whether consciously willing to move, or its neural realization, really does cause the bodily movements that it is subjectively felt to cause. Given that conscious willing must itself be caused by previous neural events, under a physicalist worldview, we can ask whether or not the RP is a signature of neural activity that is causal of willing and/or movement itself. This is an empirical question that the Libet experiments do not answer. My group and other groups have done further experiments using Libet-like paradigms in an effort to try to answer that question.

It is no doubt interesting that consistent patterns of brain activity can precede conscious awareness of wanting to move. But, in one sense, this just had to be the case, since all brain events have to be caused by, though not necessarily deterministically caused by, preceding brain events. Libet made the very strong claim that preceding unconscious computations cause all human actions. He did this on the basis of an unsurprising finding, namely, that conscious willing is preceded by brain activity in just one tiny domain of human action, that is, meaningless, repetitive, and inconsequential hand movements. He generalized from this narrow case to the general claim that the conscious feeling of willing is not the cause of any of our actions in any domain of human action or decision making. That is a pretty foolhardy and I think completely unfounded—even reckless over-generalization. Just because something applies to repetitive and inconsequential hand movements does not mean that consciousness plays no role in the outcomes that follow our conscious deliberations concerning matters of consequence, such as whom to marry or where to go to college.

Even if the RP or the LRP begins before our earliest conscious awareness of wanting to move, the brain activity that gives rise to these ERPs may have no direct relationship with the conscious feeling of willing at all. Libet's finding simply shows that the average of these brain potentials begins before the average time of becoming aware of wanting to move. There is no evidence that the brain processes that precede the feeling of willing cause either the conscious feeling of willing, or even cause the motor act. They might just be random brain events that lead later brain events to tip one way or another. Or there might be nonrandom biases in us that can be picked up by EEG that are not the direct cause of a subsequent event.

To make this point more clearly, let us consider a more recent experiment (Soon et al., 2008) in the tradition of the Libet experiment that seems even more dire for free will. In an fMRI experiment by John-Dylan Haynes and colleagues (2008), scientists were able to decode from brain data in frontal and parietal regions whether a subject would decide to move to the right or to the left up to ten seconds before they actually moved. Their ability to predict was above chance (50%) performance, but was only barely so, at about 60% in the seconds before the decision. It is unlikely that a brain state ten seconds before an arbitrary, meaningless decision, such as picking left or right, already computes that decision. Instead, an earlier brain state might simply bias that later decision.

There are many cases where pre-existing biases affect later outcomes without ruling out choice. For example, I know you are human, so I know that you have a bias to sleep at night. In fact, for most of you, I can predict with above 90% accuracy that you will be asleep tonight at 3:24 a.m. In fact, I can predict well above chance that exactly ten years from now, you will be asleep at 3:24 a.m. Does this mean your consciousness plays no role in your actions or that you lack the ability to choose? No, it means you have pre-existing (perhaps unconscious) biases that bias your later decisions, such as when to go to bed, or whether to choose left or right, or even whom to marry.

Let us look even more closely at the Libet paradigm to find other problems with it. One problem is that the timing of the beginning of the RP is not correlated with the later timing of feeling the urge or intent to move. Following the observation of John Stuart Mill (1843) that one characteristic of causal relations is "covariation of causes and effects," Patrick Haggard and Martin Eimer, two of my neuroscience colleagues, argued that the presence of a temporal covariation between the timing of the onset of the RP or the LRP and the timing of the feeling of consciously willing to move, namely, time W, would be at least consistent with a causal relationship, while a lack of temporal covariation would rule out the possibility of one or both of these brain potentials being the cause of the conscious awareness of commanding or intending to move.

In 1999, Haggard and Eimer reported that the timing of the start of the RP was not correlated with the time of the conscious feeling or urge to move, time W, but that the timing of the beginning of the LRP was correlated with the conscious urge to move. In their words, "this finding rules out the RP as the unconscious cause of the conscious state upon which W judgment depends, but it is consistent with LRP having that role."

My group (Schlegel et al., 2013) carried out an exact replication of their study with many more subjects, and we found neither a temporal correlation between the onset of the RP and the moment of conscious willing, time W, replicating Haggard and Eimer, nor a temporal relationship between the onset of the LRP and the timing of conscious willing. Thus, following the same logic, we concluded that neither the RP nor the LRP is likely to be an "unconscious cause of the conscious state upon which W judgment depends." Yes, conscious willing is preceded by brain activity, but the brain activity that gives rise to these ERPs does not causally drive conscious feelings of willing.

But does it cause the motor act? Another assumption underlying Libet's conclusions is that there is a causal connection between the RP or LRP and impending motoric actions. If the RP or LRP is not causally related to movement production or execution, then findings about them could not show that conscious willing does not play a role in producing movements. To that end, my colleagues and I carried out various versions of the Libet experiment where people had to make voluntary choices without making a motor act (Alexander et al., 2016). The results of our experiments suggest that the RP does not reflect uniquely motor-related processes. Our data are consistent with other possible explanations for the RP such as the buildup of anticipation or perhaps even spontaneous random fluctuations.

Schurger and colleagues (2012) published an account of the RP, according to which it is essentially an average of random activity that crosses a threshold just prior to movement, and it is the random crossing of this threshold that triggers the movement. Their study suggests that the RP is effectively an artifact of a random process that drifts to a threshold; when we average backward in time only among cases where the threshold was randomly crossed, it looks as if it is a nonrandom process that moves toward that threshold. If their account is correct, and finger movements in Libet-like scenarios are generated automatically upon the crossing of such a threshold, then neither our experiments nor those of Libet accurately test for free will because there would be in fact little in the way of conscious willing occurring on each trial. Furthermore, Schurger and colleagues suggest that their model can explain why a feeling of willing is consistently reported just prior to the movement. According to their model, the crossing of the threshold represents a "neural commitment to move now" and it is this event that subjects report as the feeling of willing to move at time W. Beginning at that point in time, the typical process of motor preparation and execution unfolds, accounting for the ~150-ms delay between W and the movement. In this framework, the timing of the movement is not determined until the threshold is crossed. I think future work is needed to test the Schurger et al., hypothesis more directly, but it would certainly be damning of the Libet paradigm if it turns out to be correct.

3.3 Hypnosis versus Libet

The gold standard for assessing causal relations requires manipulation of one variable while measuring changes in another variable. The ideal procedure for determining causation would allow comparison between RPs for spontaneously timed movements that were consciously intended and those that were not. Hypnosis may provide a possible mechanism by which movements can be elicited outside of reportable awareness or intention. Thus, in one experiment, my colleagues and I used hypnosis to compare RPs preceding hypnotically induced and volitionally induced movements (Schlegel et al., 2015). This involved two stages: the hypnotic induction and what is called the "post-hypnotic suggestion." Hypnotic induction is the process of inducing a trance-like state via guided imagery. A post-hypnotic suggestion is an instruction given to a hypnotized person that is to be followed after waking from the hypnotic state. We began by finding highly hypnotizable subjects. We then prepared each subject for EEG. Then we carried out a first hypnotic induction where we implanted a post-hypnotic suggestion, followed by a first task phase, then a second hypnotic induction to remove the post-hypnotic suggestion, again followed by a second task phase. The task was to press a ball while watching a movie. When subjects were conscious but acting on the basis of a post-hypnotic suggestion, they pressed the ball in their hand when a visual signal was present on the screen that they had been commanded, during the hypnosis induction phase, to obey. Importantly, they were not consciously aware of why they were pressing the ball. From their conscious point of view, pressing just happened. We gave them a cover story, saying that tests in the equipment might lead their arm muscles to contract, so that they would not suspect anything. Without getting into all the details, we found that RPs and LRPs look indistinguishable, whether or not subjects are conscious of having caused a motor act. These results suggest that the RP and LRP happen whether or not there is a conscious feeling of willing.

Libet inferred from his data that the neural processes that generate the RP cause the subsequent conscious proximal will, making it only illusorily causal of the subsequent motor act. Given the results of our own and others' recent experiments, I conclude that neither the RP nor the LRP arise from neural processes causal of conscious willing. Also, the RP does not reflect uniquely motor-related processing, while the LRP reflects a motor command sent from motor cortex to the hand. Since both the RP and LRP occur even when subjects, operating under a post-hypnotic suggestion, make a motor act, without even being conscious of having commanded that act, it seems that the RP and LRP are simply unrelated to conscious intentions to move at all. Moreover, the RP does not reflect the presence of an unconscious decision to move, since it occurs in the absence of movement, and is not time-locked to movement. It would appear to reflect a more remote process that is neither necessary nor sufficient to cause movement. One hypothesis is that the RP reflects one or more of a number of other general processes, such as anticipation or preparation, that accompany actions in the Libet paradigm but are not explicitly measured. Or perhaps, as Schurger and colleagues argue, the RP is an artifact of averaging noise relative to time W.

Given results like these, I think it is safe to say that Libet vastly overreached in his claims about free will, and that his experimental paradigm and results do not pose a threat to free will. To his credit, he did acknowledge that there might be other scenarios where conscious willing might be causal of movement. But his findings are only about a tiny class of arbitrary, meaningless actions that test proximal willing. They should not be used to draw general conclusions about all actions or about distal free will. If distal willing and imaginative deliberation are where the action is in free will, then future experiments should go beyond the Libet tradition to test whether distal intentions and willing play a causal role in subsequent action.

3.4 Libet's Confusion about Causation in the Brain

Whereas most philosophers worry about questions like whether or not free will is compatible with determinism, the neuroscientific attack on free will has emerged from a very different angle, namely, the claim that consciousness is epiphenomenal. Most people would argue that we do not exercise volitional control over our unconscious processing in any direct way, since we have no conscious access to unconscious operations. But if consciousness is not causal of our actions, presumably our actions are caused unconsciously. On that account, we are like puppets controlled by processing of which we are unaware.

If it were true that consciousness played no role in our actions—for example, if we did not go to the dentist because our tooth hurt, but instead because of unconscious processes where pain is not felt—then it would be fair, I think, to say that there is no free will. This is because consciousness is the domain of volitional operations.

In order to have free will we must have options to consider. Because we cannot objectively observe futures that have not yet happened, we are forced to subjectively "observe" possible futures that we internally "hallucinate" in the internal virtual reality of imagination. As mentioned earlier in the book, consciousness has a dual role. In one case, consciousness of the world and our bodies in that world is just the domain of highly precompiled representations (qualia) of what is intrinsically true about the world and our bodies in it, including teleological drivers or drives, such as hunger and thirst. This is the generally veridical hallucination of perceptual consciousness or experience. And in its second role, consciousness is our internal virtual reality, or imagination, where we daydream and play things out; this is true whether these are events that happened in the past, might happen in the future, or are purely imaginary, meaning that they could never really happen. For example, I can imagine what it is like to be a dog or to fly around the surface of Mars. Consciousness, in either its perceptual or imaginary role, is closely related to the concept of volition because volitional attention, as the key executive volitional operator, is the operator that operates over the operands or representations that we regard to be conscious. Without subjective experience, we would be left trying to attend to things we do not experience, which we cannot do, since to attend just is to select some subset of experience so that we then experience it more deeply and coherently. An animal lacking consciousness would be unable to volitionally attend or choose.

Thus, three processes are inseparable: consciousness, endogenous attention, and volition or will. If the unconscious is the domain of volitional unattendables, then consciousness is the domain of volitional attendables. Even in a dream or daydream, during which we seem to be conscious of nonvolitionally generated content, we feel that we are intensely attending to that content.

Often we feel that there is a "self" or executive that controls the volitional attentional operator. We feel invested in the causal efficacy of our consciousness because it is where volition, attention, and the self, as that which controls volitional attention, carry out their operations. If consciousness were epiphenomenal, then there would be no causal volitional operations, and therefore no self that could be possessed of free will. But a controlling operation can happen in the absence of a controller. There can be freedom of the will without a self or agent. But there cannot be such freedom without conscious experience because operations require operands to operate on. Without consciousness, we would be left with nonvolitional operations operating on unconscious operands. We would be left with reflex and habits but would lack the flexibility to weigh options in light of dynamically changing reasons, some of which are cognitive, such as "I have to find my children now because we have a doctor's appointment," while others are emotional and rooted in conscious desires, such as feeling hungry. Without consciously experienced drivers of action and planning, whether desires, emotions, or pressing needs, we would not feel them and would have no reason to weigh options for optimally fulfilling their demands.

Volitional operations take place over the experienced format so animals can experience their consequences virtually, and thereby know what it would be like to do them. Consciousness evolved for a purpose, so animals could plan, weigh options, and try out possible actions internally before executing one of those actions externally. As Karl Popper so beautifully phrased it, consciousness evolved so that our hypotheses could die in our stead. If the reflexes, habits, schemas, and scripts that so efficiently and unconsciously execute most of the body's decisions were adequate to solve all our problems and make optimizing decisions, consciousness would not have been needed. But because we are confronted with an open future that is itself not in the present stimulus, the body needs to make those invisible possibilities present, so it can respond to these as virtually present stimuli.

But the making of the invisible "visible" does not only concern the future. In trace conditioning it concerns maintaining the past, namely, a representation of the conditioned stimulus (CS), say an odor or image, after it has disappeared from the sensory input. If this is maintained without interruption until the unconditioned stimulus (US) appears, say, a food reward, then associative learning takes place between that trace and the reward. Trace conditioning is then similar to delay conditioning, except that in the former the trace of the CS and US overlap in time, whereas in the latter the CS and US overlap in time in the input. The existence of trace conditioning then is strong evidence for internal representations maintained in some form of working memory that can get flushed by distraction, which is in turn potential evidence for a capacity, such as attention, that can get distracted. In mammals, trace, but not delay, conditioning appears to require neural activity in prefrontal cortex as well as NMDA receptor functionality (Gilmartin and Helmstetter, 2010) there and in the hippocampus (Czerniawski et al., 2012). Remarkably, many invertebrates exhibit trace conditioning as well (Dylla et al., 2013), and this may also be dependent on NMDA channel function. To the extent that trace conditioning reflects active maintenance of internal representations, is it evidence for not just working memory, but also attention and consciousness?

Libet and his ilk have argued that the very specific conscious feeling of proximal willing cannot be causal. However, if it is not causal of the actions that we feel it to be causal of, so the argument goes, then something else must be causal of our actions. According to Libet and his like-minded colleagues, what is actually causal of our actions is unconscious activity that precedes the conscious feeling of willing. This unconscious activity is taken to both cause the subsequent conscious feeling of willing, and to cause the motor act that follows a couple of hundred milliseconds after the feeling of conscious willing. Then some scientists follow Libet in making the radical generalization from the conclusion that the conscious feeling of proximal willing is not causal of our actions to the conclusion that nothing that is consciously experienced is causal of any of our later actions. I previously provided reasons to doubt that the unconscious processing associated with the RP or the LRP is causal of either the conscious feeling of willing, or of the motor act. And I also gave reasons to doubt the validity of the generalization from the presumed causal inefficacy of feeling of willing to the epiphenomenalism of all of consciousness.

Even if I am wrong about this, let me point out that Libet's claims about causation are philosophically confused. Just because unconscious processing precedes the conscious feeling of willing does not mean that the conscious feeling of willing cannot also be causal of subsequent events. Let me give a concrete example here to drive this point home. Let us take the example of baseball. A pitcher pitches a ball over the home plate and then a batter hits the ball out of the park, and it is a home run. The fact that the pitcher pitched a ball over the home plate is certainly one cause of the resulting homerun. We know this has to be true, because if the pitcher had not pitched the ball, there would never have been a home run following from that pitch. However, the later event of the baseball batter hitting the ball in just the right way is *also* a cause of there being a home run. We know this too, because had the batter not hit the ball in just the right way, there would also not have been a home run. The fact that the pitching of the ball preceded the hitting of the ball does not mean that the pitching of the ball was the sole cause of the home run. Why? Because the hitting of the ball was also a cause of the home run. The mistake that Libet is making in his logic is to say that the fact that there was preceding unconscious neural activity (which is analogous to the pitch) implies that it is the sole cause of the later motor act (which is analogous to the home run). But this is a pretty basic logical mistake. Even if it turned out that the neural basis of whatever is measured by the RP was *necessary* for the motor act to occur, it does not mean that it was *sufficient* for the motor act to occur. If that unconscious processing were sufficient, then the motor act would have happened even if there had not been an intervening feeling of conscious willing. Nobody would say that a pitch alone is sufficient for a home run. So why do Libet and his intellectual followers assume that preceding unconscious neural activity is sufficient for the motor act? Libet's data offer no support for this claim. Therefore, there is room for the conscious feeling of willing to also be causal of subsequent events, either of the motor act or of later brain events. And assuming physicalism, the conscious feeling of willing only has to be realized in brain events that were themselves caused by prior brain events, some of which may not have been conscious. And those brain events had to be caused by prior brain events, even if nondeterministically. And so on and so on, back through time, just as the pitcher pitching the ball had to be preceded by the pitcher going to the park, and getting up in the morning, and being born, and so on and so on, back into the distant past. So Libet's claim to have proven consciousness in general to be epiphenomenal on the basis of the special case of conscious feelings of proximal willing being epiphenomenal, is not only a radical over-generalization from a special instance of consciousness to all of consciousness, it is also built on a mistaken notion of causation as sufficient, when really we should be basing our notions of causation on what is *necessary* here, not *sufficient*. To repeat, we would never say that the pitching of the ball is sufficient for a home run. So why should we say that preceding unconscious activity is sufficient for the motor act? Instead, the pitch was necessary for the home run, and the subsequent correct hit was also necessary for the home run. Similarly, preceding unconscious neural activity may be necessary for the motor act, and a conscious feeling of willing may also be necessary for that act.

To date, no experiments to my knowledge have shown that the unconscious neural activity measured by the RP is necessary for action. In fact, it appears not to be necessary since there are cases where an action happens in the absence of the build-up of a RP. In particular, arbitrary decisions appear to be preceded by a RP, whereas the more important class of decisions that follow deliberation are not preceded by a RP (Maoz et al., 2019). And my group has shown that the RP is not sufficient for motor acts, because we have shown that a RP can occur in the absence of a motor act (Alexander et al., 2016). The RP is neither necessary nor sufficient for willed acts, and when it starts it is correlated with neither the timing of W nor of M. Given these findings, it is safe to conclude that the RP, and indeed Libet's whole body of evidence, is simply irrelevant to the question of free will.

No work to date has shown that the conscious feeling of willing to move is necessary for a motor act. Indeed, my group has shown that it is not necessary, because in the case of hypnosis people make a motor movement without the associated conscious feeling of willing it to happen (Schlegel et al., 2015). In any case, the deep question is not whether conscious feelings of willing are necessary for actions that we deem to be volitional, but whether conscious feelings of willing are sufficient to cause bodily actions in a normal nervous system. Is proximal conscious willing sufficient for nonreflexive, uncued actions? We know that the human brain supports multiple neural pathways that can lead to action. Thus, it may not be very surprising if actions, even complex actions, can occur without immediate conscious intervention. To my knowledge no study has provided evidence either that proximal conscious will can be sufficient or that it is not typically sufficient to cause movement. Thus, the central and most pressing question on which the debates over Libet's studies have focused—the causal sufficiency of proximal conscious will—remains untested and unanswered.

Even if it turns out that conscious willing is not sufficient for some motor acts, and even if consciousness is not necessary for many classes of motor acts, such as reflexes, it would seem, on the face of it, that some conscious states are necessary for certain kinds of motor acts. When you describe the contents of your conscious experience right now, you might say, my nose itches, and I am feeling a bit hungry. It would seem that your subsequent motor acts of talking about what you are experiencing causally depend on what you happen to be experiencing. To try to cut conscious experience out of the causal picture here seems fundamentally misguided. Also, consciousness might play a role in setting up global distal plans of action, like needing to go to the supermarket to buy spinach, even if many of the component proximal intentions and proximal actions that go into the completion of this distal intention or plan, such as pressing the accelerator, are so automatized that they are entirely governed by unconscious processing.

Finally, Libet's conception of causation is linear and solely feed-forward, in which unconscious processing precedes and causes conscious processing, while conscious processing does not cause or precede unconscious processing. But we know that conscious processing can invoke unconscious processing. For example, I might be deliberating about a possible vacation in Mongolia, whereupon I wonder what the name of the capital of Mongolia is. I then experience the strange conscious feeling associated with having the name on the tip of my tongue. I knit my brow and try hard to recall the name, to no avail. Later, while taking a shower, the name "Ulaan Bataar" pops into my consciousness and I say "Of course, I knew that!" There are countless other examples of conscious processing invoking subsequent unconscious processing, such as this memory search, because consciousness and unconsciousness are in a tight functional cybernetic loop in the service of goal-directed problem solving.

3.5 Wegner's Theory of Apparent Mental Causation

Hume pointed out that we do not see causation because causation is invisible. Causation is an inference and a perceptual construction, based on assumptions about how successions of events are linked together in space and time. This point applies equally well to the kind of causation we attribute to our own actions. Wegner pointed out that we usually assume that our conscious feeling of willing or intending something to come to pass is the cause of that thing coming to pass, if our consciously willing that event to happen precedes its happening, and no other obvious alternative explanations lie in sight. However, in this book, we have discussed the idea that the rooster's crowing does not cause the sun to rise even though it precedes it, because both are actually driven by a hidden variable; the rotation of the earth causes dawn, which causes the rooster to crow, and the rotation of the earth also leads to the later apparent rising of the sun above the horizon.

Wegner argues that mental causation is also like this. Consciously willing event X to happen may appear to cause X to happen, but it is only apparent mental causation; according to Wegner, what is really going on is that a hidden variable (in this case, preceding unconscious computations) cause both the conscious experience of willing an action, and then also cause the later occurrence of that action. But, like Libet, he concludes that the conscious feeling of willing does not cause our actions (Figure 3.3).

The majority of Wegner's evidence for his theory of apparent mental causation comes from studies where people subjectively experience the feeling that they were the cause of an event when in fact they were not. One example involves the game "I Spy." In this study (Wegner and Wheatley, 1999), two subjects jointly moved a shared cursor around various images of objects. One of these subjects was actually an accomplice of the experimenters. There were two kinds of trials. One where the accomplice let the subject put the cursor where she wanted to, and another where the accomplice made sure to put the cursor on an object dictated by the experimenters. In addition,

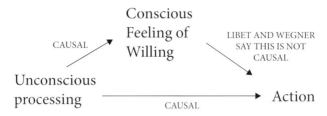

Figure 3.3 The Wegner experiments, as well as the Libet experiments, presume to show that our conscious feeling of willing is only illusorily causal of our actions. In fact, they argue, unconscious processes cause both our feeling of willing and our actions; consciousness plays no role.

subjects heard words as they did this task. Once the cursor stopped, the participants had to rate how in control they felt of the placement of the cursor, from "I allowed the stop to happen," meaning, I was not in control of its placement, all the way to "I intended to stop on this object," meaning, I was in full control of its placement. Their key finding was that if subjects heard, within a few seconds, the word corresponding to the object where the cursor would subsequently land, in cases where the accomplice was in fact in full control of its final placement, subjects nonetheless had the illusory feeling of willing that they were at least somewhat in control of its final placement.

Subjects were asked whether they believed that they in part caused an action, which they did not cause at all, and if they were primed by the name of the selected object, they said yes, they were in partial control of its placement. Wegner says this happens because the word made them think of that object prior to the cursor landing on it, so they felt that that thought led them to then place the cursor there. This then counts as an illusion of will. One believes one caused something when one in fact did not. But just as the existence of visual illusions does not prove that all vision is an illusion, the existence of various illusions of willing does not prove that all willing is an illusion. In particular, Wegner's data suggest that people can have mistaken beliefs about their wills. But a belief about one's will is not the same as that which wills or intends to act. A belief about X is not X. An incorrect belief about one's causal powers does not mean that one lacks causal powers. Just because I mistakenly believe that I can throw a ball all the way to the Moon does not imply that I cannot throw a ball at all. People might have an efficacious will, where their intentions affect future events, even when they make incorrect attributions about their will, for example, believing that they caused something when they did not.

3.6 Is the Feeling of Agency Retrodictive?

It takes time to construct our conscious experience of the world. In part, this is because there must be a preconscious buffer that compares events over some duration, in order to then infer what must have happened in the world to have generated that sequence of sensory events. For example, in the case of apparent motion between a spot followed by a displaced spot, it cannot be the case that motion was inferred starting from the first spot at time t1 at position p1, because the spot at later time t2 and shifted position p2 might never have occurred. It must therefore be the case that motion was only inferred to start at t1 and p1 after the appearance of the spot at t2 and p2, even if t2 is 200 ms after t1. If retinal activation occurs at time zero, conscious experience that is constructed in part on the basis of that activation may occur 300–400 ms after time zero (Sun et al., 2017).

This slowness of consciousness has been used as an argument that free will must be an illusion, because many brain decisions are made faster than the completion of consciousness. If the conscious feeling of having caused an action were causal of that action, and if actions are initiated before consciousness could have played a role, because they are initiated before 300 ms post retinal activation, many have argued that the feeling of agency must not be the actual cause of that action. For example, some have pointed out that a fast serve in tennis arrives so quickly that the receiver has to respond to the ball before the conscious experience of the ball could have occurred (Gray, 2004; McCrone, 1999). Indeed, it is likely that unconscious parietal "zombie agents" (Koch, 2004) respond to the ball, and that the subjective experience of having seen the ball and then hit it, is a retrodictive experience that was not the immediate cause of having returned the serve. Similarly, others (Velmans, 1991, 2000) have pointed out that this is generally the case for all sensory systems; the construction of consciousness is a process that takes too long for a slowly constructed conscious feeling (of having been the cause of a response to sensory input) to have been the actual cause of that response. For example, evoked potentials corresponding to conscious recognition of the meaning of a word, measured using electroencephalography, occur as late as 400 ms after activation at the cochlea, whereas semantic processing and initiation of responses can occur sooner than this (Van Petten et al., 1999). Dennett (1991) suggested that perception is constructed and revised over hundreds of milliseconds before a final commitment is made to what most likely happened in the world to lead to that sequence of sensory inputs. He likened this to an Orwellian rewriting of history. Episodic memory then remembers the final version of what happened as personal history, along with an indication that the actions that led to that sequence of sensory events were self-caused.

Likewise, Wegner's studies, like Libet's, are about the causal efficacy of the conscious feeling of having caused something. But why should the feeling of having caused something be necessary for having caused it? Perhaps the feeling of having caused something is not about what one will do, but about what one just did. That is, there may be an ongoing analysis of what one has caused that is not causal of what one will do, but is instead a description, rather like a narrative, about causation and authorship in the immediate past.

In this regard, we should consider the "corollary discharge" theory of Hugo von Helmholtz. The idea was framed initially in the context of eye movements. Helmholtz wondered how the brain was able to distinguish self-generated and therefore spurious motion, generated across the retina because of eye movements, from real motion of objects in the world. He had the idea that when we plan to make an eye movement there is a prediction of the motion that will occur across the retina; then, after we make the eye movement, the actual motion signal that occurred across the retina is compared to the predicted motion signal. If the predicted motion matches the motion that actually happened, then the visual system concludes that it itself is responsible for the motion and does not interpret the retinal motion signal as having arisen from moving objects in the world. It instead attributes the source of this motion to itself. In this case, no conscious experience of motion in the world is generated by the visual system. This is why we don't see the world move each time we move our eyes. In contrast, if there is a mismatch between the predicted and actual motion signals, then a percept of motion is generated under the assumption that the motion must have arisen in the world, rather than having been self-generated. Many scientists have argued that this basic neural circuit is applied in many ways in order to distinguish that which is self-generated from that which is not.

Another example would be reaching. When I reach for something, I generate a prediction of how this will feel when I execute the reach. Then I in fact execute the reach. If what I expect to happen matches what in fact happens, then my brain concludes "I just did that." But if there is a mismatch—say the wind blows hard and my expected reach is different from my planned reach—I feel that "I did not do that." I might then look for causal explanations about why my planned reach went astray, and I might attribute this to the wind blowing. In fact, some researchers think that it is this kind of neural computation that might go awry in some aspects of schizophrenia, where people have a mismatch between a planned thought and the thought that happens, then say to themselves "I did not think that" even though they in fact did think it. This feeling of not being the cause of one's own thoughts leads them to then confabulate who or what might have put the thought into their heads.

The feeling of being the cause of an action might not be about the future at all. It often appears to be about the immediate past, at least in the domains where a corollary discharge circuit is responsible for the generation of that feeling. The feeling of conscious willing might itself be at times retrospective or retrodictive. Perhaps this is the kind of subjective feeling that Wegner's or Libet's work is examining. If that is so, nobody would expect a feeling of authorship of events that already happened in the past to be causal of those events, because it is a feeling regarding past actions. An effect does not cause its causes, even if that effect is a feeling of having caused what just happened. It is a feeling of "I did that" instead of being a feeling of "I will do that."

Another example of a retrodictive assessment of what just happened occurs in the cases of Michael Gazzaniga's "interpreter." Gazzaniga (2000) carried out experiments on split-brain patients. He would show one picture in the left visual hemifield, which was only seen by the nonverbal right hemisphere and would show another picture in the right visual hemifield, which was only seen by the verbal left hemisphere. For example, he might show a chicken to the left hemisphere, and the subject would say "chicken." Or he might show a picture of a telephone to the right hemisphere. Because the right hemisphere cannot typically talk, it could not say what it had seen. However, with the left hand, it could point to what it had seen. Interesting cases occurred when the left hemisphere was shown one thing and the right hemisphere a different thing. In one example, the right hemisphere was shown a naked person, while the left hemisphere was shown a chicken. The image of the naked person amused the right hemisphere and the split-brain patient laughed. But when asked why he was laughing, the verbal left hemisphere, which had only seen a chicken, made up a cover story about what just happened. The left hemisphere essentially confabulated a story and said, "that was a funny chicken." Gazzaniga thinks that a confabulating interpreter exists in the left hemisphere and is continually concocting a causal narrative about our body's own actions, in order to try to make sense of them under the assumption that there is a unified self. This may in fact be the case and is another kind of retrodictive evaluation of what one just did. It is not prospective, namely, about the future, but is retrodictive, about the past. Even though this is a different mechanism than the corollary discharge mechanism discussed earlier, it is also retrodictive. If all that existed in our brains were retrodictive assessments that led to the conscious feeling of "I just did that" or "I just caused that" then there would not be any reason to think that consciousness plays a role in shaping future events.

But just because some feelings of being the cause of an action cannot be causal of that action does not mean that consciousness in general can never be causal of subsequent actions. It also does not rule out that there is another role for consciousness, which is not retrodictive, having nothing to do with the feeling "I just did that." There is a prospective role for consciousness, where events played out in our deliberative imaginations, for example, lead us to then carry out the tasks that we imagined doing in the future. For example, imagining what to make for dinner may lead us to the realization that we do not have the spinach that we need to make the spinach lasagna we intend to make. We then go get our car keys so that we can drive to the supermarket to buy the ingredients we need. Going to the store to buy spinach is unlikely to happen in the absence of the realization that we need spinach, and that realization arises from deliberations that take place in our conscious imagination.

In sum, just because some kinds of conscious experiences are about what one just did does not mean that all conscious experiences are retrodictive. Some conscious experiences, such as those involved in deliberation about what one will later do, may play a causal role in the outcomes considered during one's deliberations. In addition, conscious intentions can reach down into the preconscious buffer's processing, and alter the outcomes of that processing to align with our intentions (Sun et al., 2017). And finally, conscious deliberations can result in intentions and plans that lead to changes in neurally realized criteria for responses to future bottom-up input. Therefore, while some feelings of agency might be retrodictive of causal control, other conscious processes can lead to prospective changes in later neural responses.

4
The Neuroscience of Free Will

4.1 Why Did Free Will Evolve?

What were the earliest humble beginnings of free will? Why would a capacity for endogenous decision making and self-initiated action have evolved in the first place, perhaps long before the evolution of conscious imagination or even consciousness itself?

Volition is the capacity of an animal to act as an agent to fulfill its own ends, driven by its own reasons, to make decisions independently of external inputs. In humans, this capacity is highly advanced, involving complex processing that allows us to imagine and plan in our own internal virtual realities, or imaginations, before ever executing any real actions in the world. Considering the pros and cons of various possible actions before acting results in a better chance of success upon acting. But most things in life and in evolution have simple beginnings, and it is unlikely that our very distant ancestors could weigh options in light of elaborate world models in a complex imagination such as ours. Nonetheless they might have been able to initiate actions in the absence of any external impetus on the basis of internal drives or other endogenous reasons that were their own.

Even in very simple organisms, say a leech or even a paramecium, it is important not to be predictable. Any animal that is highly predictable would make easy prey, because a predator could just wait for it at the place that it was predictably going. So, even in the absence of a capacity to plan, any animal that moves will likely evolve mechanisms to act and react in ways that predators cannot foresee. One ancient example is the chemotactic behavior of certain bacteria that have a flagellum. If the flagellum is rotated one way, the bacterium moves forward, but if rotated the other way, it tumbles, orienting it in a random new direction (Berg, 1983; Sidortsov et al., 2017). If the concentration of a chemical attractant is increasing, tumbles are suppressed, causing it to swim along the gradient to the source. However, if a repellent is present, tumbling increases until a direction is randomly found along which the gradient decreases (King et al., 2008).

Once animals became metazoans, which were initially interlocked colonies of single-celled choanoflagellates (Domenici et al., 2008), they lost that kind of "run or tumble" mobility and had to invent new ways of collectively moving around. These cell collectives had to also evolve ways to move unpredictably, particularly when hunted by a predator. Both predators and prey evolved ways of predicting each other's next moves in an arms race among their perceptual, planning and motor systems.

One result of this arms race was that animals became unpredictable, driven by their own invisible plans and drives.

Even in the likely absence of complex conscious evaluation of options, many animals, such as cockroaches, have evolved escape responses that involve a form of constrained randomness. When something disturbs them, they run at a few set angles away from that thing, but which angle is selected appears to be random. This makes it very hard for a predator to predict where a cockroach will be in the next moment, making them hard to catch. How might such randomness of behavior be realized in the insect brain?

Those who study turning behavior in flies (Brembs, 2011) suggest that their brains operate in a domain called "criticality." In this domain of near chaos, a tiny difference in initial conditions can be amplified to radically different outcomes, like deciding to turn this way versus that. This is one example of a nonlinear process, where outcomes in neural processing can come to differ radically despite apparently identical inputs. In a system operating at criticality, whether the insect brain or our own, what is effectively noise in the system can lead it to end up in very different outcome states, even when starting conditions and inputs are identical. One question we return to later is what possible sources of neural noise might be and how random fluctuations might be amplified from a microscopic domain of quantum domain chance to the macroscopic domain of neural spike timing variability, and ultimately to variability in behavior.

Internally generated variability is not only important for being unpredictable. It is also important so that animals can learn. Animals try this and then try that, and the feedback that they get from the environment or from their social peers serves to reward or punish certain of these behaviors. Well-understood mechanisms reinforce those behaviors that are rewarding and down-regulate those that are not rewarding or even punishing.

But is the variability in animal behavior subject to internal control? Animals as diverse as drosophila and humans tend to increase the variability of their behavior when faced with novel situations, which might be thought of as exploratory behavior. For example, many animals begin searching for food with a random walk until the discovery of food leads them to focus on localizing the source (Berg, 1983). In other situations, where there is little novelty or the solution to a problem is familiar, responses tend to be more stereotyped. In humans we might call these habits. Because all animals face a spectrum of problems, from the very novel to the stereotypical, most animals are able to behave in a range of ways, from exploratory and flexible, to stereotyped and inflexible.

Lovely work with fruit flies suggests that they can control the degree of variability injected into their own neural processing, depending on the kind of problem that they are facing (Tse, 2013, Section 4.70). This capacity to up- and down-regulate variability in neural processing is not driven by the stimulus, but rather by processing that is internal to the fly. Thus, under identical input conditions, a fly might or might not act, or might act with high or low variability. In other words, even in much simpler nervous systems than our own, under identical starting conditions, there are times when animals decide on the basis of purely endogenous factors to do this or that. And they could have done otherwise, since their responses were probabilistic, perhaps resulting from amplification of randomness in the microscopic domain to randomness in macroscopic neural and behavioral domains.

Another important reason animals have evolved endogenous (i.e., internally generated) versus exogenous (i.e., driven by the stimulus) modes of acting and deciding is that animals have to know whether changes in the world or stimulus are driven by self-actions or events in the world. At the very least, animals have to discount self-generated changes in the input as spurious, or they might take self-generated changes in sensory input to be due to changes in the world. Even in relatively simple animals, neural circuits (e.g., the corollary discharge circuit discussed in Section 3.6) allow an animal to distinguish self-generated from non-self-generated consequences of actions. This affords the beginning of a model of the world as that which happens independently of self-generated actions and processing. And it affords the beginning of a model of one's self, as that which causes self-generated actions and processing. An animal, even an animal as simple as a fly, can learn the consequences of its actions. It can learn that it can control certain consequences of its actions—for example, that turning left will make the visual array appear to move in the opposite direction—and it can learn that it cannot control other things, like that which happens in the world independently of its own decisions.

Another reason that endogenous modes of processing evolved was to allow an animal to process identical inputs in flexible and varying ways, depending on the needs of the animal. A key instance of this is endogenous attention, which allows animals to focus on what is relevant and to ignore what is irrelevant. Given control of the sensors, such as where the eyes will look next, the brain can take control of its own future inputs for its own internal reasons. For example, if I am looking for my keys, I will look at and attend to likely places where I might have left them, but if I am looking for my kids, I will search an identical scene in very different places.

In more advanced animals that have evolved a working memory, the model of the world and the model of the self can operate entirely in the absence of external input, over internal representations. How might this have gotten off the ground? Imagine a fish that lacks working memory. It is driven by its inputs. If it sees a barracuda, it flees. But if the barracuda swims behind coral, it can no longer respond to it, because it cannot represent it, as it is no longer in the stimulus. Now imagine a new revolutionary kind of fish that has a working memory. It can represent the barracuda even though it is no longer visible. It can play out internally that the barracuda is going that way, so it will flee the opposite way. The evolution of a working memory afforded the ability to play out events before they happened, inside of an internal world model, which includes a model of the self in that world model.

This revolution in nervous system design afforded an escape from "garden paths." A garden path occurs when locally, on the basis of present input, this is the best option, and then this next thing is the best option, and so on; at the end of all these locally optimal choices, lies something bad, like the jaws of a predator. In contrast, once working memory evolved, there was the possibility of "desert paths" where locally we have to do without, and locally we have to suffer, but at the end of the process we get something desirable, such as a mate or shelter or food. This advantage is highly elaborated in advanced animals such as ourselves and allows us to pursue aims, not solely on the basis of sensory input, but also on the basis of invisible goals and complex cognitive maps of the world and ourselves.

In addition, teleological drives, such as thirst, lust, and hunger drive animals to seek out that which might not be visible in the present set of sensory inputs. Operating within an endogenous model of the world within an internal virtual reality afforded tremendous freedom to play events out before doing anything in the real world. This ability to play things out internally required the evolution of endogenous operations that in us are highly elaborated and give us our tremendous powers of imagination. Such operations are not driven by the input. They are driven endogenously. Such endogenous processes are the root of volition and freedom from being stimulus-driven and freedom to explore and act within an internal world model. Later, after internal modeling has zeroed in on an optimal path of action, the animal can attempt to enact its intended action plan in the world.

This is not an all-or-none state of affairs. In humans, endogenous volitional processes are highly elaborated; even in much simpler animals, whether fish or flies, there are endogenous operations over internal representations that are subject to control for internal reasons. Thus, free will comes in degrees. Its beginnings were humble, and, in humans, reached a degree of elaboration that gives us, in comparison to other animals, something approaching the freedom of gods.

4.2 The Two Valleys of Information Processing Death

Thoughts and mental operations, whether conscious or not, including acts of volition as well as acts of imagination, are realized in neural activity. Since thoughts can be very fast, whatever the neural realization of a thought is must also be fast, at least as fast as a thought. For example, I can ask you to recall something that has a unique solution, and you can answer me incredibly quickly. Look how fast this happens. Ready? As fast as you can, say out loud your mother's maiden name. Within a fraction of a second, you produced her name. Think of all the steps that went into this. First, your reading system decoded the words. After numerous steps of analysis, you understood a question. Then your brain commanded the recall of her name from your memory stores, almost surely involving processing in the hippocampus. Upon recall, your brain controlled the muscles of your throat and mouth so that you then said her name. There were easily dozens of steps of neural processing that went into your production of your mother's maiden name, all in under a second. Each step probably lasted on the order of tens of milliseconds. This is amazing.

What is more amazing is that you can volitionally generate possible solutions to an open-ended problem almost as fast as recalling a fact like your mother's maiden name. For example, say the name of a politician out loud. You just said some politician's name, but many politicians were also nameable by you, so there was no singular solution, as in the case of your mother's maiden name. Again, it is amazing how fast you could do this. I can add additional criteria that need to be fulfilled. If I ask you to name a European female politician, you can do that too, even though I constrained the possible answers by three separate criteria (woman, European, and politician). So, the neural code that underlies neural information processing not only has to be at least as fast as the thoughts that it realizes, it has to permit the setting of arbitrary criteria that can be met in multiple ways, all within a fraction of a second. In this chapter our goal is to understand the basics of how neurons might realize the rapid setting of criteria. Our goal is to understand the basics of a neural code that could realize the criterial causation that I argue underlies the kind of constrained indeterminism in the brain that could afford us both a first-order and second-order free will.

It turns out that neural information processing involves a delicate interplay between excitation and inhibition where timing or temporal phase relationships are of the essence. By way of analogy, think of excitation as analogous to hitting the accelerator when you drive your car, and think of inhibition as hitting the brake. You need both abilities in order to reach your destination. If you only had a brake pedal and no accelerator, you would not be able to drive. But if you had only an accelerator and no brake pedal, you would probably crash and burn; you need both to function in a controlled manner. Similarly, if you could only inhibit neurons from firing, you would have no firing at all, and therefore no ability to process information using the medium of well-timed neural firing. This would be like coma. There is not much information processing possible in a state of coma. On the other hand, if you could only excite neurons to fire, you would have lots of neural firing that carried no information at all. This would be like epilepsy, where, again, information cannot be processed because the firing of neurons is arbitrary and out of control, carrying no information.

So, in a sense, neural processing in the brain walks a narrow ridge between two valleys of information-processing death. One is the valley of too much inhibition or coma, and the other is of too much useless neural firing, or excessive excitation, which is like epilepsy. Just as in driving, we need the well-timed interplay between excitation, or hitting the accelerator, and inhibition, or hitting the brake.

Figure 4.1 depicts perhaps the simplest and most common neural circuit found in the brain. It involves a pyramidal cell, the excitatory workhorse of cortical information processing, interacting with an inhibitory interneuron. When the pyramidal cell fires, its action potential propagates down its axon toward other neurons, including other pyramidal cells (not shown here for simplicity); in addition, there is a collateral axonal fiber that excites (+) an inhibitory interneuron, which, in turn inhibits (–) or hits the brakes on further firing in the pyramidal cell. This delayed self-braking guarantees that the first neuron can send a signal to other neurons downstream, but once it has done so, it is shut off and does not fire again and again, sending the same

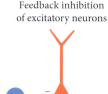

Figure 4.1 The most basic self-inhibition circuit of the human cortex involves an excitatory pyramidal cell that sends a collateral to a nearby inhibitory interneuron, which, when excited by the former's firing, inhibits that cell from firing further.

information, or no information of any use. It is this fine temporal interplay between excitation and inhibition that allows information processing to be informative and not noisy, and to be well controlled. It is this fine interplay between excitation and inhibition that allows us to catch a ball, smile, to think, and yes, to have free will.

4.3 How Neurons Function

I have argued that mental causation is realized in a neural code where neurons alter the informational criteria for the subsequent firing of other neurons or of themselves. This happens when those reset informational criteria have been met by inputs that meet those criteria at some point in the future. A concrete example occurs in the case of planning. A plan about what to make for dinner might result from deliberation in working memory about various possibilities, given various constraints. Such a plan is not only itself realized in neural activity, it can also alter subsequent neural activity. That is, conscious and unconscious operations that result in plans can be causal in the universe. The plan to, say, make spinach lasagna, can lead to action in the world by invoking the use of our muscles, say in driving to the supermarket, or it can lead to subsequent thoughts, such as "where are my car keys?"

Before we begin an analysis of how a neural code could realize this type of criterial causation, let us first review how neurons integrate information and fire. Neurons come in many shapes and sizes. The neuron idealized in Figure 4.2 is an example of a pyramidal cell. Pyramidal cells are called that because the cell body looks a bit like a pyramid. Pyramidal cells are the main workhorses of neural computation. They are always excitatory, so require inhibitory interneurons to inhibit them or to put the brake on their processing.

The anatomical differences among different types of neurons are not arbitrary, but rather belie differences in how neurons function, how they integrate information, and how they pass the informational results of their computations on to other neurons, whether locally to nearby neurons, say microns or tens of microns away (a micron or

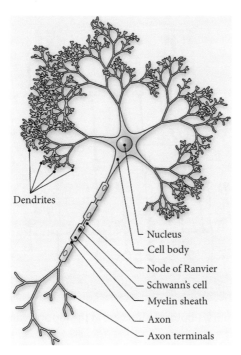

Figure 4.2 The basic anatomy of a neuron.
Source: Wikimedia Commons.

micrometer is a millionth of a meter), or on to neurons far away via long axons that carry action potentials. These axons can be centimeters long, and in some extreme cases, like the long axons that feed down from the brain to the muscles, whether in us, or in a giraffe or a whale, axons can be meters long.

For tiny nervous systems, axons are not necessary. Neural computations can be carried out locally within local neural circuits in the absence of axons and action potentials, as happens in the local information processing that happens in our retina. Only when those computations are complete, and it is necessary to ship the results of those computations far away, are axons and action potentials necessary. In fact, there is a class of neurons in the retina called "ganglion cells" whose job is to send the results of retinal computations on to other parts of the brain, via action potentials sent down their long axons, which bundle together to form our optic nerves. Thus, action potentials almost surely evolved so that signals could be sent to distant locations. Though they play a key role in neural computations, in that signals have to be sent from one neuron to another for further information processing, axons and action potentials are not necessary for neural computations, which can happen locally, as in our retina, in the absence of axons and action potentials. Even though many scientists are biased to think of the neural code as realized in action potentials, we have to be aware that this is just a bias. For example, just because information can be sent along telephone wires

176   A Neurophilosophy of Libertarian Free Will

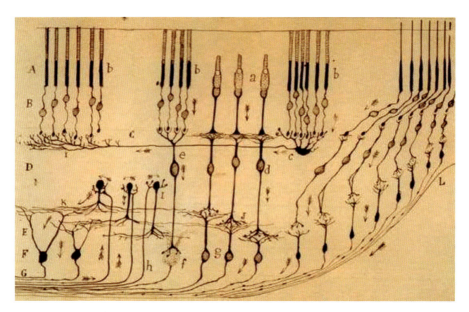

Figure 4.3 Retinal circuitry. Photoreceptors are at the top and ganglion cells axons are at the bottom.
Credit: Santiago Ramón y Cajal.

does not mean that the telephone wires are where the key information processing is taking place, or that human communication cannot happen in the absence of such long-distance links.

Neurons never exist in isolation. They always exist in circuits of interacting neurons. For example, Figure 4.3 shows a drawing of the neural circuitry in the retina drawn over a hundred years ago by the anatomist Ramón y Cajal, shown in Figure 4.4 sitting in front of his microscope. Because neurons process inputs in the context of circuits of neurons, it is almost certainly the case that information processing happens not only at the level of individual neurons, but also at the level of dynamic neural circuits.

The correct level of analysis of information processing in the nervous system is the level of circuits. Some of these circuits might exist inside a neuron, in particular, in the logical operations possible among the branches of dendrites, and some of these circuits exist among interacting neurons. Given that the neural code is a neural computational code, it is likely that the neural code is realized in both dendritic computations within individual neurons and within the computations carried out among chains of neural computations, namely, within neural circuits made up of many interacting neurons. Action potentials are a means to that end but are not necessary for small circuits. So, those who think the neural code will be decipherable, like a Morse code, by listening to firing rates or patterns, are not likely to crack the neural code.

That said, let us begin by looking at the organization of a single neuron. Figure 4.5 shows a schematic drawing of a neuron. Every neuron has an input (dendritic) end and

The Neuroscience of Free Will 177

Figure 4.4 Santiago Ramón y Cajal in the 1880s.
Source: Santiago Ramón y Cajal/Wikipedia.

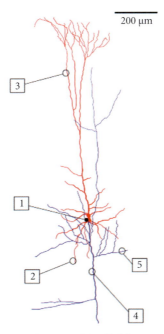

Figure 4.5 A depiction of a cortical pyramidal cell: (1) Soma, (2) Basal dendrite, (3) Apical dendrite, (4) Axon, (5) Collateral axon. Its cell body and dendrites, both apical dendrites and basal dendrites, are colored red here. And its branching axon is colored blue. The soma is typically around 20 μm long. But if you include the dendrites, the length of a pyramidal cell can be hundreds of microns long. And if you include the axon then the length can be meters long.
Source: Fabuio/Wikipedia.

an output (axonal) end. This anatomy makes apparent that neurons take input from other neurons, process those inputs (primarily via computations realized within their dendrites), then send the results of these computations on to other neurons in the form of action potential signals. These downstream neurons take action potential outputs of earlier stage neurons as their inputs for further processing. Neural outputs, at least for neurons that are far apart, typically take the form of action potential signals, which are really patterns of electrical disturbance, that race down the axon. The myelin sheath increases the ability of axons to transmit these signals, or action potentials, to distant cells with little to no signal loss, a bit like a cable's insulation protects against signal loss.

What we are especially interested in is what is going on at the synapse. The synapse is where the terminals of axons or "axonal boutons" of a presynaptic neuron terminate on a post-synaptic neuron. If we zoom in on a synapse, we can see that the synapse contains a small gap called the synaptic cleft, between the presynaptic and post-synaptic neurons. It is really tiny, on the order of 20–40 nm wide in most cases. By way of comparison, a human hair is between 80,000 and 100,000 nm wide. Since a nanometer is one billionth of a meter, and a micron or micrometer is one millionth of a meter, the synaptic cleft is 2–4% the width of a micron. Another way to put it is that the synaptic cleft is about one millionth of an inch wide. So, while the gap between the pre- and post-synaptic neurons is incredibly small, it is a gap nonetheless. In Section 4.7 we ask why there is such a space between neurons, but first we need to understand what happens when an action potential arrives at the terminal bouton of a presynaptic neuron.

In the standard case, when the electrical disturbance of an action potential reaches the end of an axon, or the axonal bouton, it triggers the release of neurotransmitter molecules into the synaptic cleft. The main excitatory neurotransmitter is glutamate and the main inhibitory one is GABA. Then there are other neurotransmitters that modulate the degree or consequences of excitation and inhibition, including famous neurotransmitters, such as acetylcholine, dopamine, serotonin, and norepinephrine.

The neurotransmitter molecules are held in tiny sacks (vesicles) in the presynaptic neuron's terminal boutons. The arrival of an action potential triggers the binding of vesicles to the presynaptic neural cell membrane, which then ejects the neurotransmitter molecules into the synaptic cleft, which is actually the outside of the presynaptic neuron. Once in the synaptic cleft, neurotransmitter molecules diffuse across the tiny gap between the pre- and post-synaptic neurons. When the neurotransmitter molecules reach the post-synaptic neuron, they typically bind to a receptor that is specialized to take exactly this type of neurotransmitter as its binding input. Speaking metaphorically, if a lock is to open it can only take keys of the right shape as inputs (Figure 4.6). A receptor is a very complex molecular machine made of proteins that float in the neuron's cell membrane, as shown in the drawing's inset. Once neurotransmitter has bound to the receptor, the receptor generally does something that affects the post-synaptic neuron in response to that act of binding. In coming chapters we will learn about different classes of receptors, and what the consequences of neurotransmitter binding to them are for the firing behavior of neurons.

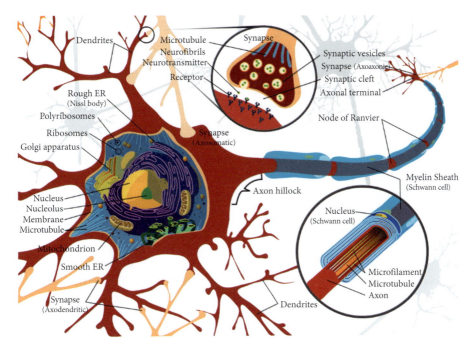

Figure 4.6 The anatomy of a neuron.
Source: https://en.wikipedia.org/wiki/Neuron

4.4 Ionotropic and Metabotropic Receptors

There are basically two main kinds of receptors. Ionotropic receptors function as tiny holes in the membrane. You can think of them as little donuts that can be either closed or open. When the neurotransmitter molecule binds to an ionotropic receptor, it typically triggers the opening of a tiny pore, through which charged atoms, or ions, such as sodium, chloride, or potassium can flow. As ions cross the membrane, both into and out of the post-synaptic neuron, there is a change in the voltage or charge differential (potential) across the membrane. Metabotropic receptors, in contrast, don't typically directly open a tiny hole in the membrane, but rather trigger secondary signaling cascades inside the post-synaptic neuron that have relatively delayed downstream effects, including sometimes the opening of other receptor pores. In either case, the binding of neurotransmitter to a receptor leads to a change of the charge inside a post-synaptic neuron, or voltage across its membrane. In the case of ionotropic receptors this change in charge will be fast, and in the case of metabotropic receptors, the changes in charge will tend to be slower.

A neuron would be at equilibrium when there is no difference in charge between the inside and outside of the membrane. This generally occurs only when a neuron is dead. When a neuron is alive, it actively keeps the voltage across its membrane far from equilibrium using ion pumps. This allows neurons to do important things, like fire.

Living neurons tend to have a negative "resting potential," which means that, even in the absence of input, neurons are far from equilibrium. In order to maintain a negative potential, there have to be more positively charged ions outside the cell than inside of it, or more negatively charged ions inside the cell than outside of it. This is accomplished by carrying out work. In particular, sodium ion pumps actively transport positively charged sodium ions out of the cell. It therefore takes expensive cellular energy (stored in the molecular "batteries" of adenosine triphosphate; ATP) to maintain this resting potential. It also means that any deviations from this resting potential tend to be brought back to this baseline resting potential within milliseconds or tens of milliseconds.

When an ionotropic receptor opens, ions flow into and out of the post-synaptic neuron. If there is a net increase in charge inside the post-synaptic neuron, it is said to depolarize. And if there is a net decrease in charge, it is said to hyperpolarize. Depolarization is typically associated with neural excitation. That means that the neuron becomes more likely to fire an action potential. Conversely, hyperpolarization is typically associated with neural inhibition. That means that a neuron becomes less likely to fire an action potential.

Let us say that the resting potential of a neuron is −70 mV. When an excitatory neurotransmitter, such as glutamate, binds to an ionotropic glutamate receptor, the pore opens and sodium rushes in. This leads to an increase in the net charge inside the cell. We can measure this bump up in potential as an excitatory post-synaptic potential (EPSP). Since sodium pumps are actively pumping sodium outside of the cell, an EPSP will tend to decay in short order. That is, in the absence of further excitatory or inhibitory input, the neuron tends to return to its resting potential, and it is then as if that EPSP had never happened. A neuron therefore functions as a "leaky integrator." It sums up EPSPs, but they decay away quickly. Neurons essentially "forget" the distant past, and only integrate over the short time window dictated by the rate of decay of an EPSP back to the resting potential. EPSPs have to all occur within a very brief time window in order to add up. For a typical pyramidal cell this integration window is typically around 25 ms.

Because a neuron "forgets" that it was excited, once it has returned to its resting potential, it functions as a coincidence detector, typically of multiple spikes. If spikes arrive close together in time, say, within 25 ms, their EPSPs can successfully add up. If they arrive outside of this narrow time window, they generally fail to integrate; that is, they fail to drive the post-synaptic neuron toward firing. If the sum of EPSPs pushes the potential above the firing threshold for the neuron, typically around −55 mV, then the neuron will fire an action potential away from the axon hillock down the axon.

The final decision whether to fire or not is made at the axon hillock. If the firing threshold is reached at the axon hillock, then an action potential is ballistically generated in an all-or-none fashion. There is no such thing as a partial action potential. It either happens or it doesn't.

However, a neuron can also be hyperpolarized by inhibitory inputs, typically triggered by the binding of GABA to GABAergic receptors. If these inhibitory ionotropic receptors open, then the net ionic charge inside the neuron is hyperpolarized, bringing the neuron further away from the threshold for firing. There is a dynamic interplay between excitation or depolarization and inhibition or hyperpolarization. In Figure 4.7, you can see how EPSPs add up and how, if they reach the firing threshold, the neuron generates an action potential. You can also see how inhibitory post-synaptic potentials (IPSPs) can add up and inhibit the cell, making it less likely to fire.

Let us now look at what happens when an action potential is generated. You can see that initially the net charge climbs massively above the resting potential. This is typically because positive ions, in particular sodium ions, rush into the post-synaptic neuron. But this change in voltage triggers the opening of other receptors that lead to the net outflux of positive charge, typically an outflow of positively charged potassium

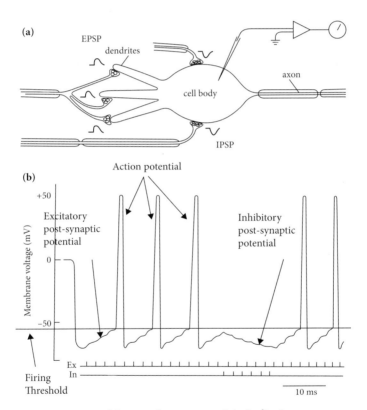

Figure 4.7 The timecourse of the membrane potential of a single neuron. Glutamatergic inputs can trigger a net positive deflection in potential, shown as an excitatory post-synaptic potential (EPSP). GABAergic inputs can trigger a net negative deflection, shown as an inhibitory post-synaptic potential. Typically, several EPSPs must arrive within a brief time window in order to reach the firing threshold of the neuron, upon which an action potential is generated.

ions, leading to the rapid collapse in potential after the peak. After firing, a neuron's potential will often overshoot, descending below the resting potential. This leads to a refractory period during which the neuron is so hyperpolarized that it cannot fire.

Once, when teaching an introductory neuroscience course, I thought I had hit upon the perfect metaphor to explain how neurons fire. I said that they function sort of like a toilet, in that there is a threshold beyond which they ballistically fire, and that there is a refractory period, after having flushed, when a toilet cannot be flushed again before returning to baseline. But after class I realized the problem with my metaphor, because one student wanted to know what the thing was that was sent down the "pipe" of the axon. At this point I realized that I had mistakenly implied that an action potential is, by analogy, a concrete thing, which it is not. Rather, it is a pattern of energy, or a disturbance, more like a wave than a physical thing. In fact, it is a wave of ionic flux into and out of the axon that travels down the axon between one meter per second, and for very large axons, as fast as 100 meters per second. Metaphors are useful, but dangerous. They can help us understand something that we do not understand in terms of something that we do understand, but they can also cause misunderstanding, if we take them too far or too literally.

4.5 Synchrony and Bursting

Our goal is to understand how will or volition might work in the brain. In particular, we want to understand how the master volitional operator (volitional attention) works in the brain. If attention and volition are to have an effect within the brain, the neural code has to be one that allows for top-down influences that alter neural function. Volitional attention is in part realized in the release of acetylcholine into the synapse, which alters neural responses. But before we discuss this, we need first to understand about different types of neural responses or firing patterns. Our goal in this chapter is to learn about two patterns: synchronous firing and bursty firing.

If we were to anthropomorphize a neuron, we might say that a neuron's goal in life is to make those downstream neurons that receive its action potentials fire. Of course, neurons don't really have goals, but let us pretend that they do. Now we also know that making a downstream neuron fire is not easy. One action potential is usually not enough to make the receiving neuron reach the firing threshold. And a single EPSP tends to decay quickly back to the resting potential of the post-synaptic neuron. Depending on the temporal integration window of a neuron, EPSPs will only sum up to the firing threshold if numerous EPSPs arrive within some few tens of milliseconds of each other. For this reason, we should think of neurons as coincidence detectors. They tend to respond best when many action potentials coincide in the time of their arrival. In the absence of such a coincidence, they are not likely to fire above their own baseline firing rate. So, neurons are sensitive to the timing or temporal pattern of that energy, not to the amount of energy impinging upon them. In a word, neurons are pattern detectors. They respond to a particular pattern of energy. That pattern is the temporal phase of action potential arrival. This is why neurons are coincidence detectors and pattern detectors. It is why information is realized in the brain in patterns of energy, or the phase of energy, rather than in old-fashioned Newtonian aspects of energy such as mass and momentum.

To put it romantically, neurons are "listening" for the particular rhythm or melody to which they are sensitive, among the noise and cacophony of irrelevant melodies with which they are continually bombarded. Since there are countless ways the same melody can be played, each of which obeys all the conservation laws of physics, such conservation laws are largely irrelevant to understanding the responses of neurons and chains of causation in the brain.

Determinists like to circularly assert that the conservation laws of deterministic physics eliminate the possibility of multiple possibilities among particles or neurons made of particles. Indeterminists like myself are backed up by the standard interpretation of quantum theory, according to which there are multiple possible paths open to particles, each of which obeys all the conservation laws, which in turn allows for the possibility of multiple possible paths open to neural chains of causation.

When a neuron fires, it is basically telling other neurons that receive its input: "Hey, I have detected a token of the vast class of possible inputs that count as the 'melody' that I was looking for in my inputs." A receiving neuron can't know which particular token met the transmitting neuron's criteria for what counts as a satisfaction of its "melody." That information gets lost because it is irrelevant. Criterial causation therefore imposes an "arrow of time" on brain events from the past into the future. The particulars of microscopic history that led to an outcome in the brain are lost. What matters is that the melody class, not token, was present. The receiving neuron is in turn "listening" for an instance of the class of satisfactions of its "melody" criteria being met. And so on and on, in a chain of criterial neural causation that can run its course via countless token chains of material causation. Any token chain would almost surely have been realized in a different chain of tokens, were we able to rewind the universe. What supervenes then on any particular token neural satisfaction of criteria for firing, or token chain of such neural satisfactions, is an equivalence class. There are infinitely many ways to play the same symphony.

But playing a symphony is an imperfect metaphor for the succession of neural processing because a symphony is precomposed and merely mechanically executed. The symphony metaphor might mislead one into thinking that all chains of causation in the brain are stereotyped, mechanistic, and even predetermined. A better metaphor would be an improvisational jazz jam session that can go in lots of directions spontaneously, while riffing on certain melodies and rhythms. If neurons are detectors of tokens of equivalence classes, not only is the history about past tokens lost, but also which chain of such token paths will be realized in the future is indeterminate. Because criteria can be met indifferently in countless possible particular neural realizations, and any particular token satisfaction of criteria might happen over others just by chance, neural and mental causation in the brain among neurons that respond criterially is indeterministic. The particular succession of past brain states that led to the present brain state is uncertain because countless past brain states could have led to the present brain state. Similarly, knowing only the present brain state, it is also uncertain which brain state will follow from the present brain state because presently realized criteria can be met in multiple token ways and because of noise. Because the brain operates criterially over equivalence classes of patterns, it riffs indeterministically. But note that this indeterminism is not utterly random. Any token must meet the criteria set. Like a good jazz ensemble, the brain riffs around a nonrandom melody. Good improvisation is playful and creative, not random. It is not random because, whatever token realization happens, it must have met the nonrandom informational criteria that were implicit among the synaptic weights of neurons evaluating their inputs for their "melody."

Now we can return to neurons and ask where the play in its responsiveness originates. Why is it a class detector as much as a "token of a class" detector? To bring it down to an individual neuron, how do we get enough EPSPs to arrive all at once so that they add up to trigger an action potential? Since the integration constant for a pyramidal cell is on the order of a few tens of milliseconds, and for some neurons even shorter than this, there are two broad classes of solution to the problem of simultaneous or coincident arrival of depolarizing inputs. One class of solutions occurs when several neurons from the previous stage of neural processing send their respective action potentials to the same downstream pyramidal cell at roughly the same time. It is as if neurons at the previous stage collaborate to make a downstream neuron fire. This class of solutions can be thought of as neural synchrony. By firing in synchrony, their outputs arrive on a downstream neuron at the same time, or close enough, depending on the temporal integration window of the receiving neuron, leading the EPSPs in the receiving neuron to add up before they have time to decay back down to the baseline of its resting potential. This coincidence of arrival will increase the likelihood that an action potential will be generated by the post-synaptic neuron.

Another class of solutions is for a very few (or even a single) neurons to fire extremely rapidly, with action potentials only a few milliseconds apart. If it fires quickly enough, then again, EPSPs can sum up, and drive the post-synaptic neuron above threshold, making it fire. When a neuron fires in machine-gun like fashion, every few milliseconds, this is called "neural bursting." So another class of solutions to the problem of successfully driving a post-synaptic neuron to fire is for the presynaptic neuron to burst. This is also called "phasic firing." It is not surprising that information processing in the brain takes advantage of both solutions to neural signaling, namely both neural synchrony and neural bursting.

Neural synchrony can be thought of as a large population or large ensemble solution to getting the next neuron to fire, because many neurons must collaborate in order to drive a downstream neuron to fire. Neural bursting can be thought of as a small population or small ensemble solution to getting the next neuron to fire, in that, in principle, even a single neuron firing very rapidly can increase the probability of post-synaptic firing.

A given pyramidal cell can typically fire in either a tonic way, a phasic way, or some combination of both patterns. A tonic pattern of firing might occur randomly around some average interspike interval. In contrast, a phasic pattern of firing might have a temporal pattern rather like a machine-gun firing brief volleys on and off. The number of spikes or action potentials per second might be the same on average, but the pattern can be very different and this temporal pattern has big effects on downstream processing.

To sum up, neurons tend to fire in one of two basic modes. In tonic firing, such as typically occurs at the baseline firing rate, neurons fire irregularly in a way that obeys "Poisson statistics." This means that the amount of variability among interspike intervals—that is, the time between two adjacent action potentials—varies as a linear function of the mean firing rate. An analogy is a bull's eye that you throw darts at again and again. If the dartboard is close, there will be a small spread around the center where the darts have hit, but if the dartboard is farther away there will be a larger spread. In this case, the variability in distance from the target increases the further away the target is. In tonic firing the variability of interspike intervals increases the higher the average firing rate. The average rate of tonic firing per unit time can increase or decrease in an analog manner, even though action potentials are themselves digital in the sense that they occur in an all-or-nothing manner.

In phasic firing, however, action potentials cluster in time in brief but rapid bursts of spikes. Bursts are preceded and followed by periods of relative quiescence. A burst occurs when two or more action potentials are generated within rapid succession, typically at >100 Hz with a preceding and subsequent silent period. Three to five spikes separated by ~5 ms (200 Hz) is common. With these two modes of firing, the nervous system can use the same neurons for at least two modes of information transmission or functional control, although there are likely to be even more modes of information processing than just these two.

Neurons typically have a baseline firing rate that is tonic. This allows neurons to deviate from baseline both in terms of an increase away from that baseline, and in terms of a decrease away from that baseline. I like to think of the baseline firing rate of a neuron as sort of like the idling of car. You need the car to idle so that you can have fast responsiveness to either excitation, namely, hitting the accelerator, or to inhibition, or hitting the brake. Because of the baseline firing rate, information can in principle be encoded in terms of both decreases in firing rate and in terms of increases. And there can be increases in the firing rate that are tonic in pattern, or phasic.

These two patterns of neural firing are not mutually exclusive. A very common type of neural spike train in visual processing areas occurs in response to the onset of a visual stimulus. At first the neuron is just firing tonically at its baseline firing rate. But once the information about the onset of the visual stimulus arrives, say, the appearance of a white disc, there is an onset transient, which is a kind of burst pattern. This is followed by an elevated firing rate as long as the stimulus is present. Often, the end of a spike train is associated with a second burst of firing, known as the offset transient, corresponding to when information about the offset of a stimulus arrives. Figure 4.8 shows an example of such a spike train pattern, associated with the onset and offset of a stimulus.

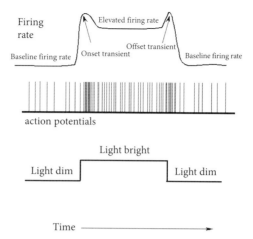

Figure 4.8 When a light is turned on and then off, neurons responsive to light, such as pyramidal cells in V1, may respond with a transient burst-like increase in firing rate upon light onset and offset, respectively.

It turns out that these onset and offset transients may be important for the neural coding of consciousness. In a stimulus known as metacontrast masking, if a flickering central bar that appears for 50 ms is abutted in space and time by 100 ms duration flanker bars that turn off when the central bar appears, and turn on when it disappears, the central bar vanishes from consciousness (Tse et al., 2005). But when the flanker bars do not abut the central bar, the central bar can be seen just fine, flickering on and off very quickly. Why does this happen? One idea is that the onset transient of the flankers exactly overlaps the offset transient of the central bar. Any downstream neuron getting input from the location of this edge of abutment between the central bar and flanker will have to decide whether to associate this transient with the offset of the bar in the middle or with the onset of the flanker. If conscious events are in part encoded in terms the presence of onset and offset transients, and if one or both of these is erased because of this ambiguity, then (at least in the case of metacontrast masking) the decision appears to be to erase the central bar from consciousness. Such bursts may in effect function as a kind of punctuation, telling a receiving neuron, "What you are about to receive or just received is a message." This type of pattern coding and decoding may help a neuron detect its favored melody above the din and noise of random and irrelevant inputs that it constantly receives. In the absence of appropriate punctuation, the input may be regarded as noise, not signal.

4.6 AMPA and NMDA Receptors

Different receptor classes dominate the two modes of neuronal firing: tonic and phasic firing patterns. We would expect the receptors that lead to tonic or phasic spiking to be associated with neural excitation, because spiking occurs when a neuron is excited. Since the main excitatory neurotransmitter is glutamate, we would expect the receptors underlying tonic or bursty firing patterns to take glutamate as their driving input. Indeed, that is the case. In the case of ionotropic glutamate receptors, tonic firing is primarily subserved by AMPA receptors that, in the aggregate, allow ions to pass through their pore to the degree that glutamate binds to them. As such, the firing rate of an excitatory neuron can increase in an analog manner. The more glutamate released into a synapse, the faster the average firing rate of the neuron.

NMDA receptors, in contrast, which are also glutamatergic receptors, subserve phasic firing or neuronal bursting. NMDA antagonists reduce bursting; that is, the frequency of pairs and triplets of spikes separated by only a handful of milliseconds decreases.

When glutamate binds to AMPA receptors they open. This depolarizes the post-synaptic neuron as the net positive charge inside the post-synaptic neuron increases. NMDA receptors stay closed initially. In order for NMDA receptors to also open, it is necessary that three facts be true. Glutamate has to bind to the NMDA receptor, another chemical called D-serine or glycine has to bind to it as well, and the post-synaptic neuron has to already be depolarized. This means that NMDA channels can only open if AMPA receptors have already allowed the post-synaptic neuron to depolarize. So, NMDA receptors are also coincidence detectors. Whereas neurons are coincidence detectors in the sense that they are waiting for the simultaneous arrival of several presynaptic action potentials, NMDA receptors, which are orders of magnitude smaller than a neuron, are waiting for these three facts to all be true. If they are all true, a single atom, which happens to be a magnesium ion and which functions like a stopper in a drain, comes unstuck from the receptor pore. It just drifts off and the receptor becomes "unplugged." When an NMDA receptor opens, positively charged calcium ions enter the post-synaptic neuron. The sudden influx of calcium ions makes NMDA receptors very different from AMPA receptors because calcium ions cannot pass through AMPA receptors. This calcium massively depolarizes the post-synaptic neuron and triggers bursting, which can also be thought of as firing at an extremely fast rate, at least for a moment.

Calcium, it turns out, is actually quite toxic for neurons, so is typically contained in little compartments called dendritic spines. Figure 4.9 shows a drawing of a pyramidal cell with dendritic spines evident as little bumps. If you see a neuron that has dendritic spines, you can infer that it is an excitatory neuron that takes glutamate as its key driving input neurotransmitter, and that it will have AMPA and NMDA receptors at the location of its spines. The main neurons that have spines are pyramidal cells and a kind of local cell that is a lot like a pyramidal cell, called a spiny stellate cell, but which lacks the long axons of a pyramidal cell.

In contrast, if you see a neuron that entirely lacks dendritic spines, you can infer that it is probably not an excitatory neuron that takes glutamate as its input. You can reasonably (though not perfectly) infer that a spineless neuron is an inhibitory interneuron. They have many different shapes, as shown here, but they all tend to be

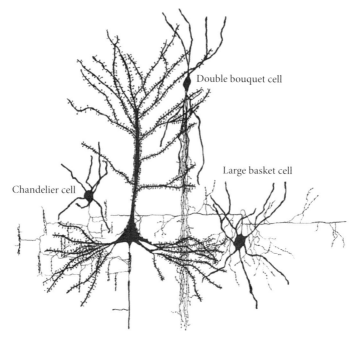

Figure 4.9 An excitatory pyramidal cell shares various spatial relationships with surrounding inhibitory interneurons of different classes.

Reproduced with permission from Elsevier, from DeFelipe, J., & Fariñas I. (1992). The pyramidal neuron of the cerebral cortex: Morphological and chemical characteristics of the synaptic inputs. *Progress in Neurobiology*, 39(6), 563–607.

smooth and lacking in dendritic spines. They also tend to release GABA on downstream neurons, inhibiting (hyperpolarizing) them, making them less likely to fire.

Interestingly, as any anesthesiologist will tell you, NMDA antagonists (as well as certain GABA agonists) in appropriate amounts can knock out consciousness, again suggesting that bursts are as important to the neural basis of consciousness as periods are to demarcating the beginning and ending of sentence structure. Another implication of this is that the key neural correlates of consciousness necessarily involve the processing and firing patterns of neurons that have spines. Bursts are thought by some neuroscientists, such as the late, great John Lisman (Lisman, 1997; Kepecs and Lisman, 2003), to propagate across an information-processing network as units of information, as we shall soon see.

4.7 Why Is There a Synaptic Cleft?

Neurons can be thought to physically realize informational criteria placed on characteristics of their input, which, if met, trigger neuronal firing. But how do they do this?

To answer this we should first consider a fundamental puzzle in neuroscience, which is why neural networks "bother" with relatively slow chemical transmission between neurons at the synapse, when electrical communication between neurons would be much faster. Put another way, why is there a synaptic cleft at all? One answer could be that evolution cannot easily come up with an unbroken reticulum because such a reticulum would have to be constructed of cells, and cells are by their very nature discrete entities. However, there are instances of networks of discrete neurons that communicate using "gap junctions," which are essentially little pores that link abutting neurons. Gap junctions allow direct transfer of charge, and therefore depolarization and hyperpolarization, from neuron to neuron, extremely quickly. Networks of neurons linked by gap junctions are tantamount to a continuous reticulum that behaves as a unit, since gap junctions allow potential to flow directly from cell to cell. Therefore, cellularity alone cannot explain why the nervous system relies on chemical transmission at most synapses. There has to be some advantage to slow chemical diffusion of neurotransmitter across the synapse, or there might be some disadvantage to the fast transfer of charge afforded by gap junctions.

An alternative answer to the puzzle of why there is a synaptic cleft arises from an understanding of neurons as criterial informational decoders of their inputs. Neurons keep their intracellular potential discrete because they each impose their own discrete set of criteria for firing on their inputs. This guarantees that neurons respond only to their own inputs, and not to the inputs of other neurons. If neurons were linked by gap junctions they could not realize discrete criteria for firing based upon summation of intracellular potential, since depolarization of one cell would automatically lead to depolarization of abutting neurons. To enact discrete criteria for firing, it is necessary to keep the summation of potential in one cell entirely separate from that in another cell. In fact, discrete criterial assessments require discrete compartmentalizations of the summation of potential, not only at the level of individual neurons, but also within neurons.

Discretization of criterial assessment may account for the compartmentalization of potential within dendritic arms and spines as well because neural computations can also happen in the dendrites. For example, one dendritic branch might only depolarize if both of the dendritic branches feeding into it also depolarize, amounting to an AND gate. Indeed, it is becoming clear that neural computation might most fundamentally be a dendritic affair, as such dendritic computations could realize basic Boolean operations.

Criteria are physically realized, in part, at the level of receptors in the post-synaptic cell, and receptors are by their very nature chemical in the criteria they set, owing to the binding of the neurotransmitter molecule with the receptor. Thus, all complex nervous systems that we know of have evolved an alternation between electrical communication (which is not criterial once a ballistic action potential has been set in motion) and chemical communication, allowing discrete summation of potential within each neuron. Physical compartmentalization of potential summation, when combined with a physical assessment of potential level relative to a threshold for the release of some subsequent physical process, such as the firing of an action potential, realizes the specification of discrete informational criteria placed on informational inputs, which, if met, change the physical state of the brain by triggering neural firing. In other words, the meeting of informational criteria changes the physical brain, and thereby the physical universe. Criterial satisfaction and flexible changing of neuronally realized criteria for future firing are how information becomes causal and how top-down mental causation also becomes possible.

Independent informational criterial assessments require compartmentalization of potential for those informational criteria that are assessed in the physical realization of threshold assessments of potential. This necessitates a means of communication between neurons that is not reliant on gap junctions, because gap junctions would decompartmentalize physical potential across neurons, and therefore make informational criterial assessments nonindependent.

Given that having a synaptic cleft is necessary if informational criteria are to be evaluated independently of the criterial assessments made by other neurons, evolution might have harnessed the existence of the synapse for other purposes as well. In other words, chemical transmission between neurons, although slow, might introduce additional advantages. Another central reason why chemical transmission at the synapse may be beneficial is that neurotransmitter diffusion across the synapse introduces a source of variability in the timing of post-synaptic neuronal responses. Variability or noise in neural activity can be harnessed by a neuronal system that realizes discrete criterial detectors to generate novel solutions that meet any given set of neuronally realized criteria. How is this variability realized within a single post-synaptic neuron? Well, variability exists in the arrival time and magnitude of single post-synaptic potentials or currents because of neurotransmitter binding to post-synaptic receptors and their consequent re-conformation. This translates, ultimately, into variability in the timing and rate of firing of post-synaptic neurons. This variability has multiple potential independent sources. First, there is variability in the amount of neurotransmitter in the synaptic cleft due to variability in the amount contained in vesicles, and therefore in the amount released presynaptically; second, there is variability in how receptors themselves respond to neurotransmitter binding; and, third, there is variability in the size of the synaptic cleft, which is the distance between the neurotransmitter release site on the presynaptic neuron to the site of receptors on the post-synaptic neuron.

Scientists (Bartol et al., 1991; Franks et al., 2003; Stiles and Bartol, 2001; Stiles et al., 1996) who have modeled the synapse using a three-dimensional random walk (meaning, a Monte Carlo algorithm mimicking Brownian motion), have found that distances greater than 300 nm lead to essentially no post-synaptic response. It is therefore most likely not a coincidence that the synaptic cleft is typically on the order of 20–40 nm (billionths of a meter), which is incredibly tiny, but a gap, nonetheless. There would be little variability in arrival times of neurotransmitter as it diffuses across the synaptic cleft if the synaptic cleft were just 1 nm wide, because the random walk of diffusion would not have much distance over which to introduce variability in arrival times of neurotransmitters. Conversely, if the cleft were too big, say, 300 nm wide, the neurotransmitter would hardly arrive, and even if it did arrive, it would take too long to get there. A reasonable hypothesis, then, is that the cleft has evolved to be the size that it is because this permits the introduction of an optimal "sweet spot" level of variability in post-synaptic potential onset time given neurotransmitter diffusion rates in brains that have our temperature and physical make-up and given the need to arrive quickly. In effect, diffusion across the synapse is one of several physical mechanisms that permit the amplification of microscopic fluctuations into macroscopic variability in spike timing.

In Sections 4.10–4.12 I consider other processes of amplification besides diffusion across the synaptic cleft that bring indeterminism from the quantum domain up to indeterminism at the level of spike timing among criterially responsive neural circuits. Brownian motion may or may not be an indeterministic process, but there are other amplification cascades in the brain that follow from undeniably quantum domain effects, such as the absorption of a single photon by a single molecule in the retina.

4.8 How Neurons Realize Informational Criteria

All informational criteria are realized in physical processes that place physical criteria on aspects of energy. In the case of neurons, the primary physical mechanism that places physical criteria on aspects of energetic inputs is that which determines whether summed potential at the axon hillock surpasses the critical threshold above which an action potential will be generated. One might say that summation of EPSPs and IPSPs, whether in a dendrite or later in the soma, cannot itself comprise an assessment of information because this summation is purely mechanistic; potential just goes up or down, and either passes the action potential threshold or not. When a neuron is considered in isolation of all the neurons that give it input, this is correct. A neuron made to fire alone in a Petri dish realizes and conveys no information. One could depolarize the neuron and it would fire once the threshold was passed. In a localistic sense, then, summation of potential at the axon hillock cannot be regarded as placing any criterial conditions on the informational content of the input into a neuron. Similarly, a neuron cannot be thought to assess information criterially when considered in isolation. It just takes chemicals, such as glucose, oxygen, neurotransmitters, and ions, as inputs. But if the threshold for firing is met if and only if certain kinds of informational facts are true about the inputs, then the mechanism underlying neuronal firing not only assesses net potential at the axonal hillock, but also assesses the occurrence of these informational facts. In this way, physical criteria placed on physical inputs can realize informational criteria placed on informational inputs. Thus, the information realized in neural firing is not realized solely in its firing, it is realized in its firing given inputs defined by its pattern of neuronal connectivity within a circuit of neurons. This is an inherently holistic or globalistic view of informational realization or mental activity. It runs counter to the dominant reductionistic bias of both science and Western culture.

A simple cell in primary visual cortex (V1) provides a straightforward example of how this might be done more generally. A simple cell in cortical area V1 fires if a luminance-defined edge or bar of light is present at a given location in the visual field. David Hubel and Torsten Wiesel argued that a simple cell could be wired up by having earlier detectors, that themselves responded best to a spot of light, all converge on a downstream neuron, namely a simple cell, which would only fire if it received simultaneous action potentials from a subset of these earlier cells. These earlier cells, found in a part of the brain called the lateral geniculate nucleus of the thalamus, feed into V1. They tend to be excited by light falling in one spot on the retina, and to be inhibited by light falling around this spot. These neurons are said to have an excitatory center, and an inhibitory surround receptive field or response field, which is just that part of the retina that leads to a change in the cell's responses. A simple cell could be constructed that fired if, say, at least three out of five on-center off-surround neurons triggered EPSPs in the simple cell within that cell's very brief temporal integration window. If these center-surround cells respond to inputs from adjacent regions of the visual field that fall along a line, the simple cell fires when a band of light of a particular spatial extent and orientation appears at a particular location in the visual field. The axon hillock in this simple cell places physical criteria on net potential within a cell before physical firing is triggered, and simultaneously places informational criteria on informational inputs for the realization of certain information (the presence of a bar of light) that occurs when the simple cell fires. The simple cell functions as a coincidence detector in that several lower-level facts (e.g., inputs from lateral geniculate neurons) must hold at the same time, before it fires above its baseline firing rate.

Coincidence is not made of energy in addition to the energy it is realized in. That is, coincidence per se does not have mass or momentum or other attributes of an amount of energy. For example, several temporally coincident action potential inputs are not made of more energy than a staggered sequence of the same number of action potentials. But coincidence detection affords the possibility of detecting spatial patterns that exist at a given time. And these spatial patterns, or spatial relationships among inputs, are likewise not made of energy in addition to the energy in which the pattern is realized. Just as the fact of temporal coincidence has no mass, orientation also has no mass. Coincidence detection therefore allows neurons to respond to relationships among material inputs. By encoding arbitrary relationships among light, sound, heat, or vibration energy detected locally at the sensory sheet, neurons make explicit information about such relationships that are only implicit in the sensory input.

An eliminative reductionist might want to fight back by arguing that the assessment of informational criteria is epiphenomenal upon the assessment of physical criteria for neuronal firing. But physical neurons are arranged such that physical criteria for firing are satisfied only when certain information is the case, so that an animal can gain information about its environment and body in order to be able to respond to things and events appropriately. Since evolution operated on perceptual, motor, and cognitive systems to optimize information processing, one could equally well argue that the particular physical implementation of informational realization that we find in brains in the form of action potentials within neural networks is arbitrary with respect to the information that needs to be realized so that an animal can eat, flee, and mate successfully.

A given physical criterion for firing, given by summation of potential at the axon hillock, can realize different informational criteria, depending on the connectivity modulated by synaptic weights and other synaptic properties at a given time. For example, given one set of inputs, a simple cell in V1 might fire to a bar of light in one location. But if its inputs changed suddenly, it might fire to a bar of light at a different retinotopic location, or even to a bar of light of a different orientation. Neural connectivity cannot change rapidly because axons cannot suddenly grow within milliseconds. But effective neural connectivity can change very rapidly by changing synaptic weights within milliseconds.

Let us say that a simple cell now does not receive inputs from five spot-of-light detectors, but from 25 such cells. We can turn the weights of most of these inputs down to zero, and have some inputs be set to one. For the presynaptic neurons whose weights are set to zero, even if they fire, they cannot depolarize the post-synaptic neuron. The inputs whose weights are set to one *can* depolarize the post-synaptic neuron. Now imagine if we can rapidly change synaptic weights from one pattern of synaptic weights to a different pattern. Even though the overall pattern of axonal connectivity has not changed, the effective pattern of connectivity has changed, since now different presynaptic neurons drive the post-synaptic neuron. I call such changes in how neurons partake in neural circuits changes in "epiconnectivity," rather than connectivity. This is why I think that learning about the fixed pattern of axonal connectivity, known as "connectomics" is not going to get us very far in unravelling the neural code. We will also need a new field of "epiconnectomics" if we are to make deep headway in understanding how mind is realized in matter.

The physical criteria for firing at the axon hillock do not change, but the informational criteria for firing change as a function of epiconnectivity. Epiconnectivity can change via extremely rapid dynamic changes in synaptic weights due to the opening or closing of ionotropic receptor pores, and slower changes in synaptic weights that depend on protein synthesis via, for example, long-term potentiation.

It seems trivial to say that neurons process information, but how do they carry information at all? Neurons carry, communicate, compute, and transform information by transforming action potential spike inputs into spike trains sent to other neurons. If I say, "Please pick up your coffee cup," and you do, then a pattern of air vibrations has been transduced into neural firing in nerves that receive input from inner hair cells; this is in turn transformed multiple times across neuronal subpopulations until the meaning has been decoded at the level of words and a proposition, allowing you to issue a motor command to carry out my request, perhaps after having considered various other possible courses of action. This can all happen in less than a second after hearing the word "cup." To try to cut information and meaning out of the causal picture here, as radical reductionists and epiphenomenalists do, by arguing that there are only particles interacting with particles, makes a fundamental error.

Of course, there are only particles interacting with particles. But assuming ontological indeterminism, countless sets of particle paths could physically follow my command given your initial physical state and the physical state of the world at the moment of the word "cup." Why did a subset of possible particle paths occur that was consistent with an information-processing view of the brain, and not other physically allowed sets of particle paths that would have been consistent with the indeterministic laws of particle physics but not consistent with an information-processing account? Because neurons place physical criteria for firing on inputs that are also informational criteria on inputs, such that only those subsets of possible particle paths that meet those criteria can occur, as only those subsets trigger neuronal firing. On this account, mental events can cause future mental and physical events by altering physically realized informational criteria for firing that can be met by future neuronal inputs. Informational criteria for neural firing are realized in physical criteria for firing within a neuron, and, at a higher level, by a neuron existing within a neural circuit such that it only deviates from its baseline firing rate if certain informational facts are true.

We considered the case of a simple cell that fires above its baseline firing rate if and only if a bar of light occurs at a particular position on the retina or in the visual field. We can imagine other neurons that fire if and only if a cat is visible. Such neurons in fact exist in the anterior inferotemporal lobe. Firing alone in a Petri dish, such a neuron would not be a "cat detector," but given the right set of neural inputs, we can create a cascade of ever more complex feature detectors, from bar detectors like simple cells, to shape detectors, ultimately to cat detectors. Even though an individual neuron is "dumb," when linked in a cascade of simple "if–then" statements realized in neural circuits, neurons can become "smart." Similarly, a single brick does not have an architecture, because this arises only through relationships among many bricks. When a cat-detecting neuron fires by virtue of a particular cascade of if–then acts of decoding having occurred among its inputs, the rest of the brain learns that a cat is present in the sensory input and can act on this information.

I have argued that top-down causation in general, and mental causation in particular, occurs because physically realized informational criteria effectively carve out, from among all sets of possible paths open at the particle level, an instance of that tiny subset that is *also* an informational path or causal chain. This is only possible because neurons physically realize informational criteria. And this, in turn, is made possible by the discrete summation of potential within neurons, which is, in turn, only possible because there is a synaptic cleft that keeps the potential from one neuron from contaminating the potential in another neuron. Thus, mental causation is possible because of the 20–40-nm synaptic cleft!

4.9 A Synaptic Reweighting Neural Code

To understand how informational criteria for firing are set up in a given neuron, it is not enough to specify how input neurons are physically connected to that neuron; it is also necessary to model how synaptic weights on inputs to that cell change dynamically, effectively changing its neural "epiconnectivity." In this chapter I describe a useful metaphor for what I think is going on with rapid synaptic reweighting as a basis for the neural code. In future chapters we cover how top-down processing might harness such a neural code for the fulfillment of high-level aims like "think of a European woman politician" or for coming up with answers to the question "What should I make for dinner?" But before moving on to top-down processing, and, in particular, top-down volitional processing involving volitional attention, I focus on what rapid synaptic reweighting might be like in the brain. We have covered AMPA and NMDA receptors, and later I argue that rapid synaptic reweighting involves the opening of just these ionotropic receptors, but for now let us develop an intuition for rapid synaptic reweighting using a useful metaphor.

A common assumption in neuroscience is that information processing in the brain is realized in action potentials and that mental causation must be realized in a succession of action potentials triggering action potentials. Many people have thought that this process might be deterministic, like Newtonian billiard balls banging into each other and making each other move, except that now action potentials trigger action potentials. This is a fundamentally incorrect way to think about how action potentials coming from presynaptic neurons trigger an action potential in a post-synaptic neuron. The process is deeply non-Newtonian and profoundly nonlinear. It is also not deterministic, but (as I argue in the next section) indeterministic. Nonetheless, action potentials triggering action potentials is no doubt part of the story of the neural code. You can think of it as the "yang" of the neural code, but there is also a "yin" of the neural code. Much recent evidence suggests that dynamic, millisecond-timescale changes in synaptic plasticity can also play the role of a neural basis for information processing.

Many neuroscientists have thought that deciphering the neural code would mean deciphering the information carried by action potentials per se, as if a train of action potentials could be deciphered like, say, the Morse code or the Enigma code. But which inputs will make a neuron fire is dependent on the synaptic weights that are imposed on incoming presynaptic action potentials at a given moment. If information is physically realized when it is made explicit (i.e., when a neuron fires and passes that information on to other neurons), then the information that a neuron will realize if it fires is implicit in its synaptic weights even before the arrival of any presynaptic action potentials. Facts about action potentials in isolation of the inputs that trigger them will not carry information about anything; a given neuron might fire identically given one set of inputs at t1 and a different set of inputs at t2. Since different information would be realized, the information cannot be localized in action potentials per se. If you know that a neuron has fired but you do not know what inputs made it fire, then you do not know what information has made it fire. But if you know that a neuron has fired given particular physical inputs, which will only occur when certain informational facts are the case, then you can know what information made it fire.

As we discussed in the last section using the example of a simple cell, if an action potential arriving at a synapse is "multiplied" by a synaptic weight of zero, it contributes nothing to the firing of the post-synaptic neuron and therefore nothing to its information processing. Therefore, observing an action potential without knowing about how it is "filtered" by synaptic weighting cannot tell you what information it conveys, if any.

Here is an analogy. How the mouth is formed determines whether the same vibrating air passing through the mouth will lead to the enunciation of, say, an "ah," "oh," or "oo" sound. The mouth can be formed into an "ah," "oh," or "oo" shape before any air is forced through it, just as neurons can be criterially reset before being driven to fire by the arrival of action potential inputs from presynaptic neurons. The bit of information "ah" versus "oh" versus "oo" does not exist in the vibrating air in isolation of the shape of the mouth through which it is filtered. Rather, this information comes into being as the vibrating air passes through either the "ah," "oh," or "oo" mouth filters. On this account, action potentials are analogous to the vibrating air, and momentary synaptic weights are like filters that determine the information expressed by action potential input.

The search for the neuronal code is likely to be more fruitful if the focus is on neuronal criterial resetting rather than on action potentials in isolation of synaptic recoding. Cracking this kind of criterial neural code poses a major challenge to neuroscience because, given present single- and multi-unit neuron-recording methods, action potentials are easy to observe, whereas dynamic synaptic resetting over thousands of synapses is not. At present, we don't really even have good methods to observe the dynamic weight of a single synapse, let alone how hundreds or thousands of them are dynamically changing in a single post-synaptic neuron. However, if this view of the neural code is correct, even if neurophysiologists were to measure only action potentials for an eternity, neuroscience would never truly crack the neuronal code. Doing so would be like trying to decipher what someone is saying by observing air vibrations as they come off the vocal cords without observing how the mouth is formed or how the mouth filters vibrations in highly specific ways. Measuring only the vibrations of the vocal cords would yield something like this: uh uhhhh uh. On the other hand, measuring only the filtering of the mouth, in the absence of the energy passed through the filter of the mouth would yield this: silence. So we need both energy passing through the system, and filtering of that energy into words, in order to realize information. We need both the yang and the yin of the neural code. Without both action potentials and the filtering imposed by rapid synaptic reweighting, we would not be able to realize information or mental events in neural activity.

The analogy can be taken further, in the sense that the shape of the mouth has to be formed before the air is passed through the mouth. Similarly, criteria for firing have to be set on a post-synaptic neuron before the arrival of presynaptic action potentials if they are to be able to make it fire as a result of meeting the informational criteria realized in those preset physical criteria for firing. Indeed, the mouth must be shaped dynamically on a continual basis in order for the mouth to be able to speak. Action potentials are therefore a necessary but not sufficient basis for neural information processing whereby neurons convey information or "talk" to each other. The current dominant bias in neuroscience that the neural code is ultimately an action potential code is misguided. Action potentials are only half the story. The other half of the story is rapid and dynamic synaptic reweighting.

Another current confusion in neuroscience is to think that one can understand how neurons communicate with one another if one understands how neurons are statically connected to one another via axons. A popular effort is to view the brain as a graph where nodes represent processing areas and edges represent information flow between nodes along axons. This is a bit like looking at the brain as an airline traffic map, where the graph nodes or hubs are airports. But something is missing from this picture. Brain areas carry out operations and operations are not represented in a graph. It is useful to look at air traffic patterns as such a graph, but airports are not carrying out operations on us. Imagine if flying to Philly turns you into an orc, while flying through San Diego turns you into an elf, and flying though New York changes your gender. Simply looking at the number of people flying between points will tell you nothing about the operations taking place. Viewing the brain as a dynamic graph is similarly limited in its usefulness.

The issue of operations is relatively neglected in neuroscience, but it an issue of fundamental importance. We can measure tuning properties of single neurons. Those tell us something important about the "nouns" of the mind (edges, shapes, faces, houses, scenes, etc.). But we cannot measure operations over these nouns, which are likely carried out at a circuit level. We are presently unable to measure the "verbs" of the mind. Shape is likely the product of such circuit-level operations (contour completion, surface and volume completion). Since we can measure x or y, we focus on those measurable nouns instead of the verb $f(x) = y$, which we cannot measure, because we lack the technology to measure every neuron in a known circuit. Since we cannot measure operations easily, we focus on representations implicit in neural tuning properties. But this is not so different than looking for our keys where the light is good, when they are lost in the dark elsewhere.

The field of connectomics aims to map out exactly how every neuron is connected to every other. But let us say I had a perfect understanding of the highway system of the United States. That would not be enough for me to understand patterns of traffic in America. It might help somewhat, in that I can guess that two points connected by bigger highways likely share more traffic between them. But just knowing the highway system will not help me understand the dynamics of traffic across the highway system, and it would not help me understand why one car follows the path that it does. So, if connectomics is rooted in a metaphor of the brain as a highway, I would have to conclude that we need a better metaphor.

Maybe the brain is less like a highway system of axons, and more like a train track system, where axons play the role of train tracks, and synapses play the role of those shunts that shift trains from one track to another. If synapses are regarded as switches that can be turned on or off, then perhaps the majority of synapses might be off at any given time, as in the simple cell example I gave at the end of the previous section. But when needed, switches could be turned on. This permits the possibility of "sculpting" neuronal "epicircuits" on the fly, to construct neural circuits that are needed at a given time, rather like switching the railroad switches on train tracks to create different track connections as needed. Depending on how the switches are set, a single stretch of railroad track, say in Ohio, can be part of an "epitrack" that links Boston to San Diego, or New York City to Mexico, and so on.

How might an epicircuit "wire up"? One possibility is that there is a form of back-propagation, such that inputs that drive some goal state are made more likely to happen again by enhancement of those synaptic weights that afforded those inputs. Such a Hebbian mechanism might in principle work its way backward through the cascade of neurons that led to that goal state, sculpting in effect an epicircuit across the processing hierarchy that led to that goal state. If true, we might say that the goal or operation is realized in neural activity as much as the neural activity is realized in pursuit of the goal.

Another mechanism evolution has developed in circuit formation is having a critical period during development when neural connectivity is especially plastic. Such a state of plasticity combined with playful, exploratory behavior allows the nervous system to find those neural paths that best afford exactly those behaviors. Then, a transition from the playful/plastic state to a more "hard-wired" adult state might take the form of reduced plasticity, perhaps realized in the substitution from a "juvenile" plastic variant of NMDA receptor subunit with an "adult," less plastic form (Larsen et al., 2011). An analogy here would be laying down grass on a new college campus in order to see what paths form between destinations, and only then laying down cement sidewalks over such use-defined paths once pedestrian use had revealed them. Recent exciting work by Gül Dölen and colleagues suggests that some psychedelics may be able to re-open at least some of the brain's critical periods, potentially permitting the unlearning of previously ossified forms of suboptimal learned patterns (Nardou et al., 2019).

The metaphor of the brain as a train track system, however, breaks down because synaptic weights, in the case of neurons, need not be limited to the case of on or off, or this way or that way, as is the case in binary train track switches or light switches. Synaptic weights can generally be modulated up and down, like dimmer switches (Cho et al., 2020). Criterial causality does not require that a response be all or none, like an action potential. Criteria can be physically realized such that they can be met to degrees or not, amounting to fuzzy or hard thresholds for criterial satisfaction.

Scientific thinking is often driven by metaphor. Often the brain is taken to be like the most complicated thing or idea that is currently available. Thus, Leibniz was convinced that the mind was like a mill, and Freud that it was like a closed hydraulic set of pumps and valves. Wilhelm Wundt founded the first psychology lab based on the metaphor that all mental events might be reducible to combinations of elements of mind, just as Mendeleyev had shown that all matter is comprised of combinations of atomic elements. Later the behaviorists thought of animals as stimulus–response machines. Since the most complicated thing at present is the internet, surely someone will argue that the brain is just like the internet.

Metaphors are useful in helping us understand something we don't understand in terms of something that we do understand, but if taken too far, lead to confusion. At the end of the day, when it comes to the brain and the mind realized in it, I think all metaphors will fail if taken too far, for the simple reason that there is nothing in the nonbiological universe that operates like a brain, especially a human brain.

The current metaphor about the brain that may be misleading us is that the brain functions like a computer; this is manifestly not so. In brains there is no software/hardware distinction. In computers there is no consciousness with teleological desires and emotions, and no computer hardware is rewiring itself on a millisecond timescale as happens with the epicircuit dynamics that result from rapid synaptic reweighting arising from, for example, the opening and closing of NMDA receptors. Moreover, whereas a CPU generally takes a single thread of input, resulting in a binary decision, the computational units of the brain (neurons) assess hundreds or thousands of inputs criterially, and then send outputs to many other such units. Computers also lack innate cybernetic setpoints relative to which discrepancies are detected so that the system can be set on a corrective trajectory, as animals express when they, for example, get hungry. While a computer program that guides a heat-seeking missile involves path correction on the basis of detected errors, the cybernetic looping is not existential, as the matter of finding food becomes for a starving animal. Computers at present shuffle ones and zeros around, and therefore lack inherent purpose at the level of the hardware or the machine language. They cannot care, although software can create that appearance. The setpoint of, say, minimizing the deviation of a missile's aim to its target, is not inherent to the substrate of zeros and ones, but imposed by a programmer in high-level software. In contrast, the setpoint of optimal hydration in an animal is not written in software. It is innate to the organism in the workings of its cells and systems. Every cell is teleological and purposive as cybernetic processes operate to fulfill cellular needs. This innate cybernetic substrate realized in hardware, not software, makes animals inherently purposive. In contrast, missiles and computers are only seemingly so. They have "as if" needs or desires rather than felt needs or desires. Thus, from top to bottom, brains do not function anything like a computer. And just because something can be described computationally does not mean that it is actually computing anything. For example, peristalsis in the esophagus can be described beautifully with differential equations, but nobody would argue that the esophagus is executing mathematical operations. We should not confuse a model of a thing with the thing itself.

If computer-like and graph-like metaphors are not adequate to account for information processing in biological systems, how might informational reparameterization and causation work at a neural level? In my 2013 book *The Neural Basis of Free Will*, I developed an understanding of the neural code that emphasizes rapid and dynamic synaptic weight resetting over neural firing as the core engine of information processing in the brain. The neural code on this view is not solely a spike code, but a code whereby information is transmitted and transformed by flexibly and temporarily changing synaptic weights on a millisecond timescale. One metaphor is the rapid reshaping of the mouth (analogous to rapid, temporary synaptic weight resetting) that must take place just before vibrating air (analogous to spike trains) passes through if information is to be realized and communicated. What rapid synaptic resetting allows is a moment by moment changing of the physical and informational parameters or criteria that have to be met before a neuron will fire. This dictates what information neurons will be responsive to and what they will "say" to one another from moment to moment. Thus, the heart of criterial causation in the brain is the resetting, by other neural inputs, of the synaptic weights that realize informational parameters that have to be adequately met by a neuron's subsequent inputs in order for that neuron to fire, which in turn will reset the parameters that will subsequently make other neurons fire.

4.10 Indeterminism in the Brain, Part 1

In this section we return to the question of indeterminism, but here we ask specifically whether brain function is in any sense indeterministic. Even if the universe is indeterministic at the level of the quantum domain, it might make no difference at all to brain function. Since, according to modern physics, the only domain that may be indeterministic is the quantum domain, the only way that the macroscopic domain of neurons can be made indeterministic is if there exists amplification of indeterminism from the quantum domain to the macroscopic domain of neurons.

Here we examine evidence for the amplification of microscopic indeterminism to the macroscopic domain of cell activity. I give numerous examples of such amplification. But even if there were only one such mechanism of amplification, it would suffice to make the behavior of the brain indeterministic. And if even one tiny corner of the universe, such as our brains, is made indeterministic by such amplification, then the entire macroscopic universe is made indeterministic, because we are agents acting in that universe at the macroscopic level, changing things in light of our creative thoughts, whether building spaceships or even just choosing to make this for dinner versus that.

In a previous section we considered the Brownian motion or random walk of neurotransmitter as it diffuses across the 20–40 nm of the synaptic cleft. This is one way that randomness from the microscopic domain could be amplified to the macroscopic domain of spike timing.

In 1827, botanist Robert Brown noticed that grains of pollen floating in water seemed to jump around. Because the water itself had no net direction of flow, as it was in a jar, this struck him as strange. At first, he thought it might have something to do with the pollen being alive, like little Mexican jumping beans. But when he put tiny inert particles into water he saw the same motion, ruling out the hypothesis that being alive had something to do with it. It was Albert Einstein, in one of his 1905 papers, who finally gave a formal explanation. Basically, the grains of pollen bump into the particles in which they are suspended, which then move the pollen around. Einstein was able to infer the size and number of atoms in a medium by looking at the magnitude and frequency of jumps of a suspended grain.

Remarkably, in verses 113–140 of his 60 BC book *On the Nature of Things*, the Roman thinker Lucretius provides the correct explanation of Brownian motion:

> Observe what happens when sunbeams are admitted into a building and shed light on its shadowy places. You will see a multitude of tiny particles mingling in a multitude of ways … their dancing is an actual indication of underlying movements of matter that are hidden from our sight … It originates with the atoms which move of themselves. Then those small compound bodies that are least removed from the impetus of the atoms are set in motion by the impact of their invisible blows and in turn cannon against slightly larger bodies. So the movement mounts up from the atoms and gradually emerges to the level of our senses, so that those bodies are in motion that we see in sunbeams, moved by blows that remain invisible.

Lucretius explains that there is amplification from an invisible domain of colliding atoms up to a level of macroscopic particle movements that we can see with our naked eye. And so it is in the synapse as well. Brownian motion affects the arrival time of neurotransmitter on, for example, AMPA and NMDA receptors, which in turn affects the timing of the opening of these ionotropic pores, which in turn affects the timing of an excitatory post-synaptic potential, which in turn affects the timing of an action potential, which in turn affects the timing of coincidences of action potentials reaching a post-synaptic neuron, which in turn affects whether the post-synaptic neuron will fire. We have all heard that a butterfly's wings flapping can, in principle, influence the formation of a storm, if amplified in just the right way. Here, the butterfly's wings flapping might be as subtle as the random motions of a molecule of glutamate in the synaptic cleft.

Brownian motion in the synaptic cleft alone is a sufficient mechanism for amplifying randomness from the atomic domain up to the domain of neural spike timing. With this mechanism alone, the entire macroscopic universe might be made indeterministic because our activities in the macroscopic universe are influenced by the amplification of random movements in the nanometer regime of the space between our neurons.

But Einstein's account of Brownian motion was a deterministic one. We therefore want to continue our search for microscopic fluctuations that can be amplified up to a macroscopic level of neural activity. In particular, we want to find quantum domain processes whose outcomes are indeterministic that get amplified up to a macroscopic level. For example, recent remarkable experiments (Cartlidge, 2020; Cho et al., 2020; Yu et al., 2020) suggest that macroscopic objects are subject to a kind of inherently indeterministic Brownian motion or "Lucretian swerve" because virtual particles collide with them.

There are other mechanisms whereby the activity of single atomic particles is amplified up to a level of spike timing randomness. Another example can be found in NMDA receptors. Remarkably, they are blocked by a single atom of magnesium, a bit like a stopper might block water from flowing down the drain. When glutamate binds to an AMPA receptor, sodium ions can flow into the cell, depolarizing it. We have learned that three conditions must be met for the NMDA receptor to open: glutamate has to bind to it, d-Serine or glycine has to bind to it as well, and the post-synaptic neuron has to already be depolarized because AMPA receptors have recently opened. If all of these conditions are met, the magnesium ion will drift out of the pore, freeing calcium ions and other ions to enter a dendritic spine, depolarizing it much more massively than is possible with AMPA receptors alone, possibly triggering a shift from tonic to bursty firing. But the departure of this single magnesium ion from the pore is a quantum domain event, whose timing is indeterministic. It can only be modeled as a probabilistic process. So, in addition to Brownian motion of neurotransmitter molecules, such as glutamate across the synapse, we now have a second possible way of amplifying quantum domain indeterminism up to a level of spike timing indeterminism.

But NMDA receptors may amplify quantum domain indeterminism to a level of indeterminism in neuronal spike timing in an even more interesting way than the timing of the release of the magnesium ion from its NMDA receptor pore. NMDA receptors may play a role in placing the operation of the brain in the domain of criticality. The sweet spot that balances dynamic excitation with inhibition occurs in a narrow range of moderate excitability. Theoretical work suggests that dynamic systems are maximally perturbable, even for small inputs, when the system operates in the narrow zone of criticality (Beggs, 2008; Bertschinger and Natschlaeger, 2004; Chialvo, 2010; Friedman et al., 2012; Kinouchi and Copelli, 2006; Roli et al, 2018; Stewart and Plenz, 2008; Tagliazucchi and Chialvo, 2013), which, theorists have shown, in turn requires a baseline spontaneous firing rate. This spontaneous activity in the absence of input is crucial for various aspects of network development and plasticity (Ben-Ari, 2001; Penn et al., 1998; Spitzer, 2006). Its signature in neural tissue is the occurrence of tens to hundreds of milliseconds of synchronized bursts called "avalanches" that are typically separated by seconds of quiescence (Spitzer, 2006). The criticality domain expresses a moderate mean level of synchrony with maximal variability of synchrony. This domain lies at the boundary between excessively low synchrony and excessively high synchrony in the population of neurons. The healthy brain therefore appears to operate where unpredictability of network response to a given input is maximal. This high-variability, borderline chaotic behavior of healthy neural networks may account for empirical evidence showing variability in neuronal responses to identical external inputs. Some theorists have argued that the brain's operation in the domain of criticality may arise in part because of the nonlinear and burst-triggering responses of NMDA receptors, in conjunction with effects of dopamine binding to the D1 receptor (Stewart and Plenz, 2006). If information is carried in perturbations of firing rate away from the baseline firing rate, this domain is maximally sensitive to perturbations, and thus is maximally capable of carrying information. In a sense, the system is set up so that the fluttering of a butterfly's wings, which is a metaphor for local fluctuations or variability in spike timing, can be amplified up to a level where it makes a difference to information processing in the brain.

This section considered three ways that microscopic indeterminism might be amplified up to a level of spike timing indeterminism: Brownian motion in the synapse, magnesium ion behavior in NMDA receptors, and the introduction of criticality or near-chaos into neural spike timing (again probably by virtue of NMDA receptor behavior). These factors alone may be enough to make not only our brains, but also even the whole macroscopic universe indeterministic. But some people have argued that there are even stranger ways that quantum domain indeterminism might play a role in brain function. We cover these possibilities in the next section.

4.11 Indeterminism in the Brain, Part 2

Quantum domain entanglement is the strange state where particles, once they have interacted, are to be described by a single quantum mechanical wave equation, even if the component particles that have interacted in the past are now far apart (i.e., spacelike separated). A consequence of entanglement or nonlocality is that an observed event or fluctuation here can be correlated with an event as far away as the other side of the universe, as long as the particles have interacted in the past and remain coherent or entangled. If all particles ultimately trace back to a singularity at the beginning of the present universe, the entire universe may be entangled.

Einstein, Podolsky, and Rosen (1935) proposed an experiment designed to reveal the absurdity of quantum theory, because it predicted such entanglement. Instead, entanglement has repeatedly been shown to occurr, just as quantum theory predicts. For example, if two photons are emitted from a calcium atom, they will move in opposite directions but maintain a net spin of zero; if one is measured to have spin in a given direction, then the other photon with which it is entangled will be found to have the opposite spin, even though this "effect" would seem to have been transferred instantaneously, or faster than the speed of light. The reality of nonlocality has now been largely settled by physics (Aspect, 2015; Aspect et al., 1982; Francis, 2012; Hanson, 2015; Kocher, 1971; Matson, 2012; Yin et al., 2013). Einstein's local realism, according to which a particle's state has definite physical values at each moment, even when not measured, which, moreover, can only be influenced by local causes transmitted no faster than the speed of light, is dead (Holmes, 2017).

For most philosophical determinists, it would seem obvious that determinism implies that each partial subset of the universe also develops deterministically, belying their incorrect local realist intuitions. But one implication of these recent results in physics is that local determinism is also dead. This follows because, for any partial finite subset of the universe, a state, say, a spin state, could take on a definite value for no apparent local causal reason because of a measurement made outside that finite subset, even if executed at the other end of the universe. Therefore, nonlocality entails that the only tenable variant of determinism left is global determinism or superdeterminism, according to which the nonlocal entanglements that would later arise among particles were determined even before the particles came into existence, presumably at the beginning, when all energy came into existence at the same moment in a hypothesized singularity. This global determinism is only possible if the universe is finite in extent. If it were infinite in extent, nonlocality and the partial finite subset argument would entail that the universe is inherently indeterministic, because no matter how big the finite partial subset considered, local causal factors could not account for event outcomes within the subset, because of nonlocal correlations with events outside the subset. Questions of global determinism and the size of the universe may not be empirically settleable, in which case believing in global determinism would become an act of faith, rather than evidence-based reason.

The universe is assumed to be 13.8 billion years old because astronomers can see light from early events that left their sources that long ago, in every direction, which is to say that we might think that we find ourselves at the center of a giant sphere of visibility twice 13.8 billion light years across. But there are likely to be events beyond this horizon of visibility. For one thing, the farthest things we can see do not look like the hypothesized first events, so it is likely that light is on its way from outside the zone of visibility, and the universe would have to get older in order for us to be able to see it on Earth (Haynes, 2020). Moreover, the universe has expanded since the Big Bang, and events that emitted light 13.8 billion years ago are now perhaps 46 billion light years away (Siegel, 2018), making the known universe 92 billion light years across.

In order to account for a static universe, Einstein posited a cosmological constant in the field equations for general relativity as a fudge factor to counteract gravitation, which would have entailed a contracting universe. He abandoned the idea after Hubble showed the universe to be expanding. In the late 1990s, very distant supernovae were observed to be dimmer than expected, implying that the universe's expansion is accelerating. The cosmological constant was reintroduced in the form of a hypothesized, but so far unobserved, dark matter/energy that many associated with the zero-point energy of the vacuum, which is itself a quantum domain phenomenon. Because of Heisenberg's uncertainty relationship, a particle, even at absolute zero, cannot occupy the trough of its possible states because this would entail a precise position and momentum. Instead, even at absolute zero, a particle would have some vibrational energy. Another consequence of this idea is that the vacuum is not empty but is instead a rather ether-like sea of virtual particles.

Because the universe is expanding, a subset of the universe containing the whole universe would soon not subsume the whole universe anymore because new space is continually being created between the stars and galaxies, and this space is thought to be full of virtual particles. The partial finite subset argument arises again at each moment because new parts of the universe come into existence outside of that subset as the universe expands. This might interestingly link indeterminism to the expansion of the universe (Wood, 2022a,b). Moreover, if the cosmic inflation hypothesis of Alan Guth is correct, and the universe grew rapidly and vastly in size in the first moments of the universe (Wood, 2021), the majority of the universe lies beyond our horizon of visibility. If such inflation happened in multiple or even infinitely many places, multiple universes might exist beyond our ability to detect them (Eicher, 2019). If nonlocal correlations stem from a shared origin, it is conceivable that a measurement in one universe might result in what seemed to be a random fluctuation in another. But really, who knows? Some researchers say that cosmic inflation preceded the "hot Big Bang" and erased any information about events prior to that event. This would mean that we have no way of knowing how the universe began (Siegel, 2021).

I do not want to stray too far into astronomy and cosmology in a book about free will and the brain. I have only raised these fascinating matters in order to address the issue of determinism versus indeterminism. At present we have no way to rule out global determinism or indeterminism, and the matter might not be settleable by scientific observation, in principle, if parts of the universe lie beyond what can be observed. Astronomers do not even understand the nature of dark energy and dark matter, which some estimate together comprise more than 95% of the universe (Bass, 2015; Naeye, 2019) and which are assumed to be central to the expansion of the universe. Think about that: physicists lack a physics for 95% of the universe.

Returning to the brain, a veritable cottage industry has emerged among physicists who have suggested that mental events somehow follow from quantum domain entanglement and nonlocality. But I believe the claim that entanglement, also known as quantum domain coherence, matters for brain function is implausible. Such seemingly radical claims are not needed to account for indeterminism at the level of information processing in the brain. Criterial detectors or decoders, such as receptors or neurons, can operate in the domain of warm brain temperatures where the kind of quantum domain coherence that would be necessary to realize entanglement would be made incoherent (Davies, 2004), unless some kind of molecular "shield" has evolved to keep coherence in place among shielded particles. I think there is no need to invoke quantum nonlocality, superposition, entanglement, coherence, electron tunneling, quantum gravity, or any new forces to understand informational causal chains in the brain. Criteria can be realized in the input–output mechanisms of relatively large-scale, high-temperature entities, such as receptors or neurons, in the absence of nonlocality effects.

What is needed, however, is some degree of noise in the system that arises from amplified microscopic fluctuations that manifest themselves as randomness concerning the timing of EPSPs and IPSPs, which in turn introduces randomness into neural spike timing. Because of such noise at the synapse and within neurons themselves, there is no guarantee that identical presynaptic input will lead to identical postsynaptic output, even if time could be "rewound" and initial conditions were truly identical. But noise could also be introduced by external factors, for example, noise in perceptual inputs, or cellular damage due to free radicals or cosmic rays, or many other possible causes that have nothing to do with nonlocal quantum level effects. While I argue that noise can be harnessed for the purposes of generating novel solutions using criterial causality, this is a far cry from notions that nonlocal quantum-level effects are in some mysterious way responsible for mental events.

In short, I think that it is improbable that any of the strange, nonlocal quantum coherence effects can have any influence on how neurons behave, or how consciousness or information is realized in neural events. The brain is, simply put, too "warm" to support this kind of quantum domain coherence, and synapses are too wide to support electron tunneling. Just because some quantum effects are mysterious, as is the physical realization of mental phenomena, does not mean they are related. This is why I doubt that quantum domain effects—beyond the variability in neural dynamics introduced by amplification of microscopic fluctuations that we discussed in the last section—are required to account for how information is processed by neurons.

Some physicists and philosophers have argued that quantum indeterminism permits a gap in physical causal chains that can be exploited by consciousness to bias which possibilities become real. The view that I developed in my 2013 book is unlike such views because consciousness, in the sense of subjective experience, is not seen to play a necessary role in determining which possibility is actualized right now. Rather, consciousness, and the entertainment of possible scenarios and courses of action in working memory, plays a role in changing the criteria for firing on neurons that might lead to future mental events. In other words, conscious experience and online manipulation of representations in working memory allow the potentiation of future mental events and actions, not present ones.

4.12 Indeterminism in the Brain, Part 3

Now that I have confessed myself to be a skeptic about quantum entanglement and nonlocality playing a role in brain function, I must also express skepticism toward my own skepticism. I now give concrete reasons that might end up proving my skepticism to be just plain wrong. As a first example, it has been shown that even massive molecules such as C_{60} (Fullerene, molecular weight 720.6468 g/mol; diameter ~0.7 nm) exhibit interference effects when passed through a double slit one molecule at a time. By comparison, neurotransmitters are typically much smaller than this (e.g., glutamate: 147.13 g/mol; GABA: 103.12 g/mol; serotonin: 176.22 g/mol; glycine: 75.01 g/mol) and the ions that pass through ionotropic receptors are even tinier (sodium: 22.99 g/mol; calcium: 40.08 g/mol; potassium: 39.10 g/mol). The diameter of an open NMDA receptor pore is only about 5.5 Å or 0.55 nm. By way of comparison, slits that are orders of magnitude larger generate interference effects when electrons are passed through them (50 × 0.3 μm). Given their small size, NMDA receptors can be (and typically are) packed together much more closely than this, which, if simultaneously open, as occurs during bursting, would create the conditions for two- or multi-slit interference. Moreover, multiple classically incompatible states can exist in a quantum superposition in microgram-scale macroscopic objects that are orders of magnitude larger than a neuron (Bild et al., 2023). So certainly wave–particle effects could in principle be expressed among neurotransmitters in the synapse. The key question is whether such effects matter in the functioning of a neuron. I am skeptical, but I admit, I do not know. If so, this would be another mechanism for introducing indeterminacy from the quantum domain to the level of variability in spike and burst timing.

Another known mechanism can be found in that part of the brain called "the retina" where a cascading avalanche of signals can follow the detection of even a single photon. How can sensors in the retina detect a single photon? If there was ever a quantum domain event, it would be the absorption of a single photon. Evolution has come up with a protein molecule called rhodopsin, which is in the photodetectors in our retina. The key subcomponent of this is called "retinal," which is basically very close to vitamin A. So, when people say vitamin A helps you see, there is a good bit of truth in that. Retinal is amazing. It changes its shape from all-trans-retinal to 11-cis-retinal if a single photon is absorbed by it.

Thus, the central foundation of our most important sensory system, vision, and ultimately of our visual conscious experience, is the isomerization and consequent shape change of a molecule that is a variant of vitamin A. As depicted in Figure 4.10, a single photon of light isomerizes a single molecule of retinal bound to rod or cone opsins. This is then amplified through a cascade of downstream processes that greatly amplify this signal, which can ultimately increase the likelihood that a neuron in the retina, called a ganglion cell, will fire and tell the rest of the brain that light has been detected at a certain location on the retina. Moreover, coherent coupling of electronic states mediated by vibrational motion (vibronic coupling) rooted in quantum domain coherence enhances the energy transfer underlying light detection (Schnedermann et al., 2018). Thus, a quantum domain process plays a central role in seeing, the most important aspect of our perception. Other scientists have recently argued that the perception of smell is similarly rooted in quantum domain processes.

Now things get even stranger in the retinas of birds. Some scientists (Hiscock et al., 2016; Hochstoeger et al., 2020; Xu et al, 2021; Zoltowski et al., 2019) have recently argued that migratory birds have a protein in their retinas that allows them to detect the orientation of the Earth's magnetic field lines. In particular, there is a cryptochrome protein of the Cry4 type, expressed in the cones of migrating birds, which many think is likely to be the magnetoreceptive protein used by birds to navigate using Earth's magnetic field lines. But it is not magnetoreceptive because it contains anything like tiny bits of iron that are magnetic. Instead, it detects light. According to the "radical pair model of the avian magnetoreceptor" it depends on long-lived electron spin

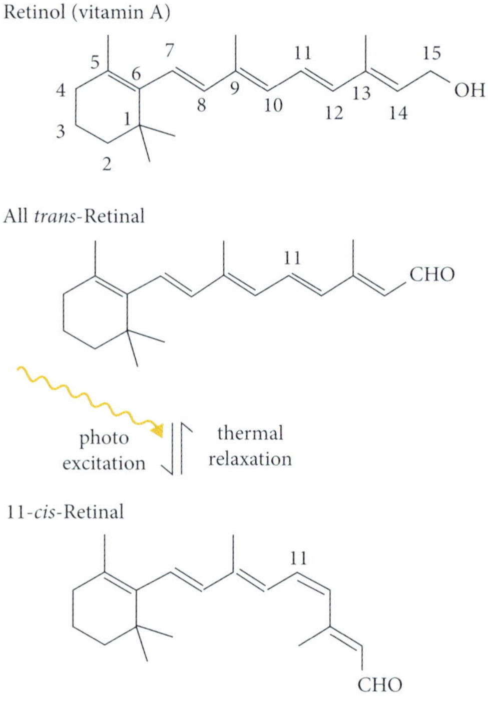

Figure 4.10 The vitamin A-like all trans-retinal molecule changes its conformation when a photon is absorbed. This quantum domain event is the beginning of a cascade of events that leads to conscious visual experience perhaps two to three hundred milliseconds later.

Reproduced with permission from Mark R. Leach, from *The Chemogenesis Web book*. https://www.meta-synthesis.com/webbook/17_photo/photo.php

coherence or entanglement. Physicists have long known that the rates and yields of reactions involving free radicals are influenced by the application of magnetic fields, a phenomenon they call the "radical pair mechanism." Evidence is accumulating that migratory birds sense the direction of the Earth's magnetic field by means of radical pairs formed by the influence of detected photons on the cryptochrome protein Cry4. Sensitivity to magnetic field orientation arises because of the radical pair's spin dynamics. In particular, it depends on the spins being coherent across the pair. So, evolution has come up with a protein that effectively shields coherent spins from decohering, despite the warm noisiness of the bird retina. This coherence or quantum domain entanglement allows migrating birds to gain information about the orientation of magnetic field lines.

Now whether birds actually consciously experience the orientation of the magnetic field lines of the Earth with associated qualia (say north looks reddish and south looks greenish), I have no idea. I would not even know how to find out the answer to the question of what it is like to see magnetic field lines. But even if this mechanism has nothing to do with consciousness, if this model of avian magnetoreception in the retina is not ultimately falsified, it will be, in my opinion, the first strong evidence of quantum domain entanglement playing a central role in brain processing.

According to the philosophical doctrine of functionalism, a particular mental state is what it is solely because of the way it functions or causally interacts with other functions that have evolved to be realized in the nervous system. The material realization of a function is irrelevant, and as long as the same function is realized across different material realizers, the realized mental state will be the same in all realizers. A strong version of this doctrine cannot hold if some functions can only arise because of the particular material constitution of neurons, synapses, clefts, and, indeed, molecules. For example, if certain functions, say, the transduction of magnetic fields into action potentials, can only be realized by quantum domain phenomena, such as spin entanglement, then function cannot be divorced from particular material realizations.

Beyond brains, it may be that quantum domain entanglement plays a central role in other biological processes. Numerous experiments in recent years have supported the conclusion that photosynthesis is afforded by quantum domain effects (Thyrhaug et al., 2018). Scientists have found that coherence between distant particles affords energy transfer or transport within the photosynthetic chain reaction. In all organisms that carry out photosynthesis, a photon triggers the excitation of an electron in a protein "antenna." Scientists noticed that coherence within the light capturing "antenna" proteins of green sulfur bacteria lasted much longer than one would expect, given the decohering influences of the warm temperatures they exist in.

Figure 4.11 shows a picture of the protein complex of these bacteria. The gray areas are protein scaffolding, and the green areas are chlorophyll proteins. Once a photon is captured, it triggers electron excitation which, in turn, triggers a change in charge in a reaction site, which is ultimately converted into chemical energy, such as the production of sugars, for the cell to store and use later as a source of energy, rather like storing energy in a battery the size of a molecule. The problem for photosynthesizing lifeforms is that electron excitation must be transferred, extremely fast and efficiently, from the antenna to the sugar-producing core before the energy associated with electron excitation is lost. Awareness of this extreme time pressure and need for efficiency triggered the interesting idea that maybe there is something like quantum computation going on in chlorophyll to optimize energy transfer. The idea is that energy from captured photons could explore every possible path from a protein's surface to the reaction center at the chlorophyll's core, in order to take the shortest and fastest path.

Engel et al. (2007) and Wang et al. (2019) showed that quantum coherence at cold temperatures (77 K) could account for the efficiency of energy transfer from the antenna to the core. Others soon observed quantum coherences at room temperatures (Collini et al., 2010; Panitchayangkoon et al., 2010, 2011). Quantum coherence has now been observed in a many photosynthetic subsystems, including protein–pigment complexes LH1 (Ferretti et al., 2014) and LH2 (Dahlberg et al., 2015; Fidler et al., 2014; Hildner et al., 2013), the reaction centers (Flanagan et al., 2016; Fuller et al., 2014; Hayes et al., 2011; Lee et al., 2007; Parkinson et al., 2007; Romero et al., 2014;

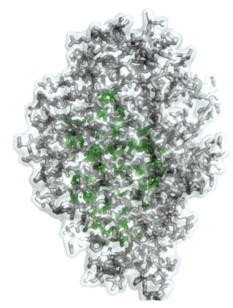

Figure 4.11 The Fenna–Matthews–Olson (FMO) bacteriochlorophyll complex, found in anaerobic, thermophilic, gram-negative green sulfur bacteria *Chlorobium tepidum*, acts as an energy 'wire' connecting a large peripheral light-harvesting antenna, the chlorosome, to the reaction center. Wave-like quantum beating signals among excitons within the FMO complex at 77 kelvin can account for the extreme efficiency of photosynthesis, because it allows the complexes to sample vast areas of phase space to find the most efficient path from the antenna to the sugar-producing core (Engel et al., 2007). Chlorophyll molecules are shown in green. Protein scaffolding is shown in gray.
Reproduced with permission from Greg Engel.

Ryu et al., 2014; Westenhoff et al., 2012) and antenna complexes from marine algae (Collini et al., 2010; Richards et al, 2012; Turner et al., 2011, 2012; Wong et al., 2012), as well as *in situ* in green sulfur bacteria (Dostál et al., 2016) and *in vivo* in purple bacteria (Dahlberg et al., 2015, 2017). Photosynthesis, which is the ultimate source of light-to-chemical energy that keeps us alive, appears to be rooted in quantum domain coherence.

At the fundamental level, all living things are creatures of the quantum domain. This is simply because atoms are possible only because of the quantized states of elementary particles. If it were not for the quantized states of electrons, they would not form discrete electron shells around the nucleus, and atoms as we know them could not exist. Since we are made of atoms, we could not exist if electron states were not quantized.

The key question we have considered here is whether quantum domain outcomes are amplified to a level where they make a difference to neural processing. The evidence for timing differences in neural firing associated with microscopic events like

Brownian motion of a neurotransmitter molecule diffusing across the synaptic cleft, or of the release of a magnesium ion from the pore of an NMDA receptor, is strong. These mechanisms alone amplify randomness from the microscopic domain to the macroscopic domain of neural spike timing randomness. And since neurons are fundamentally temporal coincidence detectors, and since the information realized in neural spiking depends on which inputs have made a post-synaptic neuron fire, information processing in the brain is surely made indeterministic by these processes of microscopic-to-macroscopic amplification. But this section considered the more radical idea that quantum domain coherence among nonlocal particles might play a role in brain function. I started out expressing my skepticism toward this idea, since so many farfetched ideas have been proposed. But then I looked at the actual data and found evidence for a role of quantum domain coherence, particularly in systems that have evolved to detect light. I think the evidence for a role of nonlocal coherence in the avian retina and in the case of light capture by plants is increasingly strong and convincing. I do not know where else quantum domain phenomena play a consequential role in biological systems. But as I mentioned, if quantum domain indeterminism is amplified up to a level of macroscopic biological relevance in even a single tiny corner of the universe, whether in our brains or in the brains of birds, then the entire known universe is made indeterministic.

4.13 What Is a Top-Down Brain Executive?

In order to have a free will, where outcomes can turn out otherwise and yet not be utterly random, it is necessary for an agent to be able to set conditions on how those outcomes will turn out. For example, it is necessary to be able to set criteria that must be met by any possible solution to a problem. If I need to build a bridge, for example, the criteria are pretty clear. The bridge has to support itself, should be as strong as possible, as cheap as possible, and should take advantage of an island in the middle of the river.
But criteria don't specify a unique solution. They constrain possible solutions. So, we might first turn off our internal editor and generate lots of solutions. We can build it out of wood, gold, stone, glass, or steel. Once we have generated a bunch of solutions, we can turn our internal editor on and decide that gold is too expensive and that wood can too easily burn. We might then conclude that steel is the strongest material for the price. We might then consider the type of bridge, and again generate many solutions. It can be a suspension bridge, a covered bridge, a draw bridge, etc. We can then turn our internal editor on again and conclude that a draw bridge is not required given that only small boats go by. We might conclude that a suspension bridge that has a support on the island in the middle of the river is the best solution. Using a "genetic algorithm" we can then start the whole process over from this new starting point. Given that it will be a steel suspension bridge, how can we best meet our specs? We can again turn off our internal editor in order to generate multiple possible adequate fulfillments of

our specs. Then we can turn our internal editor back on and sift through these ideas. We can cycle between possibility generation and editing of possibilities as many times as needed.

This kind of genetic algorithm is very much like natural selection in that there are two stages: one in which microscopic randomness (like genetic shuffling and mutation) is amplified up to a macroscopic level (of varied animal phenotypes), followed by elimination of what is suboptimal (weeding out the weak by predators). But this two-stage process is also like sexual selection, in that there is not only deselection of the weak, but active selection of the desirable; however, it does not involve generations of evaluations of some attractive ornament such as antlers or peacock tails, but rather involves generations of ideas. Through this generational interaction between creative generation of diverse ideas and the internal editor's selection/deselection of what is best/worst, we can evolve, in our minds, to an adequate solution to our problem.

Note that I said *an adequate* solution, rather than *the optimal* solution, because there are many possible solutions given any finite set of criteria or specs. It is easy to see how such a genetic process can serve as an engine of creativity in the human mind. We impose selective pressure in our imaginations, and naturally, as well as sexually, evolve toward a solution over generations of ideas.

In order to have a free will, where outcomes can turn out otherwise and yet not be utterly random, it is necessary for an agent to be able to set criteria or "specs" regarding how those outcomes will turn out. It is therefore necessary to have a neural code in place where such informational criteria can be set up. I have argued that evolution has provided us with just such a neural code. It is one rooted in the dynamic resetting of synaptic weights, such that a neuron will fire if particular informational conditions are met. But having such a neural code in place alone is not sufficient for having a free will. In addition, it is also imperative that there is an executive system in place that can set neural criteria as needed. Luckily, we also have such an executive. Rather, I would say we have a whole series of such executives in place, each of whom specializes in a particular domain of decision making.

Freely made decisions tend to result from cybernetic searches relative to an internal setpoint or goal. The need to build a bridge economically and well acts as a cognitive cybernetic setpoint. The search for a solution concerning what kind of bridge to build unfolds over durations, involving feedback and corrections along the way, as we deliberate our way creatively toward an adequate solution.

Other cybernetic deliberative searches are less cognitive and more emotional or visceral. We have an internal setpoint that emerges into consciousness, say, of feeling loneliness. We ponder how we might meet someone. Initially we might consider classes of ways to do this; we might go to a bar, call up an old flame, or join a dating service. Once we have internally evaluated how each of these options feels in our internal virtual reality of imaginative consciousness, we might go with what feels best, say, the latter option. We might then read reviews about various websites, and after subjectively, virtually experiencing how these options feel, we might join one. Then we might review possible mates, again seeing how we feel upon looking at them and reading about them. We might then contact a few who registered above an internal threshold of attraction, and over time, and with some luck, we might find an adequate solution to fulfilling our setpoint goal defined by the desire to meet someone. Notice how conscious evaluation is essential in each loop of the cybernetic cycle, as we, rather like a heat-seeking missile, home in on a potential "target." Whether cognitive or noncognitive setpoints guide us, free will unfolds cyclically, over extended durations, as we traverse trajectories of conscious and unconscious processing and action that, we hope, will take us to our eventual desired goal.

Volition never occurs at an instant. It is also inherently purposive and extended in time. The Baconian, Newtonian, Skinnerian project of limiting causal explanations to Aristotle's material and efficient causes simply fails for biological, cybernetic organisms, even ones as simple as a paramecium. We have no choice but to bring Aristotle's formal and final causes back into the domain of valid scientific and philosophical inquiry, because cybernetic reward-seeking and punishment-avoidance are inherently teleological and purposive. And consciousness, for those animals that have evolved to experience an evaluative internal world hallucination, as the domain of felt emotions and desires, is centrally about teleological drives that guide volitional attention, behavior, and thought toward goal fulfillment, whether through action or planning. That is, consciousness is inherently cybernetic and driven toward the fulfillment of organismic purposes. Because the vast majority of the universe, outside of living systems, is not cybernetic (a rock has no desires or goals, and internally hallucinates nothing), pan-psychism is a pipe dream.

Many, but not all, of the desires that guide volitional attention and other volitional operations toward goal fulfillment, cybernetically, are genetically programmed. For example, normal humans experience basic desires such as hunger, thirst, need for air or warmth, greed, lust, sleepiness, and so on. We also experience basic emotions, such as fear, anger, jealousy, loneliness, grief, love, and so on. Other cybernetic setpoints are more abstract, such as wanting to save Nature from ruination, or wanting to become a medical doctor. But even our more cognitive goals are typically infused with emotionality and desire. We want to save Nature because we love creation and can imagine both a world in which there is mass extinction with civilizational collapse, and a different world of balance and stewardship of our Earth.

Conversely, our desires and emotions are not independent of our cognition. For example, Peter Singer (1981) makes the argument that there are innate "Chomskian switches" in the domain of ethics. One of these is that we are born with a tendency to mark an in-group as "us" and everything outside that as "them." But how this switch is set depends on culture and our own reasoning. Papua New Guinea head-hunters of the distant past might have defined the in-group very narrowly as "those who speak my language." In contrast, Jains or Zen Buddhists might have defined "us" broadly to include all sentient beings in the universe. In one case, eating other human beings in some cases was condoned, whereas in the other case, eating *any* animal was regarded as immoral. Basic desires, such as the desire to eat something, or disgust at eating forbidden things, would be shaped by our ideas of what counted as food. Free will plays a role here as well, in that we can volitionally decide to stop eating meat, say, on moral grounds, despite our first-order desire to eat meat.

In the coming sections I review what we know about executive systems that permit volitional control of how bottom-up stimulus information is handled or responded to. Control is top-down if it is not driven solely by facts about the stimulus, but is also in part driven by the needs and criteria held by an executive system, say, in a working memory buffer, or by evaluation and cybernetic error correction relative to internally held setpoints, desires, goals, or beliefs. Control is volitional if the criteria to be satisfied are flexible and open to change by an executive for reasons that are its own, or if the desires and goals are its own, such as feeling hungry. I would like to argue that there is a family of such executives and teleological cybernetic desires in our brain that permit top-down control in various domains, rather like one person in a family dominating what goes on in the kitchen, and another governing decision making and actions in the family business.

4.14 Global Cortical Architecture

Our goal is to learn about the executive control systems of the brain, especially those that allow the brain to take volitional control of how it will behave via the body, or volitionally govern itself, such as what it will pay attention to, even in the absence of an overt movement by any part of the body. As a general rule, the brain is divided into a perceptual processing side and an executive control or planning side. The divide between these two functional halves, perceptual or bottom-up and executive or top-down, just so happens to fall almost exactly at the midpoint of the brain at the central sulcus. Perceptual processing tends to run back to front, whereas executive processing tends to run front to back across the cortex.

In Brodmann area 10, which is right under our foreheads, we tend to find the most abstract sorts of planning. This might include plans that are independent of the present sensory input, such as, "next year I want to learn Arabic." It might also process stacks of plans, such as "I need to go to the supermarket, but on the way I have to go to the post office to buy stamps." And if I get interrupted, say, because I run into a friend at the post office, it might remind me that I had better go to the supermarket before the kids get home. Or it might process a high-level proposition such as "I need to drink more water." A bit further back, in premotor cortex, a more concrete plan might come up with a particular path toward a particular water fountain. And by the time we reach all the way back to the motor strip, which lies in the gyrus just in front of the central sulcus, called the precentral gyrus, particular motor sequences might get activated. This might be thought of as pulling the strings on a marionette. In fact, you can think of your body as your own personal marionette, whose control is via the "strings being pulled" in motor cortex by other more anterior executive areas. Ultimately motor output neurons, such as Betz cells in layer V of the motor strip (area 4) are activated so that the neurons that they in turn activate in the dorsal horn of the spinal cord can then trigger other neurons to contract muscles appropriately.

In the case of vision, information processing tends to run from the back of the brain toward the front of the brain in various processing streams. Information that flows down the ventral stream flows down the temporal lobes. Ventral stream processing is central to our conscious experience and object recognition. Sometimes people call the ventral stream the "what" processing pathway, because it helps us know what an object is. It flows down the temporal lobes toward the hippocampus bilaterally, where objects can be identified and stored for later recognition purposes. Some of this bottom-up visual information is selected, via attention, for deeper processing. It is shunted toward frontal working memory areas where it can help frontal areas plan what to do next, in light of what is being seen and the broader context of the present situation.

There is also a dorsal stream flowing from visual input areas up into the parietal lobes. This information is not about *what* an object is, but rather it is about *where* it is and *where* it is going. So sometimes scientists call the dorsal stream the "where" or "whence" processing pathway. Because of this division of labor into two or more processing streams, you might have a neuron down in the ventral stream (in the temporal lobe) firing away, carrying the information that there is, say, a tiger out there in the world somewhere, but it doesn't know where. And at the same time, you might have another neuron up in the dorsal pathway (in the parietal) lobe firing away, carrying the information that an object of a certain size and a certain distance from me is moving in this or that direction at this or that speed, but it doesn't know what it is.

One problem is how the unconnected information in these two processing streams can be brought together, so that we can know that it is a tiger at that location moving this way or that. This is one aspect of the "binding problem." How can information that has been separated into separate parallel processing streams be brought back together into a unitary bound representation, such as the unitary moving tiger of our subjective experience? It is a bit like the problem of putting Humpty Dumpty back together again. One idea is that attention binds the outputs of these two processing streams by creating a link in frontal working memory areas, such that a new neuron or population of neurons in a working memory area, such as the dorsolateral prefrontal cortex (dlPFC), temporarily takes input from a ventral stream "tiger detector" and simultaneously from a dorsal stream "moving object detector." When such a frontal neuron or group of neurons fires, it is driven by both of these inputs, and effectively becomes a tiger-moving-at-that-location detector. Thus, attention may play the role of a binding "glue," linking diverse modularized representations across information processing streams.

There are many other processing streams than just the ventral and dorsal visual processing streams. There are analogs of the ventral and dorsal pathways for audition, touch, and the other sensory systems. In addition, there are other pathways even for vision. For example, on the medial surface of the brain there appears to be a "medial processing stream" involved in representing our location as we navigate through the world. Its information processing runs from visual input areas to retrosplenial cortex, through parahippocampal and entorhinal cortex, down into the hippocampus as well.

Having multiple processing streams allows the brain to operate in and compute in multiple coordinate systems at the same time. The coordinate system of the ventral stream appears to be in viewer-centered or egocentric coordinates, which is to say, where things are relative to me, the viewer of a scene. In contrast, the coordinate system of the dorsal stream seems to be in effector-based coordinates, that is, where things are relative to an effector, such as my hand, my head, my eyes, and so on. And the coordinate system of the medial processing stream appears to be in so-called world-centered (or allocentric) coordinates, namely, where objects are in the world, relative to each other, rather than relative to where I happen to be standing. Thus, just as we have many distinct specialist organs in our body, like the heart and the lungs, our brains appear to have many distinct information processing "mental organs" or modularized neural circuits that specialize in processing distinct types of information.

4.15 Phineas Gage and Self-Governance

Our goal in this and coming sections is to get an overview of the executive neural control circuits that permit our nervous system to govern itself. What does it mean to govern oneself? It means the ability and freedom to decide based on one's own needs, desires, and priorities, and to be able to consider many possible courses of action or thought. It means the capacity to select the best course of action or thought, based on one's own reasons and evaluations. And finally it means the capacity to stick to a self-determined course of action, as long as it makes sense to do so. Since we make decisions in various domains of thought and action, there are probably different executive processes associated with each class of our decision making, self-control, self-regulation, or self-governance.

Some executive processes you would want to be volitional, such as deliberation regarding whom to marry. In contrast, other executive decisions should probably not be volitional. As an example of the latter sort, an animal that could will to make something that smells disgusting smell delicious, might then go eat it, and then get sick and die. There are good and ancient reasons why we cannot will to make vomit or feces smell good, or will to find visible indicators of genetic dishealth or low fertility attractive. Genes that permitted that kind of volitional control would have gotten weeded out long ago. Conversely, what smells good is also probably in part innately programmed in our genes. But that does not mean that we have to be slavishly driven by such nonvolitional and perhaps innate programming. This is because there are other centers of decision making that can override nonvolitional decisions such as "hmm, that smells good," "wow, that looks attractive," or "yuck, that smells bad." Returning to our earlier example, let us say that you are a vegan on moral grounds. You might still find the aroma of barbecued meat delicious. You might find that smelling barbecued ribs makes your mouth water against your will. But you can override that desire and choose to eat vegetables for your own (in this case moral) reasons. Conversely, you might find some vegetarian dish unappetizing, but force yourself to eat it, so that you do not, say, insult the host, who put so much effort into making that just for you. You can act on the basis of your reasons rather than your desires if your executive neural circuitry is in working order.

Some psychologists (Metcalfe and Mischel, 1999) and philosophers (Frankfurt, 1971, 1989) have talked of "hot" or first-order desires, like wanting to eat ice cream because it will taste good, and other "cold" or second-order desires, like simultaneously not wanting to eat the ice cream, because you do not want to gain weight. When there is no conflict between desire and other goal-seeking systems, there is no problem. If I tell you that you must kiss that beautiful person with whom you are madly in love, you will probably say "Sure, no problem." Or if I tell you that you must not eat this vomit, you will say "OK, no problem." But if your father commands you to never again see the person with whom you are madly in love, as in *Romeo and Juliet*, there will be conflict between the desire to obey your father and your desire to see your beloved. Conversely, if your father commands you to marry an unappealing old man, as in *Fiddler on the Roof*, there will be conflict between the desire to obey your father and your desire to avoid that awful outcome. Executive control is essential in regulating our behavior and minds, especially in such cases of conflict, where prioritization and appropriate sequencing among opposing goals is required. Self-governance is most evident in cases where one or more of our brain's goal-seeking circuits must be inhibited in the service of fulfilling the aims of another of our brain's goal-seeking circuits.

It turns out that key executive circuitry lies just behind our foreheads. If we lose key frontal lobe circuitry, whether through a frontal lobotomy, the degeneration of neurons associated with frontotemporal dementia, Alzheimer's disease, or brain damage, we might well lose volitional executive control of our bodies and minds. The most famous example of such a loss is Phineas Gage, shown in Figure 4.12. He actually worked in the town where I also now work, in Hanover, NH. He was a foreman working with his crew, laying down railroad tracks in Cavendish, VT. This was before

Figure 4.12 Phineas Gage holding the iron spike that blasted through his skull.
Source: https://commons.wikimedia.org/wiki/File:Phineas_Gage_GageMillerPhoto2010-02-17_Unretouched_Color_Cropped.jpg

the invention of dynamite. He put gunpowder into a crack in the granite and laid down a long fuse. Normally he should have covered the gunpowder with some sand before tamping it down, but Phineas got distracted, and tamped the gunpowder down with his iron rod directly. This made it spark, which then blew the iron spike through his brain. The spike landed 80 feet, or more than 25 meters away, covered with his blood and brains. Incredibly Mr. Gage did not die. Instead, he remained conscious and was able to talk to the doctor about what had just happened. But he did sustain massive left frontal lobe damage. (The frontal lobes appear not to be necessary for consciousness since he was still conscious). Whereas before his accident he was responsible and capable of leading a team of men, after his accident he had a major personality change. Basically, he lost executive control of his desires, and became less able to govern himself, especially in the social and emotional domains.

In the words of Dr. John Harlow (1868), who treated Gage after his injury:

> The equilibrium or balance, so to speak, between his intellectual faculties and animal propensities, seems to have been destroyed. He is fitful, irreverent, indulging at times in the grossest profanity (which was not previously his custom), manifesting but little deference for his fellows, impatient of restraint or advice when it conflicts with his desires, at times pertinaciously obstinate, yet capricious and vacillating, devising many plans of future operations, which are no sooner arranged than they are abandoned in turn for others appearing more feasible. A child in his intellectual capacity and manifestations, he has the animal passions of a strong man. Previous to his injury, although untrained in the schools, he possessed a well-balanced mind, and was looked upon by those who knew him as a shrewd, smart businessman, very energetic and persistent in executing all his plans of operation. In this regard his mind was radically changed, so decidedly that his friends and acquaintances said he was "no longer Gage."

What does the case of Phineas Gage teach us? At one level we all have an internal Phineas Gage, who is being held in check by our capacities to self-govern and inhibit ourselves. That capacity is realized in the frontal areas and white matter tracts that he lost. We all have multiple goals at the same time, and these have to be prioritized and sequenced correctly if we are to reach our highest level goals, and not undermine them with impetuous impulsiveness. We can feel various bodily desires at the same time. For example, we can feel thirsty, tired, hungry, and feel in need of cooling down, all at the same time. In addition, we can feel various emotions at the same time. We can feel angry and ashamed and afraid all at the same time. We can also have immediate cognitive goals. For example, we might want to finish making dinner as quickly as possible, while also paying attention to an ongoing conversation. And we can also have longer-term cognitive goals, like wanting to get into college or to travel to Chile (as Phineas Gage did after his accident). Given that we can simultaneously pursue numerous goals and subgoals, how can we organize our planning to optimize the fulfillment of these different goals? And given that we have desires, emotions, conscious perception of the world, and the inner virtual reality of our imagination, we have ways of sequencing and otherwise regulating these different classes of goals.

We need ways to regulate our emotions, our desires, our thoughts, and our actions. Not surprisingly the brain appears to have developed specialized neural circuitry for each of these domains that is tantamount to having modular mental "organs" specialized for these various capacities. Each such mental capacity involves its own internal processes of regulation, control, and prioritization. And executive control processes govern the prioritization of processes across these mental organs. If we lose the capacity for such control, we might become like Phineas Gage or a disinhibited frontotemporal dementia patient. Or we might be like a two-year old with temper tantrums and impetuous wants that need to be fulfilled right now.

We all begin life unable to fully govern ourselves well. But with practice, feedback, and the wiring up of executive circuits behind our foreheads, we get better at governing ourselves. With enough practice we can even attain self-mastery.

4.16 Executive Control Circuits of the Brain

This section aims to provide a forest-level view of the executive neural circuits that permit our nervous system to govern itself. To that end, let us now look at some of the principal neural circuits of the human cortex. Below is some color-coded fMRI data from a 2011 paper by Yeo, Buckner and others (2011).

What you see in Figure 4.13 is a parcellation of the cortex into seven main cortical regions. These areas were found using functional connectivity analysis, a technique that allows researchers to see what parts of the brain co-vary in their activity patterns with each other. Even when people are at rest, just lying in the MRI scanner getting scanned, not doing any particular task at all, brain areas will co-vary if they are part of a common neural circuit. By looking across a thousand resting human brains, these authors came up with a map of what parts of the cortex are part of a common circuit. They could infer that they comprised a common circuit because neural activity varied in a positively correlated way. Note that this color-coding scheme is not based on local neural circuit architecture, like Brodmann areas, but is based on correlation of neural activity across the whole cortex. What you will immediately notice is that a given functionally defined neural network, defined by a single color here, is not located at a single location in the brain. Rather, it is distributed across the lobes of the brain.

First let us look at the light blue area. This circuit corresponds to motor output and sensory input areas that have a somatotopic representation. We can therefore assume that the blue areas correspond to circuitry associated with perception of the body, and motoric control of the body.

The next circuit we see is the red one. This is sometimes called the default mode network because a neuroscientist named Marcus Raichle noticed that it seemed to be activated when people were not doing a task in the fMRI scanner. Figure 4.14 shows

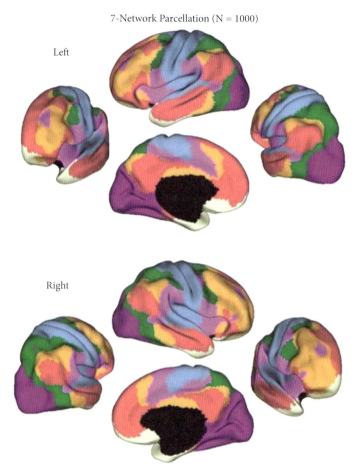

Figure 4.13 The seven colored regions represent areas of the brain that tend to covary in their neural activity. This "functional connectivity" suggests that regions of a given color subserve shared functions realized in interacting neural circuitry.

Reproduced with permission, from Yeo, B. T., Krienen, F. M., Sepulcre, J., Sabuncu, M. R., Lashkari, D., Hollinshead, M., Roffman, J. L., Smoller, J. W., Zöllei, L., Polimeni, J. R., Fischl, B., Liu, H., & Buckner, R. L. (2011). The organization of the human cerebral cortex estimated by intrinsic functional connectivity. *Journal of Neurophysiology*, *106*(3), 1125–1165.

another view of the default mode network. These brain areas co-vary in their activity because they are "talking" to each other and providing one another with inputs via long axons that connect them, as shown here. Other people noticed that these same red areas were active when people were thinking about other people, mindwandering, daydreaming, or thinking about themselves. So, it seems that the red circuit is fundamentally involved with simulating events in an internal "virtual reality," particularly concerning ourselves, other minds, and social activity. It is likely central to our capacity to imagine. And since we are social beings, much of what we imagine is social in nature, particularly concerning our own interactions with others. But as we see

The Neuroscience of Free Will 221

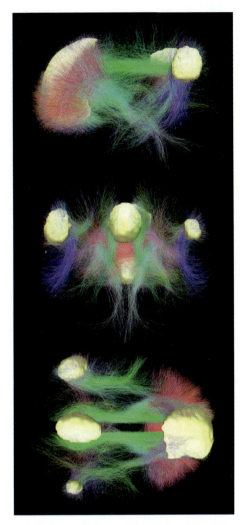

Figure 4.14 Diffusion tensor imaging shows the nodes of the default mode network (Horn et al., 2013) connected via axonal fiber tracts (anterior–posterior in green, up–down in blue, and left–right in red). Top: View of left side of head, with forehead on the left. Middle: View from behind head. Bottom: View from above head, with forehead on the right.

Source: Horn, A., Ostwald, D., Reisert, M., and Blankenburg, F. (2013). The structural-functional connectome and the default mode network of the human brain. *NeuroImage*, *102*, 142–151. doi:10.1016/j.neuroimage.2013.09.069

later, this internal virtual reality simulator can be engaged for nonsocial tasks as well. Scientists noticed that this red circuitry was downregulated when people were actively and willfully paying attention to the execution of some task.

Now let us move on to another two circuits. It was various parts of the green and yellow circuitry that seemed to become activated as the default mode network became deactivated, and vice versa, suggesting a mutually inhibitory relationship between a "task-positive" and a "task-negative" or default mode network. The green circuitry seems most involved with making and planning volitional eye movements and shifts of endogenous attention that are subject to volitional control. The yellow circuitry also seems to be involved in volitional processing, but not so much in shifts of attention as in planning, deliberation, consideration, weighing and selection of options. Since the green and yellow circuits likely operate in tandem to decide what to do and attend to next, various parts of the green and yellow circuits are sometimes called the dorsal attentional network (DAN).

In contrast, shown in violet is the ventral attentional network. This one is not subject to volitional control. It seems to subserve "exogenous" attention, which is the automatic grabbing of attention by things that suddenly move or blink, that make a sudden noise, or are otherwise distracting. Its role is to disengage us from whatever we might be volitionally attending, or nonvolitionally daydreaming about and orient us to the locus of something suddenly salient and worthy of attention. Any animal that could not get distracted by sudden sensory changes would likely end up in the belly of a predator.

Finally, at the back of the brain, shown in purple, is the largely retinotopic cortex associated with visual processing. And in light green, at the bottom of the front of the brain, in the ventromedial and orbital prefrontal regions, is neural circuitry thought to be involved in the regulation of emotion.

Granted, this is a very crude parcellation of the brain. Much finer parcellations of neural circuitry are possible and have been carried out and certain circuits are not shown here. For example, the many noncortical circuits involved in reward are not visible in this view of the cortex, though reward plays a central role in our behavior and thinking. And, also not shown here is another subcortical structure, the amygdala, which plays several roles, including the processing of potential danger and the triggering of associated emotions such as fear, or bodily reactions, such as the fight-or-flight response.

Even though this is a coarse picture of the main circuits of cortex, it does allow us to gain a forest-level view of cortex. We can see that there are two primary neural circuits associated with executive control and willing, namely, volitional control of eye movements and attention (associated with the green areas) and the volitional control of events involved in planning and deliberation (associated with the yellow areas). These volitional circuits exist in contradistinction to apparently nonvolitional ones, such as the ventral attentional or exogenous attentional network (the violet areas) or the default mode network (the red areas). In the next section we dissect the volitional circuits in a bit more detail.

4.17 Cybernetic Cingulate Cortex and Willpower

In this and in the next section we look in more detail at the areas of cortex associated with volitional control of attention and planning. In the last section I argued that the yellow and green areas are especially central to volitional control. Now let us unpack what may be going on with regard to cognition in a bit more detail. Many brain scientists assume that frontal areas are involved in regulating, controlling, or governing the rest of the brain. They do this by carrying out operations in a mental workspace of sorts, sometimes called working memory. But where do these frontal brain areas get the operands over which mental operations will take place? One path appears to come from the ventral stream at the bottom of the temporal lobe, which passes information up to the frontal lobes about attended objects and events. This affords the frontal lobes information about the perceived world, so that plans can be made concerning how to respond to goings-on in the world. But another source of information, this time about potential actions, appears to come from the dorsal stream, in the posterior parietal lobe. Some scientists believe that these posterior parietal regions realize something like a salience map that drives where the eyes and attention will go next.

Salience is an evaluation of the behavioral relevance, value, or importance of a stimulus. Before we shift our eyes or attention to the next thing, it stands to reason that there should first be an evaluation of what might be the most valuable location to which we will then shift our eyes or attention. One possibility is that posterior parietal areas realize a saliency map, which in turn feeds the most salient operands into frontal areas for the execution of mental operations, such as making decisions about what to do next, given ventral and dorsal information.

How the brain defines salience or importance is an open issue in neuroscience. Somewhere in the brain, probably in the posterior parietal lobe, there has to be a comparison of many different kinds of inputs. At any given moment, the visual system might process different sources of salience in parallel. Motion processing areas might evaluate a moving thing as salient; the amygdala might output that some potentially dangerous thing is salient; the reward system might indicate that something attractive is salient; and volitional processes might emphasize the importance of completing the task at hand. How might these conflicting salience signals be reconciled, given that we can generally only look at or carry out one action at a time? Is there a winner-take-all decision? Is there something like a weighted sum among all these inputs to a master salience map? These are all open questions in neuroscience. Once salience has been defined, attention or our eyes, heads, hands, or bodies can move to the peak of the salience map.

Some scientists have argued that the DAN should really be broken down into two subnetworks, one involved in considering and selecting among and switching between tasks, and the other associated with maintaining or sticking to a given task, as depicted in Figure 4.15. The former "fronto-parietal" circuit, which we consider in a couple of sections when we focus on the neural basis of volitional imagination, may be involved in selecting and switching among tasks appropriately. And the latter "cingulo-opercular" neural circuit linking the opercular part of the frontal lobe with medial frontal cortex, may be involved in maintaining a task or keeping us on task. The cerebellum may coordinate interactions between the fronto-parietal and cingulo-opercular circuits. We need both the volitional capacity to choose a path of action

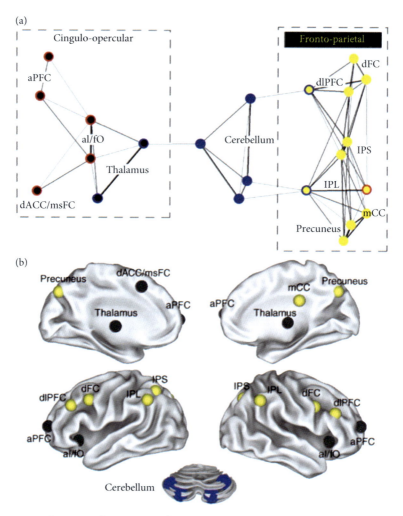

Figure 4.15 The network structure of human control networks reveals distinct fronto-parietal and cingulo-opercular control networks. Black lines indicate strong resting state functional connections between brain regions. The thickness of the lines indicates the relative connection strength. Regions sharing connections are placed close together, whereas minimally connected regions are spatially distant. For each region (circle), the central color indicates which network it belongs to (black = cingulo-opercular; blue = cerebellar and yellow = fronto-parietal). The outer color indicates the predominant control signal type of each region (red = set-maintenance; blue = error-related and yellow = start cue-related). At the displayed correlation threshold ($r \geq 0.15$), the cingulo-opercular and fronto-parietal networks are not directly connected to each other, but each network is connected to the cerebellar error-network through regions that also carry error information (the thalamus, dlPFC, and IPL). This architecture suggests that both networks might be communicating error signals (or codes) to and from the cerebellum, in parallel. (b) Distinct cingulo-opercular (black) and fronto-parietal (yellow) control networks, in addition to cerebellar regions (blue circles) are shown on an inflated surface rendering of the human brain. (Dosenbach et al., 2008).

Used with permission, from Dosenbach, N. U., Fair, D. A., Cohen, A. L., Schlaggar, B. L., & Petersen, S. E. (2008). A dual-networks architecture of top-down control. *Trends in Cognitive Sciences*, 12(3), 99–105.

Figure 4.16 The above image was taken in the Levant in 1889. Arthur Schopenhauer (1969) said "Willpower is to the intellect like a strong blind man who carries on his shoulders a lame man who can see." Using this metaphor, the cingulo-opercular circuit that keeps us on task despite errors and distractions is the strong blind man, while the fronto-parietal circuit is the lame man who can guide the former with his vision and plans.
Source: https://commons.wikimedia.org/wiki/File:Blind_man_carrying_a_paralysed_man.jpg

and the volitional capacity to persevere in pursuing it, using the fronto-parietal and cingulo-opercular circuits, respectively. The cingulo-opercular circuit may therefore be associated with the old-fashioned idea of willpower. It is often the case that activities that require staying on task activate some part of the cingulate cortex. And, in particular, if there is a mistake, where someone momentarily fails to stay on task, anterior cingulate cortex (ACC) tends to become more active (Figure 4.16).

One way to think about this would be to say that the ACC is involved in error detection. I don't think that is incorrect, but it misses the point. The error detection is in the service of staying on task. It is in the service of seeing a task through. A famous example, in this regard, is the Stroop task (Banich, 2019). The task is to say out loud the color of a word without reading it. When there is no conflict between the color of the ink, and the written word, this is easy. But when the ink color conflicts with the written color word, as when "blue" is written in red ink, people often unintentionally read the words, especially if attentionally fatigued or burdened. When people make these kinds of mistakes in the MRI scanner, their dorsal anterior cingulate cortex (dACC) shows a rapid increase in activity. But the point of detecting an error is not only to detect it, but also to correct oneself and return to the task at hand, which in this case is naming the ink color. You can also think of anterior cingulate circuitry as a sort of traffic cop saying "reading circuitry stop" and "color-naming circuitry come forward." When an error occurs, and we accidentally read a word, our internal traffic cop becomes even more driven to regulate our mental traffic correctly, according to the plan to name the ink color. But this takes effort, and our internal mental traffic cop can undergo fatigue because it presumably costs neurons ATP to actively inhibit the more automatized reading circuitry.

Now it turns out that the anterior cingulate is full of circuitry involved in error detection because it functions to keep us on task in numerous domains of thought and action, so that we can reach our diverse goals. Such circuitry is cybernetic. A cybernetic process involves the pursuit of a goal or setpoint, and an error signal that tells us if we have deviated too far and must correct. A basic example of this is a thermostat. If we set the thermostat to our desired room temperature, that will be its "goal." If the room gets colder than some tolerance, an "error" signal will be detected, and it will turn the heating unit on. But after a while, if the room becomes too warm, then it will again detect an error signal, and turn the heater off. Another example of a cybernetic process would be a heat-seeking missile. If its trajectory deviates from a path that will take it to its goal, the error will be corrected, so that the missile can hit its target. Various subcircuits in the anterior cingulate are cybernetic in that they detect errors that are then corrected in order to get back on task in pursuit of some goal. Whereas the "goals" of a thermostat or heat-seeking missile are set externally, an animal's goals or setpoints are set internally. There are different error signals associated with different neural circuits in the cingulate. Some of these error signals we consciously experience as a feeling, for example, the feeling of having made an error of some type.

We have just considered the dACC, which ramps up in activity when one makes a cognitive error, as occurs in the Stroop task. Let us now consider a different type of error signal, this time in the ventral anterior cingulate. Interestingly, the cybernetic neural circuitry in Brodmann area 25 shown in red in Figure 4.17, also known as the subgenual anterior cingulate because it is below the "genu" or bend of the corpus callosum, is neural circuitry involved in governing social emotional interactions. An error signal here is associated with feelings of guilt or shame or even self-loathing. In a healthy brain, this type of error signal induces us to correct our social mistakes. Interestingly, people who suffer from severe depression tend to have an over-active area 25 (Hamani et al., 2011).

We all make social errors now and then. Let us say you go to someone's house, and you bring a salad with bacon bits on it. Then they say, "I thought you knew we were vegetarian." You have committed a social error. People without depression will typically apologize, feel bad for a minute, and then get over it. But people with depression might dwell on an error like this for hours, days, or even weeks. Whereas people without depression can turn the "guilt" switch off, it is as if people with severe depression have a "sticky switch" that cannot be reset. They ruminate about such gaffs and

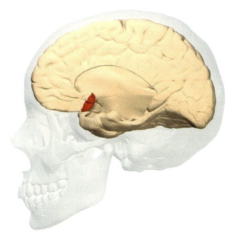

Figure 4.17 Brodmann area 25, also known as the subgenual anterior cingulate, is shown in red.

slights, in a kind of mental hell of self-disgust. Not coincidentally, I think, many of the same drugs that are used to treat obsessive compulsive disorders are also used to treat depression, in part, I think, because they both seem to involve something like a sticky switch. Depressed people can become so consumed with the consciously felt error signals of guilt, shame, and self-loathing that they choose to commit suicide to put an end to this kind of emotional hell. Mayberg and colleagues (2005) put a deep brain stimulating device in area 25, possibly deactivating its hyperactivity. In some patients with severe depression they claimed that this helps alleviate their mental torment.

Looking more broadly, we can now see that we have different types of processing going on in these volitional circuits. In the dlPFC we have working memory, planning, and mental operations. In the posterior parietal lobe we have the dorsal stream and an analysis of salient operands, some of which get fed into the frontal lobe for planning and other mental operations. In addition, we have ventral stream inputs, especially from among attended stimuli, into the working memory and planning areas of the frontal lobe. The lateral and anterior portions of the frontal lobe select a goal or plan, but this must then be executed. Once a goal has been established, anterior cingulate circuitry plays a role in cybernetically keeping us on task and helping us detect errors so that we can complete tasks that we have decided to carry out. But sometimes these cybernetic neural circuits fail to operate correctly, as in depression or OCD, and an error signal fails to turn off.

4.18 Top-Down Causation in the Brain

In discussing indeterminism in the brain, so far I have focused on amplification of microscopic to macroscopic randomness. However, macroscopic to microscopic causation can also occur in complex systems that operate far from thermodynamic equilibrium. Such so-called dissipative structures exchange energy with their environment, increasing entropy or disorder globally, while potentially increasing organization locally. These two things do not contradict each other. Life does not violate the second law of thermodynamics overall, even when it increases organization locally. For example, a cell, or our body, or even our household will excrete or dispose of waste products or garbage. This might increase the messiness of the environment, but it will create more order inside the cell membrane, or inside our bodies, or inside the walls of our house.

When several dissipative structures interact, as occurs within nested hierarchies of cooperating and competing neural circuits in the brain, nonlinear interactions can impose organization at the level of local neuronal activity that could not have been predicted on the basis of full knowledge of any subset of neural circuit activity in isolation. Nonlinear dynamic systems are chaotic and unpredictable in principle because global outcomes are dependent on initial or boundary conditions to such a degree that immeasurably small differences in those conditions can lead to radically different outcomes or trajectories of system development.

One common nonlinear mechanism occurs when winner-take-all operations lead to the capturing of the entire information-processing system by a random fluctuation at the level of an entire circuit. For example, should a burst from one neuronal subcircuit happen to arrive, just by chance, at neurons that realize a winner-take-all decision, just a couple of milliseconds before a burst from another subcircuit, the "winning" information could come to dominate subsequent information processing at all levels for a period of time because it flushes new order into the system.

This all sounds rather abstract. So let me give a metaphor from everyday life. Something analogous happens in winner-take-all social systems, where, for example, one candidate wins by chance. For example, in Florida in 2000, George W. Bush received more votes essentially by accident because of faulty ballots in Palm Beach County. This was an unpredictable and bizarre chance event caused by confusing ballots that led people to check the box for the wrong person (Pat Buchanan). Bush was then effectively installed by supreme court justice Scalia and others, who came up with dubious reasons to award him the victory. This then led to the imposition of a new social order on the whole country, and even on planet Earth, that effectively shut down or at least tried to shut down potential competitors and dictate the terms of future decisions carried out within the system. It is almost inconceivable to think of it now, but the mistaken votes of a few thousand senior citizens in Palm Beach County was a random fluctuation that flushed in a new global order, followed by 9/11 and the neoconservative's many wars in Iraq, Afghanistan, Libya, and elsewhere aimed at bolstering the hegemony of their one "indispensable" nation. This was an example not only of microscopic to macroscopic causation, but also of macroscopic to microscopic causation. Yes, the random fluctuation of votes meant for Gore, but counted toward Buchanan, involved amplification from the local to the global. But once Bush was awarded the victory, he and Cheney and colleagues imposed a new order on the entire globe that altered everything afterward.

An even more extreme example of this kind of bottom-up–top-down causation would be Hitler. After the First World War and the weakness and hyperinflation of the Weimar republic, Germany was deeply unstable. You might say it had hit a point of "criticality" where a local fluctuation could easily be amplified up to a new global ordering. At the time, there were many demagogues who wanted to lead the desperate German people out of the crisis. In normal times, such people get dampened down, ignored, or thrown into prison. But these were not normal times. Society was, so to speak, "on fire." And when you are desperate and the theater is filling up with smoke, and a man stands up and says, "I know the way out, follow me!" you follow him because he seems strong and certain, and because you are desperate to get out. You don't worry about niceties like the rule of law or democracy at that point.

But when there were dozens of such people aiming to take control at the time, both on the left and the right, why did Hitler win out? That he did was a matter of contingency. What if he had been required to serve his entire five-year term in prison after his failed attempt to take over the government of Bavaria in November 1923 (the "beer hall putsch")? Instead, some single person's brain probably decided that it was OK to let him out after just nine months, during which time he had written *Mein Kampf*. More improbably, some years prior, on September 28, 1918, British soldier Henry Tandey had a bleeding 29-year-old Hitler in his line of sights near the French village of Marcoing, but, he later told historians: "I took aim but couldn't shoot a wounded man, so I let him go." World history would have turned out radically differently had a microscopic fluctuation in Private Tandey's brain gone the other way that day. Instead, Hitler made eye contact with Tandey, nodded to him in gratitude, then limped off with his bleeding leg. Even earlier still, what if he had gotten into the Vienna Academy of Fine Arts in 1907 or 1908 as was his dream as a young man? He was gifted enough at art that, had he been admitted, he would probably not have ended up trying to take over the world. Instead, his party, the Nazi party, ended up being elected the majority party in 1932, even though Paul von Hindenburg defeated him for the Weimar presidency in that election. On January 30, 1932 Hitler succeeded in his aim to rule Germany, when Hindenburg, in a political (but in retrospect, obviously foolish) move, chose Hitler to become chancellor. There were so many contingencies that could have gone the other way. Instead, within short order, the top-down imposition of a new world order began. The Enabling Act of 1933 effectively gave Hitler dictatorial powers, and the rest is history.

Now, let us return to the brain. There are times when you don't want a local disturbance or fluctuation to be able to flush a whole new order into brain processing. Sleep might be such a case. Below a certain level of disturbance, it is more important to sleep than to be roused. But there are other cases where you do want the brain to operate in a regime where a local fluctuation can flush a whole new order into the brain's information processing. For example, if a small object suddenly moves in the visual periphery, it might be a predator, so you want to stop doing whatever you are doing and pay full attention to this potentially dangerous thing.

In society and in the brain, especially when the system is operating in the domain of criticality, causation can be thought to be "circular," as winner-take-all and other nonlinear "attractor" mechanisms impose global-upon-local causation. This imposition then constrains subsequent local neuronal behavior, which in turn realizes later local-upon-global causation by changing the dynamics of the circuits to which they belong, and so on.

Neuronal criterial causation is really an example of such "circular" causation. Criteria may be set in a top-down manner at t1. When these criteria are nondeterministically met, via bottom-up variability at t2, this solution biases subsequent future behavior in a "downwardly" causal manner. It is impossible to disentangle bottom-up from top-down causation in such a system.

Central to the possibility of top-down causation in the brain must be mechanisms whereby an idea considered in working memory, such as "think of a female, European politician," could then come to modulate synaptic weights, such that just these criteria are implemented, which can then be realized by searching memory stores for information that meets these criteria. Then, just by chance, you might end up thinking of Theresa May or Margaret Thatcher or Angela Merkel or someone else. So, it is neither determined nor utterly random. It is not determined because it could have turned out otherwise (i.e., you might have thought of a different female European politician), and it is not utterly random because it had to be a female, European politician. Another example need not involve memory, but might instead involve attention, where deciding in the frontal lobes to pay attention to, say, cars, would then lead bottom-up processing to function differently than it would have if those frontal cognitive neural circuits had decided to pay attention to people, or horses, or houses, or whatever. That you ended up paying attention to this car versus those other possible cars may have occurred by chance.

It is likely that neuromodulators and neurotransmitters released into the synapse of to-be-influenced neural circuitry by such top-down neural circuitry will play a central role in altering neural excitability and synaptic weights. This will alter informational criteria that have to be met in order for the neuron to fire above its baseline firing rate in the future. This will alter the information-processing properties of neurons and neural networks and realize a form of top-down informational causation in the brain.

The next section focuses on volitional attention, a particular example of such top-down causation in the brain, and how it might be realized via neurotransmitter release from frontal and parietal areas down into areas that process sensory input in a bottom-up manner, such as the ventral stream.

4.19 The Neural Basis of Volitional Attention

This section considers volitional attention, also known as "endogenous attention," which is a central example of top-down influence on bottom-up processing. In the last section I mentioned one key way that top-down modulation of bottom-up processing is likely realized, at a neuronal level, by the release of neuromodulating neurotransmitters into the synaptic clefts of neural circuits that process bottom-up inputs. A key example of such a modulatory neurotransmitter is acetylcholine. There are receptors that lie slightly away from the synapse that allow for the regulation of intracellular potential via changes in ligand- and voltage-gated receptor conductances. This just means that the likelihood that receptors will pass ions can change as a result of neuromodulation by acetylcholine and other neuromodulators. For example, one of acetylcholine's effects might involve altering the probabilities that NMDA receptors will open. Extra-synaptic muscarinic acetylcholine receptors are of this class and appear to play an important role in network changes that occur with changes in arousal and attention. Cholinergic neurons originating in the nucleus basalis of the basal forebrain (depicted with a purple disk in Figure 4.18), project widely across cortex. Attention may have its effects on local neural circuitry in part via the release of acetylcholine from these cholinergic neurons that binds with muscarinic and nicotinic acetylcholine receptors. When such binding occurs, some neurons may become more excitable while others might become less so. If muscarinic acetylcholine receptors lie on inhibitory interneurons, acetylcholine would increase the drive of the inhibitory network that surrounds, synchronizes, and regulates pyramidal cells. This might in turn alter the degree of synchrony or the probability of burst firing. Since neurons are ultimately spike coincidence detectors, changing synchrony or burstiness or rates of firing through such a top-down mechanism would alter information processing in a neural circuit very fundamentally. There are multiple acetylcholine-mediated

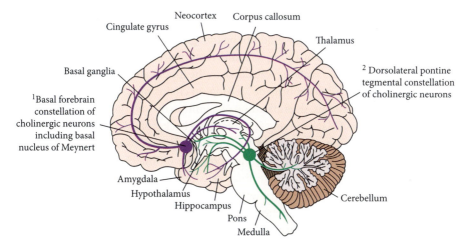

Figure 4.18 Cholinergic circuitry in the human brain originates in two brain areas. Pontine tegmental cholinergic circuitry appears to play a central role in the stages of sleep, arousal, and wakefulness or vigilance. The cholinergic circuitry originating in the nucleus basalis of Meynert plays a central role in the allocation of volitional or endogenous attention.

Source: https://brainstuff.org/

effects, many more than we can explore here, but a result of cholinergic projections from the forebrain is that attention enhances the likelihood of signal detection and transmission.

Top-down causation in the brain is realized in altering, for example, the conductances of receptors via physical injection of acetylcholine and other neurotransmitters into the synapse. This in turn alters information processing in those downstream neurons. Some scientists think that this may permit the transfer of bursts as informational packets across a network (Lisman, 1997). Top-down cholinergic, GABAergic, and other neuromodulator input can alter neural function, ultimately at the level of receptors, which is then magnified up to a level of depolarization. This then affects spiking, which in turn alters the rest of the brain.

Attention is not only realized in acetylcholine release in a top-down manner from the basal forebrain to relatively early sensory processing areas; there is evidence that basal forebrain *non*cholinergic neuronal bursting may realize top-down attentional modulation of pyramidal cells' behavior as well. In particular, it may switch pyramidal cell networks from a tonic or relatively nonbursty to a phasic or relatively bursty mode, perhaps via basal forebrain neurons' GABAergic inhibition of local inhibitory interneurons. Another possibility is that top-down attention alters the dynamics of the local inhibitory network so that it becomes more synchronized, which would increase gamma oscillations in that circuit even before the arrival of bottom-up input, changing the way that the neural circuitry will respond to bottom-up input when it later arrives.

If this view is correct, then top-down attentional alteration of bottom-up processing may be realized in the transitioning of the target cortical circuit from a tonic into a bursting mode mediated by NMDA receptor opening with concomitant increases in firing rate. Attentional binding would not be the "gluing" of features together at a location but would instead afford complete information processing at an attended location, from visual input areas all the way down to the hippocampus. The process might work something like a "bucket brigade" setting up chains of information processing that reach the hippocampus, thus affording recognition of, say, a gorilla, as opposed to localistic processing of black moving features in the background, when not attending.

In a visual processing area such as V4, neurons that received top-down cholinergic and non-cholinergic neurotransmitter release, ultimately from the basal nucleus of the forebrain, might change their sensitivity to subsequent spike inputs, altering in turn their spiking pattern and rate, which would then alter downstream neurons' behavior. A lot of difficult neuroscience research is needed to determine how the changes that attention induces in consciousness are realized in top-down control of bottom-up processing via cholinergic and noncholinergic inputs. And many questions remain, for example, what circuitry controls the basal forebrain to release neurotransmitters where it will? Is area 10, the seat of our most abstract planning, and among the cortical areas that have disproportionately expanded relative to a chimp's brain, at the top of the volitional executive hierarchy of processing? We do not yet have a complete enough understanding of the brain to fully delineate the structure of the control hierarchy among frontal executive circuits. But there is no doubt that there is top-down causation in the brain effectively realized by changing the synaptic weights of downstream neurons, which in turn alters bottom-up or stimulus-driven processing, which in turn influences subsequent top-down biasing of future bottom-up processing, and so on.

Thus, the biggest point—that patterns in energy can become causal—is rooted in the tiniest point, which is that conductances of receptors can be altered rapidly and dynamically in light of the information processing needs of the whole organism. Ultimately, patterns among energy become causal in the universe only when pattern detectors exist. In humans these have evolved in fascinating ways. In this book we consider two such pattern detectors. One, at a cellular level, is a neuron, which is sensitive to the pattern of coincidence, or coincident arrival of action potentials. In this temporal pattern, many other patterns can be encoded, such as the spatial pattern of a simple cell tuned to an oriented bar of light, or a neuron tuned to the spatial pattern of the constellation Orion, or really any other pattern at all. Then, at a much tinier level, at the level of receptors, we also considered the pattern detector realized in an NMDA receptor, which is also a coincidence detector, namely, of three facts being true: glutamate binding, glycine binding, and then also post-synaptic neuron depolarization. When NMDA receptors open they effectively change the synaptic weights linking a pre- and post-synaptic neuron, changing both the firing rate and burstiness of a post-synaptic neuron, but also altering its responsiveness to subsequent presynaptic inputs. This mechanism of dynamically altering synaptic weights is subject to top-down volitional control via the intermediation of acetylcholine and other neurotransmitters.

Amazingly, microscopic NMDA receptors may play at least five important roles in the neuronal basis of mental causation:

1. They introduce randomness to the macroscopic domain in the form of spike-timing uncertainty, which then may or may not meet present neuronally realized informational criteria.
2. They may afford the generation of many possible solutions that can meet any set of criteria.
3. They may realize rapid synaptic resetting that permits neurons to escape the impossibility of self-causation by changing the criteria for firing of neurons on the next information-processing cycle.
4. They transition neural network behavior into a burstier mode of information processing.
5. Their functioning may be necessary for consciousness, as several classes of anesthetics that block them also knock out consciousness.

Readers interested in learning more about the details of NMDA receptor function should look at *The Neural Basis of Free Will* (Tse, 2013), which goes into greater detail. Suffice it to say that top-down criterial causation can operate on the millisecond timescale of thoughts by rapidly resetting synaptic weights and altering other neural response properties. Volition is closely tied to endogenous attention, which is in part realized in alterations of neurons receiving top-down cholinergic and non-cholinergic inputs from the basal forebrain and other areas, such as the posterior parietal lobe.

I have argued here that causation was initially conceived to be a transfer of energy. Later notions of causation emphasized how energy is transformed. Criterial causation emphasizes not how energy is transferred or transformed into a different state, but rather how patterns of energy, such as coincidence, are transmitted and transformed. This section considered how a top-down process, such as what we choose to attend, based upon considerations in working memory, can come to alter the dynamics of neural circuitry, ultimately by altering the properties of synapses. Such top-down causation is made possible by altering the behavior of coincidence detectors operating at the molecular level, such as NMDA receptors.

A higher-level of coincidence detection, namely, between well-timed apical and basal dendritic activations, may play a central role in the influence of top-down on bottom-up processing (Aru et al., 2020; Larkum et al., 2022). According to Larkum and colleagues, when the apical dendrites of layer V cortical pyramidal cells are activated by top-down input, their responses to bottom-up inputs to the basal dendrites are altered. Anesthesia, they argue, disrupts apical–basal dendritic coupling, undermining consciousness (Suzuki and Larkum, 2020), perhaps by blocking cortico-cortical and cortico–thalamo–cortical feedback loops (see also Bachmann, 2015).

For me, the beauty of what evolution created, that is, basing criterial causation on the detection of patterns of coincidence, is breathtaking. Because patterns can be created and destroyed, unlike the physical substrate in which they are realized, patterns are not subject to the same physical laws that constrain amounts of energy. This permits the emergence of higher-level types of causation of pattern on pattern, or a type of causation that operates over a succession of patterns. This affords a downward and non-epiphenomenal causation, where mental events (realized in some neurons' criteria for firing having been met) only occur if elementary particles realize a particular subset of the possible paths open to them. This subset embodies not only a physical causal chain of events, but also an informational causal chain of events. Other possible paths that are open to elementary particles that do not also realize an informational causal chain are in essence filtered from potentially happening at that level by neurons because those paths fail to meet physical/informational criteria for the release of an action potential. All informational causal chains are also physical causal chains, but the vast majority of physical causal chains in Nature are not informational causal chains. What makes some physical causal chains also informational causal chains is that the physically realized criteria for some physical event happening, like the firing of a neuron, are only met when certain informational criteria are also met. If inputs to this neuron are such that action potentials sufficient to make it fire only arrive from presynaptic neurons when some informational conditions are met, then this neuron realizes informational criteria by virtue of imposing physical criteria for firing upon its physical inputs. This information is used by a physical organism to fulfill its internally set goals, whether finding food or avoiding dangers.

4.20 The Neural Circuitry of Nonvolitional Thought

This and coming sections look even more closely at the cortical neural circuits that govern human thought, some of which realize the volitional control with which we are primarily concerned when we talk about free will. But volitional thinking and imagining are just one mode of human thought. There are also other modes of thinking that are not deliberative or top-down. Among these types of nonvolitional thought are the spontaneously divergent or "jumping around" forms of thinking evident in dreaming and day-dreaming, and also in the idea-generation or brainstorming phase of creative thinking. Sometimes this kind of circuitry can dominate thinking excessively, for example, the incessant distractibility of attentional deficit hyperactivity disorder (ADHD), perhaps associated with an overly active exogenous attentional system. In an associative jumble, where every thought hyperlinks to every other possible thought, it would be very hard to maintain a goal-directed train of thought, as indeed happens in people who suffer from schizophrenia and other forms of disordered thinking. And at the other end of the spectrum of nonvolitional thinking, we have cases where instead of having excessively divergent cognition, we instead have excessively convergent cognition. An example of this occurs in the case of the ruminations of a depressed person, who returns again and again to thoughts about his or her own failings, slights against the self, and an inescapable dwelling on feelings about the self. In this obsession with aspects of the self, depression has some parallels to narcissism, except that the self, rather than being glorified and endlessly promoted, is endlessly reviled. Closely related would be other forms of nonvolitional thought that dwell on some object other than the self, as in obsessive compulsive disorder, or the sexual or romantic obsessions that lead to stalking, or the obsessions related to threat and danger, associated with various anxiety disorders.

While the main focus in a book about free will should naturally be neural circuits associated with volitional top-down control, we have to acknowledge that volition operates within an ecosystem or family of human thought processes, perhaps the majority of which are not volitional. Anyone who has fallen madly in love with someone else can attest to the fact that it is almost impossible to will oneself not to have obsessive thoughts about the person one adores. This might be regarded as a "legitimate" form of OCD, which ideally leads to the healthy outcome of family formation, but which can also go awry, as in cases of stalking. But many of the primary psychological torments of clinical populations, whether OCD, depression, or anxiety disorders, involve cases of nonvolitional thoughts that are (in a sense) imposed on a person against their will. These nonvolitional modes of cognition are generally present in every human brain but within a certain range of function, they are not debilitating and even lead to healthy outcomes. For example, it is good to be involuntarily distracted by things that move suddenly in the environment because they might be predators, but it may not be good to be excessively and incessantly distracted, as in ADHD. It is good to be forced, so to speak, to cognize about one's social errors and violations, so that one can heal relationships and correct one's behavior, but it is not healthy to excessively ruminate on these things, as occurs in depression. In healthy brains, the volitional modes of thinking that we cover in the next section are not overwhelmed by the nonvolitional modes of cognition that we are discussing here.

Let us now look at the neural circuits that underlie nonvolitional modes of thinking in the brain. I use the figures and ideas from a solid review (Christoff et al., 2016) of cortical circuitry to help us better understand how volitional circuits function within a framework of bottom-up and top-down control of one's mind and body.

Let us return to the image that we considered in Figure 4.13, of the cortex segmented into seven cortical regions where neural activity tends to vary together. We can now look more closely at the main executive circuits that we considered before and try to understand them in greater detail. Let us compare Figure 4.13 with a finer level of analysis of the different networks shown in Figure 4.19. First, we consider two nonvolitional control circuits.

The first of these is the neural circuit associated with the light green color shown here on the left lateral cortical surface. This is the "ventral attentional network." The ventral attentional network is a nonvolitional circuit associated with shifting attention automatically to sudden motion and onsets in the environment. This circuitry is very important, because it causes us to automatically orient to things of potential relevance to our survival, whether potential predators or prey. If this circuitry is too sensitive, one will constantly get distracted, as occurs in ADHD. The ventral attentional network is part of a more general salience network, that also includes the yellow circuitry, including the ACC, and the anterior insula (AI). I have argued that the anterior cingulate is involved in error detection in the service of staying on task cybernetically, but in this case, the ACC might be involved in detecting errors or deviations from the normal state of affairs that are worthy of a reorienting one's attention. The AI, also known as the frontal operculum (FO) is likely involved in interoception. Some people think that the two circuits—the ventral attentional network, and the dorsal aspect of the cingulo-opercular circuit—are really two sides of a single salience detection system that leads one to reorient one's attention or reorient what one is doing, in a bottom-up way. Other people think that these are separate interacting circuits that detect different types of salience, perhaps associated with external world versus internal world processing.

The second nonvolitional neural circuit that we consider is the default mode network. Initially, people thought that this circuit was central to spontaneous internal thought, such as daydreaming or "mind-wandering," or else thoughts about oneself and others. Since then, the story has turned out to be more complex and interesting, because there are times when parts of the default mode network are invoked in the service of deliberative, volitional thinking, especially in cases where one mentalizes about the mental states of others, or projects oneself into an imagined future, or in episodic memory retrieval. What all these processes have in common, whether volitional or nonvolitional, is internal thinking not connected with events in the outside world.

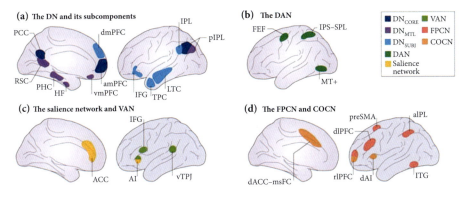

Figure 4.19 Main large-scale brain networks with relevance to spontaneous thought. The default network (DN). Medial prefrontal cortex (mPFC). The core DN subsystem (DNCORE): Anterior mPFC (amPFC), posterior cingulate cortex (PCC) and posterior inferior parietal lobule (pIPL). The DN subsystem centered around the medial temporal lobe (MTL) (DNMTL): The hippocampal formation (HF) and parahippocampal cortex (PHC), the retrosplenial cortex (RSC), the ventral mPFC (vmPFC) and the pIPL. DNSUB3: Dorsomedial PFC (dmPFC), the lateral temporal cortex (LTC), the temporopolar cortex (TPC), and inferior frontal gyrus (IFG). The dorsal attention network (DAN): Intraparietal sulcus (IPS)–superior parietal lobule (SPL), the frontal eye field (FEF) and the middle temporal motion complex (MT+). The ventral attention network (VAN): The inferior frontal gyrus (IFG), the anterior insula (AI), frontal operculum (not shown), and the ventral temporoparietal junction (vTPJ). The salience network: the AI and the anterior cingulate cortex (ACC). The frontoparietal control network (FPCN): The dorsolateral PFC (dlPFC) and the anterior IPL (aIPL), the rostrolateral PFC (rlPFC), the region anterior to the supplementary motor area (preSMA), and the inferior temporal gyrus (ITG). The cingulo-opercular control network (COCN): The dorsal ACC (dACC)–medial superior frontal cortex (msFC) and bilateral AI–frontal operculum. The rlPFC contributes to both the FPCN and COCN.

Used with permission from Christoff, K., Irving, Z., Fox, K. C. R., Spreng, R. N., & Andrews-Hanna, J. R. (2016). Mind-wandering as spontaneous thought: A dynamic framework. *Nature Reviews Neuroscience*, 17, 718–731.

That is, they are not concerned directly with present perception of the real world outside us but involve an internal simulation that we might regard as imagination. The default mode network is central to imagination because many forms of imagination involve invoking memories in the service of simulating others' minds, or one's own reactions in possible scenarios.

The authors of the review article call it the "default network" or "DN" and dissect it into three subcircuits. These are shown here in dark blue, light blue and purple. They call the dark blue subcircuit the network core, which functions as a hub for internal simulation and can invoke the light blue and purple circuits, depending on the internal reality that is being simulated at any given time. Included in this dark blue circuit are the posterior cingulate cortex (PCC) and the anterior medial prefrontal cortex (amPFC) on the medial side of the cortex; the default network core includes this part of the posterior inferior parietal lobule (pIPL) on the lateral side of the cortex.

Now let us consider another part of the default network, shown here in purple, which they call the DN-medial temporal lobe circuit or DNmtl. There is also a portion of this circuit in the pIPL, shown here, as well as the circuitry of the medial temporal lobe, that is involved in placing oneself and one's actions in a representation of space in world coordinates, including the retrosplenial cortex (RSC) so-called because it sits behind the posterior portion or "splenium" of the corpus callosum, and the parahippocampal cortex (PHC), as well as the hippocampal formation (HF). Finally, they identify what they call the DN subcomponent 3 (DNsub3), shown in light blue, which includes a more anterior portion of the IPL, as well as a portion of the dorsal medial prefrontal cortex (dmPFC), portions of the superior temporal gyrus or lateral temporal cortex (LTC), portions of the temporal pole or temporal polar cortex (TPC), and then a portion of the inferior frontal gyrus (IFG). Whereas the purple circuitry appears to be involved in simulating the placement of oneself in space or moving through the space of an internally generated world, the light blue circuitry is involved in placing oneself in others' minds or their "animacy." Note that the purple circuitry is also involved in the perception of oneself in the world as one navigates through it, whereas the light blue circuitry is centrally involved in the perception of biological motions, such as facial gestures. So, the spatial and animacy circuitry of perception of external events can also subserve the processing of these types of information in internally generated or imagined worlds.

This section discussed the neural circuits involved in human cognition that are nonvolitional. The next section goes into greater depth concerning the neural basis of volition in the human cortex. After that we discuss how volitional and nonvolitional modes of processing interact in our brains and minds.

4.21 The Neural Circuitry of Volitional Thought

This section discusses the primary volitional neural circuits that are involved in top-down governance of our actions and our minds. These are circuits that underlie human free will, by imposing constraints on thought or action paths, that we can also think of as top-down criteria for future actions or thought. Let us again compare the image of the whole cortex and areas within it that are highly correlated in Figure 4.19. The DAN, shown in green, includes the frontal eye fields (FEF), the intraparietal sulcus (IPS) of the superior parietal lobule (SPL), and it includes the middle temporal motion complex (MT+). The DAN is thought to link the shifting of attention, as well as eye movements, to salient stimuli in the outside world, defined in particular by changes in luminance associated with motion in the visual domain.

But since salience is in part specified by what one chooses to pay attention to—say, one is looking for one's dog, thus making dogs more salient—the DAN is in part subject to volitional control. Another way that this circuitry is subject to volitional control is top-down inhibition. For example, if someone very attractive should come into view, but you don't want people to know that you find them attractive, you can inhibit yourself from making an eye movement to this person, even when a part of you wants to look at them. Indeed, some people have argued that volitional attention evolved as a replication of the neural circuitry involved in making volitional saccades. They have said that it would be dangerous for a beta male, for example, to actually look at the alpha male, who might take this staring to be a threat display, possibly leading the alpha male to attack the beta male. Instead, the beta male can keep his mind's eye on his object of interest, without overtly giving away what he is attending, and so avoid the wrath of the alpha male. I don't know if volitional attention in fact evolved as a replication of volitional eye movement circuitry, but it is a reasonable idea, supported by the overlap found in brain activity when either shifting attention or the eyes. Be that as it may, the DAN is one of two volitional executive circuits that are central to human volition and free will.

The other pair of volitional circuits involved in top-down imposition of constraints on thought and action, includes the fronto-parietal control network (FPCN), shown in red, and the cingulo-opercular control network (COCN), shown in orange in Figure 4.19d. The FPCN is central to top-down cognitive control. If it couples with the DAN, it plays a role in the volitional control of attention and eye movements as one plans actions in the perceived world. And if it couples instead with the default network, it plays a role in deliberating about one's actions in the internally simulated worlds of one's imagination. This neural circuit includes part of the rostrolateral prefrontal cortex (rlPFC) behind our foreheads, that we previously considered as Brodmann area 10 and its role in our most abstract planning, such as planning what we want to do next year. It also includes the dlPFC, which we discussed in the context of working memory and the carrying out of mental operations, say, imagining a human body with a lion's head. It also includes the anterior inferior parietal lobule, which we have considered as potentially realizing a global salience map. It also includes the region anterior to the supplementary motor area (preSMA), involved in high-level planning and programming of future bodily actions, and the inferior temporal gyrus (ITG), which is part of the ventral stream concerned with representing the shapes and identities of objects in the world.

Working in close cooperation with the FPCN is the COCN. In earlier sections (4.17, 4.20, 4.21) we discussed how the former is likely involved in deciding which task to execute next, as well as volitionally switching among such tasks, whereas the cingulo-opercular circuit is likely involved in keeping one on task, and detecting errors when one has strayed from the task at hand. This circuit includes the dACC, as well as the medial superior frontal cortex (msFC) and bilateral AI (FO), from where we get the name cingulo-opercular control network. Together, the FPCN and COCN allow us to set goals internally and then cybernetically maintain ourselves on a trajectory of behavior or thought that will fulfill our goals over extended cycles of perception, evaluation, and action.

So far, we have only discussed modes of thought that occur while a person is awake. But we spend roughly a third of our lives asleep, and of that time, about two hours a night is spent dreaming, especially during the phase of sleep known to occur with rapid eye movement (REM) sleep. Volition generally plays little role in normal dreaming, so it might be thought of as a form of nonvolitional imagination. Indeed, many people have noticed that there are similarities between dreaming while asleep, and daydreaming while awake. Figure 4.20 depicts brain areas that increase in activity during REM sleep, shown in red, and areas that are down-regulated, shown in blue. During dreaming the medial temporal portion of the default network is activated, and the lateral prefrontal areas known to be involved in top-down volitional control are deactivated. This medial temporal portion of the default network can also be activated while awake, that is, when one is daydreaming.

In a remarkable study, Voss and colleagues (2014) applied alternating current to the scalp above the dlPFC, which tends to be down-regulated during REM sleep, while people were dreaming with another grounding electrode placed over the temporal lobes. When they stimulated current to flow between these electrode poles in the low-gamma or 40-Hz range, as depicted in Figure 4.21, people effectively woke up inside their dreams and could take volitional control of the contents of their dreams! Dr. Voss artificially induced lucid dreaming, where a person realizes that they are dreaming and can then make things happen in their dream that they volitionally choose to happen.

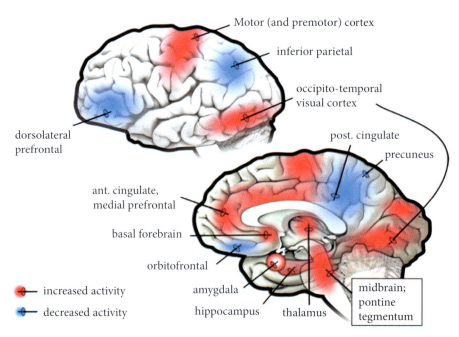

Figure 4.20 Areas of the brain in red show increased brain activity during REM sleep, whereas those in blue show decreased activity.

Used with permission from Elsevier, from Perogamvros, L., & Schwartz, S. (2012). The roles of the reward system in sleep and dreaming. *Neuroscience and Biobehavioral Reviews*, *36*(8), 1934–1951.

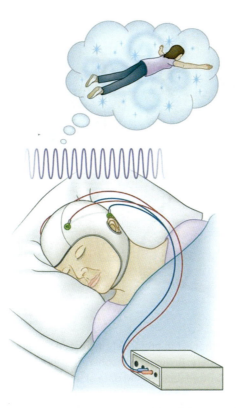

Figure 4.21 Voss and colleagues artificially induced lucid dreaming by applying alternating current in the gamma domain into the dorsolateral prefrontal cortex.

Used with permission, from Voss, U., Holzmann, R., Hobson, A., Paulus, W., Koppehele-Gossel, J., Klimke, A., & Nitsche, M. A. (2014). Induction of self-awareness in dreams through frontal low current stimulation of gamma activity. *Nature Neuroscience, 17*, 810–812.

Figure 4.22 (Dressler et al., 2012) shows areas of the brain that tend to be more active during lucid dreaming than during the normal, nonlucid dreaming of REM sleep. This involves the volitional circuitry of the lateral frontal lobe and other parts of the FPCN. So, although dreaming tends not to be volitional, lucid dreaming is one important exception where dreaming *is* volitional. And it becomes volitional by activating the very circuitry that underlies volitional processing in the lateral frontal lobes that is active when we are awake. As we can see from this lucid dreaming example, nonvolitional processes can be influenced by volitional processes.

Together, these circuits permit the brain to take volitional control of what it thinks, imagines, and does by imposing top-down constraints or criteria that have to be met by bottom-up processing. These constraints or criteria are ultimately realized in a neural code that permits the setting of criteria in synaptic weight changes, which is ultimately realized in the release of neuromodulators that change the conductances of specific channels, such as NMDA receptors. To me, it is a cognitive architecture as

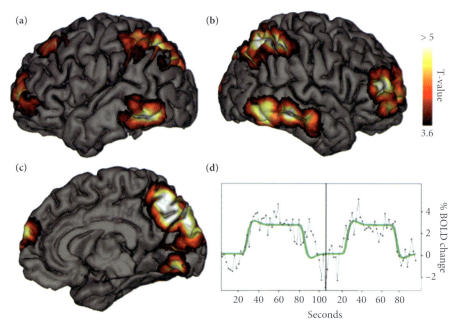

Figure 4.22 Brain areas that exhibit relatively increased activity during lucid dreaming. A: Left hemisphere. B: Right hemisphere. C: Medial view of right hemisphere. D: Predicted (green) and fitted (black) fMRI data of the peak activation in the right precuneus, showing combined analysis of two independent lucid epochs in a single subject.

Used with permission, Dresler, M., Wehrle, R., Spoormaker, V. I., Koch, S. P., Holsboer, F., Steiger, A., Obrig, H., Sämann, P. G., & Czisch, M. (2012). Neural correlates of dream lucidity obtained from contrasting lucid versus non-lucid REM sleep: A combined EEG/fMRI case study, *Sleep*, *35*(7), 1017–1020.

beautiful in its macroscopic and microscopic architecture as any cathedral or symphony ever created. Of course, it is this evolved information-processing and neural architecture that affords just such creations of the human mind.

4.22 How Volitional and Nonvolitional Circuits Interact

Now that we have a finer grain analysis of the main nonvolitional and volitional neural circuits underlying human thought and planning, we are in a position to ask how these neural circuits interact. The authors of the review article from which Figure 4.19 comes (Christoff et al., 2016), suggest that there are three primary modes of human thought: one that they regard as spontaneous or relatively unconstrained, another that they regard as constrained by nonvolitional factors, and the third, which they regard as constrained by volitional or deliberately imposed top-down constraints. This latter type would include the neural circuitry that underlies free will, which would itself include the DAN, the FPCN, and the COCN.

Let us first look at how they characterize the relationship of these main networks in the case of spontaneous thought. As schematized in Figure 4.23, in this category they would put dreaming, daydreaming, and the brainstorming stage of creative ideation. The arrows below indicate likely paths of causation, and the thick arrows indicate the dominant source of causation. In the case of spontaneous forms of thinking, they would argue that memories and associations coming out of the hippocampal

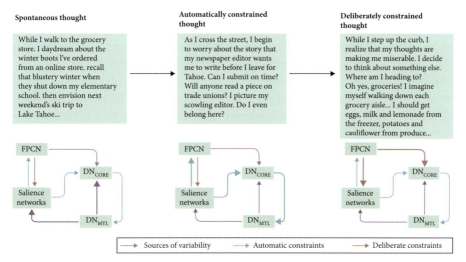

Figure 4.23 Three large-scale brain networks posited by Christoff et al. (2016) to underlie three styles of thinking: spontaneous thought, automatically constrained thought, and deliberately constrained thought. "During spontaneous, internally oriented thought, the default network (DN) subsystem centered around the medial temporal lobe (MTL) (DNMTL) exerts a relatively strong diversifying influence on the stream of thought, in the context of relatively low deliberate and automatic constraints exerted by the frontoparietal control network (FPCN), core DN subsystem (DNCORE) and salience networks. During automatically constrained, internally oriented thought, the salience networks and the DNCORE exert relatively strong automatic constraints on thought, in the context of relatively weak internal sources of variability from the DNMTL and relatively weak deliberate sources of constraint from the FPCN. Finally, during deliberately constrained, internally oriented thought, the FPCN exerts strong deliberate constraints on thought, in the context of relatively weak internal sources of variability from the DNMTL and relatively weak automatic constraints by the DNCORE and salience networks. Arrows represent influences on the dynamics of thought: sources of variability (in purple), automatic constraints (in blue) and deliberate constraints (in red). The thickness of an arrow represents the hypothesized relative strength of these influences during the corresponding part in the stream of thought."

Used with permission from Christoff, K., Irving, Z., Fox, K. C. R., Spreng, R. N., & Andrews-Hanna, J. R. (2016). Mind-wandering as spontaneous thought: A dynamic framework. *Nature Reviews Neuroscience*, *17*, 718–731.

formation as well as the spatial processing circuitry of the medial temporal lobe tend to drive cognition. There is relatively little in the way of top-down constraints imposed from the frontal executive areas, although there may be some in the case of creative problem solving. Or rather, in the case of creative problem solving, there would be an alternation between spontaneous thinking and idea generation in light of certain criteria that need to be met, followed by the invoking of a top-down editor, realized in the volitional FPCN, that sifts through the possibilities generated in the first stage, keeping only the good ideas and throwing away the not so good ones, before beginning the brainstorming phase again, and so on, until an adequate solution is reached.

Next let us look at how they characterize thought processing in the case where there is nonvolitionally constrained thinking. In this case, we see that the dominant outputs driving thought processing come from forms of bottom-up salience that specify what should be processed with highest priority. In the case of the ventral attentional network, bottom-up salience specifies what should next be attended. If this happens to be something moving suddenly in the outside world, we can talk of exogenous attentional capture. This is why we find flashing or moving advertisements on the internet so distracting. We cannot help but have our attention grabbed by such changes in luminance, and advertisers know this, which is why they do it. There are also many other sources of salience that are not subject to volitional control. Another might be the outputs of the amygdala, specifying things that are potentially dangerous or threatening. Not surprisingly, an overly active or under-inhibited amygdala may be related to anxiety disorders, such as post-traumatic stress disorder and certain forms of OCD, which result in incessant thoughts that are not subject to volitional down-regulation. Another form of such bottom-up salience might be the social error signal, associated with feelings of shame and guilt, that can happen in the case of an overly active area 25 or subgenual cingulate cortex, as discussed earlier regarding depression, when people tend to feel self-loathing concerning their social errors or ruminate about others' social slights. All of these various forms of bottom-up salience constrain processing in a way that is very difficult to control volitionally (Brewer et al., 2020).

Finally, in Figure 4.24, let us look at how they characterize thought processing in the case where there is top-down or volitionally constrained thinking. Here, the FPCN drives brain activity in the other neural circuits to meet the conditions demanded by that network. It operates cooperatively with the cingulo-opercular circuitry that keeps us on task. And it harnesses the DAN, so that we can fulfill our highest level cognitive goals in an optimized sequence when attending to the outside world. Moreover, it harnesses the internal simulation circuitry of the default network when we deliberate in our imagination. Central to top-down control is likely to be area 10 or rlPFC. This area is perhaps the highest in the pecking order of executive planning circuitry. People who have lesions in this area might have trouble forming appropriate high-level plans and sequences of actions. For example, think about how complex it is to make a cake. There are dozens of small steps that must be executed in the right way and in the right order to bake a cake. Any mistake and the result might be unpalatable. In other words, timing and sequencing matter.

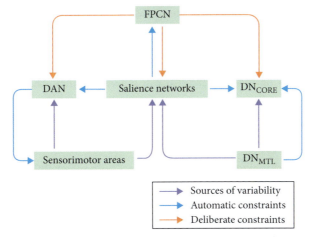

Figure 4.24 Neural model of the interactions among sources of variability, automatic constraints, and deliberate constraints. Arrows represent the influences that large-scale networks have on the dynamics of thought: networks can be sources of variability (in purple), sources of automatic constraints (in blue) or sources of deliberate constraints (in red). The default network (DN) subsystem centered around the medial temporal lobe (MTL) (DNMTL) and sensorimotor areas can act as sources of variability in thought content over time. The salience networks, the dorsal attention network (DAN) and the core DN subsystem (DNCORE) can exert automatic constraints on the output of the DNMTL and sensorimotor areas, thus limiting the variability of thought and increasing its stability over time. The frontoparietal control network (FPCN) can exert deliberate constraints on thought by flexibly coupling with the DNCORE, the DAN or the salience networks, thus reinforcing or reducing the automatic constraints being exerted by the DNCORE, the DAN or the salience networks.

Used with permission from Christoff, K., Irving, Z., Fox, K. C. R., Spreng, R. N., & Andrews-Hanna, J. R. (2016). Mind-wandering as spontaneous thought: A dynamic framework. *Nature Reviews Neuroscience*, 17, 718–731.

Certainly, what sets volitional processing apart from nonvolitional processing is the specification of top-down constraints or criteria that then influence bottom-up processing in such a way that just those constraints or criteria are met. But it would be wrong to think that executive control areas (area 10 or the dlPFC) are alone adequate for volition. In addition to having a high-level plan, you need to have ways of executing the plan. That is, you have to come up with more concrete plans than "I am going to learn Swahili." You need more immediate plans that will get you to order a book about how to learn Swahili, and, of course, you also need a motoric system that is capable of carrying such plans out using your body in the world.

The metaphor of a car is instructive. In order to drive appropriately, you need a driver or executive with a plan about where to go next and where to go long term. This would include areas such as area 10 and dlPFC. But you also need gas, or you won't be going anywhere, no matter how good your plans might be. This is analogous to the anterior cingulate circuitry that keeps us on task and that may be associated with both error detection (so that we can get back on task) and the subjectively experienced feeling of drive or willpower (Parvizi et al., 2013). If this circuitry is knocked out, people can get what is called "akinetic mutism" where they appear to lose all drive. Typically, they just lie there catatonically. It is not that they become unconscious. Rather, it is that they don't see the point of striving to do anything. Having the ACC in place gives one the willpower to see plans through. In the next two sections on willpower, we learn more precisely how this works in terms of cognitive control of the peripheral nervous system.

But having anterior cingulate circuitry in place without an ability to plan, coming from rlPFC and dlPFC, might be a bit like having a full tank of gas without having a destination in mind. Also required is a steering wheel that connects to wheels that can turn, which is analogous to having a motor system that allows one to carry out one's intentions. So free will or volition is not a single thing. In fact, volition is not a thing at all. It is a series of temporally extended and correctly sequenced, interacting processes or operations, just as driving is not a thing, but a cascade of processes that must be carried out in the right order. The concatenation of verb-like operations normally happens so seamlessly and rapidly, that they give rise to the illusion that an act of willing is a unitary noun-like command decreed instantaneously by a unitary noun-like capacity of free will.

4.23 The Neural Basis of Willpower

Here we consider the neural basis of willpower. "Willpower" is something of an old-fashioned word that is not much used by neuroscientists these days. But I think it pretty well captures the idea that there is a source of motivation and drive, as well as commitment to a goal, that helps us realize our intentions, even if having willpower alone is not enough. Obviously, we need to also have a goal in mind before we can be driven to fulfill that goal. Earlier sections raised the possibility that planning areas such as the rlPFC and dlPFC are likely to be involved in coming up with a plan or a goal, or even a stack of organized and sequenced subplans and subgoals. But the cingulo-opercular circuit that links the very anterior portion of the insula with the dACC is very likely involved in the neural realization of task maintenance and the drive needed to stay on task, so that we can see a plan through to its completion.

First let us learn a bit about what happens if this circuitry is knocked out. In one of the horrors of scientific malfeasance, tens of thousands of frontal lobotomies were performed during the 1940s and 1950s (Kean, 2022). Portuguese neurologist Antonio Moniz invented the lobotomy—from "lobe" and "otomy" (cut)—in the 1930s, and actually received the Nobel prize in 1949 for inventing this brutal practice. In America, neurologists Walter Freeman and James Watts embraced and refined the method. The surgical procedure initially involved drilling a hole through the skull and sticking a leucotome (a cannula containing a slender rotating blade) into the brain, and then letting the spikes at the end rotate, destroying a disk of tissue. Often six or more such holes were drilled in order to destroy as much frontal lobe connectivity as possible. Later, Freeman simply smashed metal icepicks into the brain through the skull above the eyelids and swept it back and forth to destroy axonal connections linking frontal areas to the rest of the brain. This was legitimized with the scientific-sounding term "transorbital lobotomy." Over 40,000 such operations were carried out in the 1940s and 1950s by Freeman and others in the U.S., and over 17,000 occurred in the UK. The majority of the victims were women hospitalized for depression. Imagine that you are a depressed woman in a hospital, and Dr. Freeman comes in confidently asserting that he must lobotomize your frontal lobes to heal you. And you, conditioned to trust your doctors agree.

Freeman described one of his victims, a 29-year-old woman, after her frontal lobotomy, as a "smiling, lazy and satisfactory patient with the personality of an oyster." She could no longer remember Freeman's name and repeatedly tried to pour coffee from an empty pot. He advised her parents to train her with ice cream as a reward, and to smack her as a punishment. Freeman proudly called the results of his procedure "surgically induced childhood." He believed that after being put into a child-like state with this procedure, patients could be retrained, using smacking and rewards to become healthy, functioning adults again. The data proved otherwise. The large majority of such patients had enduring personality damage, primarily associated with apathy and a lack of initiative or willpower, and a loss of inhibition. It is hard to believe that such a barbaric procedure was considered legitimate practice as recently as the 1950s, and that Moniz won the Nobel prize for inventing this cruel treatment.

This, along with the infamous Tuskeegee and Mengele experiments, provide all the evidence we will ever need that scientists alone cannot be trusted to do the right thing, even if they themselves believe that they are acting with the noblest of intentions. In large part, this is why experiments are now reviewed by and carried out under the supervision of internal review boards, and sometimes external review boards. Perhaps such review boards need to be introduced more broadly in our society, given the human tendency to act immorally when in positions of unchecked power.

Let us now consider what happens if the dACC is activated artificially. Unlike a lobotomy or a cingulotomy, which destroys this circuitry and induces a loss of initiative or willpower, activating this intact circuitry in the right way should activate the functionality of this circuitry. This is the orange COCN circuitry shown in Figure 4.19d. At Stanford University, Josef Parvizi and colleagues (2013) stimulated the right dACC of epilepsy patients with a very low amperage electrical current. Patients had a psychological experience of willpower, namely, of facing challenges and overcoming them, along with a bodily experience of increased heart rate and heavier breathing. In an insightful passage, one epilepsy patient in Parvizi et al. (2013; see movie in supplementary materials) describes what stimulation of his right dACC felt like:

> my chest and respiratory system started getting kinda shaky, like it was wanting to go push itself out the door .... I started getting this feeling like I was driving

into a storm. ... almost like you're headed toward a storm that is on the other side, maybe a couple of miles away, and you gotta get across the hill and all of a sudden you're sitting here thinking how am I going to figure out how to get over that, through that? ... And my chest never sits there and starts pounding like it's, you know, like you're a football player getting ready to go out and make a, try to make his first touchdown for the season or something. It's not that type of thing. It's more like this thing of trying to figure out your way out of, how you're going to get through something. It's not a matter of how you're going to production-wise do something ... You're like, am I gonna ... get through this? ... It was more of a positive type thing about push harder, push harder, push harder to try to get through this ...

Returning to Schopenhauer's metaphor (Figure 4.16), the "strong blind man" of the dACC is usually harnessed and guided by the "lame sighted man" of lateral frontal and posterior parietal circuitry. But in Parvizi's stimulation experiment, the dACC was activated in the absence of any plan for action imposed by executive control areas. In the absence of a plan, the strong blind man gropes for a solution to an ill-defined challenge that requires pushing ever harder. Note that confronting an uncertain challenge is described as a positive feeling by this patient. In a world in which we have done so much to minimize risk and challenge for our children, we may be harming their brains; In Section 4.29, we will learn about Marion Diamond's (1988) finding that challenges are enriching and can quite literally foster flourishing cortical microstructure, which, in the absence of challenge and novelty can wither.

Willpower is not only a psychological phenomenon, but also a bodily phenomenon. In fact, some neuroscientists (Critchley et al., 2003) have argued that the right dACC is effectively the encephalization, or cortical control center, of the sympathetic nervous system. Outside the central nervous system, which includes the brain and spinal cord, there is a peripheral nervous system that has two subcomponents: the sympathetic nervous system that prepares us for "fight or flight," and the parasympathetic nervous system associated with "rest and digest" processes. The main idea is that cortical activation of the right dACC invokes the sympathetic nervous system, so that we have the energy and physical power to enact our willed intentions and plans and have the energy and drive to overcome the obstacles that inevitably arise. In contrast, it may be that parts of the left ACC contain neural circuits that realize an encephalization or cortical control center for the parasympathetic nervous system. The sympathetic system may act as the gas to rev our engine so we can get things done, and the parasympathetic nervous system may act as the brake, so that we can rest and digest. We can conclude from this that the dACC is not only part of a cognitive task maintenance circuit that we have been calling the COCN, but also that it activates the body to be ready for action so that plans and goals can be achieved.

In the West there are numerous biases of which we are hardly aware. One is that the mind is separate from the body. However, in the case of willpower, the will is as much about states of body as it is about states of the mind.

4.24 The Cultivation of Willpower and Attention

Can willpower and self-control be enhanced with practice or environmental feedback? There already exist exercise regimens for training control of the mind that have remarkable effects on brain function, attentional control, and how one reacts to events that arise externally in the world or internally in the mind. Various meditation techniques afford the cultivation of will. They typically involve paying volitional attention to something pretty boring, like the breath, or a sound, a mantra, a picture, or a mandala. Each time the mind drifts off, one brings it back.

I lived in a Theravada monastery for about three months when I was in college and and know firsthand how difficult it was to stay focused on my breath. I initially felt that my mind was out of control, jumping immediately to this problem or that. I went to the head monk and explained my problem. Through a Burmese translator he told me that the mind is like a wild monkey. He said "You say 'sit monkey and don't move!' And as soon as you stop paying attention, the monkey then jumps off to climb around the many rooms of the mind." He said, "If you gently and nonjudgmentally bring the monkey back to sit down thousands of times, eventually the monkey will stay put, and your consciousness will start to transform."

Before talking about the mental effects of meditation, let us talk about some of its physical effects. Meditation and breathing techniques may evoke parasympathetic dominance. One goal of such techniques appears to be the gaining of volitional attentional control over the emotions and physiology, probably via learning that involves lateral prefrontal and parietal circuitry, which, through practice, come to better govern the ACC–sympathetic–parasympathetic axis. Scientists have to date generally focused on the deep relaxation and feelings of well-being that can follow certain meditative techniques.

There are, however, other techniques designed to elicit sympathetic rather than parasympathetic responses. For example, some schools of yoga, such as kundalini, have exercises that involve punching the air with intentionally evoked anger, as well as exercises that involve contracting the abdomen and anal sphincter in a controlled manner, in each case followed by relaxation and focus on the breath. These are the muscular and breathing responses associated with sympathetic response. Invoking them in this volitional and controlled way may bring these usually automatic or autonomic "fight-or-flight" responses under better volitional and cognitive control. I took a kundalini yoga teacher training course in which we were encouraged not simply to punch with anger, but also to feel the anger. I am convinced that intentionally evoking emotions also releases tensions associated with their chronic inhibition. Volitional control may then be gained in two ways, one by better governing circuitry associated with an emotion such as anger, and the other by releasing the anger volitionally. Certainly much loss of control in life happens because we have been repressing emotions so long that they then explode volcanically.

Training in numerous schools of the martial arts involves repeated controlled punching and fighting that were developed in Buddhist monasteries as a mental, spiritual, and emotional practice as much as a physical means of self-defense. Thus, the Western view that meditation is primarily about relaxation is incomplete. The goal is not relaxation per se, but mastery of the mind and nervous system, with particular emphasis on increasing the attentional system's range and depth of volitional control. With mastery, one can turn the body into a powerful whip of determination or, as needed, into a calm pond of inner serenity.

In all these Eastern traditions, attention to breathing is considered central to mastering one's mind. Since sympathetic and parasympathetic patterns of response typically involve stereotypical patterns of breathing, some argue that bringing the pattern of breathing under volitional attentional control affords a mechanism for gaining greater control over the autonomic nervous system (ANS). If certain mental states, such as fear, panic, or relaxation, are associated with stereotypical breathing patterns, the idea is that volitionally invoking these same breathing patterns can help one gain volitional control over the associated mental states. The causation works both ways; the emotion elicits a breathing pattern, and that pattern elicits an associated emotional state. Unlike most autonomic system responses, breathing is subject to volitional control.

For an animal to be able to function, it has to sometimes be active to eat, escape, fight, mate, care for the young, and so on. But at other times it also has to be inactive to heal, digest, sleep, and "recharge its batteries." So a balance must be struck between the sympathetic tendency toward energy expenditure in the pursuit of goals and the parasympathetic tendency toward energy conservation in the pursuit of rest and vegetative functions such as digestion. Figure 4.25 shows the outputs of the sympathetic and parasympathetic nervous systems. This balancing appears to involve phylogenetically ancient central pattern generating circuits in the vagal complex of the brainstem that regulate respiration and patterns of vocalization, probably because vocalization and respiration must be coordinated.

Although alien to a Western conception of the mind and body, the notion of willpower is tied to a specific physical location in yoga, namely the third or "manipura" chakra behind the solar plexus. This is also true in the martial arts, where willpower and the power to act are localized to the same area of the abdomen ("hara" in Japanese). When I studied Shōtōkan karate in Japan years ago, one of the strongest compliments you could pay to someone was to say that they had strong hara. Yogic, martial, and meditative exercises train mental control of this region using breathing and muscle contraction in the belief that training volitional control over this area can lead to strengthened willpower and psychological strength. In the West we colloquially refer to someone as having a "fire in the belly" when they are very determined or having "guts" when they are courageous. Perhaps different cultures have independently concluded that the solar plexus plays some special role in the exertion of will.

Even though Hindu, Buddhist, and traditional Chinese conclusions are rooted in very different assumptions than Western science, some of their discoveries and conclusions were rooted in empirical observation. Unlike Western science, emphasis was not placed on observation of the external world, but instead on observation of the internal world of experience.

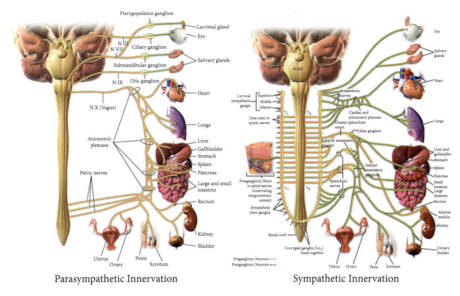

Figure 4.25 Destinations of parasympathetic and sympathetic nervous system innervation.

Used with permission from Blausen.com staff (2014). Medical gallery of Blausen Medical 2014. WikiJournal of Medicine 1(2).

Body function and health are domains where both phenomenological Eastern and scientific Western systems of observation have created complex models. It would be dogmatic to dismiss Eastern systems out of hand. Certainly, when people exert cognitive, emotional, or physical effort to overcome some obstacle they tend to knit their brows, hold or constrict their breath, and contract the muscles of the abdomen, diaphragm, and anal sphincter. This appears to be an innate human response that accompanies effortful willing, which may reflect a general preparedness for action, fighting, or resistance, as a result of sympathetic nervous system arousal.

It is likely no coincidence that behind what is colloquially called the "solar plexus" or "breadbasket" lies a large plexus of nerves called the celiac plexus. Figure 4.26 shows a 1918 figure from *Gray's Anatomy*, with an arrow added, showing where it is. It is comprised of the left and right splanchnic nerves (which carry sympathetic fight-or-flight efferent fibers that innervate the viscera and visceral sensory afferent fibers), parts of the right vagus nerve (carrying motor parasympathetic rest and digest fibers to the viscera and sensory afferent neurons carrying information about the viscera to the brain), and the celiac ganglia, which are parts of the sympathetic nervous system and the largest ganglia in the ANS. Axons from neurons in these ganglia innervate virtually the entire viscera. These neuronal connections are key in regulating the degree of fight-or-flight versus rest-and-digest operation of the body. You can see that each organ receives parasympathetic innervation, shown as fine blue lines, and also receives sympathetic innervation, shown in thick red lines, and can be thought of as the brake pedal and the gas pedal governing the activity of our body, respectively.

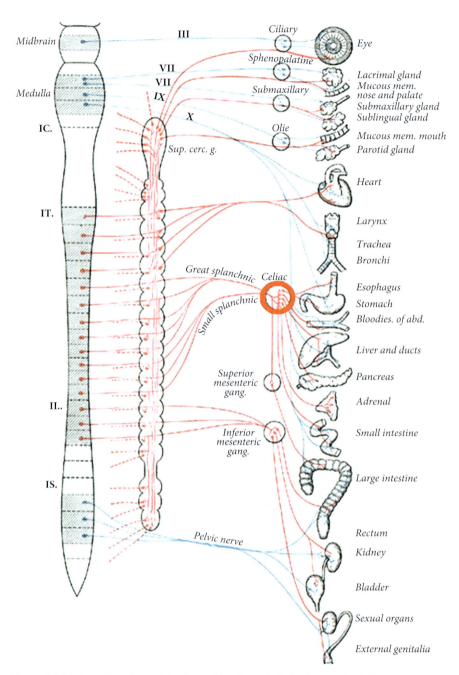

Figure 4.26 The celiac plexus is indicated by the red circle. Sympathetic innervations are shown in red. Parasympathetic innervations are shown in blue.
https://en.wikipedia.org/wiki/Splanchnic nerves

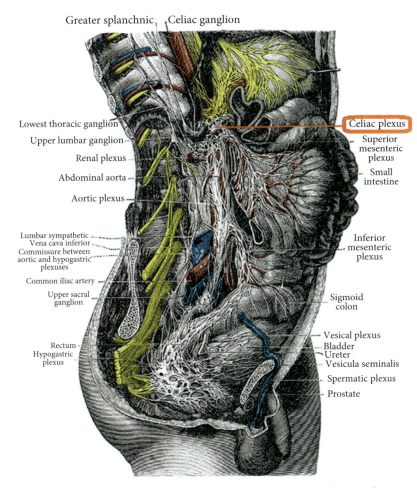

Figure 4.27 The location of the celiac plexus is indicated by the red rectangle.

While the cortex can influence the responses of the celiac plexus, these responses operate with a degree of autonomy; thus the name autonomic nervous system. One might think of the celiac plexus, shown in Figure 4.27, as one of the "two brains" or integration and control centers of the ANS, the other being the enteric nervous system embedded in the gastrointestinal lining, shown in Figure 4.28, which makes decisions about enzyme release involved in digestion, as well as motor control of the gut, including peristalsis and movements that churn food. The enteric nervous system has about one hundred million neurons, which is more than can be found in the entire spinal cord, and uses many of the same neurotransmitters. It is this "second brain" in our gut that likely gives rise to gut feelings, whose encephalized cortical center is likely the AI or FO, just as the ACC plays this role for the sympathetic and parasympathetic nervous systems. It is likely not a coincidence that the COCN links cognition with fine control of the body via both aspects of the peripheral nervous system, namely sympathetic/parasympathetic via the ACC, and enteric via the FO, so that tasks can be

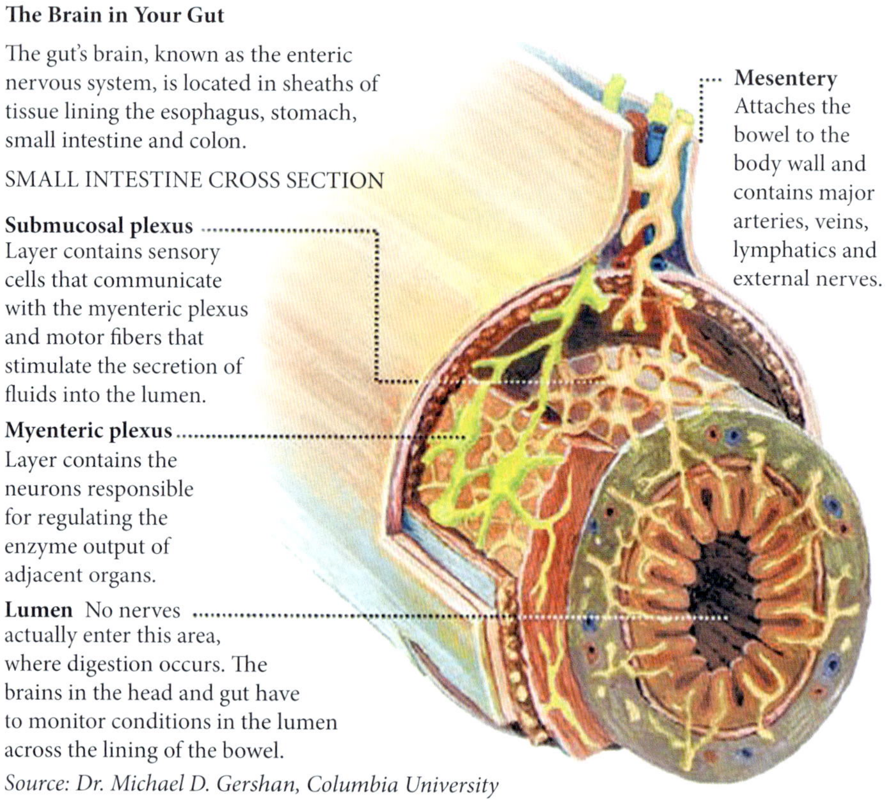

The Brain in Your Gut

The gut's brain, known as the enteric nervous system, is located in sheaths of tissue lining the esophagus, stomach, small intestine and colon.

SMALL INTESTINE CROSS SECTION

Submucosal plexus Layer contains sensory cells that communicate with the myenteric plexus and motor fibers that stimulate the secretion of fluids into the lumen.

Myenteric plexus Layer contains the neurons responsible for regulating the enzyme output of adjacent organs.

Lumen No nerves actually enter this area, where digestion occurs. The brains in the head and gut have to monitor conditions in the lumen across the lining of the bowel.

Mesentery Attaches the bowel to the body wall and contains major arteries, veins, lymphatics and external nerves.

Source: Dr. Michael D. Gershan, Columbia University

Figure 4.28 The enteric nervous system.
Used with permission from Dr. Michael Gershon.

completed as planned, while invoking appropriate body states. Free will is embodied as well as realized in the cortex.

The analytic philosophical tradition, even more so than most Western traditions, emphasizes discovering truth through reason. Naturally, its approach to assessing the truth or untruth of free will is abstract and logical. Reason has its place. Personally, I am drawn to the clarity and rigor of logic, which is why I was a math and physics major in college. But logic cannot undercover facts about the body, just as mere thinking could never tell us about the species of animals that happened to evolve. Reason would never have predicted a platypus! We have to look at what exists, because there is little about life or free will that can be deduced *a priori*, on the basis of reasonable axioms about the nature of the world. The body is not a matter of logic, and life cannot be lived solely within the head. The needs of the body, and interactions with the environment, must also be tended and attended. This is particularly so concerning free will, which is a lived, bodily phenomenon, realized in the head, the body, and its interactions with the environment. The brain may envision a plan, and exert willpower to see the plan through, but without a strong, healthy body capable of implementing the plan, there is in effect no agency. If the body is weak, exhausted, emaciated, obese or sick, the implementation of our agency may be sapped or ineffective. Anyone interested in enhancing the efficacy of human free will should therefore ask what it is that strengthens the body and makes it thrive.

In addition to good sleep, exercise, a healthy environment, and a supportive social life, an important component of physical health is a healthy diet. What the enteric nervous system "brain" does with food is not subject to volitional control, but what we choose to put in our mouths is. Philosophy, if it is to be a lived philosophy, must tend to the vehicle of our free will, which is a strong, fit, and healthy body, to the extent attainable.

Data show that two diets stand out in terms of promoting health, cognitive function, and longevity. The Mediterranean diet (Finicelli et al., 2022; Guasch-Ferré and Willett, 2021) may provide some of its benefits because of the anti-inflammatory and antioxidant properties of ingredients such as olive oil, and its high proportions of fresh fruit and vegetables. The low-carbohydrate, high-fat, moderate-protein ketogenic diet (Vidali et al., 2015; Zweers et al., 2021), in contrast, like fasting or starvation, forces the body to switch its energy source from burning carbohydrates to burning the body's own fats. Through a different pathway than the Mediterranean Diet, the Keto diet also has anti-inflammatory and antioxidant effects, and appears to have anti-cancer effects as well (Allen et al., 2014). There are many variants of these diets that are practiced, such as the Atkins diet and the Paleo diet. All have in common low sugar and little to no processed food.

These diets may yield some of their beneficial effects by up-regulating biogenesis of mitochondria, the endosymbionts in our cells that create ATP, the central energy source in all our cells. Mitochondrial biogenesis is generally a response to the body being intermittently placed in situations of energy depletion (Zong et al., 2002). Apart from the keto diet, practices that accomplish energy depletion may up-regulate the production of mitochondria, and therefore cellular energy. Such practices include fasting, intense exercise (Little et al., 2011; Wang et al., 2011), hypoxia (Gutsaeva et al., 2008; Zhu et al., 2010), and exposure to cold (van der Lans et al., 2013).

It is difficult to fit notions of life-energy like *qi* from Chinese medicine or *prana* from yogic traditions into the paradigm of Western medicine. However, one point of contact may be mitochondrial health and production of the energy required for most cellular processes, including neural function. Without ATP, neurons and other cells would die, and with their death, free will would vanish. An interesting direction for future research would be to explore whether practices said to enhance energy in tai chi or in yoga enhance either mitochondrial biogenesis or a sense of agency.

If the Eastern traditions are correct, how and why would training cortical control of the celiac plexus train willpower in the specific sense of voluntary control over the application of sympathetic and parasympathetic responses? The answer might lie in the realization that emotions and physiological responses are causally intertwined.

Although it is common to think that emotions cause physiological responses, the James–Lange theory argues the opposite, namely, that emotions tend to follow physiological responses. On this account, the ANS takes causal precedence, reacting to experiences of the world, which then trigger physiological arousal states that are then interpreted, in turn triggering emotional responses. However, as formulated, the James–Lange theory is too strong, and cannot be correct. On the other hand, the alternative view formulated in the Cannon–Bard theory of emotion, that is, that emotional and physiological responses are evoked together with causal precedence given to emotion, also has its flaws. A reasonable compromise is that there are two interacting systems, one emotional and the other physiological, that interact continuously, making claims of causal precedence pointless. As in all cybernetic systems, causation is not instantaneous or linear, but rather nonlinear, temporally extended, and, indeed, circular in its unfolding.

If emotion and physiology are normally not dissociable, but two interacting semiautonomous modes of processing input, then causality should work both ways. If true, then it is not unreasonable to assume that intentionally changing one's physiology can change one's emotional state. One sees such causation in "laughter yoga" where you force yourself to laugh artificially, then find that you feel happier and, surprisingly, are then genuinely laughing.

But training of the solar plexus in yoga and the martial arts is more ambitious than just having the goal of making us feel better. The claim is that by mastering and cultivating control over the solar plexus and breathing, one develops inner strength, psychological and emotional resilience, and willpower. If certain exercises, such as kundalini yoga's "breath of fire," do indeed train cognitive control over the sympathetic nervous system's central integration center, namely the solar plexus, then it seems reasonable that sympathetic nervous system response can itself come under greater cognitive control. Rather than automatically entering a fearful or aggressive state, one gains volitional control over the application of these states. Without the cognitive control of a cortical "rider," the autonomic "horses" might run wild, or at least be on "auto-pilot." By releasing and reining in sympathetic and parasympathetic responses at will, acts of cognitive willing gain control of the emotions, particularly fear and aggression, and the physiological responses required for exerting one's will, so to speak, volitionally, rather than reflexively or on autopilot.

4.25 The Neural Basis of Mindfulness

Using fMRI, Lazar and colleagues (2000) concluded that "the practice of meditation activates neural structures involved in attention and control of the autonomic nervous system," including the dlPFC, posterior parietal cortex, and the ACC. Such practices can decrease or increase theta activity, again suggestive of ACC activity and down- or up-regulation of sympathetic activity. If willpower is in part rooted in emotional and physiological mechanisms, then it stands to reason that training that enhances cognitive control over the application of sympathetic and parasympathetic responses will enhance one's ability to realize one's freely chosen ideas and decisions more efficiently than if one is prone to fly off the handle, panic, flee, cry, or cower inappropriately.

In another fMRI study that compared meditators with nonmeditators, either when meditating or not meditating, Brewer and colleagues (2011) found the interesting patterns of activation shown in Figure 4.29, where we can see images that provide two views of the brain. One is a sagittal (vertical) slice through the middle of the brain, and the other offers axial (horizontal) cuts through the brain. On the sagittal slices, we can see that meditators have a relatively more active dACC than nonmeditators, both when they are not meditating and when they are meditating. This is precisely the area

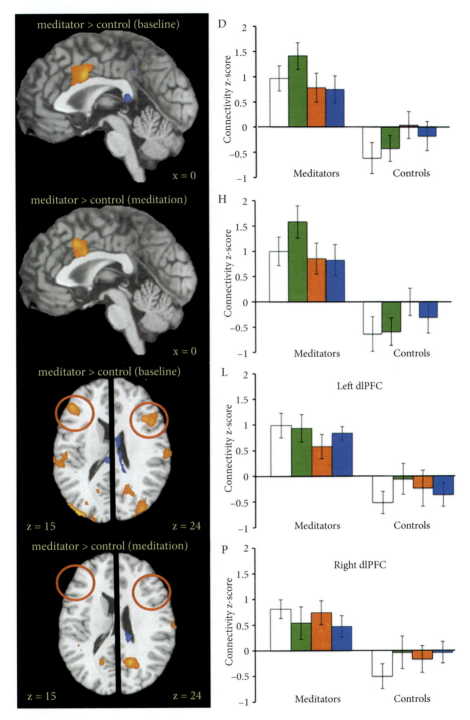

Figure 4.29 Areas of the brain where meditators show greater fMRI blood oxygen-level dependent (BOLD) signal, corresponding to greater neural activity, than non-meditators, are shown in orange. See text for details.

Used with permission from Brewer, J. A., Worhunsky, P. D., Gray, J. R., Tang, Y. Y., Weber, J., & Kober, H. (2011). Meditation experience is associated with differences in default mode network activity and connectivity. *Proceedings of the National Academy of Sciences of the United States of America*, *108*(50), 20254–20259.

associated with feelings of willpower and sympathetic response that Parvizi activated in his epilepsy patients. It is part of the COCN.

In the bottom half of the set of images in Figure 4.29, we can see two adjacent axial half-slices of the brain, at two somewhat different heights (z = 24 is higher up than z = 15). Pay special attention to the regions circled in red, which are part of the dlPFC that we have associated with the FPCN. In the case when expert meditators are not meditating, we can see that they tend to have more active dlPFC circuitry, perhaps associated with greater working memory operations or top-down control than nonmeditators. But notice that, when they are meditating, meditators do not have greater dlPFC activation than nonmeditators. This would suggest that they are not thinking about exerting more top-down control or carrying out more working memory operations than nonmeditators. Perhaps through practice they have automatized top-down control.

Things get really interesting when looking at which parts of the brain are relatively de-activated in meditators while meditating. These areas are shown in blue in Figure 4.30 in a midline sagittal slice. We have seen these areas before: ACC/amPFC (circled in red in Figure 4.30A) and PCC (circled in red in Figure 4.30B, and not circled in Figure 4.30A). These are parts of the brain involved in the default (mode) network, which are thought to play a role in mental simulations and the imagining of the self and others in imagined scenarios. So, a remarkable story emerges from this research. Meditation leads to suppression of the simulations of the self in different imagined worlds associated with the default network, and this is possibly accomplished by having a more robust dACC response, associated with staying on task and exerting willpower. Moreover, this benefit of heightened dorsal cingulate activation carries over into normal waking consciousness, even when meditators are no longer meditating. In long-term meditators, the contents of consciousness are transformed from virtual reality concerns to what is happening in the world and the body here and now.

Perhaps more remarkably, as shown in Figure 4.31, brain activation after having taken psilocybin, relative to activation after having taken a placebo, is down-regulated in the same key areas, in the ACC/amPFC and PCC (Carhart-Harris et al., 2011). Note that the top right image of Figure 4.31 resembles a horizontal flip of Figure 4.30A. This suggests that taking psilocybin down-regulates the default mode network and may diminish the kind of self-referential processing typically associated with this network. In some ways, taking psilocybin may be like taking a helicopter to a mental peak of ego dissolution that meditators take years to ascend by foot. That said, there are nonetheless major differences between the meditative and hallucinogen-induced mental states. The former appear to be more abiding into normal wakefulness, and less fraught with hallucinations.

Let us tie these findings in with the claims of Buddhism. The claim is that self-referential thinking, which we can reasonably associate in part with the default network, is a cause of suffering. I think a lot of such thinking is geared toward enhancing outcomes for oneself, relative to others, avoiding bad outcomes, or imagining good

The Neuroscience of Free Will 259

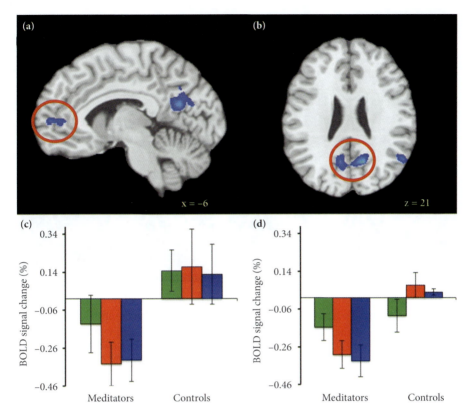

Figure 4.30 Experienced meditators show decreased default mode network activation. Areas of the brain that are more deactivated in meditators than non-meditators are shown in blue. See text for details.

Used with permission from Brewer, J. A., Worhunsky, P. D., Gray, J. R., Tang, Y. Y., Weber, J., & Kober, H. (2011). Meditation experience is associated with differences in default mode network activity and connectivity. *Proceedings of the National Academy of Sciences of the United States of America, 108*(50), 20254–20259.

and bad outcomes for others. If this addiction to the self tends to lead to suffering, then suppressing this kind of self-referential thinking, the Buddhists claim, should enhance well-being. Moreover, if the dACC or cingulo-opercular network can be strengthened through meditative practice, one should gain greater volitional control over one's bodily and mental responses to external and internal events.

In the West we place great emphasis on "potty training" to help small children master voluntary control of their rectal and urinary muscles, but we do not encourage children to cultivate further domains of voluntary control very much after this point has been reached. Other cultures encourage older children to gain control of their attentional, cingulate, and autonomic nervous systems through specific training regimens. Imagine if meditation, martial arts, and yoga were as much a part of our schooling as art or gym are today. Imagine if we were as concerned with being

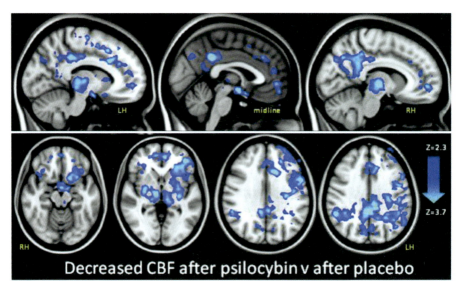

Figure 4.31 Regions where there was significantly decreased cerebral blood flow (CBF) after having taken psilocybin versus after having taken a placebo are shown in blue.

Carhart-Harris, R. L., Erritzoe, D., Williams, T., Stone, J. M., Reed, L. J., Colasanti, A., Tyacke, R. J., Leech, R., Malizia, A. L., Murphy, K., Hobden, P., Evans, J., Feilding, A., Wise, R. G., & Nutt, D. J. (2011). Neural correlates of the psychedelic state as determined by fMRI studies with psilocybin. *Proceedings of the National Academy of Sciences of the United States of America*, *109*(6), 2138–2143. doi: 10.1073/pnas.1119598109

mentally in shape as many of us are concerned with being physically in shape. Imagine if we admired someone for the degree to which they had cultivated their minds to a point of mental fitness, mastery, and health, to the same extent that we currently admire people for being physically fit and healthy. Imagine if religions were not based on beliefs that science has made now largely unbelievable, but instead were based on practices that cultivate volitional attention, self-mastery, reason, kindness, and elevated states of consciousness.

4.26 The Cultivation of Hope and Meaning

One theme of this book is that we do not only have free will in the first-order sense, which is the capacity to consider options, weigh them in light of our own reasons, and then select and enact one of them. We also have second-order free will, which is the capacity to choose to become a new kind of chooser in the future. Central to this capacity is the willpower to see a plan of action through so that our nervous system will change in the way that we want it to. For example, nearly any of us could transform our nervous system, with consistent practice, into one that can process and produce Swahili a year from now, if we set our minds to it.

Previous sections considered ways in which willpower can be cultivated. One of the most important ways is fostering a conviction that a goal is in fact attainable if one perseveres. A goal is rarely something so simple as going to a destination. Typically goals and destinations are pursued in order to realize something meaningful. We drive to New York in order to surprise our mother on her birthday, or we study hard now in order to become a doctor later. A key point, then, is that humans act for reasons that are meaningful. We are not mere information-processing devices, like a laptop.

What is the difference between information and meaning? Information can be thought of as a change or difference in input that informs one. If the reduction is from two possibilities to one certainty, say, we hear "yes" when we might have heard either "yes" or "no," that reduction in uncertainty from two possibilities to one certainty comprises one binary digit or bit of information. The meaning of that "yes" plays no role. A bit is a bit, regardless of the implications of that answer. Meaning, in contrast, is not just a difference. Biological information or meaning is about a difference that makes a difference, to use the lovely turn of phrase of biologist Gregory Bateson. If the "yes" is in answer to the question "Is today Tuesday?" not much of meaning has transpired. But if the answer is in response to "Will you marry me?" the implications are momentous.

Meaning, unlike information, can be quantified not in bits, but in terms of the degree to which a model about the world must be reconfigured or updated in light of some event. If someone says "yes" or "no" to the question "Will you marry me?," we must completely reconfigure our model concerning how we will spend the rest of our lives, whereas, if someone says "yes" or "no" to the question "Is today Tuesday?," we hardly have to update any of our mental models at all. The absence of information can be meaningful as well. If, according to our mental model, a person who wanted to marry us would answer "yes" immediately, a "no" response, or an answer of silence, would be very meaningful.

Humans are motivated to pursue goals that will realize meaningful outcomes. This is only possible relative to a causal mental model about what is going on in which the implications or consequences of incoming information can be understood. A tiny change in the informational input, such as an eyelash on your shirt, might have huge implications for you and your spouse if they believe the eyelash is from a lover, whereas a huge change in information, say, the whole visual scene getting darker because a cloud has passed overhead, might have no implications of any consequence. If we believe we can attain a goal that has meaning, for example, that we will survive a diagnosis of cancer, we will feel hopeful and strive to realize that goal. But if we believe that survival is impossible, relative to our mental model of what is going on, we will likely feel despair or acceptance and will likely give up trying. This is why hope is so central to free will, volition, and willpower, and despair so central to its destruction. If we want to cultivate will, we have to cultivate hope and a conviction that a goal is attainable.

I will now consider a horrible example to make clear that this is also true of animals. Curt P. Richter (1957) of Johns Hopkins University carried out some sickeningly cruel drowning experiments on thousands of rats that made clear the importance of hope in giving animals a will to keep trying. He noticed that rats placed in large cylinders partly filled with water tended to drown quickly, often within minutes. But just before they drowned, he rescued some by taking them briefly out of the cylinder, after which he would put them back in. Even though they had been on the verge of drowning a minute before, they would now not give up, swimming nonstop for up to three days (!) before succumbing to exhaustion and drowning. In science we are taught not to anthropomorphize animals. But how can an objective scientist look at such data and not conclude that the most conservative explanation is that the rats who had been taken out of the water and then put back in the water hoped for another rescue, whereas the unrescued rats succumbed to despair? In his own words, Richter (1957) says:

> The situation of these rats scarcely seems one demanding fight or flight—it is rather one of hopelessness; whether they are restrained in the hand or confined in the swimming jar, the rats are in a situation against which they have no defense. This reaction of hopelessness is shown by some wild rats very soon after being grasped in the hand and prevented from moving; they seem literally to "give up."
>
> Support for the assumption that the sudden death phenomenon depends largely on emotional reactions to restraint or immersion comes from the observation that after elimination of the hopelessness the rats do not die. This is achieved by repeatedly holding the rats briefly and then freeing them, and by immersing them in water for a few minutes on several occasions. In this way the rats quickly learn that the situation is not actually hopeless; thereafter they again become aggressive, try to escape, and show no signs of giving up.

He recorded the heart electrocardiogram in some dying rats, and concluded that death followed excessive *para*sympathetic, rather than sympathetic, activity:

> Contrary to our expectation, the EKG records indicated that the rats succumbing promptly died with a slowing of the heart rate rather than with an acceleration ... slowing of respiration and lowering of body temperature were also observed. Ultimately the heart stopped in diastole after having shown a steady gradual decrease in rate. As expected, autopsy revealed a large heart distended with blood. These findings indicate that the rats may have died a so-called vagus death, which is the result of over-stimulation of the parasympathetic rather than of the sympathico-adrenal system.

In the placebo effect, believing that some medicine or intervention will work accounts for some degree of its efficacy. The reverse also occurs; believing that something will turn out badly plays a causal role in it in fact turning out badly. An extreme form of this is "voodoo death," where a belief that one has been hexed to die leads to sudden death. This and other forms of death from despair appear to be rooted in hopelessness (Lester, 1972).

In the first "learned helplessness" research of Seligman and Maier (1967), a dog in a harness could not escape a shock which was preceded by the onset of a light. However, some dogs were able to turn a shock off by pressing a panel with their snout, whereas other dogs could not. The next day, dogs were placed in a two-compartment cage, one side of which would shock the dogs when the light came on. Those dogs that had previously learned that they could control the shock when in the harnesses jumped to the shockless side much more often than those that had learned that they had no control. Even though the latter dogs now had a way to escape the shock, many did not bother to escape. They just lay down and endured the shock. These animals had come to believe that they had no control over the situation because in the previous period they in fact could do nothing about getting shocked. It is as if they concluded that nothing they did made any difference, so why try? Later work (Maier, 1970) showed that these results were indeed rooted in motivational changes, rather than motoric constraint.

Seligman and others (Forgeard et al., 2011) have argued that learned helplessness mimics aspects of depression. Helplessness is an expression of learned hopelessness, in animals as in humans (Hiroto, 1974). Both depression and the passivity of hopelessness may in part be mediated via the serotonergic Raphe nucleus pathway (Maier and Seligman, 2016) which effectively inhibits escape behavior.

But Seligman's work is not primarily about learned helplessness or hopelessness. It is foremost about learned hope*fulness*. Note that the dogs that previously learned that they could control negative outcomes generalized this sense of control or agency to the new environment and overwhelmingly jumped to the shockless side. In a key variant of the experiment (Seligman et al., 1968), they reversed the order of trials. New dogs were first placed in the two-compartment box and learned that they could avoid getting shocked by jumping to the shockless side. Then, when placed in the harness, where shocks were unavoidable, they did not give up. And when later again placed in the two-compartment box, they reclaimed their ability to control the situation, by jumping to the shockless side.

It follows that early learning matters enormously. If one learns that a situation is hopeless, learned helplessness generalizes to new situations, whereas if one learns that there is hope because one can affect outcomes, this feeling of agency also generalizes. Free will is rooted in a conviction that one can make a difference through one's actions.

These findings have been generalized to many other species, including humans. In a variant of cognitive behavioral therapy, children taught to reframe negative events in terms of external, temporary factors that were not their fault were less likely to later develop depression than a control group of children not given this intervention (Peterson, 1999; Peterson and Seligman, 1984). The role of hope, hardiness, a feeling of control, and willpower in humans is no less important to our survival and success in life than it is in other animals. Further, a loss of hope is also central to human passivity, learned helplessness, grief, loneliness, depression, and loss of drive to fight for change. Exerting free will in real life is less about asserting a belief in some philosophical position than it is about feeling in one's bones that one can shape future outcomes by trying. It is about motivation and hopefulness. Free will is lived optimism.

There are even natural "experiments" involving humans that make this same point. In 1941 German U-boats repeatedly sank the ships owned by British shipping magnate Lawrence Holt. He noticed that older sailors disproportionately survived while younger ones drowned more often. This seemed to make no sense, because the younger men were physically stronger than the older men. It was also costing him a lot of money because he had to pay pensions to many young widows. He asked educator James Hogan why the younger sailors drowned more often than the older ones, and together, after interviewing many survivors, they concluded that older sailors did not give up in desperate circumstances because they were psychologically hardier, having survived difficult situations before. Even though they were thrown into cold water in the North Sea, they did not lose hope that they might be rescued, and they believed in their own ability to make it. They also found that younger sailors tended to go it alone, whereas older sailors tended to work together until rescued.

To foster the mental hardiness that the older sailors had learned through life experience, in 1941 Holt, Hogan, and German educator Kurt Hahn created Outward Bound, a school in Wales designed to teach psychological toughness and hardiness to English sailors. When asked why he founded this school, Hahn said "There is more to us than we know. If we can be made to see it, perhaps for the rest of our lives we will be unwilling to settle for less." As the school describes itself:

> Since 1941, Outward Bound has evolved but never departed from Hahn's original concept of an intense experience surmounting challenges in a natural setting, through which the individual builds his sense of self-worth, the group comes to a heightened awareness of human interdependence, and all grow in concern for those in danger and need.

I did a three-month course with Outward Bound when I was young, and it was one of the best things I have ever done in my life. By placing students in challenging situations that they must overcome, they learn what it takes to survive, to cooperate, and to endure. Students learn not to give up and to strive to attain a goal despite the inevitable setbacks and, in effect, to strengthen their willpower by gaining in hope, confidence, compassion, and conviction.

Just as hope can foster the drive needed to carry on, despite setbacks and difficulties, a loss of hope can lead to giving up. Researchers have found that parents who have lost a child have a much higher risk of dying from a heart attack than parents who have not lost a child (Espinosa and Evans, 2013; Schorr et al., 2016). Other research has shown that the rate of heart attacks increases after a diagnosis of cancer, and that the likelihood increases the more severe the diagnosis. And still other researchers have described a "broken-heart" syndrome (Hiestand et al., 2018; Li et al., 2003; Pelliccia et al., 2017), where people facing acute emotional distress develop physical heart problems, and sometimes can die of heart failure. In all cases it may be that excessive sympathetic nervous activation actually damages heart function.

The bottom line is that humans and other animals need to believe that there is a way to accomplish a goal, or they will not strive to attain it. People and other animals need hope to function healthily. This is actually the main reason I decided to write this trilogy of books on free will and make the associated online MOOC on edx.org and coursera.org, even though I knew it would be a lot of work. There are so many people from the fields of neuroscience and philosophy now saying that we lack free will. The data show, however, that people who believe this are more likely to passively conform (Alquist et al., 2013), to be less helpful and more aggressive (Baumeister et al., 2009), to be more impulsive and anti-social (Rigoni et al., 2012), to be more inclined to cheat (Vohs and Schooler, 2008) and to steal (Vohs and Baumeister, 2009), and to feel depressed. Who wants to feel like a passive puppet, where everything one would think or do was set in stone at the Big Bang, billions of years before one was born? Meanwhile, believing in free will is associated with many measures of subjective well-being, including enhanced gratitude (MacKenzie et al., 2014), better academic achievement (Feldman et al., 2016) and work performance (Stillman et al., 2010), a more satisfying love life (Boudesseul et al., 2016), lower stress (Crescioni et al., 2015), feelings of belongingness and meaningfulness (Moynihan et al., 2017), and greater happiness (Li et al., 2017). A feeling of agency over one's life is associated with these same benefits (Meyers and Diener, 1995), so the benefits of believing in free will may not arise directly from the belief per se, but because believing in free will leads people to view themselves as active agents capable of making their situation better (Gooding et al., 2018). Once I realized just how wrong some of these free will deniers are, at least in my fields of neuroscience and psychology, I felt I had to communicate to the world about how free will might be realized in the brain, in order to get the common sense-affirming message out there that we do have free will. With these three books I aim to give people both hope and strong arguments that they are agents who are in charge of their own lives and destinies, capable of changing their lives and our world for the better, which is, after all, just what people mean when they talk of having free will (Monroe and Malle, 2010). Like any goal, this project started with an idea. The rest was just work and persevering despite the inevitable setbacks. What motivated me, though, was a desire to fight the good fight and give people hope.

The cage door is open, and you can recreate your life. You are not a passive plant, rooted to the ground. You don't have to endure being shocked like a dog who believes it is helpless. You are a mind and a body with free will. You can move to where your life will be better. You have some say in the matter of what will become of you and your world.

Building on individual free will, we can also realize collective free will, because ideas and motivations can spread like wildfire between minds. Outrage against injustice and desires for freedom and justice can move people to take on the challenge of moving seemingly immovable mountains. Martin Luther King Jr. described one instance of the transformative contagion and power of collective willpower and vision the day before he was assassinated:

> We aren't going to let any mace stop us. We are masters in our nonviolent movement in disarming police forces; they don't know what to do … Bull Connor would tell them to send the dogs forth and they did come; but we just went before the dogs singing, "Ain't Gonna Let Nobody Turn Me Round." Bull Connor next would say, "Turn the fire hoses on." … Bull Connor didn't know history. He knew a kind of physics that somehow didn't relate to the transphysics that we knew about. And that was the fact that there was a certain kind of fire that no water could put out … we'd get in the jail, and we'd see the jailers looking through the windows being moved by our prayers, and being moved by our words and our songs. And there was a power there which Bull Connor couldn't adjust to; and so we ended up transforming Bull into a steer, and we won our struggle in Birmingham.

Tyrants and tyrannical governments lust for power and control. Collective action by the people is the most effective way to limit tyranny. This is why tyrants stamp out those who propagate dangerous ideas whenever they cannot stamp out the ideas themselves. Ideas can ignite an inner fire in people that can in turn ignite action among millions. The most fundamental idea, the one that precedes all others, is that we have free will; namely, we have some say in the matter of what shall become of us and our world. It is the conviction that we can make a difference that motivates us to try to change our world and others' minds. A conviction that we have free will motivates free action and free speech, and all the other acts of volition that allow our visions to affect the probabilities of events unfolding as we want them to unfold. No doubt, totalitarians and certain philosophers will try their utmost to stamp out the dangerous idea that we have free will. But this they cannot do, because people know they have free will from their lived experience (Frankl, 1962), just as they know that the sun is bright. If propagandists and shills tell you that the sun is in fact not bright, you know otherwise.

4.27 The Neural Basis of Volitional Imagination

This section considers the neural basis of volitional imagination. We have already seen areas of the brain involved in nonvoluntary modes of imagination. We saw which areas of the cortex are activated while dreaming. We then learned that people can be induced to start lucid dreaming if the dlPFC of the FPCN is stimulated using alternating current in the low gamma range through the scalp (Voss et al., 2014). We have also seen that the neural circuitry associated with mental simulation, namely, the default network, is activated when people are daydreaming or imagining in a mind-wandering sort of way.

The Neuroscience of Free Will 267

Here we focus on the neural basis of deliberation, because deliberation is, I believe, at the very heart of what it means to have free will. We can play events out in our own internal virtual reality to see what happens. Deliberating in this way is not done in a random fashion, but in light of constraints imposed by top-down cognitive areas. For example, we might play out what to make for dinner in light of various constraints, for example, that one of the guests is a vegetarian. A core idea is that parts of the default network can be harnessed by the FPCN for deliberate purposes.

In my own lab we tried to see whether this is in fact the case by looking at areas of the cortex activated by either maintaining some shapes in working memory versus brain areas activated when we have to do something with those shapes in working memory. We were motivated by the kinds of constructions seen in Figure 4.32, created by our ancestors thirty to forty thousand years ago. In this particular case, someone had to "download" a lion's head from memory, "download" a human body from memory, and then stick them together in this novel way in their mind, before going and building this "Löwenmensch" in the world.

In our study (Schlegel et al., 2013b), there were four conditions. In the first two conditions, there were four parts, such as shown in Figure 4.33, that could be put together to form a single larger shape. Subjects had to either remember the four parts, without putting them together, or they had to put them together in their minds according to certain rules.

In the other two conditions, they had to take a single conglomerated large shape and break it up in their minds into the four component subshapes, or else they just had to remember the large, conglomerated shape.

So, there were two mental operations, shown in red in Figure 4.34, which involved either constructing a shape or deconstructing a shape. And there were two maintenance conditions, shown in blue here, where subjects either remembered the four parts or remembered the single conglomerated shape.

Figure 4.32 The Löwenmensch may be as old as 40,000 years old.
Used with permission from Ulmer Museum. Photo by Yvonne Muhlheis.

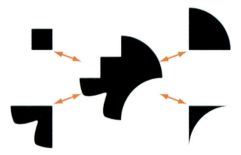

Figure 4.33 In our study (Schlegel et al., 2013b), a whole shape, such as shown in the center, was made up of four parts.

Used with permission from Schlegel, A., Kohler, P. J., Fogelson, S. V., Alexander, P., Konuthula, D., & Tse, P. U. (2013). Network structure and dynamics of the mental workspace. *Proceedings of the National Academy of Sciences of the United States of America*, *110*(40), 16277–16282.

Our goal was to see what parts of the brain were involved in mental operations, such as putting parts together, or taking wholes apart, and see what areas of the brain were involved in simply holding information in working memory. We looked at fMRI activity to determine what areas of the brain became functionally connected when maintaining information about the shapes in working memory versus when manipulating those shapes in working memory. Remember, increased functional connectivity just means that activity in two brain areas becomes more positively correlated.

In Figure 4.35, in red, you can see those areas of the brain that became more functionally connected when manipulating the shapes, either taking them apart or putting them together in one's internal mental workspace. And in blue you can see those areas of the brain that became more functionally connected when maintaining a shape or shapes in working memory, not surprisingly with the medial temporal lobes (MTL,

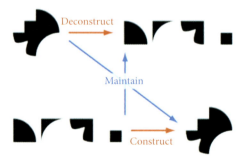

Figure 4.34 There were three working memory tasks in our study (Schlegel et al., 2013b): either the four parts could be remembered (maintained), the whole shape could be deconstructed into its parts, or the parts could be constructed into the whole shape.

Used with permission from Schlegel, A., Kohler, P. J., Fogelson, S. V., Alexander, P., Konuthula, D., & Tse, P. U. (2013). Network structure and dynamics of the mental workspace. *Proceedings of the National Academy of Sciences of the United States of America*, *110*(40), 16277–16282.

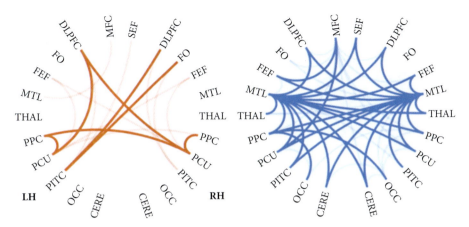

Figure 4.35 Areas of the brain that became more functionally connected when manipulating shapes in the mental workspace are shown in red, whereas areas that became more functionally connected when maintaining a shape or shapes are shown in blue.

Used with permission from Schlegel, A., Kohler, P. J., Fogelson, S. V., Alexander, P., Konuthula, D., & Tse, P. U. (2013). Network structure and dynamics of the mental workspace. *Proceedings of the National Academy of Sciences of the United States of America*, *110*(40), 16277–16282.

by the hippocampus) apparently acting as a hub linking many brain areas. But let us focus on the red connections. Basically, when subjects are carrying volitional mental operations out in the internal virtual reality of their imaginations, we can see the dlPFC and PPC (which we know to comprise the core areas of the FPCN involved in volitional top-down operations) increase in functional connectivity. But we can also see the central involvement of the precuneus (PCU), which is part of the default network core, which many researchers believe to be involved in mental simulations. We also see the involvement of the posterior temporal lobes (PITC), central to processing visual shapes, and the FO, itself central to executive control.

What does this mean? I take this to support the position that volitional mental operations involve volitional or top-down control, coming out of the FPCN, which then harnesses the internal simulation circuitry of the default network core. If free will is most fundamentally rooted in our capacity to deliberate and volitionally play out scenarios in our imagination, it is this circuitry that is at the heart of free will.

In a paper related to our 2013 paper, Beaty and colleagues (2016) sought the neural basis of creative imagination and came to a similar conclusion, namely, that creative thinking involves the volitional FPCN coupling with the main hub of the default network in the posterior cingulate/precuneus area.

Figure 4.36 shows the main figure from Beaty and colleagues' paper. On the top left you see the cortical areas that permitted significant pattern classification for a divergent versus a nondivergent thinking task. The arrow indicates PCC/PCU. On the right they use the posterior cingulate as a seed region to see which areas are functionally

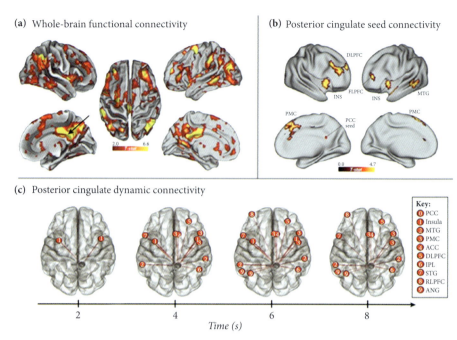

Figure 4.36 The default and executive control networks, which are commonly mistakenly thought to alternate dominance in an antagonistic relationship, actually come to cooperate during creative cognition (Beaty et al., 2018). Here the functional connectivity associated with divergent thinking is shown. "(A) Whole-brain multivariate pattern analysis contrasting alternate uses divergent thinking with object characteristic generation. Brain maps show differential functional connectivity patterns during divergent thinking. (B) The posterior cingulate cortex (PCC) shows increased connectivity with regions of the control (DLPFC) and salience (insula) networks during divergent thinking. (C) The PCC (black sphere) shows early coupling with salience network regions (bilateral insulae) and later coupling with control network regions (DLPFC). Regions labeled in black on the right show positive connectivity with the source ROI; regions labeled in gray were not significant."

Used with permission from Elsevier, from Beaty, R. E., Benedek, M., Silvia, P. J., & Schacter, D. L. (2016). Creative cognition and brain network dynamics. *Trends in Cognitive Sciences*, *20*(2), 87–95. doi: 10.1016/j.tics.2015.10.004

connected with it and they find parts of the FPCN, in particular, the rlPFC and dlPFC, and also find the AI or FO and a dorsal area near the anterior cingulate, which we know to be part of the cingulo-opercular network.

We can conclude that the neural circuitry underlying the volitional use of internal simulation that underlies human deliberation and creative thinking is now being deciphered by neuroscientists. These results offer, in essence, a forest-level view of the neural basis of free will.

Complex volitional operations, however, most likely evolved to execute actions using effectors of the body, such as the hands, long before they came to be applied within the internal virtual reality of the imagination. The incredible volitional mental operations humans can execute in their imaginations may have originated as an exaptation of the incredible dexterity of the human hand, which far surpasses that of any ape or monkey. In asking when and how human imaginative powers got off the ground, we can usefully ask when volitional dexterity of the hands evolved. The mental operations that would go into volitional manual manipulations could later be co-opted for the manipulation of internal operands in a mental workspace. It would not make much sense to evolve such mental operations with an effector unable to execute them, such as a hoof. So, it is a safe bet that mental and manual manipulations co-evolved long before being exapted for imaginary manipulations. But this could not begin until the hands were freed from locomotive burdens by bipedality.

It is now becoming clear that hand dexterity evolved long before the first evidence of stone tools (Kivell, 2015). Human levels of hand dexterity depend on thumb opposability and noncurved, shorter finger bones than found in our tree climbing ancestors. Opposition of the first and fifth digits, namely, the "opposable thumb," is unique to the genus *Homo*. According to my colleague Nate Domini at Dartmouth, who studies the evolution of the feet, hands, and bipedality, the surest signs of human-like manipulability are a saddle-shaped trapezium, which is the bone that establishes the first carpometacarpal joint, and an elongated distal phalanx of the thumb. It was the inference of human-like manipulability found in fossil specimen OH 7 based on these traits that led to its species being named *Homo habilis* ("handy man") in 1964. Human-like hand manipulability evolved at least 1.75 million years ago, and probably earlier than two million years ago with the origins of *Homo*. But some pollical (thumb) distal phalanxes might push the date back to 6 million years ago if a specimen attributed to *Orrorin tugenensis* is to be believed (Almécija et al., 2010). It is thus likely that australopiths such as *afarensis* had our high levels of dexterity.

What might australopiths have been doing with their manual dexterity? Making tools out of wood instead of stone? Chimpanzees and capuchins make perishable tools, so it seems probable that australopiths did as well. And chimpanzees touch fruits with their hands to judge their ripeness (Dominy et al., 2016), so initial enhancements in dexterity may have evolved even before bipedality. But Jolly (1970) argued that fine visuomotor control for hand-picking tiny seeds, perhaps grass seeds in the savannah, was central to the evolution of human levels of manual dexterity and the anatomy of the human hand. It may be that climate change that replaced the forests of ancient East Africa with grassland, provided the selective pressure to find a new source of food in grass grains to replace the impoverishment of food sources that come from trees. This in turn may have created a stronger selective pressure for manual dexterity.

Geladas (Figure 4.37) are the primate whose hand proportions are closest to ours, and they pick and de-husk grass seeds (Welch, 2017). Interestingly, the attentional and visuomotor demands of such dexterous feeding is privileged over either looking out for predators or carrying out social interactions visually. So geladas have evolved the largest vocal repertoire of all nonhuman primates. They are the only nonhuman

Figure 4.37 The hands of geladas are, among all extant primates, the most similar to human hands. Geladas live in the Ethiopian highlands and eat grass, which requires fine dexterity.
Source: Stefan Cruysberghs at www.scip.be

primate capable of formant variation. It is eerie to hear them "speak" to each other in a surprisingly human-like manner while they are busily picking and de-husking seeds. Thus, geladas are our best primate model for studying the origins of both hand dexterity and spoken language. This may be an example of convergent evolution of physical and cognitive traits and abilities, driven by the selective pressures of a shared niche.

To test the idea that motor operations used to control the hands and other bodily effectors may be the same operators that are used to manipulate representations in the imagination, my students and I carried out an fMRI study (Schlegel et al., 2016) in which we had people either mentally rotate a three-dimensional object using their imagination or rotate their hand as if manipulating it in the world. They had to rotate the object in one of four ways, either forward/backward or leftward/rightward. We applied a machine learning trick called multivariate pattern classification that creates a classifier that best categorizes the data into these four types of rotational responses. We then asked whether there are brain areas where a classifier created using brain data collected during motoric rotations could be used to correctly classify imagined rotation directions, and vice versa. If so, this would be evidence that a motoric operator used to manipulate the hands was used in the manipulation of imagined objects in our internal analog virtual reality. We found that we could cross-classify motoric and imaginary operations well in primary motor cortex, posterior parietal cortex, the PCU/PCC, and to a somewhat lesser degree in dlPFC and the supplementary motor area. Many of these areas are the ones we have specified as the neural correlates of volitional operations in the imagination, and indeed, the neural correlates of free will.

I take this to be direct evidence for the idea of "embodied cognition," whereby that which we think of as cognitive, such as mentally rotating objects in the internal virtual reality of our imagination, is really rooted in bodily acts that we have learned to enact by using our bodies in the real world while playing as children. An implication of this for parents is that we must allow children years of playing in the real world, using their hands to manipulate real objects, if we are to foster their capacity, later in life, to volitionally manipulate objects in their internal virtual realities. Bodily play fosters creative imagination. It could well be that limiting real-world play in children, by, for example, allowing too much screen time, has negative downstream consequences for human imagination, and therefore also for human free will.

4.28 The Relationship of Consciousness to Free Will

We intuitively understand that our volition is closely tied up with our consciousness, which is, by definition, all that we are now subjectively experiencing. Since we do not experience what lies outside of consciousness, we cannot volitionally shift our attention to it. Another way to define consciousness, then, is the set of all current operands that the operator of volitional attention is now operating on, or could operate on, in the next moment. The figure of experience is that which we are now attending, while the background of experience is that which we could turn into a figure if we shifted our attention to it.

Let us consider a bit more deeply why volition and qualia are so deeply connected. First, note that consciousness is bifurcated. We are conscious of the outside world in the form of perception. And we are also conscious of our various internal simulations or imaginings, including dreaming, daydreaming, and hallucinations. Perception might be thought of as a kind of hallucination as well, but one that is constrained to be about what is most likely really happening in the outside world and inside our body. Consciousness plays a key role in mental causation in providing a common format for endogenous attentional and other executive operations, which permit the assessment of possible behaviors and thoughts against highest-level criteria for successful attainment of goals and fulfillment of desires. Subjective experience provides an "executive summary" to planning areas that can initiate voluntary motor outputs. Qualia are those representations that can be volitionally attended, or are now being operated on by endogenous attention, giving rise to the possibility of volitional operations, such as attentional tracking, which, I argue, cannot happen in the absence of consciousness. Because volitional operations can only take place over conscious operands, whether perceived or imagined, and motor acts can follow and enact the conclusions of such volitional operations, such mental operations can play a necessary causal role in subsequent thoughts and motor acts. Because conscious operands are necessary for such volitional operations, consciousness is necessary for free will; no consciousness, no free will.

Let us consider the case of conscious visual perception. Visual perception appears to proceed in at least two stages. The first stage involves rapid and automatic operations whose outputs are briefly held in a high-capacity, parallel, short-duration buffer. Here, preprocessed outputs are made available to endogenous or volitional attention for selection for more in-depth processing. The second stage involves transfer of attentionally selected contents to one or more low-capacity visual working memory buffers. A working memory buffer permits temporally extended access to what was presented, even after it has disappeared from sight, as well as internal manipulation of those contents. Attention is not only necessary for the transfer of attentionally selected contents to working memory; attention is also required to maintain representations and to carry out further operations over them in the mental workspace. In short, the output of automatic, stimulus-driven, early modular processing comprises a "precompiled," pre-interpreted, and pre-evaluated account of events and objects in the world—as well as of the states and needs of the body. These outputs are made available to brain areas that can make cognitive inferences and plan to do something, given these facts, whether motorically or internally by, for example, volitionally shifting attention to them, or exerting effort to recall facts about them from long term memory.

On this account, conscious experience, whether perceptual or imagined, is an internal, "virtual reality" construction. In the case of perception, this construction is normally in such good correspondence with what is actually happening in the world-in-itself and in the body, that for the experiencer it is as if the world-in-itself and the body were experienced directly and without delay. However, visual illusions, dreams, and hallucinations reveal that perceptual experience is not of the world-in-itself. Rather, such experience is constructed on the basis of ambiguous, sparse, and noisy sensory inputs mediated by numerous preconscious operations that are tantamount to an inference about what is likely going on in the world, given the sensory data.

But why are there qualia at all? Couldn't volitional operations be carried out without experience? Well, if information were not in a common "qualia" format that makes explicit information about intrinsic properties of the world and our bodies in it, there would be no way to compare "apples to apples" against a common criterion assessing optimality of potential behavior. Having a highest level of assessment of multiple lower-system outputs in a common format permits the overall system to find a solution that maximizes global benefit to the animal, as opposed to locally, within the representational space of any submodule. A common format is required so that all submodules' outputs can contextualize one another, can be "time-stamped" as occurring in the same moment, presumably by the hippocampus, and can be stored in the quasi-experiential, spatiotemporal format of episodic memory. If lower-level outputs were not in a common format, there might not be a single endogenous attentional tracking operator, say, that operated on all types of input, whether visual, auditory, motoric, or emotional. Having experience be in a common qualia format allows executive, planning, attentional, and working memory processes to have all relevant information about goings-on in the world and the body at one time. In the absence of a common format, the relevance or salience of an output from one module, say, redness, might not be comparable to the output of another, say, hunger. Their relative salience, importance, or priority would not be rapidly decidable.

Consciousness evolved as a veridical hallucination that informs an animal about the goings on in the world and its body in that world so that it can act appropriately in order to fulfill its internally set goals in that world. Consciousness affords planning and action for goal fulfillment, with continual error correction, in a cybernetic experience–planning–action–experience cycle. The errors signals here can themselves be conscious, as when we feel thirst, fear, guilt, lust, hunger, and so on. Qualia evolved to encapsulate information about what is intrinsically true about objects and events in the world and regarding the states and needs of the body. What is intrinsically true about size, for example, is not available directly from the image, but has to be inferred from the image, based on contextual or global cues following size-constancy operations. An object's intrinsic properties concern its actual size, pigments, distance, motion speed and direction, material, and so forth. In addition, there are other facts that would ideally also be encapsulated, but which are inherently invisible, such as the object's value, or even intentions, if any. These local properties can generally only be correctly inferred in light of contextual cues that allow their recovery following constancy operations. Consciousness is therefore holistic in its construction, rather than a matter of detection at independent points. Or rather, consciousness is a construction based on connecting the "dots" that have been detected.

This is why we talk of sensation and perception. Sensation is about what is detected, namely, how some energy in the environment that creates a proximal stimulus at a sensory organ is transduced into neural firing. Perception is about how the dots become connected into as close a representation of the distal stimulus as possible. The preconscious and unconscious grouping or connecting operations that construct perceptual consciousness are generally so good at connecting the dots into a veridical hallucination that it is as if we experience properties of the distal object or event in itself.

If there were multiple endogenous attentional operators, it would be as if multiple minds "lived" in the same brain, as may in fact occur in split-brain patients. Executive processing and experience would be splintered. What was salient for one executive might have nothing to do with the priorities for another executive, even if they both operated over identical qualia. Executive decisions and therefore motor acts would likely conflict if there were more than one master endogenous attentional operator governing volitional acts.

Finally, if outputs of different subsystems were not in a common format, it might not be possible to bind them into a common unit for attentional tracking. This shared format allows executive processes to consider, compare, track, and select from among possible courses of action in a unified way. In the absence of a common format for planning and executive volitional operations such as endogenous attention to work on, there could be no hierarchical chain of command in volitional control of behavior.

Sometimes the hierarchy of volitional command structures breaks down, as in alien hand syndrome, where volitional hand motions seem to "have a mind of their own" and operate in a manner against the will of an executive that in a normally functioning brain would have dominion over volitional suboperators and their operations. This raises the fascinating possibility that there is a hierarchy of volitional operators, each of which operates over its specialized domain of qualia. Our volition would then not be unitary, but instead would be comprised of a family or hierarchy of micro-wills that can interact or even come into conflict, or all align in a unitary purpose, if well organized. This in turn would imply that consciousness, even in normal minds, is generally a superposition of specialized consciousnesses, each of which is the domain of some local volitional process, say, for a hand's decisions concerning what to do next.

In a normally functioning hierarchical command structure, as in a military, a corporation, a university, or a beehive, the highest-level executive issues high-level commands. In the case of Napoleon, this might be "conquer Moscow." If all subcommanders obey, Napoleon might feel like his military "body" obeyed his commands and his will. But Napoleon cannot be in charge of all the volitional local decisions that have to be made in order for this high-level command to be enacted. Napoleon lacks the information at his highest level concerning which Russian soldier to shoot. That decision has to be made by the French foot soldier himself, because only he has the required information at hand. And so on, all the way up the chain of decision making. In such an organization, it would only be required that each layer communicate with the layer above and below it. Other architectures are also possible, as when a CEO visits the factory floor and talks directly with the workers. Thus, volition may be decentralized in the sense that each layer makes decisions appropriate to that layer. Things can go awry, however, if a general starts to express volitional control that counters the intentions of Napoleon. This might feel to Napoleon like the body of his military becoming possessed by an "alien hand."

If volition is hierarchical in its enactments, and if it is true that qualia are the highly precompiled representations over which a volitional operator operates, then it follows that consciousness itself is not unitary, but is in fact a superposition of many levels or subdomains of consciousness. I believe this to be the case because attention, which I regard as the "Napoleon" of volitional operators, can be allocated at different levels in a hierarchy. I can attend to a pinkish piece of white paper viewed under reddish light and attend to the fact of its whiteness (i.e., its reflectance post-color-constancy operation) or I can attend to the fact that it looks pinkish (i.e., pre-color-constancy operation). Another way to think about this would be that there is a hierarchy of volitional attentional operators that usually act in a synchronized fashion, but which can operate independently to some extent when the highest-level commander is offline or preoccupied. For example, it sometimes happens that we find ourselves scratching and humming a tune while our mind was preoccupied with what to make for dinner. At one level we were aware of the itch or the singing in our head, but at another level the decision to scratch the itch or sing this versus that other song in our head was made without constraints imposed by the highest-level executive. Other times the executive has an intention, but when it is executed, seems to be made by some midlevel agent in the command system. For example, William James writes in his chapter on the will (chapter 26 of his *Principles of Psychology*) of lounging in his warm bed on a cold morning, cognitively wanting to get up, but in terms of body comfort, also wanting to stay in his warm bed. This might go on for an hour. But then, in a moment of inattention, he finds that he has suddenly gotten up, seemingly against his will. We might describe this as a conflict between a second- and first-order desire. When attention is drawn away from the warmth that fulfills the first-order desire to be warm, the balance turns in favor of the cognitive desire to get up.

When there are multiple things in a cluttered display that share low-level features, attentional selection is typically required to be able to gain conscious access to the identity of any particular item. Qualia comprise the representational format that can be bound into attentionally selectable and trackable objects. For example, one can listen to a symphony and choose to attentionally track the oboe. One can then listen to the same symphony again and this time choose to track the lead violin. In both cases the sensory input is the same. What differs is what features are bound into a tracked "figure" and what remains unbound as the background against which the figure moves. On this view, consciousness or experience is that domain of representations that permits volitional or endogenous attentional tracking and manipulation over sustained durations. We are given an experienced object by virtue of attentional tracking that binds local features over time into that object or figure, whether an oboe in a symphony or a bird flying against a background of trees.

It may be that lower-level outputs are placed into a common quale format so that they can all be, but need not be, attentionally tracked in the next moment, should the need arise. The link between qualia and volitional attention is very close. Again, qualia are those representations that can potentially be volitionally attentionally bound and tracked over time, and everything that can be so tracked, if need be, includes all current qualia (i.e., all that is now experienced). But this is not to say that attention is necessary to bind lowest-level features into objects, or that without attention there are no object representations at all. This is because objects can themselves be chunked as a result of past learning, and stored in memory, and even elicit priming unconsciously, in the absence of having attended to them (Cavanagh et al., 2023).

But just because qualia evolved to be the operands of volitional operations, such as volitional attentional tracking, does not mean that they cannot exist in the absence of being attentionally tracked. A normal brain is typically endogenously binding some small percentage of available qualia into tracked objects, and the rest may be comparatively unbound in a state of "qualia soup," which we experience as the background against which the tracked figure moves. Because of past chunking, it is plausible that this feature soup does not only contain unbound features, but also may contain chunked representations of features that may be as complex as an object.

If only conscious contents can be volitionally attentionally tracked, then consciousness or experience may conversely be the domain of representations that permit the possibility of endogenous attentional tracking and other forms of volitional manipulation. Consciousness, I would argue, is required for endogenous attentional allocation, shifting and tracking, volitional executive control, flexible cognitive processing and manipulation of representations in executive working memory, complex concatenations of simpler mental operations, contextually appropriate management of detected errors, and effective top-down inhibition of imminent acts. Acts that follow these types of endogenous attentional, executive operations over conscious operands, whether over external perceived operands, or internal imagined operands, are potentially causal of the motor acts that follow from the conclusion of those operations.

If volitional operations, such as attentional tracking, are only possible over conscious operands, we have free will because we are conscious. Moreover, consciousness is causal in the universe, not as a force, but because it affords mental operations that can lead us to then set about changing the world in light of our visions, plans, fears, or hopes. For example, we can imagine a flying machine and then go build what we have imagined in the world, changing the universe physically and forever. Thus, the deepest source of free will is volitional operations over conscious operands, whether invisibly choosing to attend to this or that in the world or carrying out volitional deliberations and mental manipulations in the domains of our imagination.

But why must imagination be conscious, with associated dream-like qualia? One reason is so that we can carry out volitional operations in our own private virtual reality, where virtually anything is possible. If qualia are the operands over which volitional operators can operate, imagination must be consciously experienced if our deliberations are to be subject to our willed ends. A second key reason imagination must be experienced is so that we can see how it feels when we imagine this scenario versus that alternative scenario. For example, if Tzeitel, of *Fiddler on the Roof*, imagines marrying the old rich butcher Lazar Wolf, whom her father is trying to force her to marry, versus the poor tailor Motel Kamzoil, whom she loves, in one case she might feel disgust and fear, and in the other case longing and loss. If she could not feel these evaluations, she would not act volitionally based upon them. Real or imagined perception does not only involve a construction or veridical hallucination about what is going on, but also it involves an evaluation of what is possible or of what has happened or could have happened. Our counterfactual longings and desires must be conscious so that we can experience possible futures as if they were real. We can then try to realize the future that is most desirable, or, at least, least undesirable. If the imagination were not consciously experienced, how would we know how we feel about various possibilities?

In addition, deliberation, as opposed to the free wandering of daydreaming, often involves staying on track. It involves a sometimes effortful keeping-track of a train of thought, analogous to volitionally attentionally tracking an object through space, while warding off potential distractors or distractions. Indeed, thought tracking may involve some of the same neural circuitry known to subserve perceptual attentional tracking. And if attentional tracking can only take place within the conscious format of experience, then deliberation itself must involve consciously experienced constructions as well, if they are to be kept track of and constrained to trajectories dictated by our willed goals or intentions.

Those who argue that consciousness is solely the passive recipient of conclusions and decisions reached unconsciously sometimes rely on evidence from their subjective experience while observing their own mind. For example, those who follow various Buddhist or Hindu forms of meditation, are trained to pay attention to the contents of consciousness as they arise, then, without judgment, allow what has arisen to dissipate, without being reactive to those contents. With practice, one can avoid getting swept away, say, by becoming angry or sad, as a result of thoughts, memories, and feelings that have arisen. No doubt, contents often do arise into consciousness, seemingly out of nowhere. But there is also something else present in consciousness in addition to this succession of arisings from the unconscious. And that is volitional attending itself, whether of the focused sort described as "samatha" (tranquility) in Buddhism, or the diffuse sort associated with heightened vigilance, described as "vipassana" (clear insight). In either case, attention is volitionally, effortfully applied to the contents of consciousness, like a muscle opening a jar. With years of practice, this initially effortful attentional allocation can be automatized to the point that it happens effortlessly. The irony of the claim that consciousness only passively receives contents that have arisen nonvolitionally from the unconscious is that that very insight tends to arise only in the context of non-passively exerting volitional attention to the breath or some other object or process, generally after spending years automatizing its allocation. This attentional allocation does not arise by chance from some unknown unconscious source. It arises within consciousness as a consequence of long-term commitments to a goal that takes years to realize, namely, that by volitionally attending to the contents of consciousness without being reactive, consciousness itself will be transformed. It is ironic that the automatization of a volitional process, namely, attending to the breath and the contents that arise into consciousness, is taken as evidence that there is no true volitional control over the contents of consciousness or downstream actions. Yes, after years of training, that volitional process can become nonvolitional. But to take that hard-earned nonvolitionality as evidence that there is only nonvolitional processing underlying the contents of consciousness is about as bizarre and incorrect as saying that the hard-earned effortlessness of riding a bike is evidence that all abilities are effortless.

Free will deniers who use the "passive arising" argument against the possibility of any volitional efficacy for consciousness or the reality of any non-illusory form of volition itself, are like viewers of a movie who say "See, the movie just arises, and I am nothing but a passive watcher, with no ability to create or control the contents of the movie; thus there is no volitional control, or free will." This is dishonest because a great deal of volition actually goes into creating the conditions whereby this film is played versus any other. Using this same metaphor, the reel or DVD has to be installed, a projector has to be set up, the plug has to be plugged in, the screen has to be set out properly, and the play button has to be hit. Only then does the appearance of passive viewing arise. In practice, what this means, returning to the brain, is that volitional attention must be applied in this way versus that way in order for this pattern of upwellings from the unconscious to arise versus those other possible upwellings. Because we can in fact volitionally shift attention based our own private reasons, we can effectively change the movie of what will be processed in a bottom-up manner, simply by shifting our attention to one among many possibilities of interest, or we can simply move our eyes to this location versus those other possible locations.

If consciousness just is the domain of operands over which volitional operations can take place, then we can see that far from the flow of consciousness being evidence for the absence of non-illusory volition, the flow of consciousness (meaning these operands versus those others) is evidence for the causal efficacy of volition. It is true that with practice, attention to the breath can put the mind and body into such a parasympathetic state that it seems as if all operands and all volitional operations have ceased. But just because there exist highly cultivated and unusual states of consciousness that are vacated of volition and any feelings of agency, self, or authorship does not entail in any way that all states of consciousness arise nonvolitionally or that agency is an illusion. Just because there are some illusions of will does not mean that all will is an illusion. To say so would be as misguided as asserting that all vision is illusory because there are some visual illusions.

4.29 The Neural Basis of Self-Transformation

We have the capacity to change our nervous system and can thereby choose to become a new kind of chooser in the future. There are many ways that our nervous system changes in response to what we do and what we think. We have already considered some, including meditation and other practices we might choose to build into our lives. There are many other feedback mechanisms whereby usage of a neural circuit changes its physical structure, and thereby its function. This section reviews some of the most basic and how they might operate at the level of neural circuits.

One of the most common ways that we can transform our brains and minds, simply by willing it to be so, is that we can choose to learn something. Such learning is tied up with the slogan from Donald Hebb that neurons that "fire together, wire together." The idea is that when the firing of a presynaptic neuron immediately precedes the firing of a post-synaptic neuron, the synapse linking these two neurons will strengthen. It can strengthen in various ways. It can express more receptors, such as AMPA or NMDA receptors; it can involve greater neurotransmitter release; in many cases new dendritic spines can grow. Long-term potentiation (LTP) is NMDA receptor-dependent because the calcium that enters a neuron after NMDA receptors have opened triggers a whole cascade of events inside the cell, including protein synthesis, that then goes into strengthening synapses in a process that takes hours, not milliseconds. LTP is especially strong following the high frequency arrival of spikes, as occurs during bursting, that is most likely to trigger NMDA receptor opening. In contrast, when a presynaptic spike is not predictive of the timing of spiking of a post-synaptic neuron, the synapses linking these neurons tend to weaken in a process known as long-term depression.

If it is correct that attention enhances burst transmission along epicircuits, then LTP may not just strengthen local synaptic connectivities between neuron pairs, but also it may strengthen whole epicircuits, just as many people walking over the grass can wear down new paths in it. For example, the "bucket brigade" (Section 4.19) of information processing set up by attending may become more efficient as short-term and temporary synaptic weight changes, such as the opening of NMDA receptors, get hardwired into long-term synaptic weight changes realized in structural reconformation of synapses. In this way, volitionally paying attention can alter neural wiring at the level of neurons and neural circuits. If we choose to learn something, we will, by practicing, make certain neurons fire together and thereby wire together.

A baby comes to the world with about 100 billion neurons, which is about 15% more than an adult human has (Sakai, 2020). It is as if a baby comes to the world prepared to learn many different possible worlds. The process of neural cell death (apoptosis) combined with synaptic pruning removes those possible neural circuits that are not used or adaptive for the world that the baby finds itself in. Like pruning a fruit tree, removing the weak branches allows the remaining branches to grow more robustly. The neurons and neural connectivity that remain are fine-tuned to the world in which the baby finds itself. It is the world and body that the baby learns to master. This is reminiscent of Michelangelo's comment that he sculpted the David by removing the irrelevant bits of marble from the block.

Synaptic density peaks during the preschool and kindergarten years, as shown in Figure 4.38, then declines through adolescence, gradually leveling off into adulthood (Huttenlocher, 1979). The key years when social scaffolding can most effectively intervene in the sculpting of the brain and mind thus occur prior to the start of grade school. A small child is not yet in a position to volitionally choose to sculpt his or her own neural circuits, but adults are in a position to choose to scaffold or cultivate small children's brains toward desired types of minds. For example, in the Netherlands most adults are fluent in at least four languages, because adults have decided that foreign language education should begin in preschool, in order to take

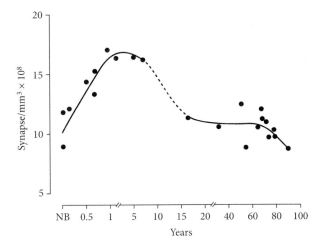

Figure 4.38 Synapse counts in layer 3 of human middle frontal gyrus as a function of age (Huttenlocher, 1979).

Used with permission from Huttenlocher, P. R. (1979). Synaptic density in human frontal cortex: Developmental changes and effects of aging. *Brain Research, 163*, 195–205.

advantage of the phenomenal language-learning capacities of small children. In contrast, most Americans are monolingual, because foreign language education in the U.S. tends to begin in 7th grade, after the closing of the critical period for learning a language as a native speaker.

Another way that volitional practice can get hardwired into the nervous system is via enhanced myelination. Recall that myelin functions a bit like the insulation around a cable, enhancing the ability of axons to transmit information without signal loss. In the central nervous system there is a kind of glial cell called an oligodendrocyte that wraps its "arms" around surrounding axons, as shown in Figure 4.39, forming the myelin around axons. There is a feedback process such that the more action potentials pass down a neighboring axon, the more oligodendrocytes will tend to wrap around it. This is a bit like muscles getting bigger the more you use them.

In one study, my group (Schlegel et al., 2012) compared Dartmouth students who learned Chinese in an intensive language course with a control group of students who

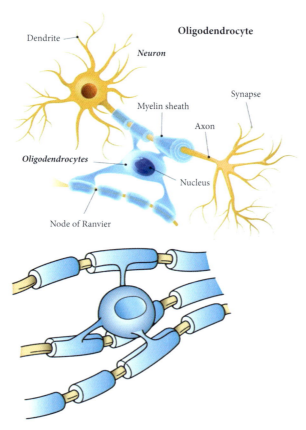

Figure 4.39 An oligodendrocyte is a type of glial cell which, in the central nervous system, creates the myelin sheath by wrapping its "arms" around neighboring axons.
Source: Designua/Shutterstock.

The Neuroscience of Free Will

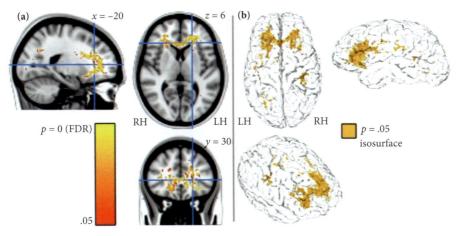

Figure 4.40 Results of whole-brain longitudinal GLM analysis of fractional anisotropy (FA) in language learning. (A) A bi-hemispheric cluster shows increases in FA in the language learning group over controls. (B) A $P = 0.05$ isosurface model from the same analysis projected onto one subject's glass brain. Additional clusters of significance can be seen along the left language pathway and in the right temporal lobe.
Used with permission from MIT Press.

did not learn a foreign language. Using a technique called "diffusion tensor imaging" we were able to localize axons that had become more organized, probably because of increased myelination. The parts of the brain that are colored yellow and red in Figure 4.40 indicate axonal tracts that became more organized in the test group, meaning that fractional anisotropy had increased, presumably because they learned the foreign language. If we choose to learn something, say Chinese, we will, by practicing, make axonal paths involved in that processing become more efficient by virtue of stronger myelination.

Experience, moreover, itself alters cortical organization throughout life. Plasticity in rat cortex is increased when rats spend even a few days in an enriched environment. For example, Diamond (1988) showed that cortical thickness differs in rats raised in an "impoverished," "standard," or "enriched" cage environment during their second month of life. The enriched group had a cage with extensive opportunities for social interaction and exploration of new objects, the standard group had fewer such opportunities, and the impoverished group had none. The enriched group had significant cortical thickening relative to the standard group, while the impoverished group exhibited relative cortical thinning.

There appear to be multiple factors that lead to increased cortical thickness. Neurons in rats with "enriched" experience show increases in number, cell body size, nuclear size, dendritic arborization and length, and the number of dendritic spines, synapses, and NMDA receptors. Increased neural growth factor release likely plays a role in this, as "enriched" brains exhibit increased level of nerve growth factor mRNA.

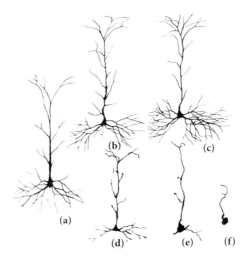

Figure 4.41 From Diamond (2001): "Two possible patterns of age-related alterations in cortical pyramidal cells. The normal mature neuron (A) may show regressive dendritic changes characterized by loss of basilar dendritic branches and eventual loss of the entire dendritic tree (D, E, F). Other neurons (B, C) may show progressive increase in dendritic branching. Drawing based on Golgi impregnations."

Such plasticity may be related to voluntary attention in particular, in that acetylcholine may be released from cholinergic basal forebrain nucleus neurons onto targeted cortical circuitry corresponding to the attended locus of information processing. This is thought to be a mechanism that realizes increased alertness, enhanced neuronal processing of relevant inputs, and enhanced learning through increased neural plasticity.

Figure 4.41, from Diamond (2001), shows what can happen to a mature pyramidal cell depending on environment and experience. The path from A to C shows increased arborization with environmental enrichment, whereas the path from A to F shows increased atrophy with environmental impoverishment. It seems that experience, behavior, social interaction, stress, and other factors, such as exercise, environmental quality, and nutrition influence brain chemistry and organization at a synaptic and dendritic level. Diamond (1988) summarized her findings in terms of five key environmental factors that lead to flourishing cortical microstructure: diet, exercise, challenge, novelty, and love.

Exercise appears to enhance release of the growth hormones that afford adult neurogenesis (Blackmore et al., 2012). This builds on earlier findings that exercise enhances expression of neural growth factors in the hippocampus (Olsson et al., 1994). It is now clear that voluntary exercise enhances brain-derived neural growth factor (BDNF), and that BDNF in turn likely fosters enhanced learning and cognitive function (Denham et al., 2014; Hopkins and Bucci, 2010; Phillips et al., 2014; Szuhany et al., 2015). One of the most straightforward ways to choose to transform your mind and brain, then, is to begin a program of physical exercise.

Concerning the centrality of love for brain health, Diamond noticed that many of her isolated rats were dying at around the 600 day mark, which would correspond to death at 60 years for a human being, even though their cages were well equipped with all the physical necessities for rat well-being. Rats who were touched, however, lived much longer. Holding her rats close and petting them not only increased their lifespans, but also increased their cortical thickness. No doubt love and touch are no less important for us human beings, and for the health of our neural circuitry.

We can choose to harness such feedback processes by taking charge of the environment in which our brains will operate in the future. We can populate our world with friends who will enrich our minds and social interactions and minimize contact with those who impoverish our life and social interactions. We can enhance our chances for exploration, love, and novelty, and minimize boredom, meanness, and drudgery. Changing our environment to foster future enrichment can enrich our neurons, so to speak, because of neural growth factors that are released when we have positive social interactions, when we pay attention, and when we exercise and explore. If you want to change your brain, then change your environment to enrich it. You are not a plant rooted to one spot. You are an animal who can move to where the nutrients are that you require.

Perhaps the most surprising mechanism allowing your brain to reconstruct itself is adult neurogenesis. Until the 1990s most neuroscientists believed that humans are born with a fixed number of neurons and then lose them throughout life. Neurogenesis, whereby undifferentiated stem cells differentiate into different kinds of neurons or glial cells, was thought to only happen in the embryo. But then stem cells were found in the adult mouse brain (Richards et al., 1992). Researchers then found that there were more neurons in the hippocampus of mice living in enriched versus nonenriched environments (Kempermann et al., 1997). To date, stem cells that are capable of generating new neurons have been found in three brain areas: the dentate gyrus of the hippocampus, an area central to learning; the subventricular zone on the lateral walls of the lateral ventricles, from whence newly born neurons are known to migrate through the brain to wherever they are needed, presumably again for learning to take place; and the amygdala. It now seems that hundreds of new neurons are born in the human hippocampus each day (Spalding et al., 2013).

Plasticity realized in such mechanisms could play a more prominent role in adult learning as modifications are made to existing processing structures. Thus, at a minimum, the brain is analogous to our muscles; if we work out particular "mental muscles" the neural substrate of those processes will get "stronger." But the brain is more flexible than this. With practice, we can learn whole new classes of things, whether a new instrument, a new language, or hang-gliding. We don't just strengthen existing "muscles,"—we can effectively grow new "mental muscles" with effort and practice. For example, if we learn a new domain of expertise, whether the sitar or Japanese, we have increased the domains of our free choice. We could say that by cultivating new representational spaces and deepening existing ones we increase the magnitude of our free will.

4.30 Chunking

Another way that learning alters our brains and minds is via chunking and automatization. Experience plays a central role in chunking of simpler representations and operations, which can in turn facilitate future volitional processes by allowing them to operate on these more complex operands. One possibility is that attention plays a role in converting criteria expressed at the level of working memory to a format expressed at the level of criterial decoders realized in dedicated neurons or groups of neurons. For example, it may take some attentional effort to convert a novel sight-read piano chord to a hand position, but with practice this becomes chunked and automatized, such that one "hard-wires" both the recognition of this novel pattern of notes and the motoric commands that realize a hand position without the need for attention.

Consciousness, therefore, may not only exist so that relatively high-level representations, in the form of qualia, can be endogenously attended and otherwise operated upon. It may exist so that attention can chunk, automatize, and hard-wire recognition of feature patterns and execute action patterns, automatizing these in order to make processing faster and potentially unconscious. Like a good teacher, attention might have the "goal" of making itself superfluous. That is, consciousness may exist for multiple reasons. Without it, chunking of volitionally glued-together chunks could not happen because without consciousness no volitional operations could take place. Consciousness is the domain over which volitional operations take place, such as volitional attentional tracking and volitional holding-together of a grouping to be learned. Moreover, imaginative deliberation takes place consciously so that we can feel what it is like to live in one versus other possible realities entertained inside of our own internal virtual reality generation system. If this were not conscious, we would not know what it feels like, so could not use that information as a basis for making a decision. If I ask you "Which tastes better to you, x or y?" and you are not conscious of the taste, because, say, x and y are chemicals that your system can only process unconsciously or, even, not at all, you would say "I can't taste either of them, so the question makes no sense."

If endogenous attention is thought of as the binding of representations in working memory, or, as Anne Treisman put it a "feature glue," it is a "glue that can harden," making future binding unnecessary. Attention might then be thought to operate in order to make itself unnecessary. To the extent that consciousness is the domain of present actual and potential future endogenous attentional bindings, one might say that one reason that we have consciousness is to make as much processing unconscious as possible. Endogenous attentional manipulation, while flexible, because any representation can be volitionally "glued" with any other, is slow and inefficient. "Pre-glued" or precompiled representations and motor sequences, while inflexible, are processed efficiently and rapidly. The unconscious is chockablock with glue-hardened patterns that were once volitionally held together by attention but that have since become automatized (Cavanagh et al., 2023). As such, the unconscious is like a vast museum collection of fossils of past volitional acts of attending. The structure of experience or consciousness will therefore change as we create more and more neo-primitive features. That is, as we master domains, we will process the world in terms of chunks and meta-chunks, whether perceptually, cognitively, or motorically. As we pre-compile chunks, they can pop out in visual or other search tasks. That which counts as a quale, then, would be that which pops out among distractors that may share low-level features, but that do not share the chunk or configuration of those features. This conscious/unconscious architecture allows attention to focus on the new and novel (Cavanagh et al., 2023).

Work in my lab has revealed that subjects can learn to efficiently locate a target defined by a particular combination of two or more features among distractors made up of a different arrangement of the same features. Initially, search times take longer the more distractors there are. But with practice, search times for such feature chunks become nearly independent of the number of distractors. This means that a complex conjunction of features that one attends repeatedly comes to "pop out" within about a week of training. This pop out can generalize to new orientations and retinotopic locations in a visual search paradigm (Reavis et al., 2018), and even to new body parts that were not themselves trained in a tactile search paradigm (Frank et al., 2022). If consciousness is the set of all current qualia, and a quale is that which pops out, we can transform our consciousness by attending. With practice, because the chunking process is one of automatization, we effectively come to master our world, both outwardly, so that, say, a stop sign becomes a perceptual unit, and inwardly, because that which we repeatedly attend comes to pop out.

This type of feature conjunction learning leads to bottom-up changes in stimulus processing. We found that as search efficiency improved, the amount of activity in the retinotopic location of the target increased relative to the amount of activity in distractor locations throughout various regions of visual cortex (Frank et al., 2014). In other words, maps of retinotopic space throughout the visual cortex contained an activity peak for target locations after learning. The effect was specific to the learned stimuli and did not result from a general improvement in visual-search performance; when trained participants were tested under the same conditions with a totally different conjunction stimulus, the neural signature disappeared (Reavis et al., 2016). We also found similar target versus distractor enhancement effects for different types of conjunction stimuli (e.g., motion-defined conjunction stimuli; see Frank et al., 2016), and that such effects can persist for years after training (Frank et al., 2018). This suggests that conjunction learning results in altered bottom-up perceptual processing of the learned conjunction stimuli, and that feature conjunction learning may be akin to certain types of single-feature perceptual learning that lead to changes in neural tuning in the visual system (Furmanski et al., 2004; Schoups et al., 2001; Schwartz et al., 2002; Shibata et al., 2012; Yotsumoto et al., 2008). Surprisingly, this signature of learned target pop out in retinotopic cortex was still evident when participants performed an attention-demanding fixation task and the irrelevant learned stimuli were presented in the periphery (Reavis et al., 2016). If attention functions as a glue that can hold together arbitrary feature combinations that we volitionally choose to bind, and if this glue can "harden," then past volitional bindings become automatized to the point that they pop out without the need for further volitional attention. Indeed, they might be processed automatically despite present acts of volition or volitionally attending. The challenge of ecological vision is made much more tractable by learning "chunks" of frequently encountered, meaningful conjunctions of features into Gestalts that can be perceived efficiently with minimal attention.

Interestingly, how well people learned such feature chunks could be predicted by how activated their caudate nucleus was on an unrelated task (Reavis et al., 2015). Specifically, individuals who showed a larger difference in activity between positive and negative feedback on an unrelated cognitive task, indicative of a more reactive dopaminergic reward system, learned visual feature conjunctions more quickly than those who showed a smaller activity difference. This finding supports the hypothesis that the reward system is involved in conjunction learning or chunking. In particular, two people might be the same in all ways except in how rewarding they tend to find learning. Perhaps not surprisingly, those who find learning rewarding will tend to be better at learning.

In one task (Frank et al., 2018) we had people learn combinations of motion paths. Learning to find a motion conjunction target to the level of pop out was associated with increased activity for the target relative to the surrounding distractors in target-present trials in early retinotopic visual cortex (V1–V3) as well as in human MT+, a central cortical motion-processing area. During retest three years later, however, we found that activity in MT+ during task performance had reverted back to pre-training baseline levels, while remaining elevated for targets relative to distractors in retinotopic cortex. This suggests that MT+ played a role in "wiring up" feature conjunction sensitivity in early visual processing areas, but that this top-down rewiring of bottom-up processing was no longer needed, once the processing of complex feature combination chunks had been automatized. Higher-level top-down processing can be thought to play the role of a good teacher. Once the bottom-up processing areas have learned to process inputs automatically, the teacher can move on to other tasks. We are both our own student and teacher and can choose to automatize our minds as we will.

4.31 Habit Formation and the Basal Ganglia

Perhaps the most potent form of chunking that we can volitionally harness is habit formation. Basically, there are two modes of responding to inputs. One is slow, volitional, and flexible, involving the conscious weighing of options; the other is fast, automatized, inflexible, and largely unconscious. The former, namely, the conscious volitional system, is realized in the cortical executive circuitry that we have considered so far, especially the FPCN. The latter is associated with habit formation, and is especially involved in chunking action patterns, whether motoric, emotional, or cognitive, in sequences that are implemented as automatized units without the need for conscious deliberation.

The habit formation system is deeply connected with the emotion and reward circuitry associated with the limbic system. The basal ganglia are essential to learning action sequences in pursuit of fulfilling goals, and those goals are most centrally realized in limbic and brainstem circuitry. The emotions and desires are teleological in that they serve to draw us toward or away from various goals. When thirsty we seek out water; when afraid we may seek out shelter or an escape route. Learning efficient action sequences or chunks in light of physically or emotionally rewarding or punishing outcomes helps animals attain their goals more efficiently in the future. It increases their chances of optimizing future rewards and minimizing future physical or emotional pain. The automatization of such motoric, emotional, and cognitive sequences is the formation of a habit of action, feeling or thought (Graybiel and Smith, 2014; Smith and Graybiel, 2016).

Reinforcement learning is a cybernetic process involving feedback. In classical conditioning, associations between experience and reward develop as a function of the order and timing of pairings (e.g., the Rescorla–Wagner (1972) model of classical conditioning, or the temporal-differences algorithm of reinforcement learning from Sutton and Barto (1981)). The animal learns a stimulus–behavior–reward mapping based on feedback from the environment. And operant conditioning, where behavior is shaped over time by successive rewards, is also rooted in dynamic feedback to an animal upon the execution of some behavior, such that errors are minimized in the service of optimizing behavior that maximizes reward.

Central to the chunking processes underlying automatization and habit formation are the basal ganglia, shown in Figure 4.42, and especially the dorsal portion, also known as the "dorsal striatum," which includes the caudate nucleus and the putamen. The dorsal striatum organizes volitional motor control, including action sequencing or concatenation, as well as selection of motor programs among multiple possible action programs.

The caudate nucleus is a key structure in learning and habit formation. Learning is fostered or guided by reward signals realized in dopaminergic inputs from the midbrain, in particular, from that subnucleus called the substantia nigra pars compacta. Used retrospectively, the basal ganglia compare predicted reward in light of expectations with the actual reward received. This difference or "prediction error" modulates the firing rates of dopaminergic neurons, which then update the predicted reward for the next cycle, by changing cortico–striatal synaptic weights (Montague et al., 1996; Schultz et al., 1997). In particular, dopaminergic neurons in the substantia nigra pars compacta change their firing rate and burstiness upward with prediction errors that are a surprise to the upside and decrease with surprises to the downside. If a reward matches the reward that was expected, little change in firing rate occurs. As prediction errors are cybernetically minimized, an optimized pattern of behavior is learned, and over time, automatized.

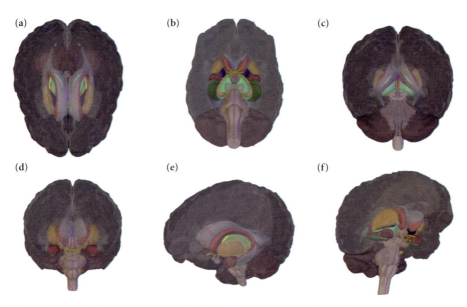

Figure 4.42 The basal ganglia are depicted from various angles: A: From above the brain (eyes on bottom). B: From below the brain (eyes at top). C: From behind the brain. D: From in front of the brain. E: From the left of the brain and slightly above. F: From the right and slightly below. Depicted: putamen is transparent gold; globus pallidus is dark purple, but viewed through the transparent putamen, looks dark gold; caudate is red. Also depicted: thalamus is light green; hippocampus is dark green; fornix is magenta; ventricles are transparent light blue; cerebellum and brainstem are lilac; amygdala is dark red. The cortex projects to the caudate and putamen (dorsal striatum), and nucleus accumbens (part of the ventral striatum) of the basal ganglia. Basal ganglia outputs project from the globus pallidus to the thalamus. The thalamus then projects back to cortex, forming a cortico-striatal-thalamocortical loop, which may comprise a central cybernetic loop through which emotional and visceral goals are reached in light of extrinsic (perceptual, motoric) and intrinsic (reward, punishment) feedback signals.
Source: Sejnowski, T. J., Poizner, H., Lynch, G., Gepshtein, S., & Greenspan, R. J. (2014). Prospective optimization. *Proceedings of the IEEE*, *102*(5). doi: 10.1109/JPROC.2014.2314297. Courtesy of Paul Wissmann.

Because predictions and expectations for reward can arise within a model of what is likely to happen, presumably represented in cortex, the basal ganglia and cortico–striatal–thalamocortical loops play a central role in updating an animal's ongoing world model. The world model is cybernetically tuned to match reality's structure and payoffs over time. The nigral–striatal–dopaminergic loop is particularly important for that aspect of an animal's world model concerned with representing reward probabilities. Because an animal's decisions should optimize the probability of reward, this dopaminergic system is central to the optimization of decision making about what to do next (Morris et al., 2006). Because the cortex and basal ganglia represent multiple sensory systems and types of planning, there are likely to be multiple corresponding working memory subsystems, each processing their own world "submodels."

How might the basal ganglia carry out a process of automatization or habit formation? To answer this we need to consider the three main types of cortico–striatal–thalamocortical loops present in mammals (Nakahara et al., 2001; Schilman et al., 2008):

1. Dorsolateral loops are involved in volitional sensorimotoric processing in light of a world model or multiple world submodels, that correspond to the various sensory systems and bodily effectors. These loops connect cognitive working memory and association cortical areas, such as the dlPFC, to the caudate of the striatum. This system links actions to reward and outcomes via a model of the world. Habit formation appears to involve a transfer of learning from this volitional, flexible associational loop to the sensorimotoric loop discussed in (2).
2. Putamen-centered loops automatize associations made under type (1) loops into habits. Sensorimotoric cortical representations loop through the putamen of the striatum and are central to habit formation. This loop links sensory information to motoric responses, and vice versa, based upon their reward value, in what is called "model-free learning." This is effectively a look-up table (Yin and Knowlton, 2006) of the type: "response x, using effector y, is linked to sensation z with predicted reward value r." Such a look-up table is fast, but inflexible, and cannot be modulated by information in a world model concerning facts that are not evident in the immediate sensorimotoric input. Such a look-up table is tantamount to a habit.
3. Ventromedial loops interact with the limbic system and are involved in motivation and emotions. These loops connect the ventral striatum, especially the ventral pallidum, via the mediodorsal nucleus of the thalamus, to orbito- and ventromedial cortex. These cortical areas are essential for processing delayed or distant rewards and damage to these cortical areas leads to a preference for immediate rewards and difficulties in delaying gratification for larger rewards in the future (Rogers et al., 1999). Note that reward is processed by neurons in this circuit in a manner that corresponds to subjective reward magnitude, rather than to the objective magnitude of the reward (Kable and Glimcher, 2007, 2010), suggesting that the neural basis of conscious feelings of reward might in part be realized in this circuitry's processing.

Sejnowski has argued that this same basal ganglia circuitry can also be used in decision-making about future actions based upon deliberation or imagination. Used prospectively, such dopamine signaling affords optimized decision making in that each of many possible future actions can be considered in turn; then the one that results in the highest dopamine release can be selected (Sejnowski, 2010; Sejnowski et al., 2014). That is, internally generated "virtual" perception and action can also teach us through reward. If an animal has an internal virtual reality or imagination within which it can play out possible actions, it can, as Karl Popper so eloquently put it, let its hypotheses die in its stead. It is likely that ventromedial loops play a central role in deliberation, imagination, decision making based on internal evaluation, and free will.

Setting aside the role of our imaginings in volitional decision making, however, we have two basic systems underlying our behavior. One is conscious, model-based, and flexible, but slow, and the other automatized, model-free, and inflexible, but fast. One role of the basal ganglia is to transform sequences volitionally "glued together" in the former system (1), into automaticities of the latter system (2), where the glue has effectively "hardened." One variety of free will then concerns what we choose to automatize in this transition from type (1) to type (2) decision making and behavior. A central danger of this process is the learning of mistakes or maladaptive patterns of action, feeling, or thought.

4.32 Second-Order Free Will and Virtue Ethics

We can volitionally harness our brain's propensity to form habits, or automatized action chunks, by consciously fostering the wiring up of what will later become unconscious good habits. We can make sure to reward ourselves for behaviors that we want to make habitual. For example, let us say we want to make exercise a habit. Rather than thinking about it endlessly, and getting frustrated with ourselves for never starting, we can instead set things up in our lives so that we will go to the gym. We can buy a gym pass and set up a regular schedule with a committed gym partner who won't let us slack off. We can start small, say with 15 minutes a day, rather than starting off with a marathon. We can build it into our schedule, consciously at first, until it becomes an automated, good habit. Exercising will naturally yield feelings of reward, and we may experience other forms of reward as well, such as compliments on our improving physique. Experiencing such rewards will get us hooked or addicted in the good way that we intended. Although we cannot cognitively will ourselves to have a good physique in a flash, or will ourselves to get hooked on exercise simply by thinking the thought, we can govern automatizing systems toward future behaviors and future desires that will realize our present cognitive goals. This is an example of externalized parameter causation. We cannot cognitively cause such habit or addiction formation, just as we cannot will ourselves to fall into or out of love. However, we can will to affect the parameters of our life such that such processes will naturally unfold. But this takes some wisdom. It takes understanding how our minds and bodies work, and how they can be harnessed. It also takes awareness of potential pitfalls, as when we automatize exercising with bad technique, or come to associate exercise with something maladaptive.

The same is true for making meditation a habit. Once the feelings of well-being kick in, we will miss meditation when we do not do it. But now, before we have started meditating, we only cognitively know that there will likely be such feelings and reward signals. So, the initial step toward harnessing the truly ancient basal ganglia (whose basic circuitry is even found in the primitive jawless fish, the lamprey; Stephenson-Jones et al., 2012) as our ally in our attempts to better the quality of our minds is to understand how our learning system works. Knowing the power of reward in shaping our behavior, and knowing that habit formation is a natural consequence of repetition and reward, we can effectively shape ourselves toward certain automaticities of mind that we initially only cognitively will to set in motion. At first this might take conscious effort, but eventually can become so automatized as to become part and parcel of our very character.

I think of the habit formation and automatization system as a great bull that can be taught and harnessed to higher ends, such as ploughing the fields of life. The bull does not understand at a cognitive level what the goal is, but it has great emotional, visceral power and can be harnessed toward good aims if guided with wisdom by the yeoman of good individual discipline and planning, or by the wisdom of a good coach or parental figure. Or the bull can go wild and wreak havoc on a person's life through self-damaging addictions or emotions that serve no higher aims.

It is instructive that the word "yoga" is etymologically related to our English word "yoke," as in the yoking of a bull. Yoga, like yoking, involves harnessing, connecting, and control. Such practices can lead to living life in a flow state, in that actions, attention, thoughts, and emotions unfold without chaos or conflict, as right acting, thinking, and feeling has become habitual. Patanjali, a founder of yoga, defined yoga (= yoking, joining, union) as the inhibition (nirodha = inhibition, quieting) of the modifications (vrtti = fluctuations) of mind (citta = consciousness). I would argue that this depends in part on the automatization of good habits of mind, and the avoidance of habit formation that undermines well-being, such as harmful addictions. This Eastern view of cultivation of the body and mind coincides well with the Western virtue ethics of Aristotle in the *Nicomachean Ethics*.

Cultures that provide strong scaffolding for a developing child's mind know this at least implicitly. They attempt to make that which is good for the child a habit or automaticity in the child, so that later, when the scaffolding is removed, the adult will have solid character. Take, for example, brushing teeth. Children do not come to the world with an innate desire to brush their teeth. Parents will start out by brushing their child's teeth for them, then later have the child do it for themselves. If there is resistance, parents make them simply do it. With my kids we would create the illusion of choice with trick questions like "Do you want to brush your teeth now or in ten minutes?" Eventually reminders are no longer necessary. You find that you have a kindergartener who wants to brush their teeth. The same is true of automatizing the saying of "thank you" and "please." The parent corrects the child possibly thousands of times, until the child comes to express politeness and respect as a matter of course. Since so much habit formation takes place before the school years start, how can society provide better scaffolding for growing minds as early as possible?

What is genetically given is not a particular outcome, but a potential for a vast range of possible outcomes. A human is born with a potential to develop language, unlike a tiger or chimpanzee. But raised by wolves, a child would not realize the innate potential to master a language. An acorn has the potential to become an oak tree, and a sunflower seed a sunflower. But planted in a desert or under a rock, both would be stunted or die. However, given ideal conditions, one becomes this, the other that. Unlike a plant that passively waits for the rain, we can water ourselves. We are ourselves part of the environment that interacts with our genetic potential and can set about making decisions that will recreate our bodies, brain, minds, and lives over time, with some luck and hard work, into that which we envision. We can view our own nervous system's capacity to learn and form habits as a powerful ally in our efforts to sculpt our minds, just as we exploit a feedback mechanism (muscle use leads to muscle growth) when we go to the gym to refashion our bodies. What starts out as a mere vision of our future self can become a newly actualized present self with consistent effort and the assistance of the right kind of scaffolding in our lives. With imagination, we can choose now to begin the process of becoming a new kind of chooser in the future.

There has been a great deal of work on the automatization of motor sequences and on perceptual learning that effectively automatizes the detection of perceptual features and conjunctions of features, such as a word. There has been much less work on the automatization of cognitive decision-making operations, although it is clear that practice can lead to reduced attentional load in a cognitive task that is, at least initially, very attentionally demanding. The automatization of decision making may draw more upon medial prefrontal areas involved in the cingulo-opercular circuit, and less upon lateral prefrontal areas, involved in the DAN. That is, the automatization of task maintenance may place less load on the cingulo-opercular circuits known to be very active in tasks that involve active task maintenance and error detection.

Initially, executive control and self-control in some new domain is likely to prove attentionally demanding, but as these processes become automatized, they likely become less so. As they become automatized to a point that they require virtually no voluntary attention, they may begin to seem effortless to a person, at which point we might consider such decision making and self-control now a veritable part of that person's character. This may offer a neuroscientific understanding of the cultivation of Aristotelian good habits, particularly those associated with executive and self-control.

Of particular interest are the implications for free will and ethics of automatized mid-level decision-making agents. For example, if a soldier who would never voluntarily choose to kill his comrades at the level of fully voluntary executive decisions has voluntarily practiced war games that have led to the wiring up of automatic decision-making agents that then decide to fire on enemy-like targets, in what sense is he responsible for, say, a "friendly fire" incident that resulted in his accidentally killing his comrades? He was on autopilot, so is he to blame? Well, yes, in part, because he trained up this "trigger-happy" automaticity instead of one that would cause him to wait a moment before shooting at people. And he was in an inattentive "zombie" mode that allowed that automaticity to act out, unchecked by deliberation among options. Responsibility for the consequences of automatized character arises less from its automatized decisions and actions than the non-automatized decision, perhaps long ago, to automatize those kinds of decision and actions. Responsibility also arises for allowing oneself to operate automatically, rather than with slower consideration and care.

Automatizing generals, majors, and lieutenants of the mind comes with certain risks. One is automatizing bad decision making. Just as we can automatize a mistake when playing the piano, if we have not practiced carefully, we can automatize poor decision making, or even a poor hierarchy of such zombie decision makers. We all have known parents who are poor role models, and then sadly watch as their children come to think and act in similarly self-undermining ways. Or we have seen, perhaps in ourselves, a tendency to repeat a certain pattern in relationships that undermines our long-term well-being. Breaking suboptimal automaticities is difficult precisely because they have become automatized. The first step is recognizing the pattern.

Another danger of giving mid-level managers of the mind discretion to act freely is that they will overstep the bounds of their permissible decision making and break the chain of command. An extreme example of this would be alien hand syndrome, where a hand starts to act of its own will, regardless of the intentions of higher executives.

Because previously voluntary, attentionally demanding, and effortful self-control and decision-making operations can be automatized, we can legitimately talk about the mechanisms of character reformation demanded by a second-order libertarian free will, whereby we are capable of choosing to have a new kind of character in the future. With appropriate practice, we automatize decision making such that we now have effectively automatized being a new kind of person. For example, if we were once a thief, and have cultivated a new kind of decision making in ourselves, we can eventually become a person who simply would not steal by default. This might not be the only way of reforming our nervous system to become the kind of chooser we intend to become. However, it is sufficient to prove the existence of just one way to show that intentions and programs of training can reform character.

But no matter how much we have chunked and automatized in our minds, even if to a point of mastery, the need for flexible, slow, deliberative processing cannot be eliminated. Automated mid-level agents can make decisions within a domain, but cannot solve novel problems, especially when solutions require sequencing or concatenation of component processes across domains, contextualized by higher-order reasons and knowledge of a world model. For example, the automated perceptual, cognitive, and motoric programs that afford good driving allow us to change lanes, pass cars, and reach our destination under normal circumstances. This automatization frees us to, say, allocate our volitional attention elsewhere, for example, to a conversation that we are having as we drive. All these processes of automatized mid-level agents involve decision making. But the automatized command chain cannot handle something outside of the script or schema learned, say, a clown skipping across the road holding a giant panda. This is when we automatically switch from "automatized volition" mode to "deliberative volition" mode. We can then consider our options, and weigh their pros and cons, in light of context and our reasons. This likely involves a transition in the basal ganglia and associated cortical areas, from reliance on type (2) to type (1) cortico–striatal–thalamocortical loops.

The beauty of mastery, however, is that anything that can be relegated to automatized mid-level agents has, generally speaking, been so relegated, allowing deliberation and volition to operate over higher-level chunks than in the non-master. Whereas the master sees higher-order patterns in the forest of possibilities, the novice sees a chaos of trees. The master therefore has a much richer freedom of will than the novice. The master attends to the goal, and the implementation takes care of itself. The novice pays attention to the implementation, and the goal is unclear. Mastery of some domain of volitional thought and action, like most attainments, takes years of practice. Freedom of the will is enhanced by choosing what volitions we will automatize with practice. Sources of distraction and inattentiveness, so rampant in our lives today, can serve to undermine the long-term learning of a deep free will. Central to our optimal self-automatization is what we choose to volitionally attend. Attention facilitates both connection and mastery, and through automatization of that which enhances our domains of volitional choice or action, enhances the depth of our free will.

Notes

Acknowledgments

1. Harari, Y. N. (2016). Yuval Noah Harari on big data, Google and the end of free will. *Financial Times*, https://www.ft.com/content/50bb4830-6a4c-11e6-ae5b-a7cc5dd5a28c; Harris, S. (2012). *Free Will*. Free Press; Coyne, J. A. (2012). Why you don't really have free will.
http://www.thinking-differently.com/phil001/wp-content/uploads/2013/03/Readings_free_will.pdf;
Sapolsky, R. (2023). https://www.econtalk.org/robert-sapolsky-on-determinism-free-will-and-responsibility/#audio-highlights
2. Nahmias, E. (2015). Why we have free will. *Scientific American*, https://www.scientificamerican.com/article/why-we-have-free-will/; Caouette, J. (2012). Free Will: Why Sam Harris needs to read more philosophy. https://aphilosopherstake.com/2012/07/29/free-will-why-sam-harris-needs-to-read-more-philosophy/; Dennett, D. (2017). Reflections on Sam Harris' "Free Will". *Rivista internazionale di Filosofia e Psicologia*, 8(3), 214–230. doi:10.4453/rifp.2017.0018

Introduction

1. Sapolsky, R. M. (2023). *Determined: A Science of Life without Free Will*. Penguin.

Chapter 2

1. This section appeared in Gregg D. Caruso and Owen Flanagan (eds.), *Neuroexistentialism: Meaning, morals, and purpose in the age of neuroscience* (Oxford University Press).
2. As an aside, there is another argument that (i) with (ii*) cannot logically entail (iii). Obviously, causes must precede effects. The usual exclusion argument is that (ii) diachronic actual elementary particle interactions preceding the moment t of (i) synchronic mental supervenience on actual particle configuration p leaves no room for mental events qua mental events to have any causal effect since those preceding physical interactions are sufficient to cause p. However, if (ii*) is taken to refer to a diachronic set of possible events preceding (i) mental supervenience on p, then there is a problem, because possibilia do not exist in the past of p; only actual events, such as those described in (ii) do. Once we have reached time t and p is not a possibility but an actuality, then all events prior to t must also be actual; events in the past are actual events that happened and are no longer possible. If they were possible, they would lie in the future. Possibilia only exist in the future relative to some actual or possible event. But p we agree is actual since supervenience makes no sense for possibilia, as in (i*), which we have rejected. Alternatively, if we want to think of the possibilia in (ii*) "collapsing" into p, where p was one among many possibilities, much like

the quantum mechanical collapse of the wave function, we are again left with the problem that the set of possibilia is not sufficient to cause p per se, because p might not have happened at all and some other possible outcome might instead have happened. However, if the possibilia in (ii*) are taken to temporally follow (i) the actual p at t, that is certainly consistent with the idea that possibilia can exist in the future of p. But then possibilia in the future of p would be seen as being sufficiently causal of p, which would entail impossible backward causation in time. Thus, the possibilia described in (ii*) can neither precede nor follow the actualia described in (i) and be sufficiently causal of them. In sum, (i) and (ii*) do not together entail (iii), whether on logical (syllogistic) grounds or on the grounds that possibilities can only exist in the future and not in the past of actual events, such as those on which mental events supervene. Again, assuming indeterminism, mental causation is not logically ruled out by Kim's argument.

3. I find the views of Levy and others who deny mental causation and free will to be nihilistic and impoverished—nihilistic because there can be no moral responsibility or self-forming acts under such views, and impoverished because they fail to recognize the astounding elaboration of modes of top-down informational causation that have evolved in biological systems, including principally the causal roles of our minds in realizing our own envisioned futures.

4. https://www.scientificamerican.com/article/are-virtual-particles-rea/

5. Note "positive feedback" here is used colloquially to mean uplifting signals received in response to some action. It does not refer to the cybernetic notion of discrepancies being enlarged on each cycle.

6. Goodall speaks about her mother here: https://www.youtube.com/watch?v=SQVVIDCXk50&ab

References

Alexander, P., Schlegel, A. Sinnott-Armstrong, W., Roskies, A., Wheatley, T., & Tse, P. U. (2016). Readiness potentials driven by non-motoric processes. *Consciousness & Cognition, 39*, 38–47. https://doi.org/10.1016/j.concog.2015.11.011

Allen, B. G., Bhatia, S. K., Anderson, C. M., Eichenberger-Gilmore, J. M., Sibenaller, Z. A., Mapuskar, K. A., Schoenfeld. J. D., Buatti, J. M., Spitz, D. R., & Fath, M. A. (2014). Ketogenic diets as an adjuvant cancer therapy: History and potential mechanism. *Redox Biology, 2*, 963–970. https://doi.org/10.1016/j.redox.2014.08.002

Almécija, S., Moyà-Solà, S., & Alba, D. M. (2010). Early origin for human-like precision grasping: A comparative study of pollical distal phalanges in fossil hominins. *PLoS ONE, 5*(7). https://doi.org/10.1371/journal.pone.0011727

Alquist, J. L., Ainsworth, S. E., & Baumeister, R. F. (2013). Determined to conform: Disbelief in free will increases conformity. *Journal of Experimental Social Psychology, 49*(1), 80–86.

Anderson, J. (2014). The impact of family structure on the health of children: Effects of divorce. *Linacre Quarterly, 81*(4), 378–387.

Aru, J., Suzuki, M., & Larkum, M. E. (2020). Cellular mechanisms of conscious processing. *Trends in Cognitive Sciences, 24*(10), 814–825. https://doi.org/10.1016/j.tics.2020.07.006

Aspect, A. (2015). Viewpoint: Closing the door on Einstein and Bohr's quantum debate. *Physics, 8*, 123. https://doi.org/10.1103/physics.8.123

Aspect, A., Grangier, P., & Roger, G. (1982). Experimental realization of Einstein–Podolsky–Rosen–Bohm gedankenexperiment: A new violation of Bell's inequalities. *Physical Review Letters, 49*(2), 91–94. https://doi.org/10.1103/physrevlett.49.91

Bachmann, T. (2015). How a (sub)cellular coincidence detection mechanism featuring layer-5 pyramidal cells may help produce various visual phenomena. *Frontiers in Psychology, 6*. https://doi.org/10.3389/fpsyg.2015.01947

Bacon, F. (1605). The advancement of learning. https://archive.org/details/advancementofl00baco/page/n7/mode/2up

Baker, L. R. (1993). Metaphysics and mental causation. In J. Heil & A. Mele (Eds.), *Mental causation* (pp. 75–95). Clarendon Press.

Balaguer, M. (2010). *Free will as an open scientific problem*. MIT Press.

Banich, M. T. (2019) The Stroop effect occurs at multiple points along a cascade of control: Evidence from cognitive neuroscience approaches. *Frontiers in Psychology, 10*, 2164. https://doi.org/10.3389/fpsyg.2019.02164

Bartlett, G. (2022). Does integrated information theory make testable predictions about the role of silent neurons in consciousness? *Neuroscience of Consciousness, 2022*(1), niac015. https://doi.org/10.1093/nc/niac015

Bartol, T. M. Jr., Land, B. R., Salpeter, E. E., & Salpeter, M. M. (1991). Monte Carlo simulation of miniature endplate current generation in the vertebrate neuromuscular junction. *Biophysical Journal, 59*, 1290–1307.

Bass, S. (2015). Vacuum energy and the cosmological constant. https://arxiv.org/pdf/1503.05483.pdf

Battersby, S. (2008, November 20). It's confirmed: Matter is merely vacuum fluctuations. *New Scientist*. https://www.newscientist.com/article/dn16095-its-confirmed-matter-is-merely-vacuum-fluctuations/

Baumeister, R. F., Masicampo, E. J. & Dewall, C. N. (2009). Prosocial benefits of feeling free: Disbelief in Free Will increases aggression and reduces helpfulness. *Personality and Social Psychology Bulletin, 35*(2), 260–268. https://doi.org/10.1177/0146167208327217

Beaty, R. E., Benedek, M., Silvia, P. J., & Schacter, D. L. (2016). Creative cognition and brain network dynamics. *Trends in Cognitive Sciences, 20*(2), 87–95. https://doi.org/10.1016/j.tics.2015.10.004

Beggs, J. M. (2008). The criticality hypothesis: How local cortical networks might optimize information processing. *Philosophical Transactions of the Royal Society A: Mathematical, Physical and Engineering Sciences, 366,* 329–343.

Ben-Ari, Y. (2001). Developing networks play a similar melody. *Trends in Neuroscience, 24,* 353–360.

Berg, H. C. (1983). *Random walks in biology.* Princeton University Press.

Bertschinger, N., & Natschlager, T. (2004). Real-time computation at the edge of chaos in recurrent neural networks. *Neural Computation, 216,* 1413–1436.

Bertulani, C. A. (2007). *Nuclear physics in a nutshell.* Princeton University Press.

BIG Bell Test Collaboration. (2018). Challenging local realism with human choices. *Nature, 557*(7704), 212–216. https://doi.org/10.1038/s41586-018-0085-3

Bild, M., Fadel, M., Yang, Y., von Lüpke, U., Martin, P., Bruno, A., & Chu, Y. (2023). Schrödinger cat states of a 16-microgram mechanical oscillator. *Science, 380*(6642), 274–278. https://doi.org/10.1126/science.adf7553

Blackmore, D. G., Vukovic, J., Waters, M. J., & Bartlett P. F. (2012). GH mediates exercise-dependent activation of SVZ neural precursor cells in aged mice. *PLoS ONE, 7*(11), e49912. https://doi.org/10.1371/journal.pone.0049912

Boudesseul, J., Lantian, A., Cova, F., & Bègue, L. (2016). Free love? On the relation between belief in free will, determinism, and passionate love. *Consciousness and Cognition, 46,* 47–59. https://doi.org/10.1016/j.concog.2016.09.003

Brembs, B. (2011). Towards a scientific concept of free will as a biological trait: Spontaneous actions and decision-making in invertebrates. *Proceedings of the Royal Society of London: Biological Sciences, 278*(1707), 930–939.

Brette, R. (2019). Is coding a relevant metaphor for the brain? *Behavioral and Brain Sciences, 42,* E215. https://doi.org/10.1017/S0140525X19000049

Brewer, J., Cortese, A., de Wit, H., Denys, D., Hanlon, C. A., Holmes, E. A., Paulus, M. P., Schwarzbach, J., & Tse, P. (2020). Interventions and implications. In P. W. Kalivas & M. P. Paulus (Eds.), *Intrusive thinking: From molecules to free will* (pp. 347–378). MIT Press.

Brewer, J. A., Worhunsky, P. D., Gray, J. R., Tang, Y. Y., Weber, J., & Kober, H. (2011). Meditation experience is associated with differences in default mode network activity and connectivity. *Proceedings of the National Academy of Sciences of the United States of America, 108*(50), 20254–20259. https://doi.org/10.1073/pnas.1112029108

Briggman, K. L., Abarbanel, H. D., & Kristan, W. B. (2006). From crawling to cognition, analyzing the dynamical interactions among populations of neurons. *Current Opinion in Neurobiology, 16,* 135–144.

Buzsáki, G. (2010). Neural syntax: Cell assemblies, synapsembles and readers. *Neuron, 68*(3), 362–385.

Carhart-Harris, R. L., Erritzoe, D., Williams, T., Stone, J. M., Reed, L. J., Colasanti, A., Tyacke, R. J., Leech, R., Malizia, A. L., Murphy, K., Hobden, P., Evans, J., Feilding, A., Wise, R. G., & Nutt, D. J. (2011). Neural correlates of the psychedelic state as determined by fMRI studies with psilocybin. *Proceedings of the National Academy of Sciences of the United States of America, 109*(6), 2138–2143. https://doi.org/10.1073/pnas.1119598109

Cartlidge, E. (2020, July 1). LIGO reveals quantum correlations at work in mirrors weighing tens of kilograms. *Physics World.* https://physicsworld.com/a/ligo-reveals-quantum-correlations-at-work-in-mirrors-weighing-tens-of-kilograms/

Caruso, G. D. (2012). *Free will and consciousness: A determinist account of the illusion of free will*. Lexington Books.

Caruso, G. D. (2015). Kane is not able: A reply to Vicens' "Self-forming actions and conflicts of intention". *Southwest Philosophy Review, 31*, 2.

Casimir, H. (1948). On the attraction between two perfectly conducting plates. *Proceedings of the Royal Netherlands Academy of Arts and Sciences, 51*, 793–795.

Cavanagh, P., Caplovitz, G. P., Lytchenko, T. K., Maechler, M. R., Tse, P. U., & Sheinberg, D. L. (2023). The architecture of object-based attention. *Psychonomic Bulletin & Review, 30*(5), 1643–1667. https://doi.org/10.3758/s13423-023-02281-7

Chalmers, D. J. (1995). Facing up to the problem of consciousness. *Journal of Consciousness Studies, 2*(3), 200–219.

Chialvo, D. R. (2010). Emergent complex neural dynamics. *Nature Physics, 6*, 744–750.

Cho, I. H., Panzera, L. C., Chin, M., Alpizar, S. A., Olveda, G. E., Hill, R. A., & Hoppa, M. B. (2020). The potassium channel subunit Kvβ1 serves as a major control point for synaptic facilitation. *Proceedings of the National Academy of Sciences of the United States of America, 117*(47), 29937–29947. https://doi.org/10.1073/pnas.2000790117

Christoff, K., Irving, Z. C., Fox, K. C., Spreng, R. N., & Andrews-Hanna, J. R. (2016). Mind-wandering as spontaneous thought: A dynamic framework. *Nature Reviews Neuroscience, 17*(11), 718–731. https://doi.org/10.1038/nrn.2016.113

Chu, J. (2020, July 1). Quantum fluctuations can jiggle objects on the human scale. *MIT News*. https://news.mit.edu/2020/quantum-fluctuations-jiggle-objects-0701

Churchland, P. (1986). *Neurophilosophy: Toward a unified science of the mind-brain*. MIT Press.

Collini, E., Wong, C. Y., Wilk, K. E., Curmi, P. M. G., Brumer, P., & Scholes, G. D. (2010). Coherently wired light-harvesting in photosynthetic marine algae at ambient temperature. *Nature, 463*, 644–664.

Crescioni, A. W., Baumeister, R. F., Ainsworth, S. E., Ent, M., & Lambert, N. M. (2015). Subjective correlates and consequences of belief in free will. *Philosophical Psychology, 29*, 1–23.

Critchley, H. D., Mathias, C. J., Josephs, O., O'Doherty, J., Zanini, S., Dewar, B. K., Cipolotti, L., Shallice, T., & Dolan, R. J. (2003). Human cingulate cortex and autonomic control: Converging neuroimaging and clinical evidence. *Brain, 126*(Pt 10), 2139–2152. https://doi.org/10.1093/brain/awg216

Czerniawski, J., Ree, F., Chia, C., & Otto, T. (2012). Dorsal versus ventral hippocampal contributions to trace and contextual conditioning: Differential effects of regionally selective NMDA receptor antagonism on acquisition and expression. *Hippocampus, 22*, 1528–1539.

Dahlberg, P. D., Norris, G. J., Wang, C., Viswanathan, S., Singh, V. P., & Engel, G. S. (2015). Communication: Coherences observed in vivo in photosynthetic bacteria using two-dimensional electronic spectroscopy. *Journal of Chemical Physics, 143*, 101101.

Dahlberg, P. D., Ting, P.-C., Massey, S. C., Allodi, M. A., Martin, E. C., Hunter, C. N., & Engel, G. S. (2017). Mapping the ultrafast flow of harvested solar energy in living photosynthetic cells. *Nature Communications, 8*, 988.

Dar-Nimrod, I., & Heine, S. J. (2011). Genetic essentialism: On the deceptive determinism of DNA. *Psychological Bulletin, 137*(5), 800–818. https://doi.org/10.1037/a0021860

Davidson, D. (1970). Mental events. In L. Foster & J. W. Swanson (Eds.), *Experience and theory* (pp. 79–91). Duckworth. Reprinted in Davidson, D. (2001). *Essays on actions and events*. Clarendon Press.

Davies, P. C. W. (2004). Does quantum mechanics play a non-trivial role in life? *Biosystems, 78*(1–3), 69–79. https://doi.org/10.1016/j.biosystems.2004.07.001

Dawkins, R. (1976). *The selfish gene*. Oxford University Press.

DeFelipe, J., & Fariñas, I. (1992). The pyramidal neuron of the cerebral cortex: Morphological and chemical characteristics of the synaptic inputs. *Progress in Neurobiology, 39*, 563–607.

Denham, J., Marques, F. Z., O'Brien, B. J., & Charchar, F. J. (2014). Exercise: Putting action into our epigenome. *Sports Medicine*, *44*(2), 189–209. https://doi.org/10.1007/s40279-013-0114-1

Dennett, D. (1991). *Consciousness explained*. The Penguin Press.

Diamond, M. C. (1988). *Enriching heredity*. The Free Press.

Diamond, M. C. (2001). Response of the brain to enrichment. *Anais da Academia Brasileira de Ciências*, *73*(2), 211–220. https://doi.org/10.1590/s0001-37652001000200006

Dirac, P. A. M. (1927). The quantum theory of the emission and absorption of radiation. *Proceedings of the Royal Society A: Mathematical, Physical and Engineering Sciences*, *114*(767), 243–265.

Domenici, P., Booth, D., Blagburn, J. M., & Bacon, J. P. (2008). Cockroaches keep predators guessing by using preferred escape trajectories. *Current Biology*, *18*(22), 1792–1796.

Dominy, N. J., Yeakel, J. D., Bhat, U., Ramsden, L., Wrangham, R. W., & Lucas, P. W. (2016). How chimpanzees integrate sensory information to select figs. *Interface Focus*, *6*(3), 20160001. https://doi.org/10.1098/rsfs.2016.0001

Dosenbach, N. U., Fair, D. A., Cohen, A. L., Schlaggar, B. L., & Petersen, S. E. (2008). A dual-networks architecture of top-down control. *Trends in Cognitive Sciences*, *12*(3), 99–105. https://doi.org/10.1016/j.tics.2008.01.001

Dostál, J., Pšenčík, J., & Zigmantas, D. (2016). In situ mapping of the energy flow through the entire photosynthetic apparatus. *Nature Chemistry*, *8*, 705–710.

Dowe, P. (1992). Wesley Salmon's process theory of causality and the conserved quantity theory. *Philosophy of Science*, *59*, 195–216.

Doyle, A. C. (1993). *The memoirs of Sherlock Holmes: The adventure of Silver Blaze*. Oxford University Press.

Dresler, M., Wehrle, R., Spoormaker, V. I., Koch, S. P., Holsboer, F., Steiger, A., Obrig, H., Sämann, P. G., & Czisch, M. (2012). Neural correlates of dream lucidity obtained from contrasting lucid versus non-lucid REM sleep: A combined EEG/fMRI case study. *Sleep*, *35*(7), 1017–1020. https://doi.org/10.5665/sleep.1974

Dretske, F. (1981). *Knowledge and the flow of information*. MIT Press.

Dylla, K. V., Galili, D. S., Szyszka, P., & Lüdke, A. (2013). Trace conditioning in insects-keep the trace! *Frontiers in Physiology*, *4*, 67. https://www.frontiersin.org/articles/10.3389/fphys.2013.00067/full

Earley, J. E. (2008). How philosophy of mind needs philosophy of chemistry. http://philsci-archive.pitt.edu/4414/1/PM_final2.pdf

Edelman, G. M., & Gally, J. (2001). Degeneracy and complexity in biological systems. *Proceedings of the National Academy of Sciences of the United States of America*, *98*, 13763–13768.

Eicher, D. J. (2019, July 1). How big is the universe? *Astronomy*. https://astronomy.com/magazine/greatest-mysteries/2019/07/2-how-big-is-the-universe

Einstein, A., Podolsky, B., & Rosen, N. (1935). Can quantum-mechanical description of physical reality be considered complete? *Physical Review*, *47*(10), 777–780. https://doi.org/10.1103/PhysRev.47.777

Engel, G., Calhoun, T., Read, E., Ahn, T.-K., Mančal, T., Cheng, Y.-C., Blankenship, R. E., & Fleming, G. R. (2007). Evidence for wavelike energy transfer through quantum coherence in photosynthetic systems. *Nature*, *446*, 782–786. https://doi.org/10.1038/nature05678

Espinosa, J., & Evans, W. N. (2013). Maternal bereavement: The heightened mortality of mothers after the death of a child. *Economics & Human Biology*, *11*(3), 371–381. https://doi.org/10.1016/j.ehb.2012.06.002

Fekete, T., & Edelman, S. (2011). Towards a computational theory of experience. *Consciousness and Cognition*, *20*(3), 807–827.

Feldman, G., Chandrashekar, S. P., & Wong, K. F. E. (2016). The freedom to excel: Belief in free will predicts better academic performance. *Personality and Individual Differences*, *90*, 377–383.

Ferretti, M., Novoderezhkin, V. I., Romero, E., Augulis, R., Pandit, A., Zigmantas, D., & van Grondelle, R. (2014). The nature of coherences in the B820 bacteriochlorophyll dimer revealed by two-dimensional electronic spectroscopy. *Physical Chemistry Chemical Physics, 16*, 9930–9939.

Fidler, A. F., Singh, V. P., Long, P. D., Dahlberg, P. D., & Engel, G. S. (2014). Dynamic localization of electronic excitation in photosynthetic complexes revealed with chiral two-dimensional spectroscopy. *Nature Communication, 5*, 3286.

Finicelli, M., Di Salle, A., Galderisi, U., & Peluso, G. (2022). The Mediterranean diet: An update of the clinical trials. *Nutrients, 14*(14), 2956. https://doi.org/10.3390/nu14142956

Flanagan, M. L., Long, P. D., Dahlberg, P. D., Rolczynski, B. S., Massey, S. C., & Engel, G. S. (2016). Mutations to *R. sphaeroides* reaction center perturb energy levels and vibronic coupling but not observed energy transfer rates. *The Journal of Physical Chemistry A, 120*, 1479–1487.

Forgeard, M. J., Haigh, E. A., Beck, A. T., Davidson, R. J., Henn, F. A., Maier, S. F., Mayberg, H. S., & Seligman, M. E. (2011). Beyond depression: Towards a process-based approach to research, diagnosis, and treatment. *Clinical Psychology (New York), 18*(4), 275–299. https://doi.org/10.1111/j.1468-2850.2011.01259.x

Francis, M. (2012, October 30). Quantum entanglement shows that reality can't be local. *Ars Technica*. https://arstechnica.com/science/2012/10/quantum-entanglement-shows-that-reality-cant-be-local/

Frank, S. M., Greenlee, M. W., & Tse, P. U. (2018). Long time no see: Enduring behavioral and neuronal changes in perceptual learning of motion trajectories 3 years after training. *Cerebral Cortex, 28*(4), 1260–1271. https://doi.org/10.1093/cercor/bhx039

Frank, S. M., Otto, A., Volberg, G., Tse, P. U., Watanabe, T., & Greenlee M. W. (2022). Transfer of tactile learning from trained to untrained body parts supported by cortical coactivation in primary somatosensory cortex. *Journal of Neuroscience, 42*(31), 6131–6144. https://doi.org/10.1523/jneurosci.0301-22.2022

Frank, S. M., Reavis, E. A., Greenlee, M. W., & Tse, P. U. (2016). Pretraining cortical thickness predicts subsequent perceptual learning rate in a visual search task. *Cerebral Cortex, 26*(3), 1211–1220. https://doi.org/10.1093/cercor/bhu309

Frank, S. M., Reavis, E. A., Tse, P. U., & Greenlee, M. W. (2014). Neural mechanisms of feature conjunction learning: Enduring changes in occipital cortex after a week of training. *Human Brain Mapping, 5*(4), 1201–1211. https://doi.org/10.1002/hbm.22245

Frankfurt, H. (1971). Freedom of the will and the concept of a person. *Journal of Philosophy, 68*(1), 5–20.

Frankfurt, H. G. (1989). Concerning the freedom and limits of the will. *Philosophical Topics, 17*(1), 119–130.

Frankl, V. E. (1962). *Man's search for meaning: An introduction to logotherapy*. Beacon Press.

Franks, K. M., Stevens, C. F., & Sejnowski, T. J. (2003). Independent sources of quantal variability at single glutamatergic synapses. *Journal of Neuroscience, 23*(8), 3186–3195. https://doi.org/10.1523/jneurosci.23-08-03186.2003

Friedman, N., Ito, S., Brinkman, B., Shimono, M., Lee DeVille, R. E., Dahman, K. A., Beggs, J. M., & Butler, T. C. (2012). Universal critical dynamics in high resolution neuronal avalanche data. *Physical Review Letters, 108*(208102), 1–5.

Fuller, F. D., Pan, J., Gelzinis, A., Butkus, V., Senlik, S. S., Wilcox, D. E., Yocum, C. F., Valkunas, L., Abramavicius, D., & Ogilvie, J. P. (2014). Vibronic coherence in oxygenic photosynthesis. *Nature Chemistry, 6*, 706–711.

Furmanski, C. S., Schluppeck, D., & Engel, S. A. (2004). Learning strengthens the response of primary visual cortex to simple patterns. *Current Biology, 14*, 573–578.

Garnefski, N., & Diekstra, R. F. (1997). Adolescents from one parent, stepparent and intact families: Emotional problems and suicide attempts. *Journal of Adolescence, 20*(2), 201–208. https://doi.org/10.1006/jado.1996.0077

Gazzaniga, M. S. (2000). Cerebral specialization and interhemispheric communication: Does the corpus callosum enable the human condition? *Brain*, *123*, 1293–1326.

Gilmartin, M. R., & Helmstetter, F. J. (2010). Trace and contextual fear conditioning require neural activity and NMDA receptor-dependent transmission in the medial prefrontal cortex. *Learning and Memory*, *17*, 289–296.

Gooding, P. L. T., Callan, M. J., & Hughes, G. (2018). The association between believing in free will and subjective well-being is confounded by a sense of personal control. *Frontiers in Psychology*, *9*, 623. https://doi.org/10.3389/fpsyg.2018.00623

Gray, J. A. (2004). *Consciousness: Creeping up on the hard problem*. Oxford University Press.

Graybiel, A. M., & Smith, K. S. (2014). Good habits, bad habits. *Scientific American*, *310*(6), 38–43. https://doi.org/10.1038/scientificamerican0614-38

Greenspan, R. J. (2009). Selection, gene interaction, and flexible gene networks. *Cold Spring Harbor Symposium on Quantitative Biology*, *74*, 131–138.

Guasch-Ferré, M., & Willett, W.C. (2021). The Mediterranean diet and health: A comprehensive overview. *Journal of Internal Medicine*, *290*(3), 549–566. https://doi.org/10.1111/joim.13333

Gutsaeva, D. R., Carraway, M. S., Suliman, H. B., Demchenko, I. T., Shitara, H., Yonekawa, H., & Piantadosi, C. A. (2008). Transient hypoxia stimulates mitochondrial biogenesis in brain subcortex by a neuronal nitric oxide synthase-dependent mechanism. *Journal of Neuroscience*, *28*(9), 2015–224. https://doi.org/10.1523/jneurosci.5654-07.2008

Hamani, C., Mayberg, H., Stone, S., Laxton, A., Haber, S., & Lozano, A. M. (2011). The subcallosal cingulate gyrus in the context of major depression. *Biological Psychiatry*, *69*(4), 301–309. https://doi.org/10.1016/j.biopsych.2010.09.034

Hanson, R. (2015). Loophole-free Bell inequality violation using electron spins separated by 1.3 kilometres. *Nature*, *526*(7575), 682–686. https://doi.org/10.1038/nature15759

Harlow, J. M. (1868). Recovery from the passage of an iron bar through the head. *Publications of the Massachusetts Medical Society*, *2*(3), 327–347.

Harris, S. (2012). *Free will*. Free Press.

Hawking, S. W. (1978). Spacetime foam. *Nuclear Physics B*, *144*(2–3), 349–362. https://doi.org/10.1016/0550-3213(78)90375-9

Hayes, D., Wen, J., Panitchayangkoon, G., Blankenship, R. E., & Engel, G. S. (2011). Robustness of electronic coherence in the Fenna–Matthews–Olson complex to vibronic and structural modifications. *Faraday Discussions*, *150*, 459–469.

Haynes, K. (2020, March 3). Is the universe infinite? *Astronomy*. https://astronomy.com/news/2020/03/is-the-universe-infinite

Hiestand, T., Hänggi, J., Klein, C., Topka, M. S., Jaguszewski, M., Ghadri, J. R., Lüscher, T. F., Jäncke, L., & Templin, C. (2018). Takotsubo syndrome associated with structural brain alterations of the limbic system. *Journal of the American College of Cardiology*, *71*(7), 809–811. https://doi.org/10.1016/j.jacc.2017.12.022

Hildner, R., Brinks, D., Nieder, J. B., Cogdell, R. J., & van Hulst, N. F. (2013). Quantum coherent energy transfer over varying pathways in single light-harvesting complexes. *Science*, *340*, 1448–1451.

Hiroto, D. S. (1974). Locus of control and learned helplessness. *Journal of Experimental Psychology*, *102*(2), 187–193. https://doi.org/10.1037/h0035910

Hiscock, H. G., Worster, S., Kattnig, D. R., Steers, C., Jin, Y., Manolopoulos, D. E., Mouritsen, H., & Hore, P. J. (2016). The quantum needle of the avian magnetic compass. *Proceedings of the National Academy of Sciences of the United States of America*, *113*(17), 4634–4639. https://doi.org/10.1073/pnas.1600341113

Hochstoeger, T., Al Said, T., Maestre, D., Walter, F., Vilceanu, A., Pedron, M., Cushion, T. D., Snider, W., Nimpf, S., Nordmann, G. C., Landler, L., Edelman, N., Kruppa, L., Dürnberger, G., Mechtler, K., Schuechner, S., Ogris, E., Malkemper, E. P., Weber, S., ... Keays, D. A. (2020).

The biophysical, molecular, and anatomical landscape of pigeon CRY4: A candidate light-based quantal magnetosensor. *Science Advances*, *6*(33), eabb9110. https://doi.org/10.1126/sciadv.abb9110

Holmes, R. (2017). Local realism is dead, long live local realism? *Physics World*, *30*(6), 21.

Hopkins, M. E., & Bucci, D. J. (2010). BDNF expression in perirhinal cortex is associated with exercise-induced improvement in object recognition memory. *Neurobiology of Learning and Memory*, *94*(2), 278–284. https://doi.org/10.1016/j.nlm.2010.06.006

Horn, A., Ostwald, D., Reisert, M., & Blankenburg, F. (2013). The structural–functional connectome and the default mode network of the human brain. *NeuroImage*, *102*, 142–151. https://doi.org/10.1016/j.neuroimage.2013.09.069

Hui, J., Wang, Y., Zhang, P., Tse, P. U., & Cavanagh, P. (2020). Apparent motion is computed in perceptual coordinates. *i-Perception*, *11*(4), 1–10. https://doi.org/10.1177/2041669520933309

Hume, D. (1739). *A treatise on human nature*. Clarendon Press.

Huttenlocher, P. R. (1979). Synaptic density in human frontal cortex: Developmental changes and effects of aging. *Brain Research*, *163*, 195–205.

Jolly, C. J. (1970). The seed-eaters: A new model of hominid differentiation based on a baboon analogy. *Man, New Series*, *5*(1), 5–26. https://doi.org/10.2307/2798801

Kable, J. W., & Glimcher, P. W. (2007). The neural correlates of subjective value during intertemporal choice. *Nature Neuroscience*, *10*(12), 1625–1633. https://doi.org/10.1038/nn2007

Kable, J. W., & Glimcher, P. W. (2010). An "as soon as possible" effect in human intertemporal decision making: Behavioral evidence and neural mechanisms. *Journal of Neurophysiology*, *103*(5), 2513–2531. https://doi.org/10.1152/jn.00177.2009

Kane, R. (2007). Libertarianism. In J. M. Fischer, R. Kane, D. Pereboom, & M. Vargas (Eds.), *Four views on free will* (pp. 5–43). Blackwell Publishing.

Kean, S. (2022). *The icepick surgeon: Murder, fraud, sabotage, piracy, and other dastardly deeds perpetrated in the name of science* (First Back Bay trade paperback edition). Back Bay Books/Little, Brown & Company.

Kempermann, G., Kuhn, H. G., & Gage, F. H. (1997). More hippocampal neurons in adult mice living in an enriched environment. *Nature*, *386*, 493–495.

Kepecs, A., & Lisman, J. (2003). Information encoding and computation with spikes and bursts. *Network*, *14*(1), 103–118.

Kim, J. (1996). *Philosophy of mind*. Westview Press.

Kim, J. (2005) *Physicalism, or something near enough*. Princeton University Press.

King, N., Westbrook, M. J., Young, S. L., Kuo, A., Abedin, M., Chapman, J., Fairclough, S., Hellsten, U., Isogai, Y., Letunic, I., Marr, M., Pincus, D., Putnam, N., Rokas, A., Wright, K. J., Zuzow, R., Dirks, W., Good, M., Goodstein, D., … Rokhsar, D. (2008). The genome of the choanoflagellate *monosiga brevicollis* and the origin of Metazoans. *Nature*, *451*(7180), 783–788. https://doi.org/10.1038/nature06617

Kinouchi, O., & Copelli, M. (2006). Optimal dynamical range of excitable networks at criticality. *Nature Physics*, *2*, 348–351.

Kivell, T. L. (2015). Evidence in hand: Recent discoveries and the early evolution of human manual manipulation. *Philosophical Transactions of the Royal Society B: Biological Sciences*, *370*(1682), 20150105.https://doi.org/10.1098/rstb.2015.0105

Koch, C. (2004). *The quest for consciousness: A neurobiological approach*. W. H. Freeman.

Kocher, C. A. (1971). Time correlations in the detection of successively emitted photons. *Annals of Physics*, *65*(1), 1–18. https://doi.org/10.1016/0003-4916(71)90159-X

Kretschmann, E., & Raether, H. (1968). Notizen: Radiative decay of non radiative surface plasmons excited by light. *Zeitschrift Für Naturforschung A*, *23*(12), 2135–2136. https://doi.org/10.1515/zna-1968-1247

Lamb, W., & Retherford, R. (1947). Fine structure of the hydrogen atom by a microwave method. *Physical Review*, *72*(3), 241–243.

Larkum, M. E., Wu, J., Duverdin, S. A., & Gidon, A. (2022). The guide to dendritic spikes of the mammalian cortex in vitro and in vivo. *Neuroscience*, *489*, 15–33. https://doi.org/10.1016/j.neuroscience.2022.02.009

Larsen, R. S., Corlew, R. J., Henson, M. A., Roberts, A. C., Mishina, M., Watanabe, M., Lipton, S. A., Nakanishi, N., Pérez-Otaño, I., Weinberg, R. J., & Philpot, B. D. (2011). NR3A-containing NMDARs promote neurotransmitter release and spike timing-dependent plasticity. *Nature Neuroscience*, *14*(3), 338–344.

Lazar, S. W., Bush, G., Gollub, R. L., Fricchione, G. L., Khalsa, G., & Benson H. (2000). Functional brain mapping of the relaxation response and meditation. *NeuroReport*, *11*(7), 1581–1585.

Lee, H., Cheng, Y.-C., & Fleming, G. R. (2007). Coherence dynamics in photosynthesis: Protein protection of excitonic coherence. *Science*, *316*, 1462–1465.

Lester, D. (1972). Voodoo death: Some new thoughts on an old phenomenon. *American Anthropologist, New Series*, *74*(3), 386–390. https://anthrosource.onlinelibrary.wiley.com/doi/pdf/10.1525/aa.1972.74.3.02a00100

Levy, N. (2011). *Hard luck: How luck undermines free will and moral responsibility*. Oxford University Press.

Li, C., Wang, S., Zhao, Y., Kong, F., & Li, J. (2017). The freedom to pursue happiness: Belief in free will predicts life satisfaction and positive affect among Chinese adolescents. *Frontiers in Psychology*, *7*, 2027. https://doi.org/10.3389/fpsyg.2016.02027

Li, J., Precht, D. H., Mortensen, P. B., & Olsen, J. (2003). Mortality in parents after death of a child in Denmark: A nationwide follow-up study. *Lancet*, *361*, 9355, 363–367.

Lieb, E. H., & Seiringer, R. (2009). *The stability of matter in quantum mechanics*. Cambridge University Press.

Lisi, M., & Cavanagh, P. (2015). Dissociation between the perceptual and saccadic localization of moving objects. *Current Biology*, *25*(19), 2535–2540. https://doi.org/10.1016/j.cub.2015.08.021

Lisman, J. E. (1997). Bursts as a unit of neural information: making unreliable synapses reliable. *Trends in Neuroscience*, *20*(1), 38–43. https://doi.org/10.1016/S0166-2236(96)10070-9

Little, J. P., Safdar, A., Bishop, D., Tarnopolsky, M. A., & Gibala, M. J. (2011). An acute bout of high-intensity interval training increases the nuclear abundance of PGC-1α and activates mitochondrial biogenesis in human skeletal muscle. *American Journal of Physiology—Regulatory, Integrative and Comparative Physiology*, *300*(6), R1303–R1310. https://doi.org/10.1152/ajpregu.00538.2010

MacKenzie, M. J., Vohs, K. D., & Baumeister, R. F. (2014). You didn't have to do that: Belief in free will promotes gratitude. *Personality and Social Psychology Bulletin*, *40*, 1423–1434. https://doi.org/10.1177/0146167214549322

Maechler, M. R., Heller, N. H., Lisi, M., Cavanagh, P., & Tse, P. U. (2021a). Smooth pursuit operates over perceived not physical positions of the double-drift stimulus. *Journal of Vision*, *21*(11), 6. https://doi.org/10.1167/jov.21.11.6

Maechler, M. R., Cavanagh, P., & Tse, P. U. (2021b). Attentional tracking takes place over perceived rather than veridical positions. *Attention, Perception & Psychophysics*, *83*(4), 1455–1462. https://doi.org/10.3758/s13414-020-02214-9

Maier, S. F. (1970). Failure to escape traumatic electric shock: Incompatible skeletal–motor responses or learned helplessness? *Learning and Motivation*, *1*(2), 157–169. https://doi.org/10.1016/0023-9690(70)90082-2

Maier, S. F., & Seligman, M. E. (2016). Learned helplessness at fifty: Insights from neuroscience. *Psychological Review*, *123*(4), 349–367. https://doi.org/10.1037/rev0000033

Maoz, U., Yaffe, G., Koch, C., & Mudrik, L. (2019). Neural precursors of decisions that matter—an ERP study of deliberate and arbitrary choice. *Elife, 8*, e39787. https://doi.org/10.7554/eLife.39787

Massendari, D., Lisi, M., Collins, T., & Cavanagh, P. (2018). Memory-guided saccades show effect of a perceptual illusion whereas visually guided saccades do not. *Journal of Neurophysiology, 119*(1), 62–72. https://doi.org/10.1152/jn.00229.2017

Matson, J. (2012). Quantum teleportation achieved over record distances. *Nature.* https://doi.org/10.1038/nature.2012.11163

Mayberg, H. S., Lozano, A. M., Voon, V., McNeely, H. E., Seminowicz, D., Hamani, C., Schwalb, J. M., & Kennedy, S. H. (2005). Deep brain stimulation for treatment-resistant depression. *Neuron, 45*(5), 651–660. https://doi.org/10.1016/j.neuron.2005.02.014

McCormick, K. (2022). The spooky quantum phenomenon you've never heard of. *Quanta.* https://www.quantamagazine.org/the-spooky-quantum-phenomenon-youve-never-heard-of-20220622/.

McCrone, J. (1999). *Going inside: A tour round a single moment of consciousness.* Faber & Faber.

Metcalfe, J., & Mischel, W. (1999). A hot/cool-system analysis of delay of gratification: Dynamics of willpower. *Psychological Review, 106*(1), 3–19. https://doi.org/10.1037/0033-295X.106.1.3

Mill, J. S. (1843) *A system of logic, ratiocinative and inductive: Being a connected view of the principles of evidence and the methods of scientific investigation.* Cambridge University Press.

Minsky, C. (2019, October 24). The universe is made of tiny bubbles containing mini-universes, scientists say. *Vice.* https://www.vice.com/en/article/j5yngp/the-universe-is-made-of-tiny-bubbles-containing-mini-universes-scientists-say

Monroe, A. E., & Malle, B. F. (2010). From uncaused will to conscious choice: The need to study, not speculate about people's folk concept of free will. *Review of Philosophy and Psychology, 1*, 211–224. https://doi.org/10.1007/s13164-009-0010-7

Montague, P. R., Dayan, P., & Sejnowski, T. J. (1996). A framework for mesencephalic dopamine systems based on predictive Hebbian learning. *Journal of Neuroscience, 16*(5), 1936–1947. https://doi.org/10.1523/jneurosci.16-05-01936.1996

Morris, G., Nevet, A., Arkadir, D., Vaadia, E., & Bergman, H. (2006). Midbrain dopamine neurons encode decisions for future action. *Nature Neuroscience, 9*(8), 1057–1063. https://doi.org/10.1038/nn1743

Moynihan, A. B., Igou, E. R., & van Tilburg, W. A. P. (2017). Free, connected, and meaningful: Free will beliefs promote meaningfulness through belongingness. *Personality and Individual Differences, 107*, 54–65. https://doi.org/10.1016/j.paid.2016.11.006

Myers, D. G., & Diener, E. (1995). Who is happy? *Psychological Science, 6*, 10–19. https://doi.org/10.1111/j.1467-9280.1995.tb00298.x

Naeye, R. (2019, April 25). Cosmic conundrum: Just how fast is the universe expanding? *Astronomy.* https://www2.astronomy.com/magazine/news/2019/04/cosmic-conundrum-just-how-fast-is-the-universe-expanding

Nakahara, H., Doya, K., & Hikosaka, O. (2001). Parallel cortico-basal ganglia mechanisms for acquisition and execution of visuomotor sequences—a computational approach. *Journal of Cognition and Neuroscience, 13*(5), 626–647. https://doi.org/10.1162/089892901750363208

Nardou, R., Lewis, E. M., Rothhaas, R., Xu, R., Yang, A., Boyden, E., & Dölen, G. (2019). Oxytocin-dependent reopening of a social reward learning critical period with MDMA. *Nature, 569*, 116–120. https://doi.org/10.1038/s41586-019-1075-9

Oizumi, M., Albantakis, L., & Tononi, G. (2014). From the phenomenology to the mechanisms of consciousness: Integrated information theory 3.0. *PLoS Computational Biology, 10*(5). https://doi.org/10.1371/journal.pcbi.1003588

Olsson, T., Mohammed, A. H., Donaldson, L. F., Henriksson, B. G., & Seckl, J. R. (1994). Glucocorticoid receptor and NGFI-A gene expression are induced in the hippocampus after environmental enrichment in adult rats. *Molecular Brain Research*, *23*, 349–353.

Otto, A. (1968). Excitation of nonradiative surface plasma waves in silver by the method of frustrated total reflection. *Zeitschrift Für Physik A Hadrons and Nuclei*, *216*(4), 398–410. https://doi.org/10.1007/BF01391532

Özkan, M., Tse, P. U., & Cavanagh, P. (2020). Pop-out for illusory rather than veridical trajectories with double-drift stimuli. *Attention, Perception & Psychophysics*, *82*(6), 3065–3071. https://doi.org/10.3758/s13414-020-02035-w

Panitchayangkoon, G., Hayes, D., Franstead, K. A., Caram, J. R., Harel, E., Wen, J., Blankenship, R. E., & Engel, G. S. (2010). Long-lived quantum coherence in photosynthetic complexes at physiological temperature. *Proceedings of the National Academy of Sciences of the United States of America*, *107*, 12766–12770.

Panitchayangkoon, G., Voronine, D. V., Abramavicius, D, Caram, J. R., Lewis, N. H. C., Mukamel, S., & Engel, G, S. (2011). Direct evidence of quantum transport in photosynthetic light-harvesting complexes. *Proceedings of the National Academy of Sciences of the United States of America*, *108*, 20908–20912.

Papineau, D. (2009). The causal closure of the physical and naturalism. In A. Beckermann, B. P. McLaughlin, & S. Walter (Eds.), *The Oxford handbook of philosophy of mind* (pp. 53–65). Oxford University Press.

Parker, I. (2003). *Biophotonics, Vol. 360, Part 1*. Academic Press.

Parkinson, D. Y., Lee, H., & Fleming, G. R. (2007). Measuring electronic coupling in the reaction center of purple photosynthetic bacteria by two-color, three-pulse photon echo peak shift spectroscopy. *Journal of Chemical Physics B*, *111*, 7449–7456.

Parvizi, J., Rangarajan, V., Shirer, W. R., Desai, N., & Greicius, M. D. (2013). The will to persevere induced by electrical stimulation of the human cingulate gyrus. *Neuron*, *80*(6), 1359–1367. https://doi.org/10.1016/j.neuron.2013

Pearl, J. (2000). *Causality*. Cambridge University Press.

Pelliccia, F., Kaski, J. C., Crea, F., & Camici, P. G. (2017). Pathophysiology of Takotsubo syndrome. *Circulation*, *135*(24), 2426–2441. https://doi.org/10.1161/circulationaha.116.027121

Penn, A. A., Riquelme, P. A., Feller, M. B., & Shatz, C. J. (1998). Competition in retinogeniculate patterning driven by spontaneous activity. *Science*, *279*, 2108–2112.

Pereboom, D. (2001). *Living without free will*. Cambridge University Press.

Pereboom, D. (2014). *Free will, agency, and meaning in life*. Oxford University Press.

Perogamvros, L., & S. Schwartz. (2012). The roles of the reward system in sleep and dreaming. *Neuroscience & Biobehavioral Review*, *36*, 1934–1951.

Peterson, C. (1999). Personal control and well-being. In D. Kahnemann, E. Diener, & N. Schwarz (Eds.), *Well-Being* (pp. 288–301). Russell Sage Foundation.

Peterson, C., & Seligman, M. E. (1984). Causal explanations as a risk factor for depression: Theory and evidence. *Psychological Review*, *91*(3), 347–374. https://doi.org/10.1037/0033-295X.91.3.347

Phillips, C., Baktir, M. A., Srivatsan, M., & Salehi, A. (2014). Neuroprotective effects of physical activity on the brain: A closer look at trophic factor signaling. *Frontiers in Cellular Neuroscience*, *8*, 170. https://doi.org/10.3389/fncel.2014.00170

Pollnau, M. (2018). Phase aspect in photon emission and absorption. *Optica*, *5*(4), 465. https://doi.org/10.1364/OPTICA.5.000465

Pollnau, M. (2019). Are absorption and spontaneous or stimulated emission inverse processes? The answer is subtle! *Applied Physics B*, *125*(2), 25.https://doi.org/10.1007/s00340-019-7133-z

Powers, W. T. (1973a). Feedback: Beyond behaviorism. *Science*, *179*, 351–356.

Powers, W. T. (1973b). *Behavior: Control of perception*. Benchmark Publications.

Powers, W. T. (1978). Quantitative analysis of purposive systems: Some spadework at the foundations of scientific psychology. *Psychological Review, 85*(5), 417–435. https://doi.org/10.1037/0033-295X.85.5.417

Rahnev, D. (2019). The Bayesian brain: What is it and do humans have it? *Behavioral and Brain Sciences, 42*, e238. https://doi.org/10.1017/S0140525X19001377

Rauch, D., Handsteiner, J., Hochrainer, A., Gallicchio, J., Friedman, A. S., Leung, C., Liu, B., Bulla, L., Ecker, S., Steinlechner, F., Ursin, R., Hu, B., Leon, D., Benn, C., Ghedina, A., Cecconi, M., Guth, A. H., Kaiser, D. I., Scheidl, T., & Zeilinger, A. (2018). Cosmic Bell test using random measurement settings from high-redshift quasars. *Physical Review Letters, 121*(8), 080403. https://doi.org/10.1103/physrevlett.121.080403

Reavis, E. A., Frank, S. M., Greenlee, M. W., & Tse, P. U. (2016). Neural correlates of context-dependent feature conjunction learning in visual search tasks. *Human Brain Mapping, 37*(6), 2319–2330. https://doi.org/10.1002/hbm.23176

Reavis, E. A., Frank, S. M., & Tse, P. U. (2015). Caudate nucleus reactivity predicts perceptual learning rate for visual feature conjunctions. *Neuroimage, 110*, 171–181. https://doi.org/10.1016/j.neuroimage.2015.01.051

Reavis, E. A., Frank, S. M., & Tse, P. U. (2018). Learning efficient visual search for stimuli containing diagnostic spatial configurations and color–shape conjunctions. *Attention, Perception, and Psychophysics, 80*(5), 1110–1126. https://doi.org/10.3758/s13414-018-1516-9

Rescorla, R. A., & Wagner, A. R. (1972). *A theory of Pavlovian conditioning: Variations in the effectiveness of reinforcement and nonreinforcement*. Appleton-Century-Crofts.

Richards, G. H., Wilk, K. E., Curmi, P. M. G., Quiney, H. M., & Davis, J. A. (2012). Coherent vibronic coupling in light-harvesting complexes from photosynthetic marine algae. *Journal of Physical Chemistry Letters, 3*, 272–277.

Richards, L. J., Kilpatrick, T. J., & Bartlett, P. F. (1992). De novo generation of neuronal cells from the adult mouse brain. *Proceedings of the National Academy of Sciences of the United States of America, 89*(18), 8591–8595. https://doi.org/10.1073/pnas.89.18.8591

Richter, C. P. (1957). On the phenomenon of sudden death in animals and man. *Psychosomatic Medicine, 19*(3), 191–198. https://doi.org/10.1097/00006842-195705000-00004

Rigoni, D., Kühn, S., Gaudino, G., Sartori, G., & Brass, M. (2012). Reducing self-control by weakening belief in free will. *Consciousness and Cognition, 21*(3), 1482–1490.

Rogers, R. D., Owen, A. M., Middleton, H. C., Williams, E. J., Pickard, J. D., Sahakian, B. J., & Robbins, T. W. (1999). Choosing between small, likely rewards and large, unlikely rewards activates inferior and orbital prefrontal cortex. *Journal of Neuroscience, 19*(20), 9029–9038. https://doi.org/10.1523/jneurosci.19-20-09029.1999

Roli, A., Villani, M., Filisetti, A., & Serra, R. (2018). Dynamical criticality: Overview and open questions. *Journal of Systems Science and Complexity, 31*, 647–663. https://doi.org/10.1007/s11424-017-6117-5

Romero, E., Augulis, R., Novoderezhkin, V. I., Ferretti, M., Thieme, J., Zigmantas, D., & van Grondelle, R. (2014). Quantum coherence in photosynthesis for efficient solar-energy conversion. *Nature Physics, 10*, 676–682.

Ross, C. E., & Mirowsky, J. (2013). The sense of personal control: Social structural causes and emotional consequences. In C. S. Aneshensel, J. C. Phelan, & A. Bierman (Eds.), *Handbook of the sociology of mental health* (pp. 379–402). Springer Science + Business Media. https://doi.org/10.1007/978-94-007-4276-5_19

Rothman, T. (2022). The forgotten mystery of inertia. *American Scientist, 105*(6), 344. https://www.americanscientist.org/article/the-forgotten-mystery-of-inertia

Ryu, I. S., Dong, H., & Fleming, G. R. (2014). Role of electronic-vibrational mixing in enhancing vibrational coherences in the ground electronic states of photosynthetic bacterial reaction center. *Journal of Chemical Physics B, 118*, 1381–1388.

Sakai, J. (2020). Core concept: How synaptic pruning shapes neural wiring during development and, possibly, in disease. *Proceedings of the National Academy of Sciences of the United States of America*, *117*(28), 16096–16099. doi.org/10.1073/pnas.2010281117

Schaffer, J. (2015). What not to multiply without necessity. *Australasian Journal of Philosophy*, *93*(4), 644–664.

Schilman, E. A., Uylings, H. B., Galis-de Graaf, Y., Joel, D., & Groenewegen, H. J. (2008). The orbital cortex in rats topographically projects to central parts of the caudate–putamen complex. *Neuroscience Letters*, *432*(1), 40–45. https://doi.org/10.1016/j.neulet.2007.12.024

Schlegel, A. A., Rudelson, J. J., & Tse, P. U. (2012). White matter structure changes as adults learn a second language. *Journal of Cognitive Neuroscience*, *24*(8), 1664–1670.

Schlegel, A., Alexander, P., Sinnott-Armstrong, W., Roskies, A., Tse, P. U., & Wheatley, T. (2013a). Barking up the wrong free: Readiness potentials reflect processes independent of conscious will. *Experimental Brain Research*, *229*(3), 329–335. https://doi.org/10.1007/s00221-013-3479-3

Schlegel, A., Kohler, P. J., Fogelson, S. V., Alexander, P., Konuthula, D., & Tse, P. U. (2013b). Network structure and dynamics of the mental workspace. *Proceedings of the National Academy of Sciences of the United States of America*, *110*(40), 16277–16282. https://doi.org/10.1073/pnas.1311149110

Schlegel, A., Alexander, P., Sinnott-Armstrong, W., Roskies, A., Tse, P. U., & Wheatley, T. (2015). Hypnotizing Libet: Readiness potentials with non-conscious volition. *Consciousness and Cognition*, *33C*, 196–203. doi: 10.1016/j.concog.2015.01.002

Schlegel, A., Konuthula, D., Alexander, P., Blackwood, E., & Tse, P. U. (2016). Fundamentally distributed information processing integrates the motor network into the mental workspace during mental rotation. *Journal of Cognitive Neuroscience*, *28*(8), 1139–1151. https://doi.org/10.1162/jocn_a_00965

Schnedermann, C., Yang, X., Liebel, M., Spillane, K. M., Lugtenburg, J., Fernández, I., Valentini, A., Schapiro, I., Olivucci, M., Kukura, P., & Mathies, R. A. (2018). Evidence for a vibrational phase-dependent isotope effect on the photochemistry of vision. *Nature Chemistry*, *10*, 449–455. https://doi.org/10.1038/s41557-018-0014-y

Schopenhauer, A. (1969). *The world as will and representation*. Courier Dover Publications. (First edition 1819.)

Schorr, L., Burger, A., Hochner, H., Calderon, R., Manor, O., Friedlander, Y., Lawrence, G. M., & Paltiel, O. (2016). Mortality, cancer incidence, and survival in parents after bereavement. *Annals of Epidemiology*, *26*(2), 115–121. https://doi.org/10.1016/j.annepidem.2015.12.008

Schoups, A., Vogels, R., Qian, N., & Orban, G. (2001). Practising orientation identification improves orientation coding in V1 neurons. *Nature*, *412*, 549–553.

Schultz, W., Dayan, P., & Montague, P. R. (1997). A neural substrate of prediction and reward. *Science*, *275*(5306), 1593–1599. https://doi.org/10.1126/science.275.5306.1593

Schurger, A., Sitt, J. D., & Dehaene, S. (2012). An accumulator model for spontaneous neural activity prior to self-initiated movement. *Proceedings of the National Academy of Sciences of the United States of America*, *109*(42), E2904–E2913. https://doi.org/10.1073/pnas.1210467109

Schwartz, S., Maquet, P., & Frith, C. (2002). Neural correlates of perceptual learning: A functional MRI study of visual texture discrimination. *Proceedings of the National Academy of Sciences of the United States of America*, *99*, 17137–17142.

Searle, J. R. (1990). Is the brain a digital computer? *Proceedings and Addresses of the American Philosophical Association*, *64*(3), 21–37.

Sejnowski, T. J. (2010). Learning optimal strategies in complex environments. *Proceedings of the National Academy of Sciences of the United States of America*, *107*(47), 20151–20152. https://doi.org/10.1073/pnas.1014954107

Sejnowski, T. J., Poizner, H., Lynch, G., Gepshtein, S., & Greenspan, R. J. (2014). Prospective optimization. *Proceedings of the IEEE*, *102*(5). https://doi.org/10.1109/JPROC.2014.2314297

Seligman, M. E., & Maier, S. F. (1967). Failure to escape traumatic shock. *Journal of Experimental Psychology*, *74*(1), 1–9. https://doi.org/10.1037/h0024514

Seligman, M. E., Maier, S. F., & Geer, J. H. (1968). Alleviation of learned helplessness in the dog. *Journal of Abnormal Psychology*, *73*(3), 256–262. https://doi.org/10.1037/h0025831

Shibata, K., Chang, L. H., Kim, D., Náñez, J. E., Kamitani, Y., Watanabe, T., & Sasaki, Y. (2012). Decoding reveals plasticity in V3A as a result of motion perceptual learning. *PLoS ONE*, *7*, e44003.

Sidortsov, M., Morgenstern, Y., & Be'er, A. (2017). Role of tumbling in bacterial swarming. *Physical Review E*, *96*, 022407.

Siegel, E. (2018, March 2). If the universe Is 13.8 billion years old, how can we see 46 billion light years away? *Starts with a Bang!* https://medium.com/starts-with-a-bang/if-the-universe-is-13-8-billion-years-old-how-can-we-see-46-billion-light-years-away-db45212a1cd3

Siegel, E. (2021, October 13). Surprise: The Big Bang isn't the beginning of the universe anymore. *Big Think*.https://bigthink.com/starts-with-a-bang/big-bang-beginning-universe/

Simons, D. J., & Chabris, C. F. (1999). Gorillas in our midst: Sustained inattentional blindness for dynamic events. *Perception*, *28*(9), 1059–1074. https://doi.org/10.1068/p281059

Simons, D. J., & Levin, D. T. (1997). Change blindness. *Trends in Cognitive Sciences*, *1*(7), 261–267. https://doi.org/10.1016/S1364-6613(97)01080-2

Singer, P. (1981). *The expanding circle: Ethics and sociobiology*. Clarendon Press.

Smith, K. S., & Graybiel, A. M. (2016). Habit formation. *Dialogues in Clinical Neuroscience*, *18*(1), 33–43. https://doi.org/10.31887/DCNS.2016.18.1/ksmith

Soon, C., Brass, M., Heinze, H-J., & Haynes, J-D (2008). Unconscious determinants of free decisions in the human brain. *Nature Neuroscience*, *11*, 543–545. https://doi.org/10.1038/nn.2112

Spalding, K. L., Bergmann, O., Alkass, K., Bernard, S., Salehpour, M., Huttner, H. B., Boström, E., Westerlund, I., Vial, C., Buchholz, B. A., Possnert, G., Mash, D. C., Druid, H., & Frisén, J. (2013). Dynamics of hippocampal neurogenesis in adult humans. *Cell*, *153*(6), 1219–1227. https://doi.org/10.1016/j.cell.2013.05.002

Spitzer, N. C. (2006). Electrical activity in early neuronal development. *Nature*, *444*, 707–12.

Stephenson-Jones, M., Ericsson, M. J., Robertson, B., & Grillner, S. (2012). Evolution of the basal ganglia: Dual-output pathways conserved throughout vertebrate phylogeny. *Journal of Computational Neurology*, *520*, 2957–2973. https://doi.org/10.1002/cne.23087

Stewart, C. V., & Plenz, D. (2006). Inverted-U profile of dopamine–NMDA-mediated spontaneous avalanche recurrence in superficial layers of rat prefrontal cortex. *Journal of Neuroscience*, *26* (31), 8148–8159. https://doi.org/10.1523/jneurosci.0723-06.2006

Stewart, C. V., & Plenz, D. (2008). Homeostasis of neuronal avalanches during postnatal cortex development in vitro. *Journal of Neuroscience Methods*, *169*, 405–416. https://doi.org/10.1016/j.jneumeth.2007.10.021

Stiles, J. R., & Bartol, T. M. Jr. (2001). Monte Carlo methods for simulating realistic synaptic microphysiology. In E. de Schutter (Ed.), *Computational neuroscience: Realistic modeling for experimentalists* (pp. 87–127). CRC Press.

Stiles, J. R., van Helden, D., Bartol, T. M. Jr., Salpeter, E. E., & Salpeter, M. M. (1996). Miniature endplate current rise times less than 100 microseconds from improved dual recordings can be modeled with passive acetylcholine diffusion from a synaptic vesicle. *Proceedings of the National Academy of Sciences of the United States of America*, *93*, 5747–5752.

Stillman, T. F., Baumeister, R. F., Vohs, K. D., Lambert, N. M., Fincham, F. D., & Brewer, L. E. (2010). Personal philosophy and personnel achievement: Belief in free will predicts better job performance. *Social Psychological and Personality Science*, *1*, 43–50. https://doi.org/10.1177/1948550609351600

Strawson, G. (1994). The impossibility of moral responsibility. *Philosophical Studies: An International Journal for Philosophy in the Analytic Tradition*, *75*(1–2), 5–24. http://www.jstor.org/stable/4320507

Sun, L. W., Hartstein, K. C., Frank, S. M., Hassan, W., & Tse, P. U. (2017). Back from the future: Volitional postdiction of perceived apparent motion direction. *Vision Research*, *140*, 133–139. https://doi.org/10.1016/j.visres.2017.09.001

Sutton, R. S., & Barto, A. G. (1981). Toward a modern theory of adaptive networks: Expectation and prediction. *Psychological Review*, *88*, 135–170.

Suzuki, M., & Larkum, M. E. (2020). General anesthesia decouples cortical pyramidal neurons. *Cell*, *180*(4), 666–676.e13. https://doi.org/10.1016/j.cell.2020.01.024

Szuhany, K. L., Bugatti, M., & Otto, M. W. (2015). A meta-analytic review of the effects of exercise on brain-derived neurotrophic factor. *Journal of Psychiatric Research*, *60*, 56–64. https://doi.org/10.1016/j.jpsychires.2014.10.003

Tagliazucchi, E., & Chialvo, D. R. (2013). Brain complexity born out of criticality. In J. Marro, P. L. Garrido, & J. J. Torres (Eds.), *Proceedings of the 12th Granada Seminar—Physics, computation, and the mind: Advances and challenges at interfaces*. American Institute of Physics.

Teel, K.S., Verdeli, H., Wickramaratne, P., Warner, V., Vousoura, E., Haroz, E.E., Talati, A. (2016). Impact of a father figure's presence in the household on children's psychiatric diagnoses and functioning in families at high risk for depression. *Journal of Child and Family Studies*, *25*(2), 588–597. https://doi.org/10.1007/s10826-015-0239-y

Thyrhaug, E., Tempelaar, R., Alcocer, M. J. P., Žídek, K., Bína, D., Knoester, J., Jansen, T. L. C., & Zigmantas, D. (2018). Identification and characterization of diverse coherences in the Fenna–Matthews–Olson complex. *Nature Chemistry*, *10*, 780–786. https://doi.org/10.1038/s41557-018-0060-5

Tononi, G. (2004). An information integration theory of consciousness. *BMC Neuroscience*, *5*(1), 42. https://doi.org/10.1186/1471-2202-5-42

Tononi, G. (2008). Consciousness as integrated information: A provisional manifesto. *The Biological Bulletin*, *215*(3), 216–242.

Tononi, G., Boly, M., Massimini, M., & Koch, C. (2016). Integrated information theory: From consciousness to its physical substrate. *Nature Reviews Neuroscience*, *17*(7), 450–461. https://doi.org/10.1038/nrn.2016.44

Tse, P. U. (2013). *The neural basis of free will*. MIT Press.

Tse, P. U., Martinez-Conde, S., Schlegel, A., & Macknik, S. (2005). Visibility and visual masking of simple targets are confined to areas in the occipital cortex beyond human V1/V2. *Proceedings of the National Academy of Sciences of the United States of America*, *102*(47), 17178–17183.

Tse, P. U., Reavis, E. A., Kohler, P. J., Caplovitz, G. P., & Wheatley, T. (2013). How attention can alter appearances. In L. Albertazzi (Ed.), *Handbook of experimental phenomenology: Visual perception of shape, space and appearance* (pp. 291–316). Wiley.

Turkheimer, E. (2011). Genetics and human agency: Comment on Dar-Nimrod and Heine (2011). *Psychological Bulletin*, *137*(5), 825–828. https://psycnet.apa.org/doiLanding?doi=10.1037%2Fa0024306

Turkheimer, E., & Waldron, M. (2000). Nonshared environment: A theoretical, methodological, and quantitative review. *Psychological Bulletin*, *126*, 78–108.

Turner, D. B., Wilk, K. E., Curmi, P. M. G., & Scholes, G. D. (2011). Comparison of electronic and vibrational coherence measured by two-dimensional electronic spectroscopy. *Journal of Physical Chemistry Letters*, *2*, 1904–1911.

Turner, D. B., Dinshaw, R., Lee, K-K., Belsley, M. S., Wilk, K. E., Curmi, P. M. G., & Scholes, G. D. (2012). Quantitative investigations of quantum coherence for a light-harvesting protein at conditions simulating photosynthesis. *Physical Chemistry Chemical Physics*, *14*, 4857–4874.

van der Lans, A. A., Hoeks, J., Brans, B., Vijgen, G. H., Visser, M. G., Vosselman, M. J., Hansen, J., Jörgensen, J. A., Wu, J., Mottaghy, F. M., Schrauwen, P., & van Marken Lichtenbelt, W. D. (2013). Cold acclimation recruits human brown fat and increases nonshivering thermogenesis. *Journal of Clinical Investigation*, *123*(8), 3395–403. https://doi.org/10.1172/JCI68993

van Inwagen, P. (1983). *An essay on free will.* Oxford University Press.
Van Petten, C., Coulson S., Rubin S., Plante E., & Parks M. (1999). Time course of word identification and semantic integration in spoken language. *Journal of Experiential Psychology: Learning, Memory, and Cognition, 25,* 394–417.
Velmans, M. (1991). Is human information processing conscious? *Behavioral and Brain Sciences, 14,* 651–669.
Velmans, M. (2000). *Understanding consciousness.* Routledge.
Vidali, S., Aminzadeh, S., Lambert, B., Rutherford, T., Sperl, W., Kofler, B., & Feichtinger, R. G. (2015). Mitochondria: The ketogenic diet—A metabolism-based therapy. *International Journal of Biochemistry & Cell Biology, 63,* 55–59. https://doi.org/10.1016/j.biocel.2015.01.022
Vohs, K. D., & Baumeister, R. F. (2009). Addiction and free will. *Addiction Research and Theory, 17*(3), 231–235. https://doi.org/10.1080/16066350802567103
Vohs, K. D., & Schooler, J. W. (2008) The value of believing in free will. *Psychological Science, 19*(1), 49–54.
Volek, J. S., Sharman, M. J., Love, D. M., Avery, N. G., Gómez, A. L., Scheett, T. P., Kraemer, W. J. (2002). Body composition and hormonal responses to a carbohydrate-restricted diet. *Metabolism, 51*(7), 864–870. https://doi.org/10.1053/meta.2002.32037
Voss, U., Holzmann, R., Hobson, A., Paulus, W., Koppehele-Gossel, J., Klimke, A., & Nitsche, M. A. (2014). Induction of self-awareness in dreams through frontal low current stimulation of gamma activity. *Nature Neuroscience, 17*(6), 810–812. https://doi.org/10.1038/nn.3719
Wang, L., Allodi, M. A., & Engel, G. S. (2019). Quantum coherences reveal excited-state dynamics in biophysical systems. *Nature Reviews Chemistry, 3,* 477–490. https://doi.org/10.1038/s41570-019-0109-z
Wang, L., Mascher, H., Psilander, N., Blomstrand, E., & Sahlin, K. (2011). Resistance exercise enhances the molecular signaling of mitochondrial biogenesis induced by endurance exercise in human skeletal muscle. *Journal of Applied Physiology, 111*(5), 1335–1344. https://doi.org/10.1152/japplphysiol.00086.2011
Wegner, D. M. (2002). *The illusion of conscious will.* MIT Press.
Wegner, D. M., & Wheatley, T. (1999). Apparent mental causation: Sources of the experience of will. *American Psychologist, 54*(7), 480–492. https://doi.org/10.1037/0003-066X.54.7.480
Welch, C. (2017). Where the world's only grass-eating monkeys thrive. *National Geographic.* https://www.nationalgeographic.com/magazine/2017/04/gelada-monkeys-grass-eating-guassa-ethiopia-bleeding-heart/
Westenhoff, S., Palecek, D., Edlund, P., Smith, P., & Zigmantas, D. (2012). Coherent picosecond exciton dynamics in a photosynthetic reaction center. *Journal of the American Chemical Society, 134,* 16484–16487.
Wheeler, J. A. (1955). Geons. *Physical Review, 97*(2), 511–536. https://doi.org/10.1103/PhysRev.97.511
Wong, C. Y., Alvey, R. M., Turner, D. B., Wilk, K. E., Bryant, D. A., Curmi, P. M. G., Silbey, R. J., & Scholes, D. G. (2012). Electronic coherence lineshapes reveal hidden excitonic correlations in photosynthetic light harvesting. *Nature Chemistry, 4,* 396–404.
Wood, C. (2021, November 10). Laws of logic lead to new restrictions on the Big Bang. *Quanta.* https://www.quantamagazine.org/cosmologists-close-in-on-logical-laws-for-the-big-bang-20211110/
Wood, C. (2022a, August 9). How the physics of nothing underlies everything. https://www.quantamagazine.org/how-the-physics-of-nothing-underlies-everything-20220809/
Wood, C. (2022b, September 26). Physicists rewrite a quantum rule that clashes with our universe. *Quanta.* https://www.quantamagazine.org/physicists-rewrite-a-quantum-rule-that-clashes-with-our-universe-20220926/?mc_cid=fa30821f35

Woodward, J. (2003). *Making things happen: A theory of causal explanation*. Oxford University Press.

Xu, J., Jarocha, L. E., Zollitsch, T., Konowalczyk, M., Henbest, K. B., Richert, S., Golesworthy, M. J., Schmidt, J., Déjean, V., Sowood, D. J. C., Bassetto, M., Luo, J., Walton, J. R., Fleming, J., Wei, Y., Pitcher, T. L., Moise, G., Herrmann, M., Yin, H., … Hore, P. J. (2021). Magnetic sensitivity of cryptochrome 4 from a migratory songbird. *Nature*, *594*, 535–540. https://doi.org/10.1038/s41586-021-03618-9

Yeo, B. T., Krienen, F. M., Sepulcre, J., Sabuncu, M. R., Lashkari, D., Hollinshead, M., Roffman, J. L., Smoller, J. W., Zöllei, L., Polimeni, J. R., Fischl, B., Liu, H., & Buckner, R. L. (2011). The organization of the human cerebral cortex estimated by intrinsic functional connectivity. *Journal of Neurophysiology*, *106*(3), 1125–1165. https://doi.org/10.1152/jn.00338.2011

Yin, H. (2020). The crisis in neuroscience. In W. Mansell (Ed.), *The interdisciplinary handbook of perceptual control theory* (pp. 23–48). Academic Press.

Yin, H. H. (2013). Restoring purpose in behavior. In G. Baldassarre & M. Mirolli (Eds.), *Computational and robotic models of the hierarchical organization of behavior* (pp. 319–347). Springer. https://doi.org/10.1007/978-3-642-39875-9_14

Yin, H. H., & Knowlton, B. J. (2006). The role of the basal ganglia in habit formation. *Nature Reviews Neuroscience*, *7*(6), 464–476. https://doi.org/10.1038/nrn1919

Yin, J., Cao, Y., Yong, H. L., Ren, J. G., Liang, H., Liao, S. K., Zhou, F., Liu, C., Wu, Y. P., Pan, G. S., Li, L., Liu, N. L., Zhang, Q., Peng, C. Z., & Pan, J. W. (2013). Lower bound on the speed of nonlocal correlations without locality and measurement choice loopholes. *Physical Review Letters*, *110*(26), 260407. https://doi.org/10.1103/PhysRevLett.110.260407

Yotsumoto, Y., Watanabe, T., & Sasaki, Y. (2008). Different dynamics of performance and brain activation in the time course of perceptual learning. *Neuron*, *57*, 827–833.

Yu, H., McCuller, L., Tse, M., Kijbunchoo, N., Barsotti, L., Mavalvala, N., Betzwieser, J., Blair, C. D., Dwyer, S. E., Effler, A., Evans, M., Fernandez-Galiana, A., Fritschel, P., Frolov, V. V., Matichard, F., McClelland, D. E., McRae, T., Mullavey, A., Sigg, D., … Zweizig, J. (2020). Quantum correlations between light and the kilogram-mass mirrors of LIGO. *Nature*, *583*(7814), 43–47. https://doi.org/10.1038/s41586-020-2420-8

Zeidler, E. (2011). Vacuum polarization in quantum electrodynamics. *Quantum field theory: Vol. III. Gauge theory: A bridge between mathematicians and physicists*. Springer.

Zeki, S. (2008). The disunity of consciousness. *Progress in Brain Research*, *168*, 11–18. https://doi.org/10.1016/S0079-6123(07)68002-9

Zhu, L., Wang, Q., Zhang, L., Fang, Z., Zhao, F., Lu, Z., Gu, Z., Zhang, J., Wang, J., Zen, K., Xiang, Y., Wang, D., & Zhang, C. Y. (2010). Hypoxia induces PGC-1α expression and mitochondrial biogenesis in the myocardium of TOF patients. *Cell Research*, *20*(6), 676–687. https://doi.org/10.1038/cr.2010.46

Zoltowski, B. D., Chelliah, Y., Wickramaratne, A., Jarocha, L., Karki, N., Xu, W., Mouritsen, H., Hore, P. J., Hibbs, R. E., Green, C. B., & Takahashi, J. S. (2019). Chemical and structural analysis of a photoactive vertebrate cryptochrome from pigeon. *Proceedings of the National Academy of Sciences of the United States of America*, *116*(39), 19449–19457. https://doi.org/10.1073/pnas.1907875116

Zong, H., Ren, J. M., Young, L. H., Pypaert, M., Mu, J., Birnbaum, M. J., & Shulman, G. I. (2002). AMP kinase is required for mitochondrial biogenesis in skeletal muscle in response to chronic energy deprivation. *Proceedings of the National Academy of Sciences of the United States of America*, *99*(25), 15983–15987. https://doi.org/10.1073/pnas.252625599

Zweers, H., van Wegberg, A. M. J., Janssen, M. C. H., & Wortmann, S. B. (2021). Ketogenic diet for mitochondrial disease: A systematic review on efficacy and safety. *Orphanet Journal of Rare Diseases*, *16*, 295. https://doi.org/10.1186/s13023-021-01927-w

Name Index

For the benefit of digital users, indexed terms that span two pages (e.g., 52–53) may, on occasion, appear on only one of those pages.

Note: Figures are indicated by *f* following the page number

Aristotle 80, 293

Bacon, Francis 125–26
Balaguer, Mark 81–82, 135–36, 137–38
Bartlett, G. 62
Bateson, Gregory 46–47, 261
Beaty, R.E. 269–70, 270*f*
Bell, John Stewart 113
Berryhill, Marian xiii–xiv
Besio, Walt xiii
Block, Ned 93
Bohm, David 113
Bohr, Niels 74, 113
Brewer, J.A. 256–58, 257*f*, 259*f*
Brown, Robert 200
Buckner, R.L. 220*f*
Bush, George W. 228

Caplovitz, Gideon xiii
Caramazza, Alfonso xiii–xiv
Carhart-Harris, R.L. 258, 260*f*
Caruso, G.D. 135
Cavanagh, Patrick xiii–xiv
Chabris, Christopher 54
Chalmers, D.J. 65–66
Choe, Eunhye xiii
Christoff, K. 237*f*, 242–43, 243*f*, 245*f*
Clinton, Bill 146
Coyne, Jerry xiv
Craig, Sienna xi

Davidson, D. 90
de Montaigne, Michel 39
Dennett, D. 165
Descartes, Rene 53, 118–19
Desrochers, Theresa xiii–xiv
Diamond, M.C. 283, 284*f*, 284, 285
Dölen, Gül 198
Domini, Nate 271
Dresler, M. 240, 242*f*

Edelman, David xiii

Edelman, S. 62
Ehrlich, Clint xiv, 97
Eimer, Martin 156
Einstein, Albert 74, 113, 200, 201–2, 203, 204
Engel, Greg 209–10, 210*f*

Fekete, T. 62
Finn, Kelly xiii
Fischer, John Martin 85–86
Fogelson, Sergei xiii
Frank, Sebastian xiii
Frankfurt, Harry 79
Freeman, Walter 246–47
Frege, Gottlob 64
Freud, Sigmund 27

Gage, Phineas 217*f*, 217–19
Gazzaniga, Michael 166–67
Gleiser, Marcelo xi–xii, 19
Goodall, Jane 147–48, 148*f*
Greenlee, Mark xiii–xiv
Gronas, Misha xi
Guth, Alan 205

Haggard, Patrick 156
Hahn, Kurt 264
Harari, Yuval xiv
Harlow, John 218
Harris, Sam xiv
Hartstein, Kevin xiii
Haynes, John-Dylan 155–56
Hebb, Donald 280
Heisenberg, Werner 74, 114, 115, 204
Heller, Nate xiii
Helmholtz, Hermann von 165–66
Hitler, Adolf 23, 135, 229
Hogan, James 264
Holt, Lawrence 264
Horowitz, Vladimir 22–23
Hsieh, Po-Lang xiii
Hubble, Edwin 204

Name Index

Hubel, David 192
Hume, David 75, 76–77, 163

James, William 31, 276–77
Jolly, C.J. 271

Kane, Robert 80–82, 135–36, 137–38, 141
Kant, Immanuel 34, 37
Kim, Jaegwon xiii, 86–87, 89–90, 93, 97–98, 102–4, 125–26
King, Martin Luther Jnr. 23, 265–66
Kitaoka, Akiyoshi 34–35, 35f
Kohler, Peter xiii
Kurosawa, Akira 30–31

Laplace, Pierre 111
Larkum, Matthew 43, 234
Lazar, S.W. 256
Lee, Bruce 146–47
Levin, Daniel 55
Levy, Neil 92, 135, 136–37
Libet, Bemjamin 33, 151–54, 155, 158, 160–63
Lingau, Angelika xiii–xiv
Lisman, John 188
Liu, Sirui xiii
Lucretius 201

Maechler, Marvin xiii
Maier, S.F. 263
Mayberg, H.S. 226–27
Mazer, Jamie xiii–xiv
Mele, Al xiii, 87
Michelangelo 281
Mill, John Stuart 124–25, 156
Missal, Marcus xiii
Miyazaki, Hayao 25
Mograbi, Gabriel xiii, 48
Moniz, Antonio 246–47

Nadelhofer, Thomas 96
Nahmias, Eddy 96–97
Nakayama, Ken xiii–xiv
Napoleon 276
Newton, Isaac 11

Obama, Barack 146

Papineau, D. 90
Parvizi, Josef 247
Patanjali 293
Pearl, Judea 50–51, 122
Peirce, Charles Sanders 31
Pereboom, Derek 105–6, 135

Plante, Cody xiii–xiv
Plato 27, 37
Podolsky, Boris 203
Popper, Karl 56, 160, 291–92
Powers, William 4, 5f, 6, 8–9, 18

Raichle, Marcus 219–21
Ramón y Cajal, Santiago 176, 177f
Reavis, Eric xiii
Richter, Curt P. 261–62
Rosen, Nathan 203
Russell, Bertrand 64

Saleki, Sharif xiii
Schaffer, Jonathan 97
Schlengel, Alex xiii, 267–69, 269f, 282–83
Schöpenhauer, Arthur 225f
Schurger, A. 157, 158
Schwarzbach, Jens xiii–xiv
Searle, J.R. 64
Sejnowski, T.J. 291–92
Seligman, M.E. 263
Shannon, Claude 44–45, 46–48, 61, 67
Sheinberg, David xiii–xiv
Simons, Daniel 54–55
Singer, Peter 213–14
Sun, Linwei xiii

Tandey, Henry 229
Tononi, Giulio 61–63
Treisman, Anne 286–87
Tse, Helga xi
Tse, Kim Fung xi
Turkheimer, Eric 28

van Inwagen, Peter 85, 135
Voss, U. 240, 241f

Wang, L. 209–10
Washington, George 146
Watts, James 246–47
Wegner, Dan 33, 151, 163–64, 165
Wheeler, John 116
Wiener, Norbert 4, 6
Wiesel, Torsten 192
Wittgenstein, Ludwig 64, 133
Woodward, John 50–51, 122
Wright, Orville and Wilbur 147, 149
Wundt, Wilhelm 199

Yarbus, Alred 69
Yeo, B.T. 220f

Subject Index

For the benefit of digital users, indexed terms that span two pages (e.g., 52–53) may, on occasion, appear on only one of those pages.

Note: Figures are indicated by *f* following the page number

abstractions 103–4
acetylcholine 230–32
action, quantization of 114, 117
action potentials 175–76
 effect at axonal bouton 178
 generation of 180–82
 and neural code 195–97
actualia 90–92
addiction 144
adequacy 98–99
adult neurogenesis 284, 285
Adventure of Silver Blaze, The (Doyle) 45–46
advertising 25
agency 15–16, 23
 and meaning 49
 requirement for libertarian free will 77–78
 retrodictive nature of 164–67
 Wegner's "I Spy" study 163–64
AI systems 48
akinetic mutism 245–46
alien hand syndrome 275–76, 295
Allegory of the Cave, The, Plato 37
AMPA receptors 186–88
amplification 115, 200, 210–11
 Brownian motion 200–2
 in natural selection 211
 in NMDA receptors 202–3
amygdala 231*f*
anterior cingulate cortex (ACC) 72, 223–25, 236, 237*f*, 245–46, 253–54
 dorsal
  activity in meditators 256–58, 257*f*
  cybernetic circuitry 226
  error detection 225–26
 ventral 226–27
anterior inferotemporal lobe neurons 194
anterior insula (AI, frontal operculum) 236, 237*f*, 239, 253–54
 role in volitional imagination 268–69
anterior medial prefrontal cortex (amPFC) 173*f*–74, 237–38
apical–basal dendritic coupling 234
apical dendrites 177*f*

apparent causation, Wegner's theory 163–64
apparent motion 40–41, 54, 165
Aristotle 80, 293
arms races, evolutionary 169–70
attention 278–79
 binding of processing streams 215
 cultivation of 249–56
 dorsal attentional network 221–22, 223–25
 hierarchical structure 276–77
 role in chunking 286–87
 role in learning 280–81
 ventral attentional network 222
 visual perception 273–74
 see also volitional attention
attentional areas of the brain 72
attentional deficit hyperactivity disorder (ADHD) 235, 236
attentional tracking 277–78
 deliberation 278
attractor states 67
automatically constrained thought 243*f*, 244
automatization 22, 24, 55–56, 278–79, 286, 292–93
 of decision making 294–96
 habit formation 144
 mastery 22, 23–24, 295–96
 and qualia 59
 and responsibility 294–95
 risks of 295
autonomic nervous system (ANS) 248, 250, 251*f*
 effects of meditation 249
 interaction with emotions 255–56
 solar plexus (celiac plexus) 251–54, 252*f*
 see also parasympathetic nervous system; sympathetic nervous system
avalanches 202–3
axonal boutons 178
 neurotransmitter release 178
axons 175*f*, 175–76, 177*f*, 179*f*
axon terminals 175*f*

babies, learning 281
Bacon, Francis 125–26

318 Subject Index

bad luck 147, 148–49
Balaguer, Mark 81, 135–36, 137–38
basal dendrites 177f
basal ganglia 231f, 289–91, 290f, 292
   role in decision making 291–92
   role in habit formation 291
baseline neuron firing rate 185, 186f
Bateson, Gregory 46–47
Beaty, R.E 269–70, 270f
behavior, variability of 170–71
behaviorism 8
belief in free will, benefits of 265
beliefs 30–31, 63–64, 262
   about causal powers 164
   false 39
Bell, John Stewart 113
biases 155–56
binding problem, processing streams 215
blindness, motion-induced 41
Block, Ned 93
Bohm, David 113
Bohr, Niels 113
bottom-up causation 7, 108, 115, 200, 210–11
   Brownian motion 200–2
   in natural selection 211
   in NMDA receptors 202–3
   requirement for libertarian free will 108
bottom-up processing 8–9
bottom-up salience 244
bottom-up-top-down causation 228–29
brain-derived neural growth factor (BDNF) 284
brain function, indeterministic
   amplification 200–3
   quantum domain effects 203–11
brainstorming 243–44
breathing, volitional control 69
breathing patterns 250
Brewer, J.A. 256–58, 257f
Brodmann area 10 214–15, 239, 244
Brodmann area 25 226–27, 227f
"broken-heart" syndrome 264–65
Brown, Robert 200
Brownian motion 190–91, 200–2
Buddhism 258–59
bursting, neural (phasic firing) 42–43, 184–85, 186f
   NMDA receptors 186–88
   onset and offset transients 185–86, 186f
   role in long-term potentiation 280–81
   and volitional attention 232
Bush, George W. 228

Cajal, Ramón y 176, 177f
calcium, role in phasic firing 187
Cannon–Bard theory of emotions 255–56

Casimir effect 115
catastrophizing 39
caudate nucleus 288, 289, 290f
causal adequacy 98–99, 102
   temporal factors 99–100
causal chains 7, 63–64, 66, 93–94, 95, 234
   informational 78, 105
   non-informational 106
   physical 106–7
causal closure 86–87, 88, 89–90, 92
   qualified definitions of 90
causal instantaneity, fallacy of 140
causal sufficiency 84, 98–99
causation 44, 50–51
   apparent, Wegner's theory 163–64
   circular 9–10, 10f, 230
   covariation of causes and effects 156
   criterial see criterial (parameter) causation
   cybernetic 5f, 6
   energy transfer conception 111–12
   informational 128–34
   interventionist models 122
   linear paradigm 6, 7, 9, 11
   mental 52–53, 104–5
      exclusion argument against 86–107
   necessary conditions for 161–62
   open- versus closed-loop 9, 11
   parameters 12–13
   role of patterns 93–94
   sufficient causes 84, 98–99, 161–62
celiac plexus (solar plexus) 250, 251, 252f, 253f, 256
cerebellum 223–25, 224f, 231f
chandelier cells 188f
change, as argument for indeterminism 118–19
character formation 141–43, 145, 295
chemotaxis 169
children
   attentiveness 55
   habit formation 293
   importance of play 272–73
   learning 281
   parenting of 24–25, 26, 121
   synaptic density 281f, 281–82
chimpanzees, manual dexterity 271
cholinergic neurons 230–32
Christoff, K. 236, 237f, 242–43, 243f
chunking 59–60, 142–43, 277, 286–88
   habit formation 288–92
cingulate cortex 223–25
   see also anterior cingulate cortex
cingulate gyrus 231f
cingulo-opercular circuit (COCN) 223–25, 224f, 237f, 239, 246, 253–54
   dACC 247

Subject Index

circular causation 9–10, 10f, 230
closed-loop causation 9–10, 11, 128
   decision making 140
closure 91
coercion, freedom from 77
cognitive inferences of reality 38
cognitivism 8–9
cognitive behavioral therapy 263–64
coincidence detection 182–83, 192
collateral axons 177f
collective free will 265–66
commitments 26
compatibilism 75–76, 77
   consequence argument against 85–86
   and exclusion argument against mental causation 88
computer metaphor for the brain 61, 66–68, 199
confabulation 166–67
conflicting desires 217, 276–77
conjunction learning 287–88
connectomics 197–98
consciousness 6, 8, 10–11, 14, 53–54, 59–60, 158–60
   apical–basal dendritic coupling 234
   and attentional tracking 277–78
   automaticities 55–56
   causal relationship to motor acts 162
   changes 118–19
   and chunking 286
   cybernetic nature of 213
   definitions 54, 273
   dendritic integration theory 43
   imagination 56, 278
   imposition of parameters 13
   information integration theory 61–66
   intentionality 65
   micro-consciousnesses account 62–63
   neural correlates 188
   pan-psychism 60, 66
   prioritization 13–14
   qualia 57–59
   and quantum effects 206
   relationship to free will 273–80
   relationship with unconscious processing 13–14, 163
   retrodictive experience 164–67
   role of NMDA receptors 233
   role of ventral stream 215
   slowness of 164–65
   source of content 278–80
   as source of free will 278
   subdomains of 275–77
   as a virtual reality construction 274, 275
   visual perception 273–74
   volitional attention 54–56
   world model 56–57
consequence argument 85–86
constellations 44, 130
constitutive luck 134, 136, 142
   and criterial causation 145–46
constraints 12–13, 143–44
   freedom from 21, 26
   freedom within 21–23, 26
   genetic 100–1
control
   external 18
   individual nature of 18
control-system model of the brain 6, 10–11
control systems 4–6, 5f
   hierarchical structure 9–10
convergent evolution 100–1, 115
coordinate systems, processing streams 216
corollary discharge theory 165–66
corpus callosum 231f
correspondence theory of truth 31–32, 33–34
cortical architecture 214–16
cortical thickness 283–84
cortico–striatal–thalamocortical loop 290f, 290–91
cosmic inflation hypothesis 205
cosmological constant 204
counterfactual relationships 96–97
creativity 121–22
criteria, setting of 211–12
criterial (parameter) causation 2, 7, 78, 83–84, 96–98, 120–21
   biological causal sequences 100–1
   causal adequacy 98–99
   comparison with traditional interventionalist models 122–23
   counter to luck argument 137–49
   information loss 99–100, 103
   inputs and outputs 101
   relational nature of properties 102
   reparameterization 121–22, 123–25
   role in evolution 125
   role in scientific modeling 125–27
   and type 1 libertarian free will 82
   and type 2 libertarian free will 82–83
criticality 170
criticality domain 202–3
critical period, neural development 198
cryptochrome Cry4 207–8
cultivation 10
cybernetic causation 5f, 6, 127–28
cybernetic processes
   dorsal anterior cingulate cortex 226
   reinforcement learning 289

Subject Index

cybernetic searches 212–13

Davidson, D. 90
daydreaming 239–40, 243–44
decision making
    automatization 294–96
    role of basal ganglia 291–92
    temporal duration 140, 146
decisions
    criteria for 138–39
    morality 140–41
    self-forming 81–82, 138
    torn 81, 135–38, 141
decoding 42, 44–45, 66, 104
    and belief 63–64
    information as 128–34
    mental events as 106
    neural acts of 132
    and theories of information 63–64
default mode network 219–21, 220f, 221f, 236–37, 237f, 245f
    activation during dreaming 239–40
    decreased activity in meditators 258, 259f
    psilocybin effects 258, 260f
    role in volitional imagination 268–70
    subcircuits 237–38
    see also DN core subsystem; DN-medial temporal lobe circuit; DN subcomponent 3
delay conditioning 160
deliberately constrained thought 243f, 244
deliberation 16, 27, 267, 278, 286
    role of basal ganglia 291–92
delusions 39
de Montaigne, Michel 39
dendrites 175f, 177f, 179f
    apical–basal coupling 234
    neural computation 189
dendritic branching 284f
dendritic integration theory 43
dendritic operations, decoding 42–43, 44–45
dendritic spines 187–88
depolarization 180
depression 226–27
    hopelessness 263
    ruminations 235
Descartes, Rene 53
desert paths 171–72
desires 8, 13, 67, 121–22, 127–28, 144, 213–14
    conflicting 217
    first-order 217
    and meaning 47
    second-order 79–80, 217
determinism 1–2, 23, 73–75, 109
    consequence argument against 85–86
    energy transfer conception of causation 111–12
    and exclusion argument against mental causation 87–88
    interpretations of quantum mechanics 113
    Laplace's demon argument 111
    and nonlocality 204
    and the "now" 118
    positions on free will 75–76, 77
    stochastic 74, 114–15
deterministic dogmatism 117–18
deterministic theories 74
Diamond, M.C. 283–84, 284f, 285
diets 255
differences, meaningfulness of 45–47, 50
digitalization of mind 49
dissipative structures 227–28
distal free will 142
distal willing 17–18, 151–52
DN core subsystem 173f–74, 237–38, 243f, 245f
    role in volitional imagination 268–70
DN-medial temporal lobe circuit (DNmtl) 237f, 238, 243f, 245f
DN subcomponent 3 (DNsub3) 237f, 238
Dölen, Gül 198
dopaminergic neurons 289
dorsal anterior cingulate cortex (dACC) 225–26, 247–48
    activity in meditators 256–58, 257f
dorsal attentional network (DAN) 221–22, 223–25, 237f, 238–39, 244, 245f
    see also cingulo-opercular circuit; fronto-parietal circuit;
dorsal medial prefrontal cortex (dmPFC) 237f, 238
dorsal stream 215, 222–23, 227
dorsal striatum 289
dorsolateral cortico–striatal–thalamocortical loops 291
dorsolateral prefrontal cortex (dlPFC) 215, 227, 239, 268–69
    activity in meditators 257f, 258
double bouquet cells 188f
double-slit experiment 112, 117
    with large molecules 206–7
downward mental causation 96, 106–7
dreaming 239–40, 243–44
    areas of brain activity 240f
    lucid 240–41, 241f, 242f
dualism 1, 60

Ehrlich, Clint 97
Eimer, Martin 156
Einstein, Albert 113
    cosmological constant 204
Einstein–Podolsky–Rosen experiment 203
electroencephalography (EEG), Libet experiment 152–54

embodied cognition 272–73
emotions 8, 13, 213–14
    executive control circuits 222
    interaction with physiological
        responses 255–56
endogenous attention *see* volitional attention
energy 128
    phase relationships 131
energy transfer conception of causation 111–12
enhanced myelination 282–83
enrichment 285
    cortical response 283–84
entanglement *see* quantum domain entanglement
enteric nervous system 253–54, 254*f*
epicircuits 198
epiconnectivity 193
epistemology 112
equivalence classes 101, 103–4, 131
    informational 133–34
error detection 225–26
    social errors 226–27
error signals 8
    control theory 4–6, 5*f*
escape responses 169–70
event outcomes, consideration and biasing of
        probabilities of 109
event-related potentials (ERPs), Libet
        experiment 152–54
evolution
    of consciousness 160
        convergent 100–1, 115
    of free will 169–72
    of qualia hallucinations 57
    role of criterial causation 125
    of volitional attention 238–39
    of volitional imagination 270–71
excitation, neural 173–74
excitatory neurons 186–88
excitatory neurotransmitters 178
excitatory post-synaptic potentials
        (EPSPs) 180, 181*f*
exclusion argument against mental
        causation 86–88
    counter argument 88–107
executive systems 70, 106, 212–14, 219–22,
        220*f*, 275
    location in the brain 214
    self-governance 216–19
exercise 284
    habit formation 292
existence 36
exogenous attention 222
external control 18
extra-synaptic receptors 230–32
eye movements, corollary discharge theory 165–66

eyes, volitional and nonvolitional control 69

feature detection 194
Fenna–Matthews–Olson (FMO)
        bacteriochlorophyll complex 209, 210*f*
firing threshold 180–81, 181*f*, 182–83, 191–92
first-order desires 144, 217
first-order free will *see* type 1 libertarian free will
Fischer, John Martin 85–86
flies
    turning behavior 170
    variability of neural processing 170–71
fornix 290*f*
Frank, S.M. 287–88
Frankfurt, Harry 79
freedom
    and commitment 26
    from constraints 21, 26
    within constraints 21–23, 26
    and mastery 22–24
    and parenting 24–25, 26
    self-mastery 27–28, 29–30
freedom of action 78, 79, 80–81, 82
Freeman, Walter 246–47
free will
    belief in, benefits of 265
    collective 265–66
    and consciousness 278
    definition 71, 143
    distal 142
    first-order 260
    see also type 1 libertarian free will
    and learning 285
    necessary conditions for 84
    possible positions on 75–76
    relationship to consciousness 273–80
    second-order 27–29, 260, 292–96
    see also type 2 libertarian free will
    strong 77
    weak 77
    see also libertarian free will
"free-won't" 30
frontal eye fields (FEF) 72, 237*f*, 238
frontal lobes
    role in self-governance 217–19
    sources of information 222–23
frontal operculum (FO, anterior insula) 236, 237*f*,
        239, 253–54
    role in volitional imagination 268–69
fronto-parietal control network (FPCN) 223–25,
        224*f*, 237*f*, 239, 243*f*, 244, 245*f*
    role in habit formation 288–89
    role in lucid dreaming 241
    role in volitional imagination 268–70
frontopolar cortex 72

fulfillment 26, 142, 145–46
    pathways to 6–7, 11
fullerene, double-slit experiment 206–7
functional connectivity analysis 219
functional imaging studies 287–88
    of feature conjunction learning 287–88
    Haynes et al. experiment 155–56
    of meditation 256–58, 257*f*
    of mental and manual rotational responses 272
    psilocybin effects 258, 260*f*
    of shape manipulation 267–69, 268*f*, 269*f*
functionalism 209
future, open nature of 119–20

GABA 178, 181
Gage, Phineas 217*f*, 217–19
ganglion cells 175–76, 176*f*
gap junctions 188–89
garden paths 171–72
Gazzaniga, Michael 166–67
geladas 271–72, 272*f*
genetic code 100
genomes 100–1
given luck 147
global cortical architecture 214–16
global determinism 204
globus pallidus 290*f*
glutamate 178
glutamate receptors 186–88
goals 146–47, 246, 261, 265
"God of the gaps" argument 117–18
Goodall, Jane 147–48, 148*f*
graph, brain as 197
gray disks illusion 72, 73*f*
guilt 141, 226–27
Guth, Alan 205

habit formation 144, 288–92
    second-order free will 292–96
habits 170
Haggard, Patrick 156
Hahn, Kurt 264
hallucinations 37–38, 57, 158–59
    see also qualia
hands
    alien hand syndrome 275–76, 295
    evolution of manual dexterity 270–72
hard incompatibilism 75–76
Haynes, John-Dylan 155–56
health, benefits of hope 265
healthy diets 255
Hebb, Donald 280
Heisenberg uncertainty principle 110, 114, 115, 204
Helmholtz, Hugo von, corollary discharge theory 165–66

hierarchical structure 232–33, 275–77
    conscious adjustment of setpoints 13
    control systems 9–10
hippocampal formation (HF) 237*f*, 238
hippocampus 231*f*, 290*f*
    neurogenesis 285
Hitler, Adolf 229
Hogan, James 264
Holt, Lawrence 264
homeostasis 4, 127
Homo habilis 271
homunculus concept 70
hope 261
    health benefits of 265
    Richter's rat drowning experiments 261–62
    survival value of 263–64
hopelessness 263–65
Horowitz, Vladimir, attainment of mastery 22
Hubel, David 192
Hume, David 76–77, 163
humor, expression in logic 48–49
hyperpolarization 180, 181
hypnosis, readiness potential experiment 157–58
hypothalamus 231*f*

identity of indiscernibles principle, Leibniz 102
illusions 37–38, 39–41
    3 gray disks 72, 73*f*
imagination 14–15, 56, 147–48, 149, 158–59, 167
    as a conscious experience 278
    default mode network 219–21, 236–37
    evolution of 171–72, 270–71
    prediction 32
    role of basal ganglia 291–92
    volitional, neural basis 266–73
incompatibilism 15, 75–76, 77
    positions on free will 80–81
indeterminism 1–2, 7, 12, 15, 73–75
    brain function
        amplification 200–3
        quantum domain effects 203–11
    and exclusion argument against mental causation 88, 90
    experimental evidence 117–18
    inputs and outputs 101
    and libertarian free will 76
    microscopic-to-macroscopic amplification 115
    positions on free will 75–76, 80–81
    requirement for libertarian free will 108
inferior frontal gyrus (IFG) 237*f*, 238
inferior temporal gyrus (ITG) 237*f*, 239
information
    absence of 46
    causal power of 105, 107
    decoding 42, 63–64

difference from meaning 261
etymological roots 41
ontological conception 61
    see also information integration theory
as pattern decoding 128–34
as a process 44, 50
role of differences 45–47
informational causation 128–34
informational classes 131–32
informational criteria, realization by
    neurons 191–94
informational equivalence classes 133–34
information integration theory (IIT) 61–62
    phi values 62, 64–65
    problems with 62–66
information loss 99–100, 103
information theory 44–45, 61
in-groups 213–14
inhibition, neural 173–74
inhibitory interneurons 187–88, 188*f*
inhibitory neurotransmitters 178
inhibitory post-synaptic potentials (IPSPs) 181*f*
instincts 121–22
integration windows, EPSPs 180, 182–83
intentionality 65
interpreter, Gazzaniga's theory 166–67
interventionist models of causation 50–51, 122
intraparietal sulcus (IPS) 237*f*, 238
ionotropic receptors 179, 180
irony, expression in logic 48–49

James, William 276–77
James–Lange theory of emotions 255–56
Jolly, C.J. 271

Kane, Robert 80–82, 135–36, 138
Kant, Immanuel 37
Kim, Jaegwon, exclusion argument 86–88
    counter argument 88–107
King, Martin Luther Jr. 265–66
kundalini yoga 249, 256

Lamb shift 115
language learning
    critical period 281–82
    fractional anisotropy study 282–83, 283*f*
Laplace, Pierre, demon argument 111
large basket cells 188*f*
Larkum, Matthew 43, 234
Laser, the, Jonathan Schaffer 97
lateralized readiness potential (LRP)
    causal relationship to motor acts 156–57
    Libet experiment 154
    timing, relationship to conscious will to
        move 156
lateral temporal cortex (LTC) 237*f*, 238

Lazar, S.W. 256
learned helplessness 263
learning 170, 171
    babies and children 281–82
    feature conjunction 287–88
    fractional anisotropy study 282–83, 283*f*
    long-term potentiation 280–81
    and magnitude of free will 285
    reinforcement 289
Leibniz, Wilhelm 102
Levy, Neil 92, 136–37
libertarian free will 1, 76
    necessary conditions for 77–79, 95–96, 108
        bottom-up causation 108
        consideration and biasing of probabilities of
            event outcomes 109
        reality of indeterminism 108
        top-down causation 108
    types 1 and 2 76–84, 110
    see also free will; type 1 libertarian free will;
        type 2 libertarian free will
Libet experiment 151–54, 152*f*
    critique of conclusions 155–57
        claims about causation 160–63
        hypnotic induction experiment 157–58
light, nature of 36–37, 129
limbic system 289, 291
linear causality 6, 7, 9, 11
lobotomy 246–47
local realism 203–4
logic 254–55
    and truth 32–34
logical operations, and meaning 48–49
long-term potentiation (LTP) 280–81
love 29
    obsessive nature of 235–36
    role in brain health 285
Löwenmensch 267*f*, 267
lucid dreaming 240–41, 241*f*
    areas of brain activity 242*f*
luck 146
    bad 147, 148–49
    constitutive 134, 136, 142
    creation of 146–49
    fast and slow 146–47
    given 147
    present 134, 136–37, 146–47
luck argument against free will 134–37
    counter argument 137–49
luck pincer (Levy) 136–37, 140
Lucretius 201
lurking variables 50

macroscopic-to-microscopic (top-down)
    causation 7, 108–9, 227–30
    requirement for libertarian free will 108

magnesium ions, role in NMDA
    receptors 187, 202
magnetoreceptors 207–9
Maier, S.F. 263
manipulationist models of causation 50–51, 122
manual dexterity, evolution of 270–72
martial arts training 250, 256
mastery 22–24, 295–96
meaning 44, 46–47, 50, 261
    and agency 49
    and AI systems 48
    expression in logic 48–49
    and purpose 47–48
medial superior frontal cortex (msFC) 239
medial temporal lobe, DNmtl 237f, 238
meditation 249–50, 278–79
    fMRI studies 256–58
    habit formation 292–93
medulla 231f
Mele, Al 87
mental causation 52–53, 104–5
    downward 96
    exclusion argument against 86–88
        counter argument 88–107
mental models 38
metabotropic receptors 179
meta free will *see* type 2 libertarian free will
metaphors 182, 199
    Allegory of the Cave, The, Plato 37
    computer 48, 61, 66–67, 199
    driving a car 71–72, 245–46
    graph 197
    mouth reshaping 196–97
    movie viewing 279
    riders and horses 27
    train track 198
    winner-takes-all systems 228–29
micro-consciousnesses 62–63
microscopic-to-macroscopic (bottom-up)
        causation 7, 108, 115, 200, 210–11
    Brownian motion 200–2
    in natural selection 211
    in NMDA receptors 202–3
    requirement for libertarian free will 108
middle temporal motion complex (MT+) 237f,
        238, 288
migratory birds, magnetoreceptors 207–9
Mill, John Stuart 156
mind–body problems 51, 53
    mental causation 52–53
    neural code 52
    realization of mental events 51–52
mindfulness 256–60
    see also meditation
misconceptions 2, 7
mitochondrial biogenesis 255

modulatory neurotransmitters 230–32
Moghrabi, Gabriel 48
monisms 1, 60
    information-based 61–66
    pan-psychism 60, 62, 66, 213
    virtual reality 60–61
Moniz, Antonio 246–47
Moon, patterns on 130
morality 140–41
motion
    apparent 164–65
    illusion of 40
motion-induced blindness 41
motor strip 214–15
MT+ *see* middle temporal motion complex
multiple universes 205
muscarinic receptors 230–32
myelin sheath 175f, 176–78, 179f, 282f, 282
    enhanced myelination 282–83

Nahmias, Eddy 96–97
naturalism 1
natural selection 100–1, 211
necessary conditions for causation 84, 161–62
negative-feedback loops 4–6, 5f, 127–28
neural bursting (phasic firing) 42–43, 184–
        85, 186f
    NMDA receptors 186–88
    onset and offset transients 185–86, 186f
    role in long-term potentiation 280–81
    and volitional attention 232
neural circuits 173–74, 174f, 176, 197–98
neural code 43, 52, 94–95, 104–5, 107, 174,
        176, 212
    and action potentials 195–97
    criterial nature of 120
    onset and offset transients 185–86, 186f
    synaptic reweighting 195–200
neural plasticity 78–79
    critical period 198
neural processing
    excitation and inhibition 173–74
    musical metaphors 183–84
    speed of 172–73
neural synchrony 42–43, 183–84
neurogenesis 284, 285
neuron response
    reparameterization 123
    temporal coincidence 96, 99–100
neurons 174–78
    acts of decoding 132
    anatomy 175f, 177f, 179f
    baseline firing rate 185
    as coincidence and pattern detectors 182–83
    depolarization 180
    discrete criterial assessment 189–90

feature detection 194
firing 181–82
   firing threshold 180–81, 181f, 182–83, 191–92
   hyperpolarization 180, 181
   membrane potential, time course of 181f
   patterns of firing 184–85, 186f
   realization of informational criteria 191–94
   resting potential 180
neurotransmitters 178
   modulatory 230–32
   possible wave–particle effects 206–7
New Year's resolutions 145
nigral–striatal–dopaminergic loop 290–91
NMDA antagonists 188
NMDA receptors 186–88, 233
   amplification 202–3
   multi-slit interference 206–7
   roles 233
      in long-term potentiation 280
nodes of Ranvier 175f, 179f, 282f
noise, neural 170, 190–91, 205–6
nonlinear systems 227–28
nonlocality 113–14, 203–6
nonvolitional actions 69–70
nonvolitional thought 235–36
   interaction with volitional circuits 243f, 245f
      automatically constrained thought 244
      deliberately constrained thought 244
      in planning 244–46
      spontaneous thought 243–44
   neural circuits 236, 237f
      default mode network 236–37
      ventral attentional network 236
   see also dreaming; unconscious
"now," as argument for indeterminism 118
nucleus basalis of Meynert 230–32, 231f
nucleus of a neuron 175f, 179f

objective truth 31–34
obsessions 235–36
obsessive compulsive disorder (OCD) 235–36
oligodendrocytes 282f, 282
online lectures 19
onset and offset transients 185–86, 186f
ontology 112
open-loop causation 9, 11, 128
operant conditioning 289
operations 197
opportunism 146–48
Orion 130
Outward Bound 264
overdetermination 92, 102
overspecification 97, 98, 99, 102

pain 8
pan-psychism 60, 62, 66, 213

Papineau, D. 90
parahippocampal cortex (PHC) 237f, 238
parameter causation see criterial causation
parameters 12–13
parasympathetic nervous system 248, 250, 251f
   effect of meditation 249
   and the solar plexus 251, 252f
   vagus death 262
parenting 24–25, 26, 121
   habit formation 293
parsimony 97
passive rising argument, consciousness 278–80
past, closed nature of 119–20
Patanjali 293
paths to fulfillment 6–7, 11
pattern decoding 128–34
   see also decoding
pattern detectors 233
   neurons as 182–83
patterns 44, 103–4, 234
   constellations 44, 130
   global nature of 129
   on the Moon 130
   role in causation 93–94
perception 35f, 57, 275
   of light 36–37
   vision 39–40, 215, 222
   visual illusions 39–41
perception–action cycle 58, 65
perceptual consciousness 14
perceptual inferences of reality 37–38
perceptual processing, location in the brain 214
Pereboom, Derek 105–6
phase causation 66
phase relationships 131
phasic firing (neural bursting) 42–43, 184–85, 186f
   NMDA receptors 186–88
   onset and offset transients 185–86, 186f
   role in long-term potentiation 280–81
   and volitional attention 232
phi values, IIT 62, 64–65
photons, double-slit experiment 112, 117
photosynthesis, quantum domain effects 209–10, 210f
physical, the, nature of 128–29
physical exercise 284
   habit formation 292
physical health 254–55
physicalism 110–11
physiological responses, interaction with emotions 255–56
placebo effect 262
planning 174, 244–46
   cortical localization 214–15
   executive control circuits 221–22

Subject Index

plasticity 283–84, 285
Plato, *Allegory of the Cave, The* 37
play, importance of 272–73
pleasure 8
Podolsky, Einstein–Podolsky–Rosen experiment 203
pons 231*f*
Popper, Karl 56, 160
positive feedback 144
possibilia 90–92
posterior cingulate cortex (PCC) 173*f*–74, 237–38
posterior inferior parietal lobule (pIPL) 173*f*–74, 237–38
posterior parietal cortex 72, 268–69
posterior temporal lobes, role in volitional imagination 268–69
potential
 harnessing of 28–30, 145–46, 293–94
 low, implications for free will 146
Powers, William 9, 18
 control theory 4–6, 5*f*
pragmatism 31
precentral gyrus 214–15
precuneus 268–69
predictability, dangers of 169
prediction 32
prefrontal cortex 72, 153*f*
premotor area (PMA) 153*f*, 214–15
present luck 134, 136–37, 146–47
 and criterial causation 145–46
pre-supplementary motor area (preSMA) 237*f*, 239
primary motor cortex (M1) 153*f*
prioritization 13–14
probabilistic behavior 112–13, 170–71
processing streams 215–16
 binding problem 215
 coordinate systems 216
 visual 215
proximal willing 17–18, 151
 Libet experiment 151–54
psychedelic drugs 198
 psilocybin, fMRI studies 258, 260*f*
purpose 47–48, 126–27
putamen 289, 290*f*
putamen-centered cortico-striatal-thalamocortical loops 291
pyramidal cells 173–74, 174*f*, 177*f*, 187, 188*f*
 apical–basal dendritic coupling 234
 attentional modulation 232
 dendritic branching 284*f*

qualia 13–14, 57–59, 273, 274–75, 277, 278
quantization of action 114, 117
quantum contextuality 113
quantum domain entanglement 203–6
 avian magnetoreceptors 207–9
 and functionalism 209
 neurotransmitters 206–7
 in photosynthesis 209–10, 210*f*
 in the retina 207–8, 208*f*
quantum theory 74, 112–14
 and Kim's exclusion argument 90–91
 nature of reality 115–17

radical pair model, avian magnetoreceptors 207–8
Raichle, Marcus 219–21
randomness 67–68, 76–77, 94–96, 110, 205–6
 Brownian motion 200–2
 and criterial causation 120
rapid eye movement (REM) sleep 239–41
 areas of brain activity 240*f*
rats, Richter's drowning experiments 261–62
readiness potential (RP)
 associated brain areas 153*f*
 causal relationship to motor acts 156–57, 162
 hypnotic induction experiment 157–58
 Libet experiment 152–54, 152*f*
 Schurger et al. account 157
 timing, relationship to conscious will to move 156
reality 34, 36
 cognitive inferences of 38
 indeterministic nature of 117
 perception of 35, 35*f*
 perceptual inferences of 37–38
 quantum theory 115–17
 visual illusions 39–41
realization thesis, Kim's exclusion argument 87, 90
 indeterministic restatement 91
reason 36, 254–55
reasons 144
Reavis, E.A. 287–88
receptors 178, 179*f*
 AMPA and NMDA 186–88
 extra-synaptic 230–32
 ionotropic 179, 180
 metabotropic 179
 see also NMDA receptors
reductionism 126–27
 and pattern decoding 129
redundancy 100
reference 64
refractory period 181–82
reinforcement learning 289
relational causation 102
reparameterization 12–13, 84, 121–22, 123–25
 and informational causation 132
 role in neural causation 94–95

repeller states 67
respect 29
responsibility 81, 86, 294–95
　and criterial selection 139
　and luck argument 135, 136–37
resting potential 180
retina 175–76, 176f
　quantum domain effects 207–8, 208f
retinal 207, 208f
retrodictive experience 164–67
retrosplenial cortex (RSC) 237f, 238
reward circuits 72, 288, 289–91
reward signals 8
Richter, Curt P. 261–62
Rosen, Einstein–Podolsky–Rosen experiment 203
rostrolateral prefrontal cortex (rlPFC) 237f, 239, 244
rotational responses, fMRI study 272

salience, bottom-up 244
salience detection 223, 236, 238–39, 245f
scaffolding 24–25, 141, 293
Schaffer, Jonathan, the Laser 97
schizophrenia 235
Schlegel, A. 267–69, 272
Schöpenhauer, Arthur 225f
Schurger, A. 157
Schwann's cells 175f, 179f
science
　models of reality 104
　and truth 31, 32–33
second-order desires 144, 217
second-order free will see type 2 libertarian free will (meta free will)
Sejnowski, T.J. 291–92
self 30, 159–60
self-control, cultivation of 249–56
self-discipline 10, 13
self-forming decisions 81–82, 141–43, 145
　criterial account 138, 139
　habit formation 144
　New Year's resolutions 82–83
self-generated actions, recognition of 171
self-governance 216–19
　Phineas Gage 217–19
self-mastery 27–28, 29–30
self-referential thinking 258–59
self-scaffolding 141
self-transformation 29–30, 80, 84, 141–42, 144, 295
　neural basis 280–85
Seligman, M.E. 263
sensation 275
setpoints 9, 127, 212–13
　conscious alteration of 13
　control theory 4–6, 5f

Shannon, Claude 44–45, 66–68
shape manipulation, fMRI study 267–69, 268f, 269f
Singer, Peter 213–14
slow luck 146–49
social errors 226–27
sodium ion pumps 180
solar plexus (celiac plexus) 250, 251, 252f, 253f, 256
spatial phase 131
spiny stellate cells 187
split-brain patients, Gazzaniga's studies 166–67
spontaneous firing 202–3
spontaneous thought 243f, 243–44
stem cells, presence in the brain 285
stochastic determinism 74, 114–15
strong free will 77
　criteria for 77–79
　see also libertarian free will
Stroop task 225–26
subgenual anterior cingulate 226–27, 227f
subjective truth 30–31, 33–34
substantia nigra pars compacta 289
sufficient causes 84, 98–99, 161–62
superdeterminism 204
superior parietal lobe (SPL) 237f, 238
supervenience relationship, mental and physical events 51–52
　and Kim's exclusion argument 91
supplementary motor area (SMA) 153f, 153–54
sympathetic nervous system 248, 250, 251f
　and the solar plexus 251, 252f
　volitional control of 249
synapses 178
　anatomy 179f
　neurotransmitter release 178
　receptors 178
synaptic cleft 178, 179f, 194
　Brownian motion in 201
　functions 188–89
　　discretization of criterial assessment 189–90
　　as source of variability 190–91
　width of 190–91
synaptic density, changes with age 281f, 281–82
synaptic reweighting 195–200, 232–33
synaptic weights 68, 104–5, 106–7, 192–93, 196
synchrony, neural 42–43, 183–84

tastes 143–44
teleological states 67
temporal coincidence 96, 99–100
temporal phase 131
temporopolar cortex (TPC) 237f, 238
thalamus 231f, 290f
thermodynamics 112, 227–28

thinking
  modes of thought 242–43, 243f
  self-referential 258–59
  see also nonvolitional thought; volitional thought
time
  direction of 118, 119–20, 183
  irreversibility of 117
tonic firing 184–85
  AMPA receptors 186–88
Tononi, G. 61, 62–63
top-down causation 7, 108–9, 227–30
  requirement for libertarian free will 108
top-down control 214
  see also executive systems
top-down inhibition 238–39
top-down processing 8–9
torn decisions 81–82, 135–38, 141
trace conditioning 160
Treisman, Anne 286–87
trust 29
truth 30, 33–34, 104
  correspondence theory of 31–32
  as logical coherence 32
  objective 31–34
  pragmatic notion of 31
  subjective 30–31
turning behavior, flies 170
type 1 libertarian free will 15, 76, 78, 80–81, 110
  criterial causation 82
  and responsibility 139
type 2 libertarian free will (meta free will) 15–17, 27–29, 76, 78–80, 110, 141–43, 260, 292–96
  criterial causation 82–83
  habit formation 144
  necessary conditions for 95–96
  and responsibility 139

uncertainty 31, 113
  and information theory 44–45
uncertainty principle 110, 114, 115, 204
unconscious 286–87
  as source of conscious content 278–80
unconscious processing 10–11, 38
  dynamic relationship with consciousness 13–14, 163
universe
  age and size of 204
  expansion of 204–5
universes, multiple 205
unobservable events 75
unpredictability, evolution of 169–70

vacuum, properties of 115–16, 204
van Inwagen, Peter 135
  consequence argument 85
variability in neural activity 190–91

variability of behavior 170
  control of 170–71
ventral anterior cingulate cortex (vACC) 226
ventral attentional network (VAN) 222, 236, 237f
ventral stream 215, 222–23, 227
ventromedial cortico–striatal–thalamocortical loops 291–92
virtual particles 115, 116
virtual reality monism 60–61
vision
  executive control circuits 222
  processing streams 215
visual cortex, information realization 192
visual illusions 39–41
visual perception 273–74
vitamin A 207
vocal repertoire, geladas 271–72
volition 14, 169, 213, 216–17
  and attainment of mastery 22, 23–24
  automatization of 22
  brain processes 71–73
  etymological roots 41
  hierarchical structure 275–77
  relationship to consciousness 158–60
volitional actions 69–70
volitional attention 54–56, 171, 182, 278–79
  evolution 238–39
  executive control circuits 221–22
  hierarchical structure 276–77
  neural basis 230–34
volitional circuits 221–27
volitional control 213–14
  see also executive systems
volitional imagination 266
  Beaty study 269–70, 270f
  evolution 270–71
  Löwenmensch 267f, 267
  shape manipulation study 267–69, 268f, 269f
  see also imagination
volitional thought 241–42
  interaction with nonvolitional circuits 243f, 245f
    automatically constrained thought 244
    deliberately constrained thought 244
    in planning 244–46
    spontaneous thought 243–44
  lucid dreaming 240–41, 241f, 242f
  neural circuits 237f
    cingulo-opercular control network 239
    dorsal attentional network 238–39
    fronto-parietal control network 239
Voss, U. 240, 241f

"walking-back" arguments 17
Watts, James 246–47
weak free will 77
Wegner, D.M. 163–64

Wheeler, John 116
Wiener, Norbert 4, 6
Wiesel, Torsten 192
"will," etymological roots 41
willed actions *see* volitional actions
willpower 223–25, 225*f*, 246, 260–61
    cultivation of 249–56
    effect of lobotomy 246–47
    role of dorsal anterior cingulate cortex 247–48
    and the solar plexus 250

winner-takes-all systems 228–29
wisdom 29
Wittgenstein, Ludwig 133
working memory 14–15, 227
    evolution of 171–72
    fMRI study 267–69, 268*f*, 269*f*
    and trace conditioning 160
world model 56–57, 65, 290–91

Yarbus, Alfred 69
yoga 249, 250, 256, 293